KU-605-141

Mediterranean Spain
Costas del Azahar, Dorada & Brava

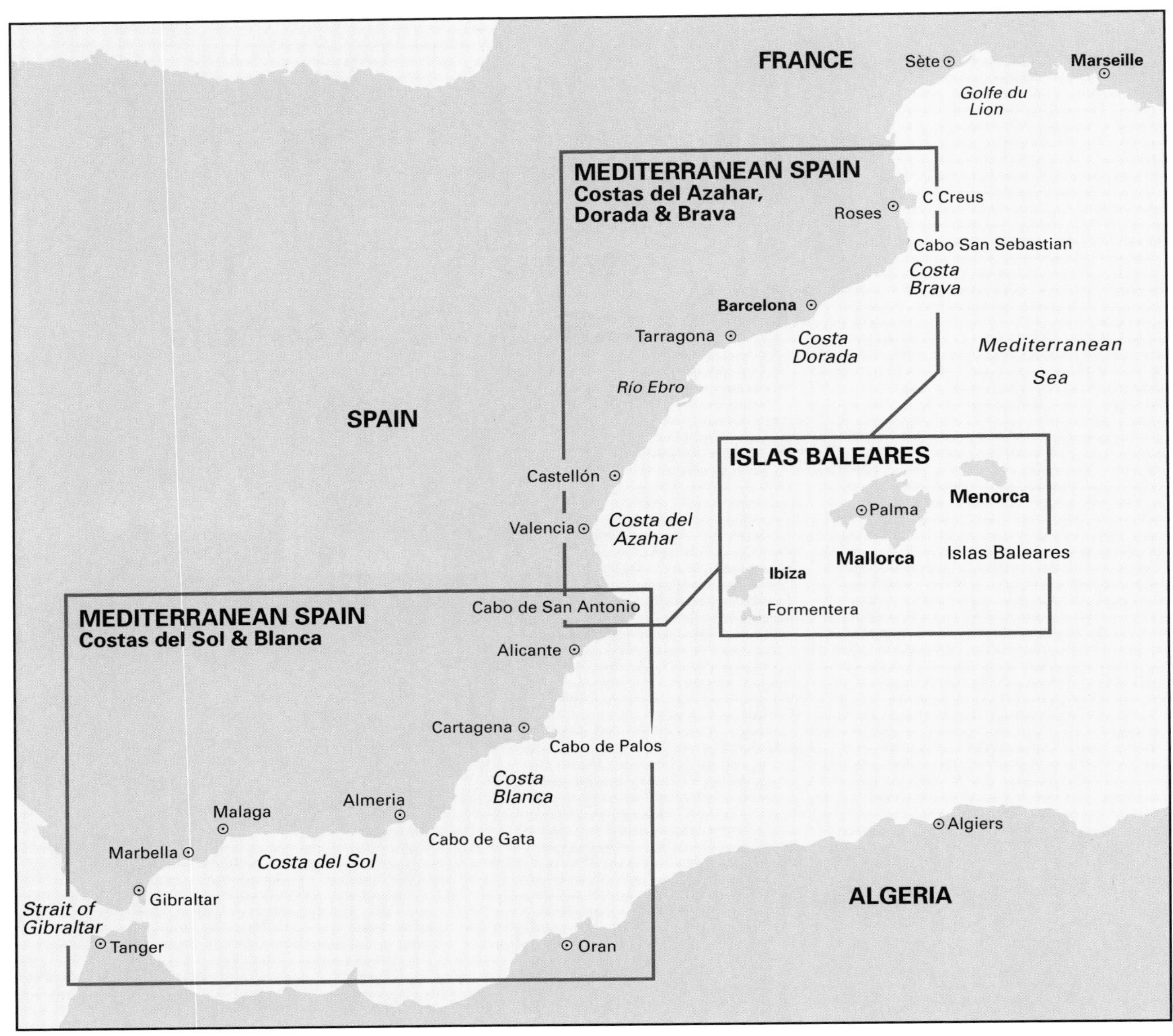
FRANCE
Sète
Marseille
Golfe du Lion
MEDITERRANEAN SPAIN
Costas del Azahar, Dorada & Brava
C Creus
Roses
Cabo San Sebastian
Costa Brava
Barcelona
Tarragona
Costa Dorada
Mediterranean Sea
Río Ebro
SPAIN
ISLAS BALEARES
Castellón
Menorca
Palma
Valencia
Costa del Azahar
Mallorca
Islas Baleares
Ibiza
Formentera
MEDITERRANEAN SPAIN
Costas del Sol & Blanca
Cabo de San Antonio
Alicante
Cartagena
Cabo de Palos
Costa Blanca
Malaga
Almeria
Algiers
Marbella
Cabo de Gata
Costa del Sol
Gibraltar
ALGERIA
Strait of Gibraltar
Tanger
Oran

Mediterranean Spain
Costas del Azahar, Dorada & Brava

ROYAL CRUISING CLUB
PILOTAGE FOUNDATION
Robin Brandon
Revised by John Marchment

Imray Laurie Norie & Wilson Ltd
St Ives Cambridgeshire England

Published by
Imray Laurie Norie & Wilson Ltd
Wych House St Ives Huntingdon
Cambridgeshire PE27 5BT, England 2002
☎ +44 (0)1480 462114, *Fax* +44 (0)1480 496109
E-mail ilnw@imray.com
Web www.imray.com

1st edition 1989
2nd edition 1995
3rd edition 1999
4th edition 2002

ISBN 0 85288 621 7

British Library Cataloguing in Publication Data.
A catalogue record for this book is available from the British Library.

This work, based on surveys over a period of many years, has been corrected to June 2002 from land-based visits to the ports and harbours of the coast, from contributions by visiting yachtsmen and from official notices. The air photographs were taken by Anne Hammick in September, 1997.

CORRECTIONS

The RCC Pilotage Foundation would be glad to receive any corrections, information or suggestions which readers may consider would improve the book. Letters should be addressed to the Editor, Mediterranean Spain, care of the publishers.

CORRECTIONAL SUPPLEMENTS

This pilot book will be amended at intervals by the issue of correctional supplements which will be published on our website www.imray.com and may be downloaded free of charge. Printed copies are also available on request from the publishers at the above address.

Printed in Great Britain by Butler & Tanner Ltd,
Frome, Somerset

CAUTION

Every effort has been made to ensure the accuracy of this book. It contains selected information and thus is not definitive and does not include all known information on the subject in hand; this is particularly relevant to the plans, which should not be used for navigation. The RCC Pilotage Foundation believes that this selection represents a useful aid to prudent navigation, but the safety of a vessel depends ultimately on the judgement of the navigator, who should assess all information, published or unpublished.

POSITIONS

Positions given in the text and on plans are intended purely as an aid to locating the place in question on the chart, and unless otherwise specified use the same datum as the ***largest scale Spanish chart of the area currently available***. They should not be used as waypoints

PLANS

The plans in this guide are not to be used for navigation. They are designed to support the text and should always be used with navigational charts.

Where lights on the plans are identified by a number in red (the international index number, as in the *British Admiralty List of Lights* or, ***where the light has no international number, the five figure number listed in Faros y Señales de Niebla Parte II of the Instituto Hidrográfico de la Marina at Cadiz)*** the reader should refer to the relevant list of lights in the text for details. All bearings are from seaward and refer to true north. Symbols are based on those used by the British Admiralty – users are referred to *Symbols and Abbreviations (NP 5011)*.

Contents

Foreword

The fact that it is just 3 years since the last edition of this book was published highlights two issues: there are a great many more yachts being kept and used on this coast and the authorities have made a great effort to provide new facilities to meet this demand. Thus although much of the content of the previous edition is retained, there are significant amounts of new material which make it worthwhile to have a new edition.

The work entailed in keeping track of all the new developments and the improvements to existing facilities is substantial and not always a very glamourous task. The Pilotage Foundation is indebted to John Marchment for the time and effort he has devoted to collating and incorporating the many changes into this book. In addition to making use of official sources of information on facilities, John has had a lot of input from many yachtsmen and other friends and we are grateful to those who have taken the trouble to send us much useful information.

We are always pleased to receive feedback on the content of this book and advice of any changes that may occur. Such comments can either be in writing to the publisher or by email to the *director@rccpf.org.uk*. Correctional supplements will be published from time to time on the Imray website *www.imray.com*. Supplements can be downloaded from the website or supplied in hard copy on request to Imray.

Francis Walker
Director RCC Pilotage Foundation
July 2002

Acknowledgements
A full revision of this volume has been undertaken both with visits and the many inputs from interested yachtsmen and women. These include Barrie Buckley, Mike and Christina Francis, Graham Hutt, Claire and Jimmy James, Henry Roberts, D Scott-Bayfield and David and Pat Teall.

The photographs Anne took in 1997 are, for the most part, still suprisingly accurate and any major changes will be stated in their captions.

Since January 2001 there appears to have been a large injection of money into the marine field and many extension plans, on hold for some years, are now going ahead especially in the northern half of this fascinating coast. A number of new marinas have been started and even a new lighthouse built! All this means that changes are ongoing all the time and I must acknowledge the stalwart efforts of the staff of Imray who have put up with my numerous changes at very late stages with good humour.

John Marchment
Weymouth July 2002

In 1976 an American member of the Royal Cruising Club, Dr Fred Ellis, indicated that he wished to make a gift to the Club in memory of his father, the late Robert E. Ellis, of his friends Peter Pye and John Ives and as a mark of esteem for Roger Pinkney. An independent charity known as the RCC Pilotage Foundation was formed and Dr Ellis added his house to his already generous gift of money to form the Foundation's permanent endowment. The Foundation's charitable objective is 'to advance the education of the public in the science and practice of navigation' which is at present achieved through the writing and updating of pilot books covering many different parts of the world.

The Foundation is extremely grateful and privileged to have been given the copyrights to books written by a number of distinguished authors and yachtsmen including the late Adlard Coles, Robin Brandon and Malcolm Robson. In return the Foundation has willingly accepted the task of keeping the original books up to date and many yachtsmen and women have helped (and are helping) the Foundation fulfill this commitment. In addition to the titles donated to the Foundation, several new books have been created and developed under the auspices of the Foundation. The Foundation works in close collaboration with two publishers – Imray Laurie Norie and Wilson, and Adlard Coles Nautical – and in addition publishes in its own name short run guides and pilot books for areas where limited demand does not justify large print runs. Several of the Foundation's books have been translated into French, German and Italian.

The overall management of the Foundation is entrusted to Trustees appointed by the Royal Cruising Club, with day to day operations being controlled by the Director. All these appointments are unpaid.

In line with its charitable status, the Foundation distributes no profits, which are used to finance new books and developments and to subsidise those covering areas of low demand.

Introduction

The five coasts of Mediterranean Spain

Following the divisions used by the Spanish, the six hundred mile coastline is considered in five sections. They are the Costa del Sol between Gibraltar and Cabo de Gata, where the coast turns north east to Cabo de la Nao; Costa Blanca between Gato and Nao; Costa del Azahar between Nao and the Ebro Delta; Costa Dorada between the Ebro, past Barcelona to Blanes; and the cliffs and inlets of the Costa Brava which runs from Blanes up to the French border. These divisions do not correspond with the provinces of Andalucia, Murcia, Valencia and Catalunya (each of which is divided into several districts) which are shown on the end-papers. This volume is concerned with Costas del Azahar, Dorada and Brava; the other two are considered in *Mediterranean Spain – Costas del Sol & Blanca.*

A description of the coast is given in each section. In general terms, however, the coastline has changed greatly since Robin Brandon first surveyed it. Where developers have been able to get to it, they have done so, either for tourism or industry. Many of the old hospitable fishing villages and ports have been overrun. An effort is made to separate yachts from the fishing fleets. The number of marinas has increased. However there are still anchorages, *calas* and cliffs which the developers have not reached. This is especially true along Costa Brava; along the other *costas* much passage-making is past tourist beaches and developments strung between towns. As in the *Islas Baleares*, cheek-by-jowl existence is a part of cruising life and the deserted anchorages and uncrowded harbours of the first editions of this guide have gone. It is now prudent to check ahead for the availability of a berth, particularly in July and August.

In the Mediterranean, yachts are usually in commission from May to October, the north European holiday season. Whilst there is then little chance of a gale, there are few days when there is a good sailing breeze. In winter, whilst it is true that off-shore the Mediterranean can be horrid, there are many days with a good sailing breeze and the weather is warmer and sunnier than the usual summer in the English Channel. Storms and heavy rain do occur but it is feasible to dodge bad weather and slip along shore from harbour to harbour as they are not far apart. In general the climate is mild and, particularly from January to March, very pleasant. A great advantage is that there are no crowds and the local shops and services are freer to serve the winter visitor. Many *clubs náutico,* which have to turn away visitors in summer, welcome visitors. Local inhabitants can be met, places of interest enjoyed and the empty beaches and coves used in privacy.

History

There are many traces of prehistoric inhabitants but recorded history starts with a group of unknown origin, the Ligurians, who came from N Africa and established themselves in southern Spain about the 6th century BC with the Carthaginians at Málaga and the Phoenicians who had been trading in the area since the 12th century BC and living in various small colonies dotted along the coast.

In 242BC a force of Carthaginians under Hamilcar Barca, who had previously been driven from Sicily by the Romans, captured and held the south of Spain until 219BC when the Romans occupied the land. The Romans were displaced in the Barbarian invasion of the 5th century AD. There followed a period of development and construction when many of the present towns were established. The Barbarians – the Suevi, Vandals and Alans – were, in turn, overrun by the Visigoths who held the area from the 5th to the 8th century AD.

In AD711 a huge force of Moors and Berbers under Tarik-ibn-Zeyab crossed the Strait of Gibraltar and captured the whole of Spain except for a small enclave in the N. The Moors took over the S and the Berbers the N. By the 10th century AD huge strides had been made in education and development and Cordoba which had become independent was renowned throughout Europe as a seat of learning.

By the 13th century, the Moors and Berbers had been driven out of the country by a long series of wars undertaken by numerous Spanish forces supported by the armies of the nobles of France. Granada alone remained under the Moors until 1491 when they were finally driven out by Isabella of Castile and Ferdinand of Aragon who united Spain under one crown

Then followed a period of world-wide expansion and, when the crown went to the house of Hapsburg in the 16th century, of interference in the affairs of Europe which continued when the house of Bourbon took over in the 18th century.

Over the years the country has been in constant turmoil. Wars and rebellions, victories and defeats, sieges and conquests were common occurrences but none were quite as terrible as the Civil War which started in 1936 and lasted for two-and-a-half years, leaving nearly a million dead. Since then the country has moved away from a dictatorship into the different turmoils of democracy and the European Union – but the Civil War has not been forgotten. Though the country is governed centrally from Madrid, provinces have considerable local autonomy. Along the Mediterranean coast, it is perhaps in Catalunya that the most independent views are found.

Local economy

Along all the coasts tourism is of course a significant factor in the economy but this coastal development is, in a manner of speaking, skin-deep. Inland, agricultural patterns remain though some of them have been drastically developed, for instance by the introduction of hydroponics supported by kilometres of plastic greenhouses. The four autonomous provinces vary considerably between themselves. Catalonia is the most highly developed industrially and Murcia, perhaps, the least. All have fishing fleets, inshore and mid-range, working out of many ports and they, together with a supporting boat building industry, help provide the skills on which marinas depend.

Language

The Castillian spoken in Andalucía sounds different to that spoken further north, principally in that the *cedilla* is not lisped. In Catalunya, Catalan is actively promoted. Though close to Spanish, there are Catalan alternatives for Castilian Spanish, some of which have French overtones, such as: *bondia* – good morning (rather than *buenos días*), *bon tarde* – good afternoon (*buenos tardes*), *s'es plau* – please (*por favor*).

Many local people speak English or German, often learnt from tourists, and French is taught as a second language at school.

Place names appear in the Spanish or Catalan form with the spelling normally used on British Admiralty charts. It should be noted that there are often variations.

Currency

The unit of currency is the Euro. Major credit cards are widely accepted. Bank hours are normally 0830 to 1400, Monday to Friday, with a few also open 0830 to 1300 on Saturday. Most banks have credit card machines.

Regional weather – the Western Mediterranean

General

The weather pattern in the basin of the western Mediterranean is affected by many different systems. It is largely unpredictable, quick to change and often very different at places only a short distance apart. See Appendix III for Spanish meteorological terms.

Winds

Winds most frequently blow from the west, northwest, north and east but are considerably altered by the effects of local topography. The Mediterranean is an area of calms and gales and the old saying that in summer there are nine days of light winds followed by a gale is very close to reality. Close to the coast normal sea and land breezes are experienced on calm days. Along the Costa Brava, northwest, north and northeast winds are most common, especially in winter, though winds from other directions frequently occur. This area is particularly influenced by the weather in the Golfe du Lion and is in the direct path of the northwesterly *tramontana* (see below), making it particularly important to listen to regular weather forecasts.

The winds in the Mediterranean have been given special names dependent on their direction and characteristics. Those that affect this coast are detailed below.

Northwest – *tramontana*

This wind, also known as the *maestral* near Río Ebro and the *mistral* in France, is a strong, dry wind, cold in winter, which can be dangerous. It is caused by a secondary depression forming in the Golfe du Lion or the Golfo di Génova on the cold front of a major depression crossing France. The northwesterly airflow generated is compressed between the Alps and the Pyrenees and flows into the Mediterranean basin. In Spain it chiefly affects the coast to the north of Barcelona, the Islas Baleares, and is strongest at the northern end of the Costa Brava.

The *tramontana* can be dangerous in that it can arrive and reach gale force in as little as fifteen minutes on a calm sunny day with virtually no warning. Signs to watch for are brilliant visibility, clear sky – sometimes with cigar-shaped clouds – very dry air and a steady or slightly rising barometer. On rare occasions the sky may be cloudy when the wind first arrives although it clears later. Sometimes the barometer will plunge in normal fashion, rising quickly after the gale has passed. If at sea and some way from land, a line of white on the horizon and a developing swell give a few minutes' warning. The only effective warning that can be obtained is by radio – Marseille (in French) and Monaco (in French and English) are probably the best bet. See page 15 for transmission details.

The *tramontana* normally blows for at least three days but may last for a week or longer. It is frequent in the winter months, blowing for a third of the time and can reach F10 (50 knots) or more. In summer it is neither as strong nor as frequent.

West – *vendaval*

A depression crossing Spain or southern France creates a strong southwest to west wind, the *vendaval* or *poniente*, which funnels through the Strait of Gibraltar and along the south coast of Spain. Though normally confined to the south and southeast coasts, it occasionally blows in the northeast of the area. It is usually short-lived and at its strongest from late autumn to early spring.

East – *levante*

Encountered from Gibraltar to Valencia and beyond, the *levante*, sometimes called the *llevantade* when it blows at gale force, is caused by a depression located between the Islas Baleares and the North African coast. It is preceded by a heavy swell (*las tascas*), cold damp air, poor visibility and low cloud which forms first around the higher hills. Heavy and prolonged rainfall is more likely in spring and autumn than summer. A *levante* may last for three or four days.

South – *siroco*

The hot wind from the south is created by a depression moving east along or just south of the North African coast. By the time this dry wind reaches Spain it can be very humid, with haze and cloud. If strong it carries dust, and should it rain when the cold front comes through the water may be red or brown and the dust will set like cement. This wind is sometimes called the *leveche* in southeast Spain. It occurs most frequently in summer, seldom lasting more than one or two days.

Clouds

Cloud cover of between 4/8ths and 5/8ths in the winter months is about double the summer average of 2/8ths. Barcelona, however, seems to manage a year round average of 3/8th to 5/8ths. The cloud is normally cumulus and high level. In strong winds with a southerly component complete cloud cover can be expected.

Precipitation

Annual rainfall is moderate and decreases towards the north from about 760mm at Gibraltar to 560mm at Barcelona. The rainy seasons are autumn and winter and in most areas the summer months are virtually dry. The Costa Brava however usually manages about 25mm of rain during each summer month. Most of the rain falls in very heavy showers of one or two hours duration.

Thunderstorms

Thunderstorms are most frequent in the autumn at up to four or five each month, and can be accompanied by hail.

Waterspouts

Waterspouts occur in the Strait of Gibraltar in winter and spring, usually associated with thunderstorms.

Snow

Snow at sea level is very rare but it falls and remains on the higher mountain ranges inland. Snow on the Sierra Nevada is particularly noticeable from the sea.

Visibility

Fog occurs about four days a month in summer along the Costa de Sol but elsewhere is very rare.

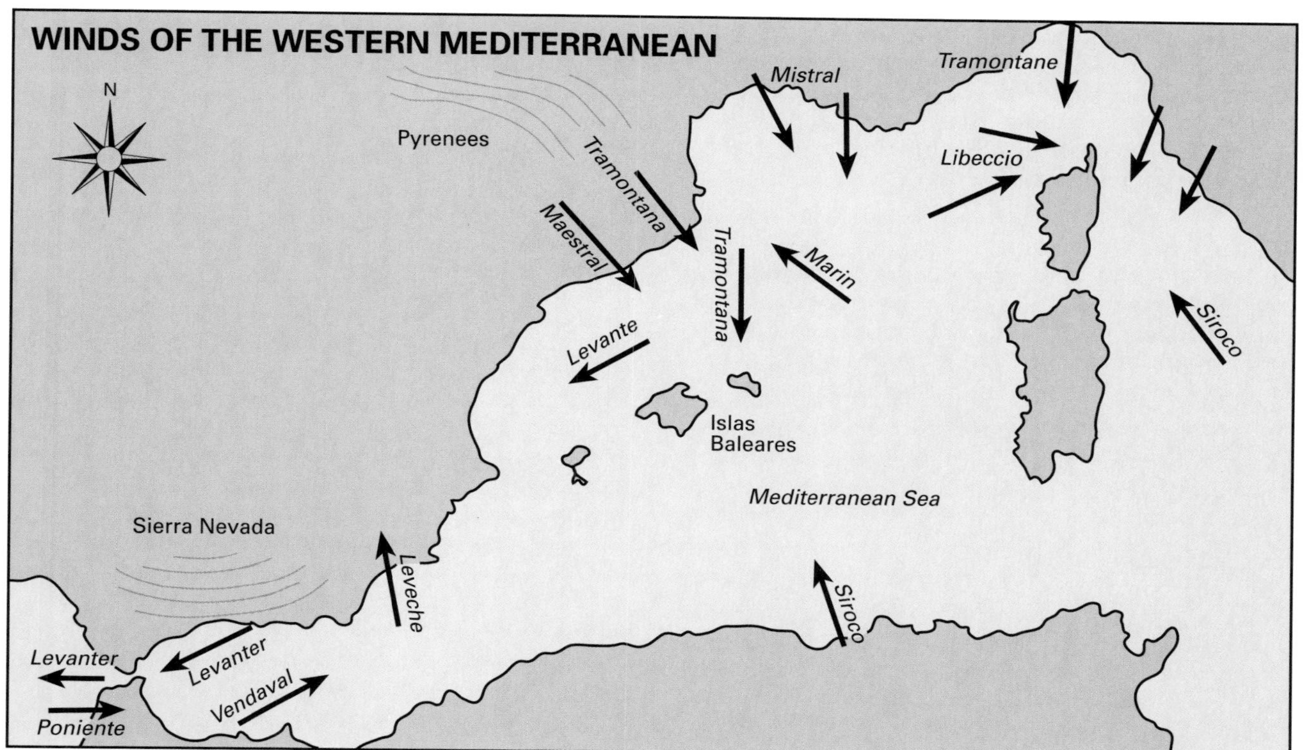

Occasionally dust carried by the southerly *siroco* reduces visibility and industrial areas such as Valencia and Barcelona produce haze.

Temperature
Winter temperatures at Gibraltar average 10°C–15°C, rising steadily after March to average 20°C–29°C in July and August. Afternoon (maximum) temperatures may reach 30°–33° in these month. At Barcelona, summer temperatures are much the same as at Gibraltar but winter temperatures are lower, 6°C–13°C.

Humidity
The relative humidity is moderate at around 60% to 80%. With winds from west, northwest or north low humidity can be expected; with winds off the sea, high humidity is normal. The relative humidity increases throughout the night and falls by day.

Local Variations

In the northeastern area, the common winds are between northwest and northeast. Gales may be experienced for 10% of the time during the winter, dropping to 2% in July and August, sometimes arriving with little warning and rapidly building to gale force

Radio equipment and weather forecasts
– see pages 7 and 14.

The Sea

Currents
There is a constant E-going surface current of 1 to 2 knots, passing through the Straits of Gibraltar and continuing the Costa del Sol and the African coast, replacing water lost by evaporation. Northeast of Cabo de Gata up to the border with France, a significant inshore counter-eddy runs roughly SSW at 1 to 1½ knots. The shape of the coast produces variations in both direction and strength, especially around promontories.

Tides
Tides should be taken into account at the west end of the Costa del Sol and are noted in the introduction to that section. From Alicante to the border with France, the tide is hardly appreciable.

Swell
Winds between NE and SE can produce a dangerous swell on the E coast. Swell has a nasty capability of going round corners and getting into *calas.*

Scouring and silting
Many harbours and anchorages are located in sandy areas where depths can change dramatically in the course of a storm or a season. Dredging is a common feature but there is no certainty that depths will be maintained. Charts and drawings are no sure guide. When approaching or entering such areas, it is of great importance to sound carefully and to act on the information received.

Sea temperature
Sea temperatures in February are around 14°C on the Costa del Sol and 12°C on the Costa Brava. In summer, along the Costa Blanca it can rise to 20°C. Winds from the south and east tend to raise the temperature and those from the west and north to lower them.

Practicalities and preparation

OFFICIAL ADDRESSES

Spanish embassies and consulates
London – 20 Draycott Place, London SW3 2RZ. ☎ 020 7589 8989, *Fax* 020 7581 7888
Manchester – Suite 1a, Brook House, Manchester. M22 2BQ ☎ 0161 236 1213
Edinburgh – 63 North Castle Street, Edinburgh EH2 3LJ. ☎ 0131 220 1843, *Fax* 0131 226 4568
Washington DC – 2375 Pennsylvania Ave., NW, Washington DC 20037. ☎ 452 0100, *Fax* 728 2317
New York – 150 E 58th Street, New York, NY 10155 ☎ 212 355-4080
Plus many others.

Spanish national tourist offices
London – 22-23 Manchester Square W1M 5AP. ☎ 020 7486 8077.
New York – 666 Fifth Avenue, New York, NY 10103. ☎ 212 265-8822

British and American embassies in Madrid
British Embassy – Calle Fernando el Santo 16, 28010 Madrid. ☎ (91) 700 8200, *Fax* (91) 700 8272
American Embassy – Calle Serrano 75, 28006 Madrid. ☎ (91) 587 2200, *Fax* (91) 587 2303
If using the telephone, see the note on page 10.

British Consulates
Alicante British Consulate Plaza Calvo Sotelo 1/2 – 1 03001 Alicante. *Mail* Apartado 564, 03001, Alicante. ☎ (96) 521 61 90, 521 60 22 *Fax* (96) 514 05 28
Barcelona British Consulate-General Edificio Torre de Barcelona Avenida Diagonal 477 13th Floor 08036 Barcelona. ☎ (93) 366 6200
Málaga British Consulate Edificio Duquesa Calle Duquesa de Parcent 8 29001 Málaga. ☎ (95) 221 75 71 / 221 23 25 *Fax* (952) 22 11 30

Formalities
Note Value Added Tax (VAT) is called *Impuesto de Valor Agregado* (IVA) and the standard rate is 16%.

Harbour organisation
At local level, the ultimate authority for the workings of a harbour is the *capitán de puerto* whose office is the *capitanía.* In fishing ports there may also be a *guarda de puerto*; in this case the *capitán* looks after the waters of the harbour and delegates berthing arrangements to the *guarda.*

At ports where there is an organised yachting presence, there is almost always a *club náutico,* a marina or both, and arrangements for handling yachts are delegated to them. For the visiting yacht, the first point of reference is the marina if there is one; and if not, the *club náutico.*

Documentation
Spain is a member of the European Union. Other EU nationals may visit the country for up to 90 days with a passport but no visa, as may US citizens. EU citizens wishing to remain in Spain may apply for a *permiso de residencia* once in the country; non-EU nationals can apply for a single 90-day extension, or otherwise obtain a long-term visa from a Spanish embassy or consulate before leaving home.

In practice the requirement to apply for a *permiso de residencia* does not appear to be enforced in the case of cruising yachtsmen, living aboard rather than ashore and frequently on the move. Many yachtsmen have cruised Spanish waters for extended periods with no documentation beyond that normally carried in the UK. If in doubt, check with the authorities before departure.

Under EU regulations, EU registered boats are not required to fly the Q flag on first arrival unless they have non-EU nationals or dutiable goods aboard. Nevertheless, clearance should be sought either through a visit to or from officials or through the offices of the larger marinas or yacht clubs. Passports and the ship's registration papers will be required. A Certificate of Competence (or equivalent) and evidence of VAT status may also be requested – see Appendices IV and V. Other documents sometimes requested are a crew list with passport details, the radio licence and evidence of insurance. Subsequently, at other ports, clearance need not be sought but the *guarda civil* may wish to see papers, particularly passports. Marina officials often ask to see yacht registration documents and the skipper's passport, and sometimes evidence of insurance.

Temporary import and laying up
A VAT paid or exempt yacht should apply for a *permiso aduanero* on arrival in Spanish waters. This is valid for twelve months and renewable annually, allowing for an almost indefinite stay. Possession of a *permiso aduanero* establishes the status of a vessel and is helpful when importing equipment and spares from other EU countries.

A boat registered outside the EU fiscal area on which VAT has not been paid may be temporarily imported into the EU for a period not exceeding six months in any twelve before VAT is payable. This period may sometimes be extended by prior agreement with the local customs authorities (for instance, some do not count time laid up as part of the six months). While in EU waters the vessel may only be used by its owner, and may not be chartered or even lent to another person, on pain of paying VAT (but see Appendix VI). If kept in the EU longer than six months the vessel normally becomes liable for VAT. There are marked differences in the way the rules are applied from one harbour to the next, let alone in different countries – check the local situation on arrival.

See Appendix V for information on documentation and the EU fiscal area. The purely practical side of laying up is covered on page 9.

Chartering
There is a blanket restriction on foreign-owned and/or skippered vessels based in Spain engaging in charter work. See Appendix VI.

Light dues
A charge known as Tarifa G5 is supposedly levied on all vessels. Locally based pleasure craft (the status of a charter yacht is not clear) pay at the rate of 5 Euros per square metre per year, area being calculated as LOA x beam. Visiting pleasure craft pay one tenth of that sum and are not charged again for ten days. Boats of less than 7m LOA and with engines of less than 25hp make a single payment of 30 Euros per year. In practice, this levy appears seldom to be raised.

Insurance
Many marinas require evidence of insurance cover, though third party only may be sufficient. Many UK companies are willing to extend home waters cover for the Mediterranean, excluding certain areas.

Flag etiquette
A yacht in commission in foreign waters is legally required to fly her national maritime flag; for a British registered yacht, this is commonly the Red Ensign. If a special club ensign is worn it must be accompanied by the correct burgee. The courtesy flag of the country visited, which normally is the national maritime flag, should be flown from the starboard signal halliard. The flag for Spain is similar to the Spanish national flag but without the crest in the centre.

General regulations

Harbour restrictions
All harbours have a speed limit, usually 3 knots. The limits are not noted in the text and none are known which are less than 3 knots. There is a 5 knot speed limit within 100m of coast, extending to 250m off bathing beaches.

In most harbours anchoring is forbidden except in emergency or for a short period while sorting out a berth.

Garbage

It is an international offence to dump garbage at sea and, while the arrangements of local authorities may not be perfect, garbage on land should be dumped in the proper containers. Marinas require the use of their onshore facilities or holding tanks.

Scuba diving

Inshore scuba diving is strictly controlled and a licence is required from the *militar de marina*. This involves a certificate of competence, a medical certificate, two passport photographs, the passport itself (for inspection), knowledge of the relevant laws and a declaration that they will be obeyed. The simplest approach is to enquire through marina staff. Any attempt to remove archaeological material from the seabed will result in serious trouble.

Spearfishing

Spearfishing while scuba diving or using a snorkel is controlled and, in some places, prohibited.

Water-skiing

There has been a big increase in the use of high powered outboards for water-skiing over the past decade, accompanied by a significant increase in accidents. In most of the main ports and at some beaches it is now controlled and enquiries should be made before skiing. It is essential to have third party insurance and, if possible, a bail bond. If bathing and water-skiing areas are buoyed, yachts are excluded.

Harbours, marinas and anchorages

In spite of the growth in both the number and size of marinas and yacht harbours there is still a general shortage of berths, particularly in July and August. Check in advance whether a berth will be available (mobile phones are replacing VHF for this function).

Harbour charges

All harbours and marinas charge, at a scale which varies from season to season and year to year. July and August are normally considered to be 'high season', with some harbours citing May, June and September as 'mid season'. High season charges may be double (and in some places almost treble) those for the low season. Long term contracts may work out a third less than the daily rate. Some marinas include water, electricity, harbour dues, light dues and IVA (at 16%) in their general charge, others charge separately; their published information does not always specify all the charges. Marinas are in competition with each other in an unsettled market and charges fluctuate at short notice. Prices increase from southwest to northeast. In 2001, mean daily rates for a 10 x 3·5m boat, high season/low season, in Euros per day and without IVA added, were very roughly as follows: Costa del Sol, 10/6; Costa Blanca, 15/10; Costa del Azahar, 15/10; Costa Dorada, 20/10 and Costa Brava 26/13 but departures from the mean are sometimes great. The percentage increase in prices for a 15m also vary greatly, even within the boundaries of a single *costa;* the range is between 65% and 110%. A further complication is that harbours are beginning to charge by beam times length or even by beam alone. It is not practical either to generalise further on harbour dues or to give detailed charges, let alone give an opinion on value for money but the foregoing may provide some guidance for financial planning. Where a relatively expensive or cheap berth has been found, this is noted. *El Mercardo Náutico* (The Boat Market), which generally appears every other month during the summer, carries tariffs and is probably the most up-to-date guide to be found.

Large yachts

Many harbours are too small, or too shallow, for a large yacht, which must anchor outside whilst its crew visit the harbour by tender. It is essential that the skipper of such a yacht wishing to enter a small harbour telephones or radios the harbour authorities well in advance to reserve a berth (if available) and receive necessary instructions.

Berthing

Due to the vast numbers of yachts and limited space available, berthing stern-to the quays and pontoons is normal. This situation is reflected in the increasing practice of marinas to charge on the basis of beam.

For greater privacy berth bows-to. This has the added advantages of keeping the rudder away from possible underwater obstructions near the quay and making the approach a much easier manoeuvre. An anchor may occasionally be needed, but more often a bow (or stern) line will be provided, usually via a lazyline to the pontoon though sometimes buoyed. This line may be both heavy and dirty and gloves will be found useful. Either way, have plenty of fenders out and lines ready.

Most cruising skippers will have acquired some expertise at this manoeuvre arriving but if taking over a chartered or otherwise unfamiliar yacht it would be wise both to check handling characteristics and talk the manoeuvre through with the crew before attempting to enter a narrow berth. Detailed instructions regarding Mediterranean mooring techniques will be found in *Mediterranean Cruising Handbook* by Rod Heikell.

Mooring lines – surge in harbours is common and mooring lines must be both long and strong. It is useful to have an eye made up at the shore end with a loop of chain plus shackles to slip over bollards or through rings. Carry plenty of mooring lines, especially if the boat is to be left unattended for any length of time.

Gangplanks – if a gangplank is not already part of the boat's equipment, a builder's scaffolding plank, with holes drilled at either end to take lines, serves well. As it is cheap and easily replaced it can also be used outside fenders to deal with an awkward lie or ward off an oily quay. A short ladder, possibly the bathing ladder if it can be adapted, is useful if berthing bows-to.

Moorings

Virtually all moorings are privately owned and if one is used it will have to be vacated should the owner return. There are generally no markings to give any indication as to the weight and strength of moorings so they should be used with caution. Lobster pot toggles have been mistaken for moorings.

Anchorages

There are a large number of attractive anchorages in *calas* and off beaches, even though many have massive buildings in the background and crowds in the foreground. Previous editions of this guide commented on some of them in the text. In this edition much of that information is presented by photographs. Where known, particular hazards are mentioned but an absence of comment in the text or on the sketch charts does not mean there are no hazards. There are always hazards approaching and anchoring off the shoreline. The sketch charts are derived from limited observation and not from a professional survey; depths, shapes, distances etc. are approximate. Any approach must be made with due care paid to current and predicted circumstances. Good seamanship is essential; detailed pilotage remains a matter for the ship's master. If possible, have a lookout up the mast or at the bow with *Polaroid* sunglasses, approach an anchorage down-sun and bear in mind what the azimuth of the sun will be at the time of departure.

The weather can change and deteriorate at short notice, especially along the Costa Brava. During the day the sea breeze can be strong, especially if there is a valley at the head of an anchorage. Similarly a strong land breeze can flow down a valley in the early hours of the morning. If anchored near the head of a *cala* backed by a river valley and there is a thunderstorm or heavy downpour in the hills above, take precautions against the flood of water and debris which will pour into the *cala*.

Many *cala* anchorages suffer from swell even when not open to its off-shore direction. Swell tends to curl round all but the most prominent headlands. Wash from boats entering and leaving, as well as from larger vessels passing outside, may add to the discomfort. If considering a second anchor or a line ashore in order to hold the yacht into the swell, consider the swinging room required by yachts on single anchors should the wind change.

In a high sided *cala* winds are often fluky and a sudden blow, even from the land, may make departure difficult. This type of anchorage should only be used in settled calm weather and left in good time if swell or wind rise.

Whatever the type of *cala*, have ready a plan for clearing out quickly, possibly in darkness. It is unwise to leave an anchored yacht unattended for any length of time.

Many yachtsmen collect picture postcards (particularly aerial views) to augment the photographs in a book such as this. They are potentially useful aids but it is essential to check that a particular photograph is of the place stated, for instance by comparison with a chart or an identified photograph. Many *calas* have more than one name and a popular name may be given to more than one *cala*. A *cala* illustrated in the guide may not be the *cala* with the same name on a chart, a map or a postcard.

Choice of anchor – many popular anchorages are thoroughly ploughed up each year by the hundreds of anchors dropped and weighed. At others the bottom is weed-covered compacted sand. Not without good reason is the four-pronged grab the favourite anchor of local fishermen, though difficult to stow. A conventional fisherman-type anchor is easier to stow and a useful ally. If using a patent anchor – Danforth, CQR, Bruce, Fortress etc. – an anchor weight (or Chum) is a worthwhile investment and will encourage the pull to remain horizontal.

Anchoring – once in a suitable depth of water, if clarity permits look for a weed-free patch to drop the anchor. In rocky or otherwise suspect areas – including those likely to contain wrecks, old chains etc. – use a sinking trip line with a float (an inviting buoy may be picked up by another yacht). Chain scope should be at least four times the maximum depth of water and nylon scope double that. It is always worth setting the anchor by reversing slowly until it holds, but on a hard or compacted bottom this must be done very gently in order to give the anchor a chance to bite – over enthusiasm with the throttle will cause it to skip without digging in.

Preparation – the yacht

A yacht properly equipped for cruising in northern waters should need little extra gear, but the following items are worth considering if not already on board.

Radio equipment – in order to receive weather forecasts and navigational warnings from Coast Radio Stations, a radio capable of receiving short and medium wave Single Sideband (SSB) transmissions will be needed. Do not make the mistake of buying a radio capable only of receiving the AM transmissions broadcast by national radio stations, or assume that SSB is only applicable to transmitting radios (transceivers).

Most SSB receivers are capable of receiving either Upper Side Band (USB) or Lower Side Band (LSB) at the flick of a switch. The UK Maritime Mobile Net covering the Eastern Atlantic and Mediterranean uses USB, and again it is not necessary to have either a transceiver or a transmitting licence to listen in. All Coast Radio

Stations broadcast on SSB – whether on USB or LSB should be easy to determine by trial and error.

Digital tuning is very desirable, and the radio should be capable of tuning to a minimum of 1kHz and preferably to 0·1kHz. Several companies (including Sony, Grundig and Roberts) market suitable SSB receivers in the UK via high street retailers and marine outlets.

Ventilation – modern yachts are, as a rule, better ventilated than their older sisters though seldom better insulated. Consider adding an opening hatch in the main cabin, if not already fitted, and ideally another over the galley. A wind scoop for the forehatch helps increase the draught, particularly if the open hatch is not forward facing.

Awnings – an awning covering at least the cockpit provides much relief for the crew, while an even better combination is a bimini which can be kept rigged whilst sailing, plus a larger 'harbour' awning, preferably at boom height or above and extending forward to the mast.

Cockpit tables – it is pleasant to eat civilised meals in the cockpit, particularly while at anchor. If nothing else can be arranged, a small folding table might do.

Refrigerator/ice-box – if a refrigerator is not fitted it may be possible to build in an ice-box (a plastic picnic coolbox is a poor substitute), but this will be useless without adequate insulation. An ice-box designed for northern climes will almost certainly benefit from extra insulation, if this can be fitted – 100mm (4in) is a desirable minimum, 150mm (6in) even better. A drain is also essential.

If a refrigerator is fitted but electricity precious, placing ice inside will help minimise battery drain.

Hose – at least 25 metres. Standpipes tend to have bayonet couplings of a type unavailable in the UK – purchase them on arrival. Plenty of 5 or 10 litre plastic carriers will also be found useful.

Deck shower – if no shower is fitted below, a black-backed plastic bag plus rose heats very quickly when hung in the rigging. (At least one proprietary model is available in the UK).

Mosquito nets – some advocate fitting screens to all openings leading below. Others find this inconvenient and rely on mosquito coils and other insecticides and repellents. For some reason mosquitoes generally seem to bother new arrivals more than old hands. If bothered, anchoring well out may decrease the problem.

Preparation – the crew

Clothing

Sunburn is an even more serious hazard at sea, where light is reflected, than on land. Lightweight, patterned cotton clothing is handy in this context – it washes and dries easily and the pattern camouflages the creases! Non-absorbent, heat retaining synthetic materials are best avoided. When swimming wear a T-shirt against the sun and shoes if there are sea-urchins around.

Some kind of headgear, preferably with a wide brim, is essential. A genuine Panama Hat, a *Montecristi,* can be rolled up, shoved in a pocket and doesn't mind getting wet (they come from Ecuador, not Panama, which has hi-jacked the name). A retaining string for the hat, tied either to clothing or around the neck, is a wise precaution whilst on the water.

Footwear at sea is a contentious subject. Many experienced cruisers habitually sail barefoot but while this may be acceptable on a familiar vessel, it would be courting injury on a less intimately known deck and around mid-day bare soles may get burnt. Proper sailing shoes should always be worn for harbour work and anchor handling. Ashore, if wearing sandals the upper part of the foot is the first area to get sunburn.

At the other end of the year, winter weather can be wet and cold. Foul weather gear as well as warm sweaters etc. will be needed.

Shoregoing clothes should be on a par with what one might wear in the UK – beachwear is not often acceptable in restaurants and certainly not on more formal occasions in yacht clubs.

Medical

No inoculations are required. Minor ailments may best be treated by consulting a *farmacia* (often able to dispense drugs which in most other countries would be on prescription), or by contact with an English-speaking doctor (recommended by the *farmacia*, marina staff, a tourist office, the police or possibly a hotel). Specifically prescribed or branded drugs should be bought in Britain in sufficient quantity to cover the duration of the cruise. Medicines are expensive in Spain and often have different brand names from those used in Britain.

Apart from precautions against the well recognised hazards of sunburn and stomach upsets, heat exhaustion (or heat stroke) is most likely to affect newly joined crew not yet acclimatised to Mediterranean temperatures. Carry something such as *Dioralyte* to counteract dehydration. Insect deterrents, including mosquito coils, can be obtained locally.

UK citizens should complete form E111 (see the Department of Health's leaflet *T4 Health Advice for Travellers*, to be found in most travel agents), which provides for free medical treatment under a reciprocal agreement with the National Health Service. Private medical treatment is likely to be expensive and it may be worth taking out medical insurance (which should also provide for an attended flight home should the need arise).

General information

Repairs and chandlery

There are many marinas equipped to handle all aspects of yacht maintenance from laying up to changing a washer. Nearly all have travel-hoists and the larger have specialist facilities – GRP work, electronics, sailmaking, stainless welding and so forth. Charges may differ widely so, if practicable, shop around.

The best equipped chandleries will be found near the larger marinas, where they may equal anything to be found in the UK (though generally with higher prices). Smaller harbours or marinas are often without a chandlery, though something may be found in the associated town. Basic items can sometimes be found in *ferreterias* (ironmongers).

Laying up

Laying up either afloat or ashore is possible at most marinas, though a few have no hard-standing. Facilities and services provided vary considerably, as does the cost, and it is worth seeking local advice as to the quality of the services provided and the security of the berth or hard-standing concerned.

In the north of the area, the northwesterly *tramontana* (*mestral*) can be frequent and severe in winter and early spring, and this should be borne in mind when selecting the area and site to lay up. Yachts with wooden decks and varnished brightwork will need protection from the winter sun, and ideally arrangements should be made for the former to be hosed down each evening. The paperwork associated with temporary import and laying up is detailed on page 5.

Yacht clubs

Most harbours of any size support at least one *club náutico*. However the grander ones in particular are basically social clubs – often with tennis courts, swimming pools and other facilities – and may not welcome the crews of visiting yachts. Often there is both a marina and a club, and unless there are special circumstances the first option for a visitor is the marina. That said, many *club náuticos* have pleasant bars and excellent restaurants which appear to be open to all, while a few are notably helpful and friendly to visitors. The standard of dress and behaviour expected is often more formal than that expected in a similar club in Britain.

Electricity

The standard is 220 volt, 50 Hz, generally via a two-pin socket for which an adapter will be needed, though some marinas provide 380 volt supplies to berths for yachts over 20–25m. If using 110 volt 60 Hz equipment seek advice – frequency may be a greater problem than voltage. If the yacht is not wired for mains, a 25m length of cable and a battery charger may be useful.

Bottled gas

Camping Gaz is widely available from marinas, supermarkets or *ferreterias* (ironmongers), the 1·9kg bottles identical to those in the UK. Its availability is therefore not listed in the text under individual harbour facilities.

Getting 4·5kg *Calor Gas* bottles refilled is much more difficult and can normally only be carried out at REPSOL/CAMPSOL depots. Where one is located near a harbour this is normally mentioned under harbour facilities, otherwise enquire of the staff. A test certificate may be required if the cylinder is more than five years old. A simpler option is to carry the appropriate fitting and regulator to permit the switch from *Calor Gas* to *Camping Gaz* – both are butane, the only real differences being the connector and regulator. Yachts fitted for propane systems should consult the Calor Gas Boating Industry Liaison Officer.

Fuel

Diesel (*gasoleo*, *gasoil* or simply diesel) is sold in two forms throughout Spain, *Gasoleo B* which attracts a lower tax and is only available to fishing craft, and *Gasoleo A* which is available to yachts. Not all harbours, and in particular fishing harbours, stock *Gasoleo A*. A limited number also have a pump for petrol (*gasolina*). *Petróleo* is paraffin (kerosene). Credit cards are widely, but not universally, accepted – if in doubt, check first.

Fresh water

In many places drinking water (*agua potable*) is scarce. Expect to pay for it, particularly if supplied by hose, and do not wash sails and decks before checking that it is acceptable to do so. In those harbours where a piped supply is not available for yachts a public tap can often be found – a good supply of 5 or 10 litre plastic cans will be useful.

Water quality is generally good. However it varies from place to place and year to year. Always check verbally and taste for salinity or over-chlorination before topping up tanks. If caught out, bottled water is readily available in bars and supermarkets.

Ice

Block ice for an ice-box is widely obtainable – use the largest blocks that will fit – while chemical ice is sometimes available in blocks measuring 100 x 20 x 20cms. The latter must not be used in drinks, the former only after inquiry from those who have tried the product. Cube or 'small' ice is widely obtainable and generally of drinks quality, particularly if bought in a sealed bag. An increasing number of marinas and yacht clubs now have ice machines which are usually as good as the water which is put into them.

Food and drink

There are many well stocked stores, supermarkets and hypermarkets in the larger towns and cities and it may be worth doing the occasional major stock-up by taxi. Conversely, some isolated anchorages have nothing. As a rule, availability and choice varies with the size of the town. Even the smallest has something and most older settlements (though not all tourist resorts) have a market with local produce at reasonable prices. Alcohol is cheap by UK standards with, unsurprisingly, Spanish wines good value. Spanish gin and vodka are also good value; Scotch whisky can only come from Scotland but the genuine article is often lower in price than in the UK. Shop prices generally are noticeably lower away from tourist resorts.

Most shops, other than the largest supermarkets, close for *siesta* between 1400 and 1700 and remain closed on Sunday though some smaller food shops do open on Sunday mornings. In larger towns the produce market may operate from 0800 to 1400, Monday to Saturday; in smaller towns it is more often a weekly affair. An excellent way to sample unfamiliar delicacies in small portions is in the form of bar snacks, *tapas* or the larger *raciónes. Tapas* once came on the house but are now almost invariably charged – sometimes heavily.

Security

Crime afloat is not a major problem in most areas and regrettably much of the theft which does occur can be laid at the door of other yachtsmen. Take sensible precautions – lock up before leaving the yacht, padlock the outboard to the dinghy, and secure the dinghy (particularly if an inflatable) with chain or wire rather than line. Folding bicycles are particularly vulnerable to theft, and should be chained up if left on deck.

Ashore, the situation in the big towns is no worse than in the UK and providing common sense is applied to such matters as how handbags are carried, where not to go after the bars close etc., there should be no problem.

The officials most likely to be seen are the *guardia civil*, who wear grey uniforms and deal with immigration as well as more ordinary police work, the *aduana* (customs) in navy blue uniforms, and the *policía*, also in blue uniforms, who deal with traffic rather than criminal matters.

Time

Spain keeps Standard European Time (UT+1), advanced one hour in summer to UT+2 hours. Changeover dates are now standardised with the rest of the EU as the last weekends in March and October respectively.

Unless stated otherwise, times quoted are UT.

Telephones and Fax

Telephone kiosks are common, both local and *teléfono internacional*, and most carry instructions in English. Both coins and phonecards, available from tobacconists (*estancos*), are used. If no kiosk is available marina offices have telephones and many have faxes. Most bars and hotels have metered telephones and the latter usually have faxes, though these are seldom metered.

When calling from within Spain, dial the whole code (beginning with the figure 9) whether or not the number you are calling has the same code. In some areas the number of digits to be dialled is nine, in others eight. To make an international call, dial 00 followed by the relevant country code (44 for the UK). If calling the UK do not dial the first figure of the number if it is 0.

To reach the international operator dial 025. A telephone number beginning with the figure 6 indicates a mobile telephone which will have no area code and its own code for calling its international operator. The number for information is 1003 and the land based emergency services can be contacted by this route.

To call Spain from abroad, dial the international access code (00 in the UK) followed by the code for Spain (34), then the area code (which begins with 9 except for mobile phones) followed by the individual number.

Warning Apart from a major re-organisation of area codes, individual numbers in Spain change surprisingly often.

Mail

Letters may be sent *poste restante* to any post office (*oficina de corréos*). They should be addressed with the surname (only) of the recipient followed by *Lista de Corréos* and the town. Do not enter the addressee's initials or title: that is likely to cause misfiling. Collection is a fairly cumbersome procedure and a passport is likely to be needed on collection. Alternatively, most marinas and some *club náuticos* will hold mail for yachts, but it is always wise to check in advance if possible. Uncollected letters are seldom returned.

Mail to and from the UK should be marked 'air mail' (*por avión*) but even so may take up to ten days so if speed is important communicate by fax or email. Post boxes are yellow; stamps are available from tobacconists (*estancos*), not from post offices though the latter will accept and frank mail. Almost every town has a post office; ask – *donde esta el Correo?*

Tourist offices

There is at least one tourist office in every major town or resort. Their locations vary from year to year – ask at the Port or Marina Office.

Transport and travel

Every community has some form of public transport, if only one *autobús* a day and many of the coastal towns are served by rail as well.

Taxis Are easily found in the tourist resorts though less common outside them, but can always be ordered by telephone. Car hire is simple, but either a full national or international driving licence must be shown and many companies will not lease a car to a driver over 70 years old.

Air Barcelona and Valencia have year round international flights and seasonal charter flights; Gibraltar has year round connections with the U.K. Other airports, Málaga, Murcia, Alicante, Reus (Tarragona) and Gerona, have international scheduled and charter flights in summer and year-round connections within Spain.

National holidays and *fiestas*
There are numerous official and local holidays, the latter often celebrating the local saint's day or some historical event. They usually comprise a religious procession, sometimes by boat, followed by a *fiesta* in the evening. The *Fiesta del Virgen de la Carmen* is celebrated in many harbours during mid-July. Dates of some local *fiestas* are included in the harbour information. Official holidays include:

1 January	*Año* (New Year's Day)
6 January	*Reyes Magos* (Epiphany)
19 March	*San José* (St Joseph's Day)
	Viernes Santo (Good Friday)
	Easter Monday
1 May	*Día del Trabajo* (Labour Day)
(early/mid-June)	Corpus Christi
24 June	*Día de San Juan* (St John's Day, the King's name-day)
29 June	*San Pedro y San Pablo* (SS Peter and Paul)
25 July	*Día de Santiago* (St James' Day)
15 August	*Día del Asunción* (Feast of the Assumption)
11 September	Catalan National Day
12 October	*Día de la Hispanidad* (Day of the Spanish Nation)
1 November	*Todos los Santos* (All Saints)
6 December	*Día de la Constitución* (Constitution Day)
8 December	*Inmaculada Concepción* (Immaculate Conception)
25 December	*Navidad* (Christmas Day)

When a holiday falls on a Sunday it may be celebrated the following day.

Technical information

Rescue and emergency services

In addition to VHF Ch 16 (MAYDAY or PAN PAN as appropriate) the marine emergency services can be contacted by telephone at all times on **900 202 202.**

The National Centre for Sea Rescue is based in Madrid but has a string of communications towers. On the spot responsibility for co-ordinating rescues lies with the *capitanías marítimas* with support from the Spanish Navy, customs, *guardia civil* etc. Lifeboats are stationed at some of the larger harbours but the majority do not appear to be all-weather boats.

The other emergency services can be contacted by dialling **1003** for the operator and asking for *policía* (police), *bomberos* (fire service) or *Cruz Roja* (Red Cross). Alternatively the police can be contacted direct on **091**.

Hazards

Restricted areas
Restricted areas are noted in the coastal sections.

Night approaches
Approaches in darkness to harbours backed by a town are often made difficult by the plethora of background lights of all colours and characteristics – fixed, flashing, occulting, interrupted. Strong shore lights make weaker navigation lights difficult to identify and unlit features such as exposed rocks or the line of a jetty are masked in the shadows. If possible, avoid closing an unknown harbour in the dark.

Skylines
Individual buildings on the coast – particularly prominent hotel blocks – are built, demolished, duplicated, change colour, change shape, all with amazing rapidity. They are not nearly as reliable landmarks as might be thought. If a particular building on a chart or in a photograph can be positively identified on the ground, well and good. If not, you may be in the wrong place; but on the other hand it may have been demolished, or be obscured.

Tunny nets and fish farms
During summer and autumn these nets, anchored to the sea bed and up to 6 miles long, are normally laid inshore across the current in depths of 15–40m but may be placed as far as 10 miles offshore. They may be laid in parallel lines. The outer end of a line should be marked by a float or a boat carrying a white flag with an 'A' (in black) by day, and two red or red and white lights by night. There should also be markers along the line of the net.

These nets are capable of stopping a small freighter but should you by accident, and successfully, sail over one, look out for a second within a few hundred metres. If seen, the best action may be to sail parallel to the nets until one end is reached.

Areas where nets are laid are noted in the coastal sections. However reports from the 2000 season saw no nets east of Punta Sabinal but many *calas* and bays had fish farms proliferating. These latter are often lit with flashing yellow lights but great care should be taken when entering small *calas* at night. The positions of present fish farms will be indicated in the appropriate places but their positions change frequently and new ones spring up virtually overnight!

Commercial fishing boats

Commercial fishing boats should be given a wide berth. They may be:

- Trawling singly or in pairs with a net between the boats.
- Laying a long net, the top of which is supported by floats.
- Picking up or laying pots either singly or in groups or lines.
- Trolling with one or more lines out astern.
- Drifting, trailing nets to windward.

Do not assume they know, or will observe, the law of the sea – keep well clear on principle.

Small fishing boats

Small fishing boats, including the traditional double-ended *llauds*, either use nets or troll with lines astern and should be avoided as far as possible. At night many *lámparas* put to sea and, using powerful electric or gas lights, attract fish to the surface. When seen from a distance these lights appear to flash as the boat moves up and down in the waves and can be mistaken for a lighthouse.

Speed boats etc.

Para-gliding, water-skiing, speedboats and jet-skis are all popular, and are sometimes operated by unskilled and thoughtless drivers with small regard to collision risks. In theory they are not allowed to exceed 5 knots within 100m of the coast or within 250m of bathing beaches. Water-skiing is restricted to buoyed areas.

Scuba divers and swimmers

A good watch should be kept for scuba divers and swimmers, with or without snorkel equipment, particularly around harbour entrances. If accompanied by a boat, the presence of divers may be indicated either by International Code Flag A or by a square red flag with a single yellow diagonal, as commonly seen in North America and the Caribbean.

Navigation aids

Marine radiobeacons and aerobeacons

Details will be found in both island and harbour details as appropriate.

Lights

The four-figure international numbering system has been used to identify lights in the text and on plans, those of the Mediterranean falling in Group E (Gibraltar is Group D). As each light has its own four figure number, correcting from *Notices to Mariners* or the annual *List of Lights and Fog Signals*, whether in Spanish or English, is straightforward. Certain minor lights with a five figure number are listed in the Spanish *Faros y Señales de Niebla* Part II but are not included in the international system.

Positions correspond to the largest scale Spanish chart of the area currently available. All bearings are given from seaward and refer to true north. Where a visibility sector is stated this is always expressed in a clockwise direction.

Harbour lights follow the IALA A system and are normally listed in the order in which they become relevant upon approach and entry, working from Gibraltar towards France.

It should be noted that, whilst every effort has been taken to check the lights agree with the documents mentioned above, the responsibility for maintaining the lights appears to rest with the local *capitania* and, depending on their efficiency, this can mean some lights may be defective or different from the stated characteristics at times.

Buoyage

Buoys follow the IALA A system, based on the direction of the main flood tide. Yellow topped black or red rusty buoys 500m offshore mark raw sewage outlets. Many minor harbours, however, maintain their own buoys to their own systems. Generally, yellow buoys in line mark the seaward side of areas reserved for swimming. Narrow lanes for water-skiing and sailboarding lead out from the shore and are also buoyed.

Harbour traffic signals

Traffic signals are rare, and in any case are designed for commercial traffic and seldom apply to yachts.

Storm signals

The signal stations at major ports and harbours may show storm signals, but equally they may not. With minor exceptions they are similar to the International System of Visual Storm Warnings.

Charts

See Appendix I. Current British Admiralty information is largely obtained from Spanish sources. The Spanish Hydrographic Office re-issues and corrects its charts periodically, and issues its own Notices to Mariners weekly. Corrections are repeated by the British Admiralty in due course. Spanish charts tend to be short on compass roses – carry a chart plotter or rule which incorporates a protractor.

Before departure – Spanish charts can be obtained through certain British agents, notably Imray Laurie Norie & Wilson Ltd, Wych House, The Broadway, St Ives, Huntingdon, Cambs PE27 5BT ☎ 01480 462114 *Fax* 01480 496109, *email* orders@imray.com. However stocks held are very limited and it may take time to fill an order. It may be simpler to order directly from the Instituto Hidrográfico de la Marina, Tolosa Latour 1, DP 11007 Cádiz ☎ 956 599412 *Fax* 956 275358 and pay by Eurocheque.

In Spain
British Admiralty chart agents in the area are Deposito Hidrografico, Avienda Marques de l'Argenteria, S Barcelona ☎ 933 105 209 *Fax* 933 102 374.

Spanish charts can be obtained from the following depots.

Alicante Valnautica S.A. – E.N.Rumbo Plaza Joaquín M. Avenida López, 4.
Alicante Unidad Provincial del Instituto Geografico Nacional, Plaza San Juan de Dios 3
Almería Valnautica S.L., Barrio de Pescadaría, Nuevas Naves de Armadores, Nave 13
Barcelona Librería Náutica Calle Fusteria 12
Barcelona Depósito Hidrográfico S.L. Avenida Marques de L'Argentera 5.
Barcelona J.L.Gandara y Cia., S.A., Plaza del Mar, 1 y 2.
Barcelona Librería Náutica Força VI, Balmes 69 (also stocks other pilot books including Imray publications).
Barcelona Servicio Regional del Ign en Cataluña, Carrer de la Marquesa 12.
Cartagena Valnautica S.L., Equi-Nautica, Calle Campos 13
Castellon Unidad Provincial del Instituto Geográfico Nacional, Calle Trinidad 5 – 3°
Castellon Valnautica S.L., Yatescuela, Calle Moncada 13
Denia Valnautica S.L. – A.N.Marina Plaza de Benidorm 9
Málaga J.L.Gandara y Cia. S.A. Muelle de Heredia 2
Marbella Valnautica S.L. Avenida Severo Ochoa 20 – 1°
Murcia Unidad Provincial del Instituto Geográfico Nacional, Calle Pinares, 1 bajo
San Feliu de Guixols Náutica Hipocampo, Calle San Ramón 49
Tarragona J.L.Gandara y Cia., S.A. Calle Apodaca 32
Valencia Unidad Provincial del Instituto Geográfico Nacional, Calle J.Ballester 39 – 5°, Edificio Servícios Múltiples
Valencia Valnautica S.L., E.N.Baleares, Avenida Baleares 3

Pilot books
Details of principal harbours and some interesting background information appear in the British Admiralty Hydrographic Department's *Mediterranean Pilot Vol 1 (NP 45)*. Harbour descriptions are also to be found in *Guía del Navigante – La Costa de España y el Algarve* (PubliNáutic Rilnvest SL) is produced in English and Spanish. Published annually, it carries many potentially useful advertisements for marine-related businesses.

For French readers, *Votre Livre de Bord – Méditerranée* (Bloc Marine) and *Les Guides Nautiques-Baléares* (Edition Eskis) may be helpful.

In German there are *Spanische Gewässer, Lissabon bis Golfe du Lion* (Delius Klasing), *Die Baleares* (Edition Maritim) and others, though possibly out of date in some aspects. See also Appendix II.

Horizontal Chart Datum – satellite derived positions
Positions given by GPS and other modern satellite navigation systems are normally expressed in terms of the World Geodetic System 1984 (WGS 84) Datum. New editions of British Admiralty charts are either based on WGS 84 Datum or carry a note giving the correction necessary to comply with it, but charts published by other nations' hydrographic offices may use a different datum when covering the same area. Charts of various scales published by the same national authority may also use different datum references, particularly when the printing of one chart predates another. In practice, this means that care must be taken when plotting a position expressed in latitude and longitude, or when transferring such a position from one chart to another, particularly when no reference can be made to physical features.

See also the note regarding waypoints on the verso.

Magnetic variation
Magnetic variation is noted on the coastal sections.

Traffic separation zones
There are traffic separation zones in the Straits of Gibraltar.

Radio and weather forecasts
Details of coast radio stations, weather forecasts, Weatherfax and Navtex follow. See individual harbours details for port and marina radio information. All times quoted are UT (universal time) unless otherwise specified. Only France Inter, Radio France International, BBC Radio 4 and one of the two Monaco stations observe local time (LT), thus altering the UT transmission times when the clocks change.

VHF
When calling a Spanish coast radio station on VHF use Ch 16 – the CRS will then specify which channel to switch to for further communication. When calling a marina or another vessel use Ch 9.

Coast radio stations
Coast radio stations on the Spanish Mediterranean coast are remotely controlled from the Centro Regional de Comunicaciónes Radiomarítimas (CCR) at Valencia, Spain. Several CRS were discontinued in late 1996 and others became VHF only.

In addition to the stations listed there is Pozuelo del Rey (Madrid) (EHY) which operates a comprehensive commercial service on the HF band. Full details will be found in the *Admiralty List of Radio Signals Vol 1 Part 1 (NP281/1)*.

Spanish coast radio stations no longer broadcast traffic lists on VHF. On receipt of traffic, vessels within VHF range will be called once on Ch 16, after that the vessel's call sign will be included in scheduled MF traffic lists.

See *Radio Equipment*, page 7, for information regarding radio receivers.

Weather forecasts

Only Gibraltar, both stations in Monaco, the UK Maritime Mobile Net and of course BBC Radio 4 transmit forecasts in English.

Most MRCCs and some CRS broadcast weather forecasts on VHF for local areas. Some, like Valencia for example, broadcast every H+15 on Ch 10; others less frequently after a call on Ch 16 quoting the working frequency. These are usually in Spanish and English.

Monaco

Weather forecasts

8728, 8806kHz at 0715, 1830 in French and English

4363kHz, VHF Ch 20, 24 at 0903, 1403, 1915 LT in French and English

VHF Ch 23 cont bcst (H24). Gale warnings, synopsis, 12 fcst and outlook, in French and English, for areas up to 5n miles offshore from Saint Raphael to Menton. Bulletins updated 3 times a day

Storm warnings

4363kHz, VHF Ch 20, 24 every H+03 (during hours of service) in French and English (winter 0600–2200, summer 0500–2100)

Navigational warnings

4363kHz, VHF Ch 20, 24 at 0803 LT. Urgent navigational warnings in French; also available in English on request

Valencia (CCR Group 1)

Palma 1755kHz, Cabo Gata 1764kHz. VHF Cartagena Ch 04, Alicante Ch 01, Cabo la Nao Ch 02, Castellón Ch 28, Tarragona Ch 27, Bagur Ch 23, Menorca Ch 82, Palma Ch 07, Ibiza Ch 03.

Storm warnings

1755kHz at 0803, 1203, 1703. 1764kHz at 0833, 1233, 1733 in Spanish

Weather forecasts

1755, 1764kHz at 0803, 0833, fcst valid for 18hrs in Spanish; 1755, 1764kHz at 1203, 1233, fcst valid for 60hrs in Spanish; 1755, 1764kHz at 1703, 1733, fcst valid for 36hrs.

VHF Ch 04 at 0910, 2110; 24hr fcst for Cabo Tiñoso to the Spanish/French border, in Spanish

VHF Ch 04 at 1410; 48hr fcst for Cabo Tiñoso to the French/Spanish border, in Spanish

Navigational warnings

1755kHz at 0803, 1203, 1703; 1764kHz at 0833, 1233, 1733. VHF Ch 04 at 0910, 2110 (Cabo Tiñoso to the Spanish/French border)

Barcelona (MRCC)

VHF Ch 10, 16

Weather forecasts

VHF Ch 10 at 0700, 1000, 1600, 2100 LT in Spanish and English

Navigatinal warnings

VHF Ch 16 at 0700, 1000, 1600, 2100 in Spanish and English

Tarragona (MRCC)

VHF Ch 13

Weather forecasts

VHF Ch 13 at 0630, 1030, 1630, 2130 LT in Spanish and English

Navigational warnings

VHF Ch 13 at 0630, 1030, 1630, 2130 LT in Spanish and English

Alger (7TA), Algeria

Weather forecasts

1792kHz at 0903, 1703. 12h fcst in French; 0903, 1705 gale warnings, synopsis, 12h fcst and outlook for a further 12h in French for all areas

Storm warnings

2691kHz on receipt at the end of the next two silence periods. 0918, 2118. Gale warnings in French for all areas

Navigational warnings

1792kHz at 0918, 2118 and on request. In French for Algerian coastal waters, Western Mediterranean south of 40°N, west of a line from the Algerian–Tunisian frontier to C Spartivento (38°52'N 8°52'E)

Gibraltar Broadcasting Corporation

Weather forecasts

1458kHz, 91·3, 92·6, 100·5MHz Mon–Fri 0530, 0630, 0730, 1030, 1230. Sat 0530, 0630, 0730, 1030. Sun

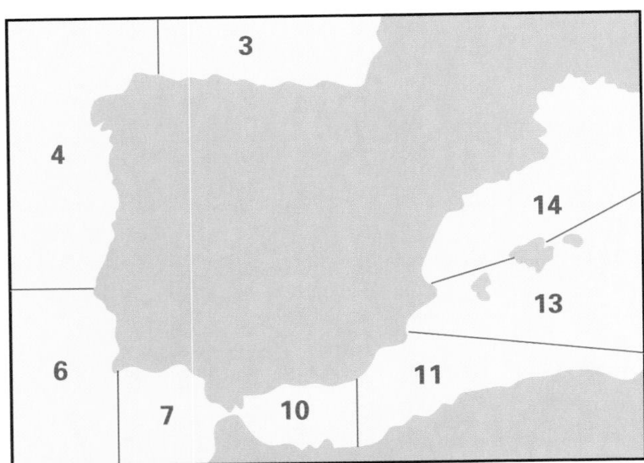

SPANISH WEATHER FORECAST AREAS

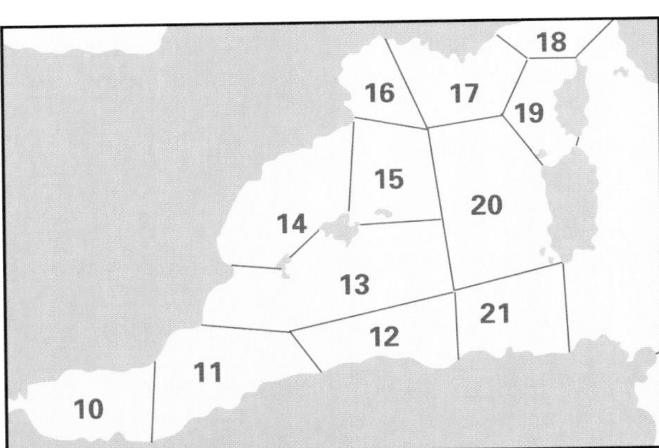

FRENCH WEATHER FORECAST AREAS

Mediterranean sea areas bear the following names in French forecasts and are usually given in this order: 511–Alboran, 512–Palos, 513–Alger, 514–*Cabrera*, 515–*Baleares*, 516–*Minorque*, 521–*Lion*, 522–*Provence*, 523–*Sardaigne*, 524–Annaba, 525–Tunis, 531–*Ligure*, 532–*Corse*, 533–*Elbe*, 534–*Maddalena*, 535–Circeo, 536–Carbonara, 537–Lipari.

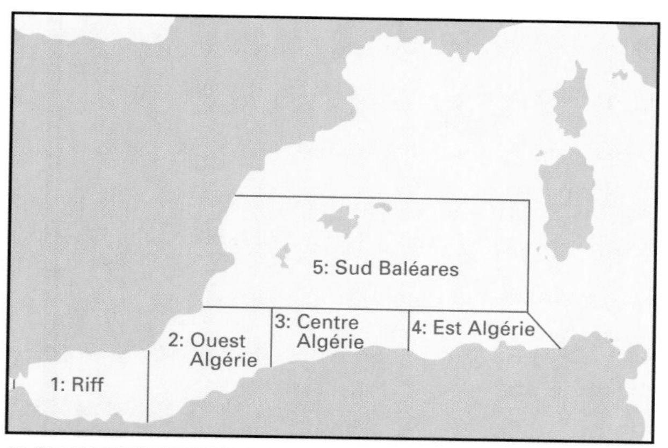

ALGERIAN WEATHER FORECAST AREAS

0630, 0730, 1030. General synopsis, situation, fcst, wind direction and strength, sea state, visibility for area up 5n miles from Gibraltar in English.

BFBS Gibraltar

Weather forecasts

93·5, 97·85MHz Mon–Fri 0745, 0845, 1005, 1605 LT. Sat 0845, 0945, 1202 LT. Sun 0845, 0945, 1202, 1602 LT. Shipping fcst, wind, weather, visibility, sea state, swell high water and low water times for local waters within 5 miles of Gibraltar in English

89·4, 99·5MHz Mon–Fri 1200 (UK LT). Shipping fcst, wind, weather visibility, sea state, swel high water and low water times for local waters within 5 miles of Gibraltar in English

UK Maritime Mobile Net

In addition to 'official' weather forecasts, that given by the UK Maritime Mobile Net covering the Eastern Atlantic and Mediterranean is reported to be useful. The Net can be heard on 14303kHz SSB on the Upper Side Band at 0800 and 1800 UT daily, the forecast following about 30 minutes later. On Saturday there is sometimes a preview of the coming week's weather prospects. It is not necessary to have either a transceiver or a transmitting licence to listen to the Net – see Radio equipment, page 7.

BBC Radio 4, UK

Weather forecasts 198kHz at 0048, 0535, Sat 0556. Topical Lesiure fcst for the Uk and other parts of Europe

Occasionally the synopsis provides advance warning of the approach of an Atlantic depression which could lead to a northwesterly *tramontana.*

German language

Offenbach (Main)/Pinneberg (DDH) (DDK), Germany

4583, 7646kHz at 0415, 1610, 5 day fcst in English

4583, 7646kHz at 1015, 2215, 2 day fcst in English. Route Alboran–Tunis

4583, 7646kHz at 1115, 2315 2 day fcst in English. Route Eastern Tunis–Rhodes/Cyprus

4583, 7646kHz at 1550 24hr fcst in English.

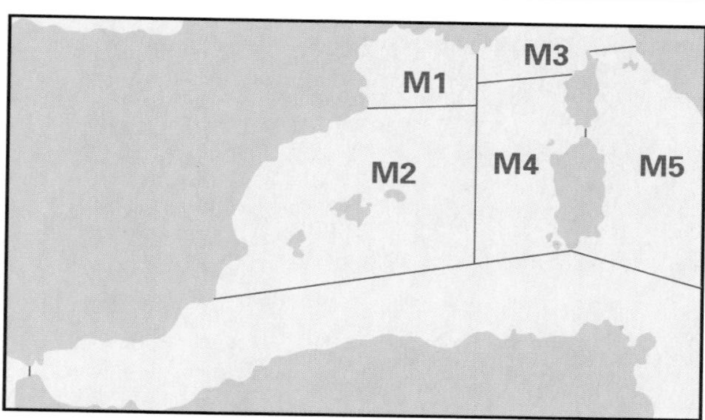

GERMAN WEATHER FORECAST AREAS

NON-RADIO WEATHER FORECASTS

A recorded marine forecast in Spanish is available by telephoning (906) 36 53 71. The 'High Seas' bulletin includes the Islas Baleares.

Spanish television shows a useful synoptic chart with its land weather forecast every evening after the news at approximately 2120 weekdays, 1520 Saturday and 2020 Sunday. Most national and local newspapers also carry some form of forecast.

Nearly all marinas and yacht harbours display a synoptic chart and forecast, generally updated daily (though often posted rather late to be of use).

WEATHERFAX

Rome (1265) broadcast weatherfax transmissions for reception via SSB and computer or dedicated weatherfax receiver. Refer to the Admiralty *List of Radio Signals Vol 3 Part 1 (NP 283/1)* for times and frequencies.

NAVTEX

Navtex is transmitted on the standard frequency of 518kHz. The Mediterranean and Black Sea fall within NAVAREA III.

Valencia (Cabo de la Nao), Spain

Identification letter X

Weather forecasts

Cabo de la Nao at 0750, 1950. Gale warnings, synopsis, 24h fcst in English

Navigational warnings

At 0350, 0750, 1150, 1550, 1950, 2350 in English.

La Garde (CROSS), France

Identification letter W

Weather forecasts

Fort Ste Marguerite at1140, 2340 in English

Navigational warnings

At 0340, 0740, 1140, 1540, 1940, 2340 in English

Key to symbols

English	Spanish
harbourmaster/ port office	*Capitán de Puerto*
fuel	*gasoil, gasolina*
yacht chandler	*efectos navales*
crane	*grua*
travel-lift	*grua giratoria*
yacht club	*Club Náutico*
showers	*ducha*
information	*información*
post office	*correos*
slipway	*grada*
anchorage	*fondeadero*
anchoring prohibited	*fondeadero prohibido*
yachts	*yates*

Costa del Azahar

Introduction

General description
This 115M section of coast, which stretches from a point just to the N of Cabo de San Antonio to a few miles to the S of the Río Ebro, is called the Costa del Azahar (Orange Blossom Coast) because of the huge areas of orange groves which stretched along the coast of Valencia. Sections of this coast have since been industrialised and both sea and air pollution are such that it might easily be called the Costa Negra (Black Coast) in places! Where industry does not exist the coast is pleasant and to a large extent unspoilt even by tourist development though construction of large apartment blocks continues apace.

From the high cliffs and mountains immediately to the N of Cabo San Antonio, of which Montaña Mongó is a conspicuous feature, the coast becomes low and flat. This whole section of coast has, in general, straight sandy beaches, sometimes with low cliffs or sand dunes behind them and with mountain ranges some distance inland. The only exceptions are near Cabos Cullera, Oropesa and Irta where there are mountainous features on the coast. A number of rivers flow into the sea, most of which do not dry out in summer. The Arabs brought prosperity to the area by building and organising the irrigation system and introducing the orange and lemon trees which they planted in huge orchards but it is perhaps due to the lack of natural harbours the larger towns are of comparatively recent origin.

Visits
Details of interesting places to visit are given in the section dealing with the harbour concerned. There are large numbers of caves, some of which were occupied by prehistoric man, located in the hills which lie inland of the S section of this coast.

The old town of Sagunto is an exceptional place and it should be visited even if not going to the harbour itself; it can easily be reached from Valencia. Onda, where the famous blue *azulejas* tiles are made, also has a ruined castle which can be visited. It lies inland from Castellón de la Plana. For those who like walking, the Monasterio del Desierto de las Palmas which lies behind Benicasim should be visited. Inland from Vinaroz lies the exceptional town of Morella which has remains of Iberian, Celtic, Greek, Carthaginian, Roman and Arab civilisations.

Many other places of interest lie further inland and can be visited by taxi, bus and some by train. Details are best obtained from the local tourist office.

Pilotage and navigation

Restricted areas
It is forbidden to anchor in an area immediately to the W of the Islote Columbrete Grande. There is an oil terminal at Castellón de la Plana. Offshore, oil drilling platforms and wells have been established some 15M to E of Cabo Tortosa. Although the coast is generally free from dangers, there are shoal areas off shore. Even where there may be adequate depth for vessels, in heavy weather uncomfortable or even dangerous seas may occur well off shore because of the sea bed rising gently and evenly towards the shore.

Gales – harbours of refuge
Gales are rare and hardly ever occur in summer. The *levante* from the E, preceded by heavy swell and rain, is possibly the worst. In the event of onshore winds and heavy seas, Valencia, Sagunto and Castellón de la Plana are the safest to enter.

Magnetic variation
1°35'W (2002) decreasing 7' annually.

Puerto de Dénia

38°51'N 0°08'E

Charts
British Admiralty *1458, 1700, 1701*
French *7296, 4719*
Spanish *4751, 833, 834*

Lights
To the southeast
0180 **Cabo de San Antonio** 38°48'·1N 0°11'·8E Fl(4)20s175m26M White tower and building 17m
Harbour
0184 **Dique Norte head** 38°50'·8N 0°07'·6E Fl(3)G.11·5s13m5M White tower, green top 7m
0187 **Dique Norte elbow** Fl.G.2s4m4M White tower, green top 3m (582m from head)
0187·5 **Dique Norte Spur head** Fl.2s4m3M White tower 3m 226°-vis-134·5°
0185 **Dique Sur head** Fl(2)R.9s9m5M White tower, red top 7m
0188 **Dique Sur elbow** Fl(4)R.11s5m4M White tower, red top 3m
0188·5 **Pier head** Iso.R Red tower 3m

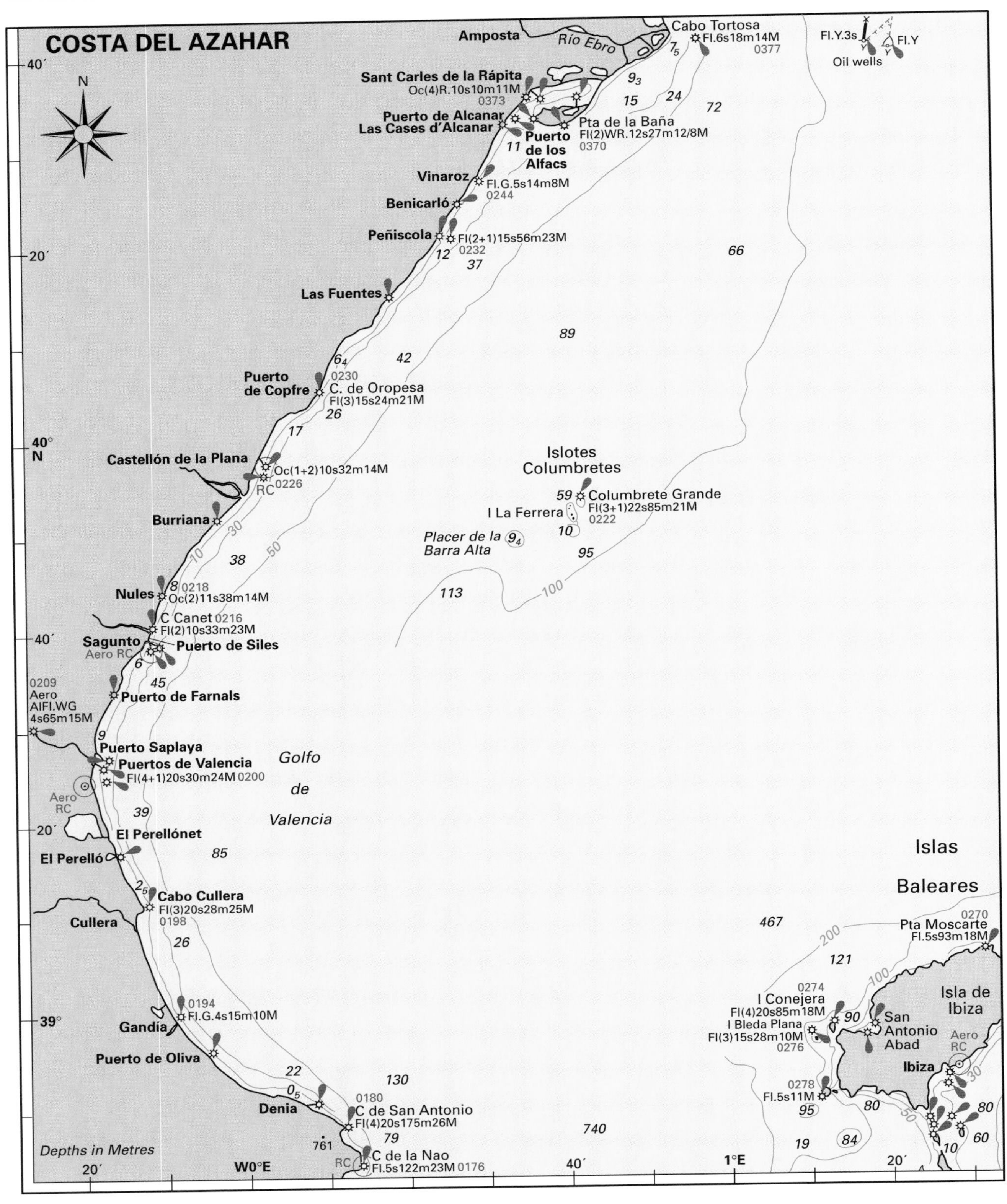

0186 **Ldg Lts 228°** *Front* Fl.R.2·5s10m4M Metal column with platform 10m 198°-vis-258°
0186·1 *Rear* 150m from front Oc.R.6s14m4M Metal column with platform 10m 198°-vis-258°

To the northwest

0198 **Cabo Cullera** 39°11'·1N 0°13'·0E Fl(3)20s28m25M White truncated cone 16m

Port communications

VHF Ch 9. *Club náutico* ☎ 96 578 09 89 *Fax* 96 578 08 50.
VHF Ch 9. Marina de Denia ☎ 966 424 307 *Fax* 966 424 387

Planning guide (Costa del Azahar)

Distance (miles)	*Harbours & Anchorages*	*Headlands*
	Puerto de Denia (page 17)	Cabo de San Antonio
11M	⚓ *Cala Almadraba*	
	Puerto de Oliva (page 21)	
5M		
	Puerto de Gandía (page 24)	
10M	⚓ *El Broquil*	Rio Jucar
	Puerto de Cullera (page 25)	
	⚓ *S of Cabo Cullera*	
8M	⚓ *Cabo Cullera*	Cabo Cullera
	⚓ *N of Cabo Cullera*	
	Puerto El Perelló (page 28)	
2M		
	Puerto de Perellónet (page 30)	
11M		
	Puertos de Valencia (page 31)	
4M		
	Puerto Saplaya (page 33)	
5M		
	Pobla Marina (page 35)	
6M		
	Puerto de Sagunto (page 36)	
1·5M		Cabo Canet
	Puerto de Siles (page 38)	
13M		
	Puerto de Burriana (page 40)	
8M		
	Puerto de Castellón de la Plana (page 41)	
9M	⚓ *Olla de Benicasim*	
	⚓ *S of Cabo Oropesa*	
	Puerto de Copfre (page 44)	
11M		Cabo Oropesa
	Puerto de las Fuentes (page 46)	
8M		
	Puerto de Peñíscola (page 47)	
4M	⚓ *N of Peninsula de Peñíscola*	
	Puerto de Benicarló (page 50)	
4M		
	Puerto de Vinaroz (page 52)	
6M	**Islotes Columbretes** (page 54)	
	Puerto de les Cases d'Alcanar (page 61)	

General

A fishing, ferry and commercial harbour occupied by all invaders from the Greeks (600BC) onwards; the latest are the tourists. Repair and other facilities are good. The old town, castle and the surrounding area are attractive. Sandy beaches on either side of the harbour, those to the N being best.

There is now a new Marina de Denia just to port on entering with 400 more berths with depths of 3 to 4m, but the port is still crowded in high season.

Work is going on on the SW side of Espigón Central and there is an (unlit?) E cardinal buoy just to starboard of the leading lines off the *espigón* end.

Approach

From the SE Round the high, steep-sided, flat-topped promontory of Cabo de San Antonio and follow the coast keeping a mile offshore to avoid shoals. In the closer approach, Castillo de Dénia will be seen on a small hill behind the harbour and the Dique del Norte. Do not cut the corner but make for a position 200m to NE of the head of this *dique*.

From the NW The low sandy coast is backed by high ranges of mountains. Montaña Mongo which lies behind this harbour, and the vertically faced Cabo de San Antonio which lies beyond it can be seen from afar. In the closer approach the Castillo de Dénia on its small hill and the long Dique del Norte will be seen. Keep at least 1M off the coast owing to shoals and make for a position 200m to NE of the head of Dique del Norte.

The head of the Dique del Norte has been washed away and underwater obstructions may still remain up to 100m to NE of the present visible head.

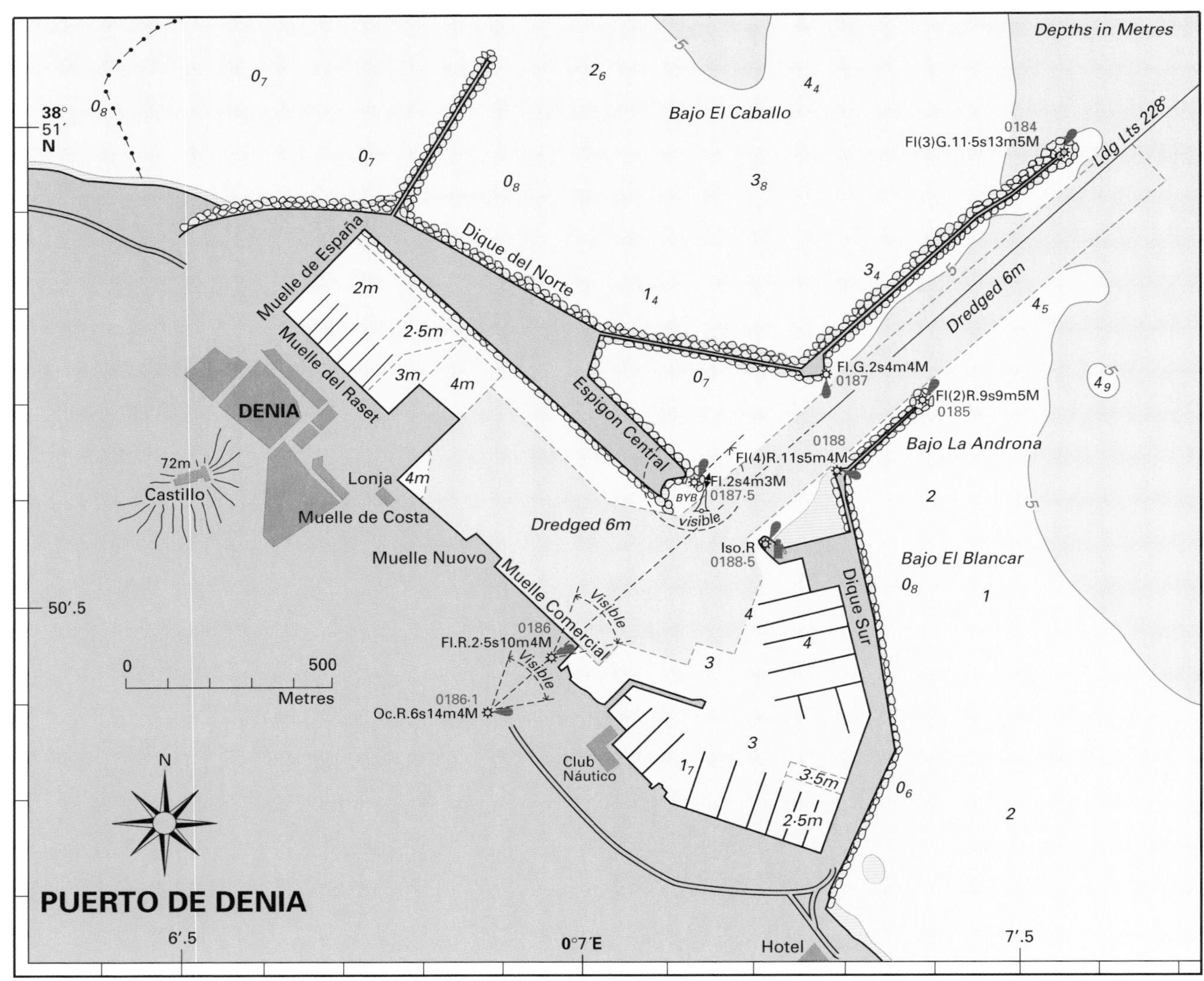

Anchorage in the approach

Anchor 300m to the E of the head of Dique del Norte in 7m, sand.

Entrance

From at least 200m to NE, approach the entrance on a SW course, give the head of Dique del Norte 30m and follow it in at this distance off.

Berths

There are now three marinas in the harbour. The Municipal Marina, at the NW end, is for small craft (<7m) only and it is for private berth holders only. The yacht club is still available for visiting yachts (call *club náutico* on Ch 9) but is expensive. There is now a new marina, immediately to port on entering (call *Marina de Denia* on Ch 9), which has nearly 400 berths and although farther away from the town it is planned have all facilities built nearby during the 2001 season.

Charges

Medium; at the *club náutico*, high.

Facilities

All ship work bar radar.
Two slipways, maximum 100 tonnes.
Cranes up to 12 tonnes.
Chandler's shop behind the shipyard.
Water from taps around the yacht harbour and on the Muelle de Atraque.
Gasoleo A and petrol in the port and, for members only, the *club náutico*.
Ice factory to the E of the Castillo de Dénia. Ice is also available from the yacht club.
The Club Náutico de Dénia has a large modern clubhouse with bar, lounge, restaurant, showers and so on. It is responsible for the S corner of the harbour. An introduction may be required.
A good range of shops in the town and an excellent market.
Launderettes in the town.

Communications

Bus service. Dénia is one terminus of the coastal narrow gauge rail system. Ferries to Islas Baleares.
☎ Area code 96. Taxi ☎ 578 34 98.

Puerto de Denia. Photographed before the Dique Sur Yacht Harbour was built

⚓ Cala del Almadraba

Cala del Almadraba. Anchor off the beach in 3m. Open between NW and E – use only when the wind is off shore.

Puerto de Oliva

38°56'N 0°05'W

Charts

British Admiralty *1701*
French *4719*
Spanish *834*
Navicarte *E10*

Lights

0190 **Dique de Abrigo** 38°56'·1N 0°05'·4W Fl(2)G.5s7m4M White tower, green top 4m
0190·2 **Contradique** Fl(3)R.12s7m4M White tower, red top 4m

Port communications

Capitanía VHF Ch 9 ☎ 962 850 596 *Fax* 962 839 000.
Club náutico ☎ 962 853 423 for bookings.

General

This is a modern artificial yacht harbour that has been built out from the coast between Denia (12M) and Gandia (5M) and is not overlooked by high-rise buildings. The harbour and entrance have to be dredged of silt dumped in flash floods from the small river which flows at the head of the harbour.

Undredged, the natural level seems to be about 1m only. Long sandy beaches on each side of the harbour.

Approach

It is most important to sound carefully and go slowly when entering, leaving or manoeuvring inside this harbour. In bad weather the area of the Algar de la Almadraba 7M to SE should be avoided because of heavy seas.

From the south Round the high, steep-to Cabo San Antonio which is backed by Montaña Mongó (753m). Pass the breakwaters of the Puerto de Denia and keep 4M off the coast to avoid rough seas over the shallow area, Algar de la Almadraba. The breakwaters and conspicuous *club náutico* of this harbour will be seen in the close approach.

From the north Round Cabo Cullera which is conspicuous and looks like an island in the distance. Follow the coast at 2M passing the breakwaters of the Puerto de Gandia which, with its cranes, and harbour-works, will easily be recognised. The breakwaters and *club náutico* of this harbour are also conspicuous in the close approach from this direction.

Anchorage in the approach

Anchor 200m to NE of the entrance in 10m, sand.

Entrance

Approach the entrance on a SW course. Round the head of the Dique de Abrigo leaving it 15m to starboard. Enter at a very slow speed while sounding carefully.

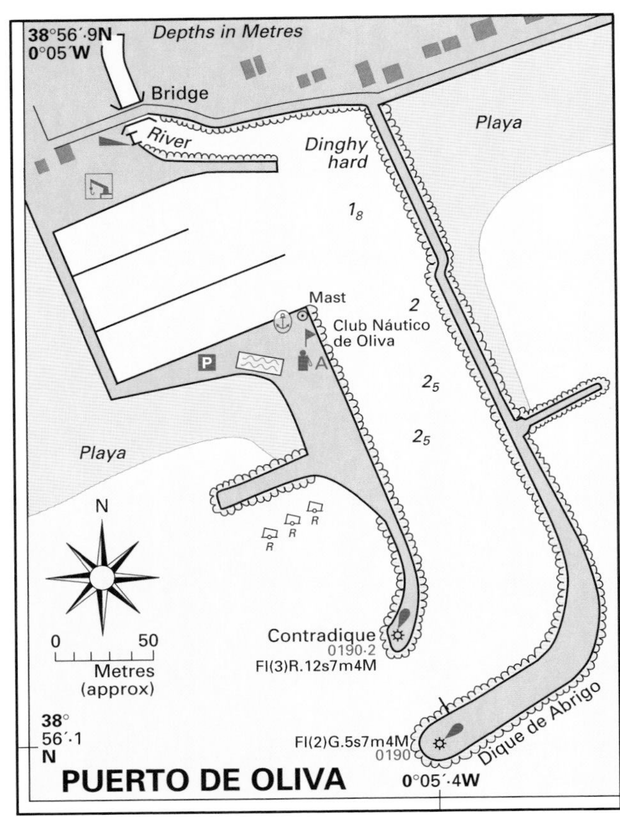

Berths

Secure to a vacant berth beside the *club náutico* and ask at the office for a visitor's berth.

Puerto de Oliva

Charges
High.

Facilities
Maximum length overall 12m.
Small slipway to SE of the *club náutico* and another at NW corner of the harbour.
5-tonne crane at NW end of the harbour.
Water taps on pontoons and quays.
220v AC sockets on pontoons and quays.
Gasoleo A.
Small ice from *club náutico* bar.
Club Náutico de Oliva has bars, lounges, terrace, swimming pool, showers/WC etc.
Basic provisions from shops nearby; more shops in the town of Oliva 1½M inland.

Communications
Bus and rail service from Oliva.

Puerto de Gandía
39°00'N 0°09'W

Charts
British Admiralty *1458, 1701*
French *7296, 4719*
Spanish *4752, 834*
Navicarte *E10*

Lights
0194 **Dique Norte head** 38°59'·8N 0°08'·7W Fl.G.4s15m10M Gteen triangular concrete tower 12m
0193 **Contradique head** Fl(2)R.7s9m6M Red triangular concrete tower 8m
0196 **Muelle Sur head** Fl(3)R.11s5m2M Red concrete column 3m
0196·2 **Dársena Deportiva** Fl(2)G.7s5m2M Green concrete column 2m
0196·25 **Contradique head** Fl(2+1)G.14·5s5m2M Green concrete column, red band 2m
0196·3 **Muelle corner** Fl(3)G.10s5m2M Green concrete column 3m
0196·35 **Muelle Frutero corner** Fl(4)R.12s5m2M Red concrete column 3m

Port communications
VHF Ch 9. Real Club Náutico de Gandía ☎/*Fax* 962 841 050.

General
A commercial and fishing port with a large ship-breaking yard. It is easy to approach and enter and offers good protection except in gales from SE. The self-contained yacht harbour is on the N side of the complex.

In 1485 the Dukedom of the Borgia was founded nearby by the ancestors of the famous Italian family. The harbour is known for the large amount of oranges it exports.

The Palace of the Dukes of Gandía, the Collegiate Church, the Castillo de Bayrén, Cova de Parpalló and, a little distance away the monastery of San Jerónimo de Cotalba, are all worth visiting. There is a long sandy beach to N of the harbour. Local holidays are: St Francis Borgia, 9–10 October and St Joseph, 19 March.

Puerto de Gandía

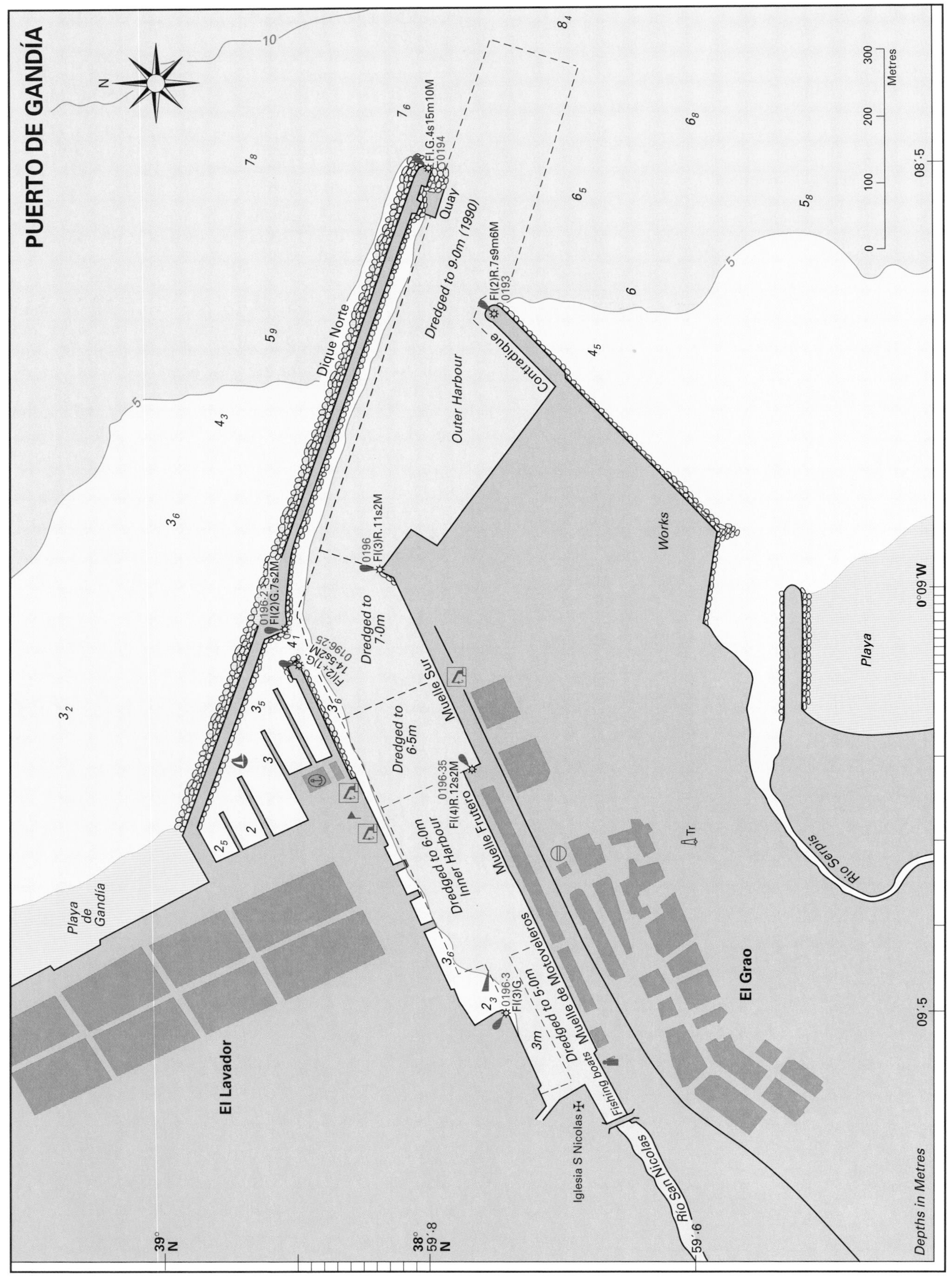
PUERTO DE GANDÍA
N
Fl.G.4s15m10M
0194
Quay
Dredged to 9.0m (1990)
Fl(2)R.7s9m6M
0193
Contradique
Dique Norte
Outer Harbour
0196
Fl(3)R.11s2M
0196.2
Fl(2)G.7s2M
Fl(2+1)G.
14·5s2M
0196·25
Dredged to 7·0m
Dredged to 6·5m
Muelle Sur
0196·35
Fl(4)R.12s2M
Muelle Frutero
Dredged to 6·0m
Inner Harbour
Dredged to 5·0m
Muelle de Motoveleros
0196·3
Fl(3)G
Fishing boats
Iglesia S Nicolas
Río San Nicolas
El Lavador
Playa de Gandía
El Grao
Works
Tr
Playa
Río Serpis
0 100 200 300
Metres
08'·5
0°09'·0W
09'·5
39° N
38° 59'·8 N
59'·6
Depths in Metres

Approach

From the south The coast from Cabo San Antonio (167m, which has a vertical cliff-face and is backed by Montaña Mongó, 753m) becomes low and sandy with ranges of hills in the hinterland. Pass the long breakwater of Puerto de Denia and keep an eye on depths and the chart if you close the shore. A high peak, Montaña Monduber (841m), will be seen to the W of this port, which will be recognised by the houses, cranes and the *diques*.

From the north Having rounded the conspicuous Cabo Cullera, which has the appearance of an offshore island when viewed from afar, the coast becomes low, flat and sandy. Gandia may be seen standing isolated in a flat plain at the foot of a valley, the blocks of flats being conspicuous from this direction. Keep clear of a fish farm some 2 miles north of the breakwater which has 4 buoys Fl(3)Y.9s3M with cross topmarks.

Anchorage in the approach

Anchor 500m to SW of the head of Dique Norte in 7m sand. Sound carefully in the approach due to silting.

Entrance

To the S of the entrance the Río Serpis deposits silt and depths decrease steadily. The harbour is periodically dredged but sound carefully when entering.

Approach Dique Norte on a W course, leaving the Dique Norte 50m to starboard. The narrow entrance is reduced by rod-fishermen operating from the *dique*. Follow Dique Norte at this distance and pass Dique Sur. The yacht harbour entrance lies ahead between two lit pier heads just beyond a building on the Dique Norte. Entering involves an S-bend, first to starboard then to port.

Berths

Ask at the *club náutico*.

Anchorages

Anchoring in the outer harbour is forbidden.

Charges

High.

Facilities

Maximum length overall 25m.
70-tonne travel-lift.
10-tonne crane at the *club náutico*. More powerful cranes are available at the Muelle Comercial. Contact *capitán de puerto*.
A small slipway on the N side of the harbour.
Engine repairs, GRP, painting, joinery in the port.
Two small chandlers near the harbour and two others in the town of Gandia.
Water from taps on the quay and pontoons by the *club náutico* and on the Muelle Comercial and pontoons. Check with notices to see if it is considered to be drinkable.
220v AC on pontoons.
Gasoleo A by the yacht club.
Ice from a factory at the N end of the bridge over the Río San Nicolás.
Club Náutico de Gandia has several bars, lounges, terraces, a restaurant, snack bar, showers, swimming pool, etc.
A few shops near the *club náutico*, some more to the W and S of the harbour and very many in the town of Gandia where there is a daily market.
Laundry and launderettes in the town of Gandia.

Communications

Rail and bus services. Taxi ☎ 284 30 30.

⚓ **El Broquil**

El Broquil. A river accessible by small boats in calm weather without swell. 1–1·5m in the canal which silts. No facilities.

Puerto de Cullera

39°09'N 0°14'W

Charts

British Admiralty *1701*
French *4719*
Spanish *834*
Navicarte *E09*

Lights

0197·2 **Malecón Sur** near head Fl(2)R.5s10m3M Red round tower on square base 7m
0197 **Malecón Norte head** 39°09'·1N 0°14'·0W Fl.G.3s10m5M Green round tower on square base 7m

To the north

0198 **Cabo Cullera** 39°11'·1N 0°13'·0W Fl(3)20s28m25M White conical tower 16m

Port communications

VHF Ch 9. Club Náutico de Cullera ☎ 961 521 154/961 217 778.

General

This harbour lies about 1M up the Río Júcar. The approach is easy but the entrance into the river mouth can only be undertaken in good conditions and is not possible with winds between NE and SE. There is very good shelter once inside, alongside an attractive old town which has many shops and good communications. A huge development consisting of high apartment blocks has been built around the hills to NE of the town to cater for the thousands of holiday-makers. The remains of an old castle and the Ermita de la Virgen del Castillo on the hill nearby, with a fine view, should be visited. The fine sandy beaches on either side of the Sierra de Cullera are very crowded in the high season. The Saturday following Easter is a holiday in honour of Nuestra Señora del Castillo. In July and August there is a regatta.

The site has been occupied since the fourth century BC and there are ruins of a city wall dating from this period. Like several places with an isolated mountain and marshy land around, it claims to be the site of Hemeroskopeion, the first Phoenician town in Spain.

Beacon

A black post with a black ▲ topmark (5·5m) on the rock Escollo del Moro (0·7m) marks a shallow patch of rocks which is located ¼M to NNE of the entrance.

Approach

From the south The low, flat, sandy coast is backed by mountain ranges which recede from the coast as one proceeds to the N. The isolated feature, the Sierra de Cullera (222m) which is surrounded by flat lands, appears as an offshore island in the distance.

In the closer approach the town of Cullera will be seen at the SW foot of this feature. The entrance to the river has two low rocky training walls with some coastal buildings and apartment blocks nearby and an isolated factory chimney which should be approached on a bearing of 280°.

From the north Having passed the very conspicuous harbour walls of Valencia the countryside is low and flat and the coast sandy. There are a number of high-rise buildings in groups along the coast and more under construction. Again the Sierra de Cullera appears as an offshore island in the distance. Round the steep-cliffed Cabo Cullera which has a conspicuous lighthouse and is steep-to, keeping on a S course and changing to SW after 1½M to avoid the Escollo del Moro (0·7m) marked by a black beacon with a ▲ topmark (5·5m). In the closer approach the rocky training walls should be seen.

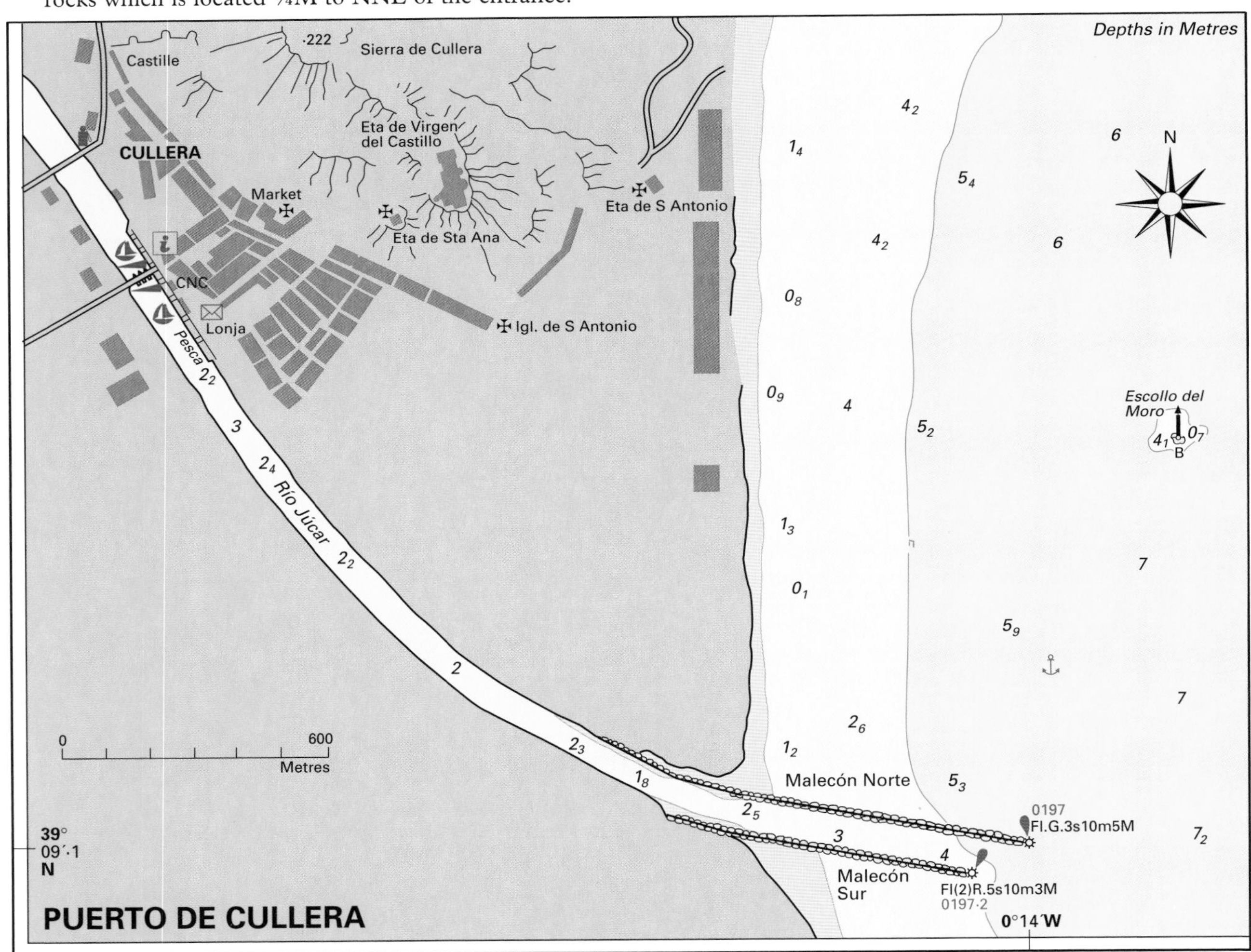

Río Júcar (river mouth)

Anchorage in the approach
Anchor 400m to NE of the entrance in 7m, sand and mud.

Entrance
Line up the two rocky training walls, approach on 280° and enter between. The depths in the river vary with the amount of water flowing and the silt deposited. Anchorage in the river is forbidden.

Berths
Berth alongside the quay on the starboard hand with bow upriver just inside the entrance or just short of the lower road bridge and check with the Club Náutico de Cullera. Yachts without masts may prefer to secure above the lower road bridge. If all berths are taken secure outside a suitable yacht.

Charges
Low.

Facilities
A small shipyard above the road bridge can carry out simple repairs. There are several engine mechanics.
15-tonne crane below the lower bridge.
A small slipway by the lower road bridge and another above it, both on the NE bank.
Limited chandlery from the shipyard and from a shop near the *club náutico*.
Taps on pontoons and quays also a water point above the lower road bridge and also near the mouth of the river. Water on quay by the *club náutico* is not drinkable.
220v AC points below the lower road bridge.
Gasoleo A and petrol from garage 300m beyond the upper road bridge on the way to Valencia.
The Club Náutico de Cullera is on the NE bank below the lower road bridge.
A number of shops nearby and a large market.
Launderette in the town.

Puerto de Cullera

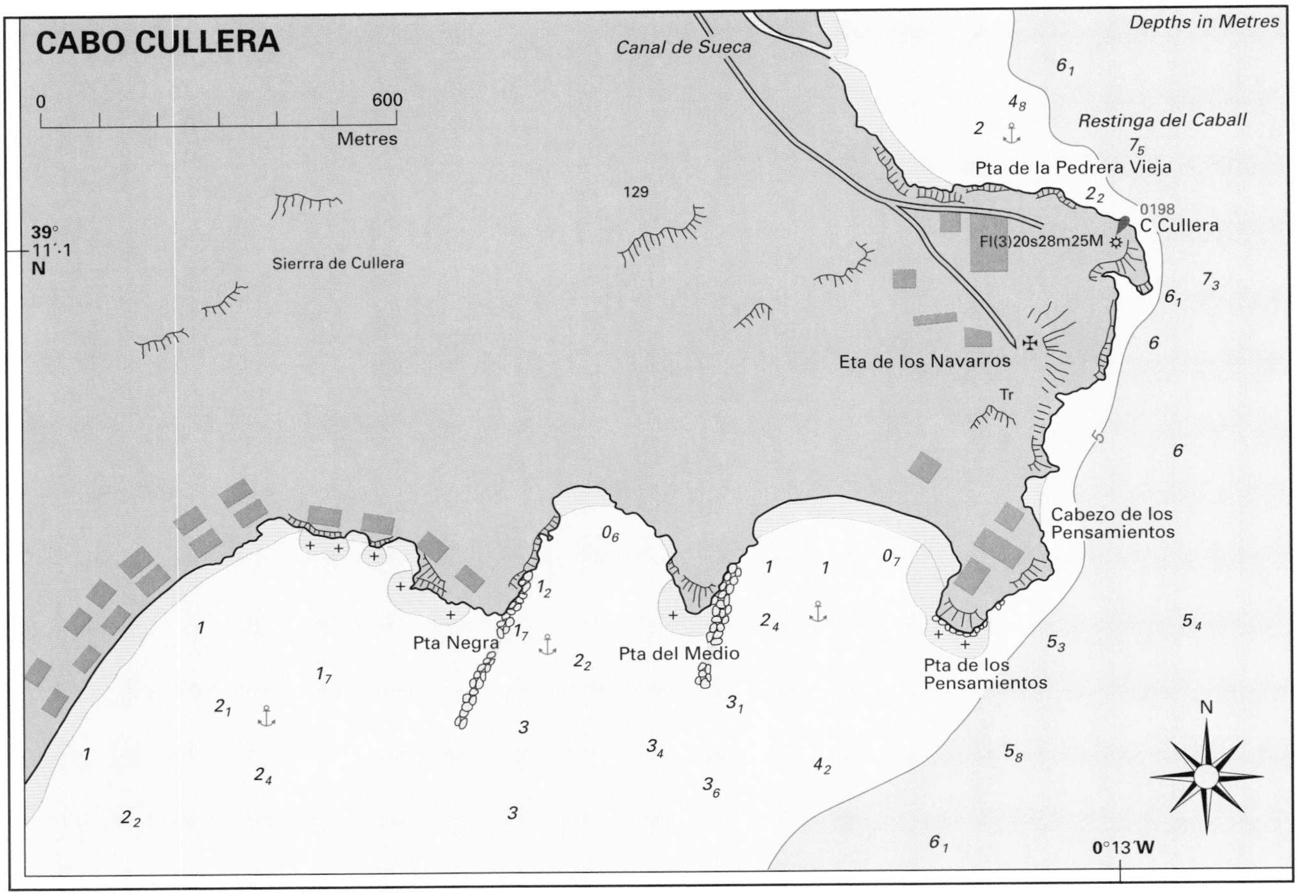

CABO CULLERA

0 600
Metres

Depths in Metres
Canal de Sueca
Restinga del Caball
Pta de la Pedrera Vieja
0198
C Cullera
Fl(3)20s28m25M
39°
11'·1
N
Sierrra de Cullera
129
Eta de los Navarros
Tr
Cabezo de los
Pensamientos
Pta Negra
Pta del Medio
Pta de los
Pensamientos
N
0°13'W

⚓ S of Cabo Cullera

South of Cabo Cullera. A spacious anchorage in sand S of the range of hills which culminates at Cabo Cullera. It is open to SE with swell from NE but is otherwise well protected.

⚓ N of Cabo Cullera

A rather exposed anchorage open to NE with swell from NW and SE. Anchor close inshore under the protection of Punta la Pedrera Vieja in 4m sand but sound carefully because the depths can change after strong winds. The road to the conspicuous lighthouse also leads to Cullera (2½M) There are a few shops in the area to S of Cabo Cullera (½M). Good sandy beaches nearby.

⚓ Cabo Cullera

Looking NW. The rather exposed anchorages on one or other side are usually in a lee but swell from both NE and SE can reach round to the other side of the point.

Puerto El Perelló

39°17'N 0°16'W

Charts

British Admiralty *1701*
French *4719*
Spanish *476, 834*
Navicarte *E09*

Lights

To the south
0198 **Cabo Cullera** 39°11'·1N 0°13'·0W
Fl(3)20s28m25M White conical tower 16m
Harbour
0199 **Dique de Levante head** 39°16'·8N 0°16'·3W
Fl(3)G.15s8m4M Green tower 3m
0199·2 **Dique de Poniente head** Fl(3)R.11s7m4M
Red tower 5m

Port communications

VHF Ch 9. Club Náutico El Perelló ☎ 961 770 386, ☎/*Fax* 961 770 412.

General

This artificial harbour has been built in the mouth of the largest river which drains the huge inland

Puerto El Perelló

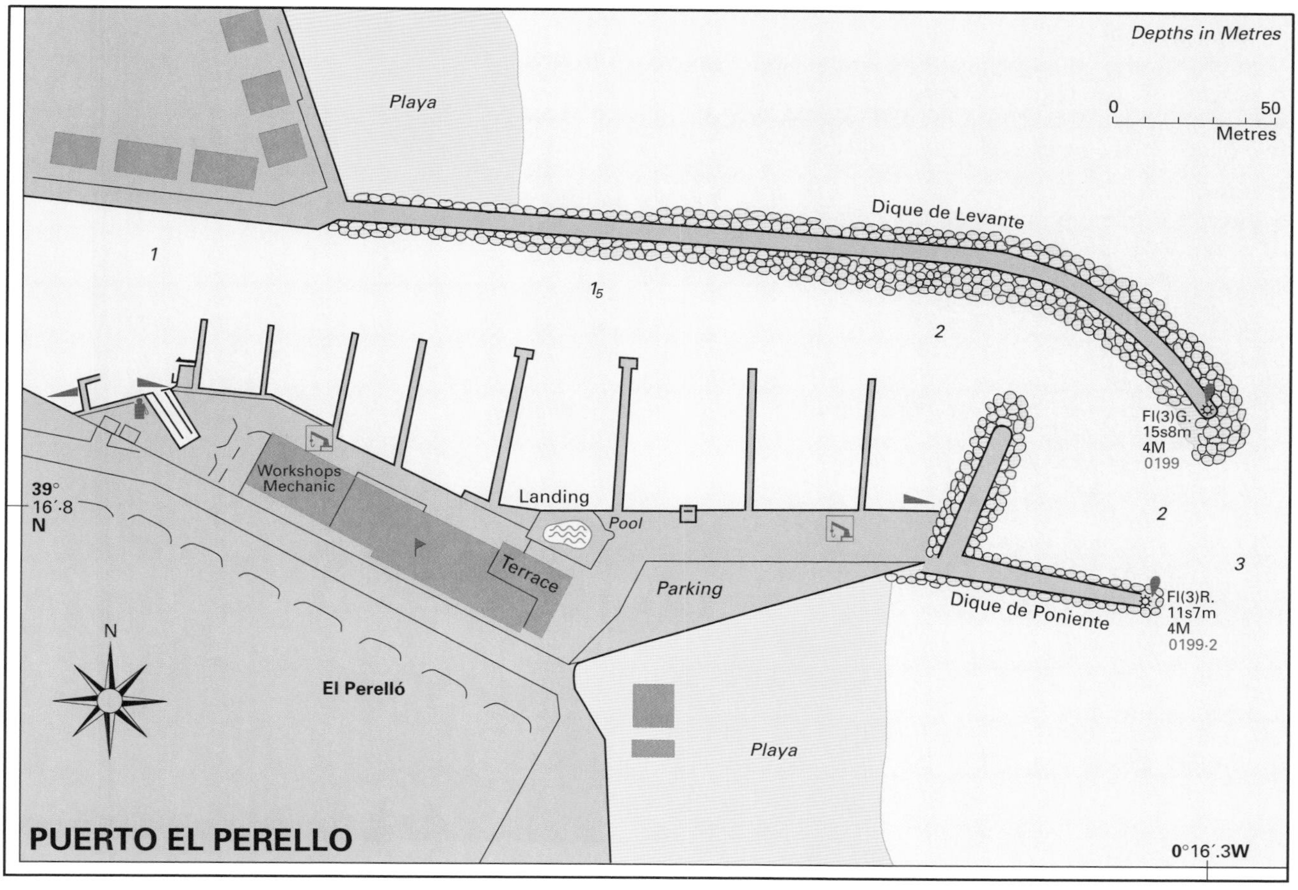

Depths in Metres

0 50 Metres

Playa

Dique de Levante

1

1₅

2

Fl(3)G. 15s8m 4M 0199

2

3

Workshops Mechanic

Landing

Pool

Terrace

Parking

Dique de Poniente

Fl(3)R. 11s7m 4M 0199·2

39° 16′·8 N

N

El Perelló

Playa

PUERTO EL PERELLO

0°16′.3W

lagoon, swamp and rice fields of La Albufera. Approach and entrance is not difficult with offshore winds but it is not advisable with Easterly winds. Space is limited and facilities are confined to everyday requirements.

There are large areas of rice fields inland, frequented by aquatic birds, and sandy beaches on either side of the harbour.

Approach

From the south Cabo Cullera with its lighthouse is unmistakable. The coast N of it is low and flat and has sandy beaches. High-rise apartment blocks are visible either side of this harbour and its breakwaters can be seen when close-to.

From the north Between the massive breakwaters of Puerto de Valencia and Perelló the coast is low and flat with sandy beaches. The houses at El Saler, the large Parador of Luis Vives, the Torre Nueva and some high-rise buildings near the Puerto El Perellónet may be identified. In the close approach the apartment blocks and breakwaters of El Perelló will be seen.

Anchorage in the approach

Anchor ½M to E of the harbour entrance in 10m, mud and sand.

Entrance

The entrance is narrow and shallow and silts easily. After rain the river may be in spate and a strong current will flow through the harbour. With onshore winds seas may break in the entrance. Sound carefully because depths may change with the flow of water and silting.

Approach the entrance on a SW course and leave the head of the Dique Norte 15m to starboard. Follow this *dique* round into the harbour leaving the two heads of the *contradique* 20–30m to port.

Berths

Secure to the first pontoon on the port-hand side in a vacant berth and ask to the *club náutico* for a berth.

Charges

Low.

Facilities

Maximum length overall 12m.
A 15-tonne crane near the second pontoon and a 3-tonne crane near the slipway.
10-tonne slipway to NW of the *club náutico*.
Engine repairs.
Water taps on quays and pontoons.
220v AC point on quays and pontoons.
Gasoleo A and petrol.
Small ice from the bar at the *club náutico*.
Club Náutico El Perelló has a restaurant, bar, terrace, lounge, swimming pool, shower/WC and sports room.
Shops in the village can supply everyday requirements.

Communications

Bus service along the coast and rail service from Sollana 7M inland.

Puerto El Perellónet

39°19'N 0°17'W

Charts

British Admiralty *1701*
French *4719*
Spanish *834*
Navicarte *E09*

General

A smaller version of Puerto El Perelló and situated 2M to NW of it. Only suitable for small boats and dinghies. The entrance is dangerous with onshore winds and/or swell. Facilities are very limited.

Approach

From the south Cabo Cullera with its lighthouse on top and surrounded by apartment blocks is easily identified. Northwards the low, flat sandy coast is broken by the Puerto El Perelló which has two breakwaters with light towers; Puerto El Perellónet is 2M N.

From the north Puerto de Valencia is easily recognised by its high, long breakwater. A group of apartment blocks and houses at El Salar may be seen as well as a large hotel, the Parador Luis Vives. The lone Torre Nueva lies 2M to NW of this harbour which can be recognised by some apartment blocks and a lone tower-block.

Anchorage in the approach

Anchor in 10m sand ½M to E of the harbour entrance.

Entrance

The mouth of this harbour is difficult to locate but the apartment blocks and a tower block indicate the area. The sandbanks at the entrance shift from time to time. Approach the entrance on a SW course. There will be a strong current in the river after heavy rain and depths may be changed by this or by strong onshore winds. Sound carefully in the approach and entrance.

Puerto El Perellónet

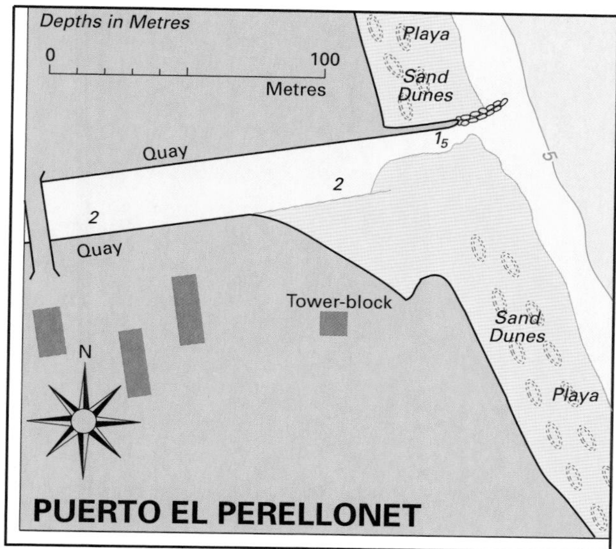

Berths
Secure to port-hand side (SW) bows-to quay with anchor from stern, a trip-line is advised. If the current is strong find a vacant place to lie alongside.

Facilities
Water from café/bars.
A limited range of shops 2M to SE at El Perelló.

Puertos de Valencia

Commercial harbour
39°27'N 0°18'W
Yacht Harbour
39°25'·5N 0°19'4W

Charts
British Admiralty *562, 518, 1701*
French *7276, 4719, 4720*
Spanish *4811, 481A, 476, 481, 835*
Navicarte *E09*

Lights
0200 **Lighthouse Nuevo Dique del Este North End** 39°27'·0N 0°18'·1W Fl(4+1)20s30m24M Pyramid stone tower on 8-sided base 22m
0200·4 **Nuevo Dique del Este head** Fl.G.5s21m5M Green column on white base 9m
0201·1 **Contradique** S Q(6)+LFl.15s17m3M S card
0201·11 **Contradique** E Fl(2)R.7s21m3M Red tower 9m
0206 **Muelle Transversal de Levante NW elbow** Fl(3)G.9s1M (lit when bridge is open)
0206·5 **SE Elbow** Fl(3)G.9s1M (lit when bridge is open)
0207 **Muelle Transversal de Poniente. NW elbow** Fl(2)R.7s1M (Lit when bridge is open)
0207·5 **SE elbow** Fl(2)R.7s1M (lit when bridgei s open)
0208·6 **Real Club Náutico Harbour Dique del Este head** Fl(2)G.7s11m3M Green round tower 4m
0208·65 **Contradique head** Fl(2)R.7s8m1M Red tower 4m
0208·7 **Entrance** Fl(3)G.9s5m1M Green tower 3m
0208·75 **Canal (starboard)** Fl(4)G.11s5m1M Green tower 3m
0208·8 **Entrance (port)** Fl(3)R.9s5m1M Red tower 3m
0209 **Aeropuerto de Manises** 39°29'·6N 0°28'·2W Aero AlFl.WG.4s65m15M On control tower 15m Occasional

Air radiobeacon
Valencia *PND* (·––·/–·/–··) 340kHz 50M 39°26'·58N 0°21'W

Port communications
Commercial: Pilots VHF call Ch 16, work Ch 11, 12, 14 and 20.
Real Club Náutico: VHF Ch 9 ☎ 963 679 011 *Fax* 963 677 737.

General
Valencia is now the third largest city in Spain. The port complex consists of a large cargo-handling, shipbuilding and ship-breaking port with the separate Real Club Náutico Yacht Harbour to the south outside of the main harbour but sharing a wall. Yachts should not enter the main harbour except in an emergency. Major works are in progress.

The yacht harbour is clear of the noise, dirt and heavy wash experienced in the commercial harbour but it does not have many of the facilities necessary

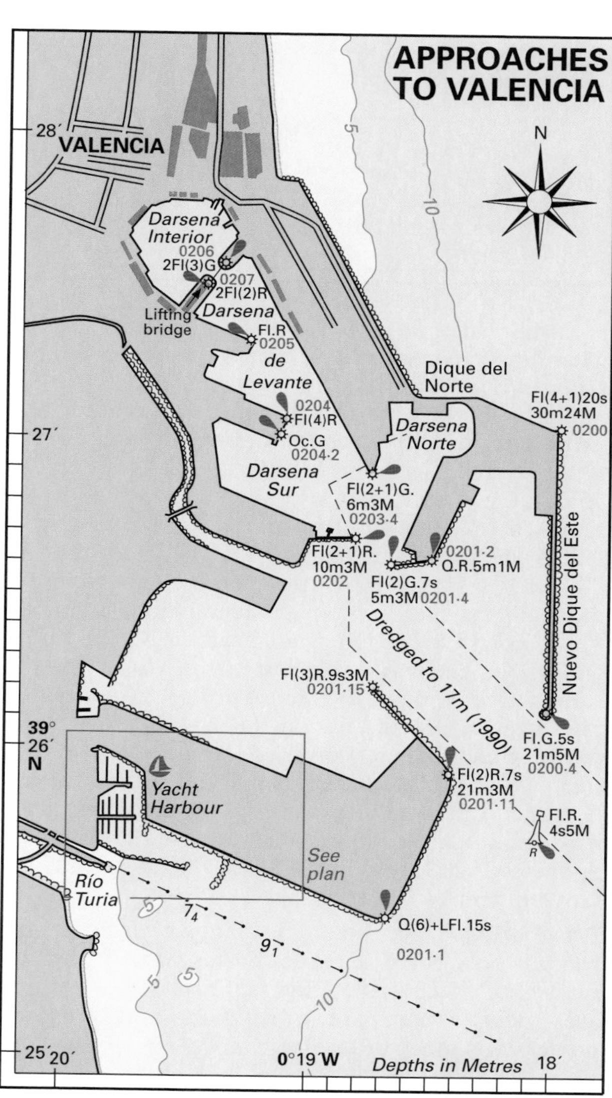

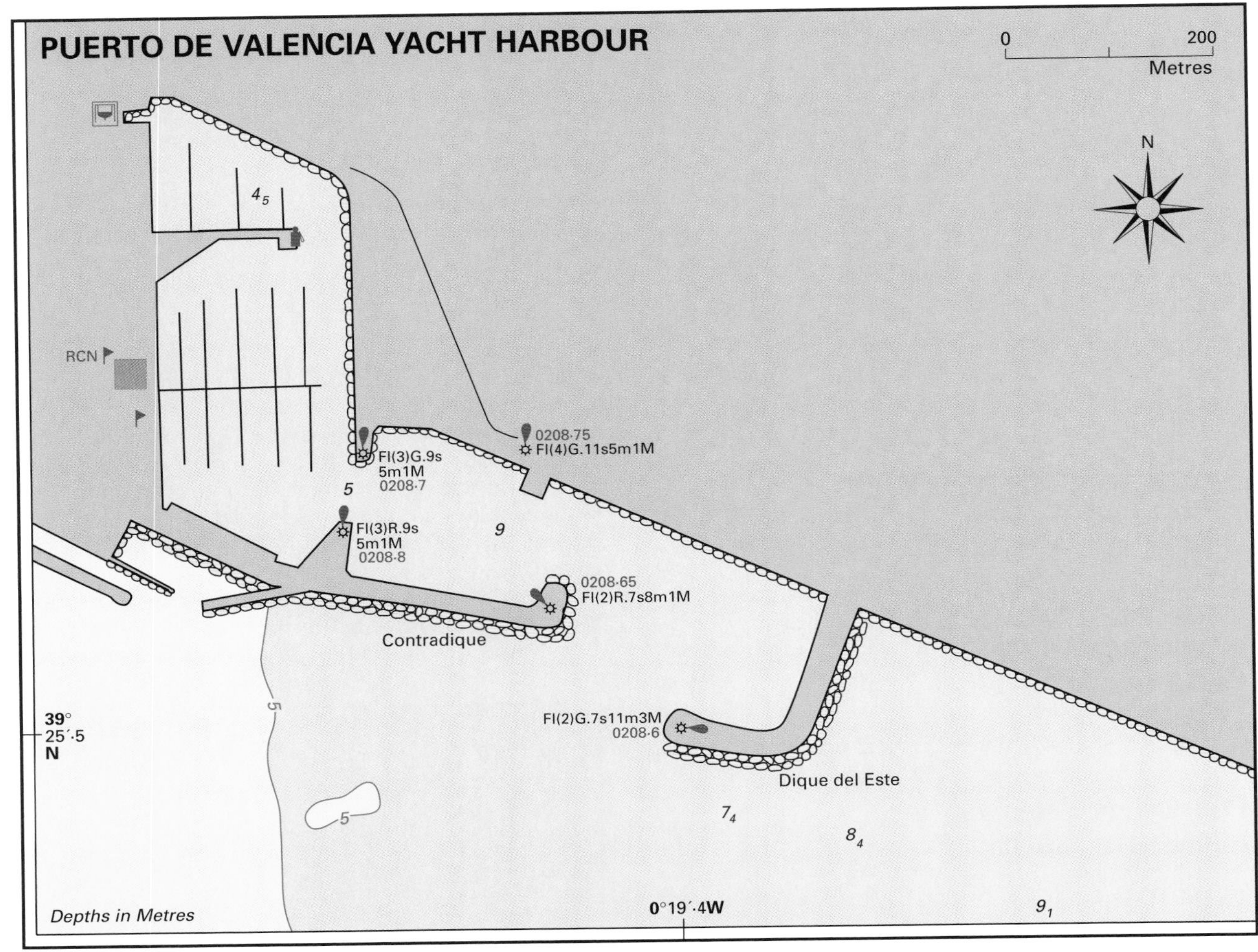

to sustain life afloat. It is a long way from the city where those facilities lie; the nearest supermarket at Nazaret is about 2km.

The city has had a long, complicated and turbulent history commencing with a Greek settlement followed in 139BC by the Romans. In 75BC it was sacked by Pompey and subsequently rebuilt as Valentía Edetanorum, a Roman colony. It fell to the Barbarian Goths in AD413 and then to the Moors in 714. In 1012 Valencia became an independent kingdom under several kings including the famous El Cid (Rodrigo Diaz de Rivar) whose widow Ximena was driven out by the Moors; they in turn were driven out by Jaime I in 1238. It remained under the house of Aragón for the next 400 years during which time it prospered. However in 1808 its people rose against the French and it suffered much damage in the ensuing wars and in the subsequent rebellions against the Spanish crown. During the Spanish Civil War it was the seat of the Republican Government of Spain.

Local holidays The Fallas de San José from 17–19 March are world famous fiestas which include masses of flowers and huge satirical statues which are burnt. There are other fairs and religious processions throughout the year.

Approach

From the south The conspicuous isolated mountainous feature Sierra de Cullera is easily identified. From here the coast is straight, low, flat and sandy and is backed by the inland lake La Albufera and associated marshes. There are several groups of high-rise buildings under construction along this coast but the mass of buildings of Valencia and its industrial fog and smoke can be seen several miles off as can the high Nuevo Dique del Este.

From the north The 1700m pier extending from beside Puerto de Sagunto is conspicuous. The low sandy coast is lined with houses and inland the valleys slope to the ranges of hills further away. The high Nuevo Dique del Este is conspicuous.

Entrance to the Yacht Harbour

The Real Club Náutico harbour is on the southwest side of the *contradique*, alongside the mouth of the diverted Río Turia. If coming from the north, give the harbour walls and entrance a good berth (commercial vessels have right of way) and when safely past the entrance, go for the head of the Dique Este. Enter and make the 90° turn to port towards the entrance of the yacht harbour itself.

Puerto de Valencia (yacht harbour)

Berths

The visitors pontoons are the 2 outside ones on entering but if in any doubt call or phone and/or moor to the fuel berth and ask at the office in the workshop area.

Charges

High.

Facilities

Maximum length overall 60m.
Major repairs can be undertaken in the commercial harbour to both hull and engines. There are also workshops attached to the club.
Hard-standing and a small slipway beside the *club náutico*.
50-tonne travel-lift.
10-tonne and 3-tonne cranes near the *club náutico*. Cranes up to 80 tonnes in the commercial harbour.
Some chandlery at the yacht harbour; otherwise a number of shops in Avda de Puerto on the way to the city from the commercial harbour.
Water points on the quays and pontoons.
Electricity 220v AC from supply points on all yacht pontoons and quays.
Gasoleo A and petrol.
Ice can be ordered from the club bar, for delivery next day, or from the bar at SW of yacht harbour.
The Real Club Náutico de Valencia is well appointed and has a restaurant and a swimming pool. Ask at the office for use of its facilities.
A number of small provision shops just to W of the commercial port on the way to the city.

Communications

Rail and bus services. International airport some 5M away. Services by sea to the Islas Baleares and other Mediterranean ports. Taxi ☎ 963 571 313/963 479 862 or via the yacht club.

Puerto Saplaya (Puerto de Alboraya)

39°31'N 0°19'W

Charts

British Admiralty *518, 1701*
French *7276, 4719, 4720*
Spanish *4811, 481A, 476, 481, 835*
Navicarte *E09*

Lights

0209·5(S) **Espigón No 1** Q(3)10s3M Cylindrical post ♦ 5m
0209·6 **Dique Sur head** Fl(4)R.12s8m4M White tower, red bands 5m
0209·7 **Dique Nordeste head** 39°30'·7N 0°19'·0W Fl.G.4s9m4M White tower green bands 5m
26190(S) **Buoy** 39°32'·8N 0°16'·9W Fl(2)10s3m3M – isolated danger

Port communications

VHF Ch 9. *Club náutico* ☎ 963 713 611.

General

This is an artificial marina with blocks of apartments and houses lining a series of waterways. A number of berths are reserved for visitors and is probably more convenient for Valencia than the yacht

Puerto Saplaya

harbour there. It has good protection and the usual facilities. The harbour mouth tends to silt up and has to be dredged frequently. With strong winds and swell from N through SE entry could be dangerous. Vast sandy beaches on both sides of the harbour.

Approach

From the south Puerto Saplaya is three miles north of the huge harbour breakwaters protecting Valencia. The group of high blocks of flats located behind Puerto Saplaya will be seen from just past Valencia and, nearer in, two rocky groynes will be seen. The breakwaters at the entrance to Puerto Saplaya are low and their heads have light towers. Do not mistake the light tower of Espigón No. 1 for the entrance.

From the north Puerto de Sagunto is unmistakable due to the 1700m-long jetty extending from beside the harbour. The breakwaters and high-rise buildings of Puerto de Farnals are also very conspicuous. In the closer approach the high block of flats and the breakwaters of Puerto Saplaya are easily recognised.

Anchorage in the approach

Anchor in 7m, sand, ½M to SE of the entrance to the harbour, paying attention to the foul ground, Algar de Albuixech, lying N of the anchorage.

Entrance

Approach the harbour entrance at slow speed heading NW. Sound continuously as the entrance

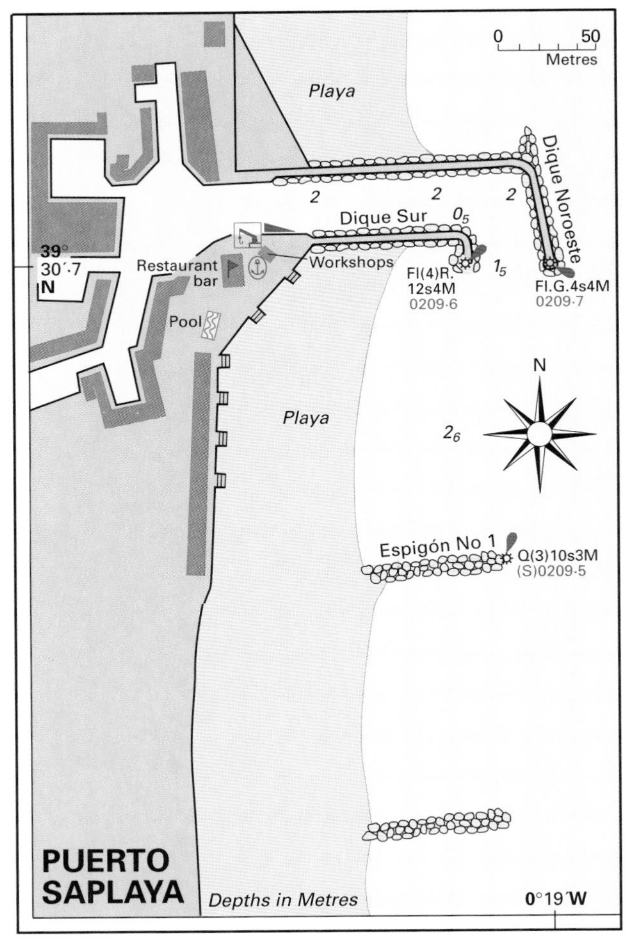

can silt up. Keep clear of the head of Dique Sur where there are shallows and enter leaving Dique Nordeste 15m to starboard. Follow this *dique* at 15–20m around and into the harbour.

Berths

Secure alongside quay on the port-hand side near the crane and ask at the *club náutico*.

Facilities

Maximum length overall 12m.
Two slipways near root of Dique Nordeste.
2-tonne crane near *club naútico* workshop area.
A mechanic at the workshop near the *club náutico*.
Water taps on the quay.
220v AC sockets on the quays.
Gasoleo A and petrol.
Small ice from the bar of the *club náutico*.
Club Náutico de Saplaya is at the root of the Dique Nordeste. It has a lounge, restaurant, bar, terrace, swimming pool etc.
Several shops and a small supermarket around the complex.

Communications

Buses and rail services to Valencia and elsewhere.

Pobla Marina (Puerto de Farnals)

39°34'N 0°17'W

Charts

British Admiralty *518, 1701*
French *7276, 4720*
Spanish *481A, 481, 835*
Navicarte *E09*

Lights

0210 **Escollera de Levante head** 39°33'·5N 0°16'·7W Fl(3)G.12·5s9m5M White and green tower 5m
0210·5 **Contradique S head** Fl.R.3·5s8m3M White and red tower
0210·7 **Dique Sur head** Fl(2)R.9s5m5M Red round post

Port communications

VHF Ch 9, 04, 27. *Club náutico* ☎ 961 463 223 *Fax* 961 462 587.
Capitanía ☎ 961 463 262.

General

A 835 berth parking lot built in front of a mass of high-rise buildings on a long stretch of sandy coast. The entrance silts and would be difficult or dangerous in strong E to S winds and swell. There is no club house but the club maintains an office. Large sandy beaches on each side of the harbour.

The Monastery of St Mary at El Puig lies about 2M inland. It was founded in the 12th century and remodelled in the 18th. It has a 6th-century Byzantine statue of St Mary.

Approach

From the south The huge outer breakwaters of Puerto de Valencia are conspicuous and easily recognised. 3M further N the low breakwaters of Puerto Saplaya which is backed by large apartment buildings should be identified. The breakwaters and blocks of high-rise buildings of Puerto de Farnals can be seen in the close approach with a red latticework tower near the entrance.

From the north The coast from Castellón de la Plana is low and flat with sandy beaches. The harbours of Burriana and Sagunto will be recognised by the industrial development behind them. The steelworks at Sagunto are particularly noticeable because of the smoke. The group of high-rise apartment blocks behind the breakwater of Puerto de Farnals will be seen in the closer approach.

Anchorage in the approach

Anchor in 10m, sand, with the harbour mouth ½M to NW. Do not anchor further out because of foul ground.

Entrance

The harbour mouth is subject to silting and though frequently dredged, depths are variable. Approach the head of the Escollera de Levante at slow speed, sounding. Keep 25m from the Muelle and do not veer to port into the shallow area off the beach. There may be a line of red or yellow buoys in high season but they were not present during a March 2001 visit.

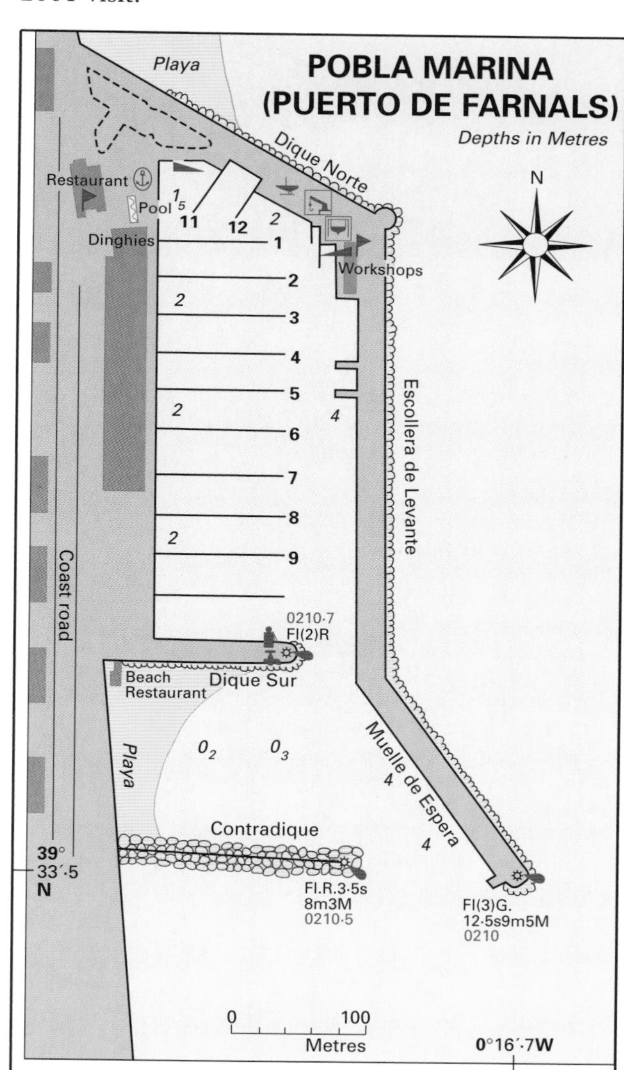

Pobla Marina

Berths

On passing the Dique Sur turn to port and moor in the waiting berth (W of the fuel berth) while sorting out a berth with the *capitanía*.

Facilities

Maximum length overall 18m.
Boat yard: hull and engine repairs.
50-tonne travel-hoist.
5-tonne crane.
A small hard-standing for yachts.
Slipways at NW and NE corners of the harbour.
Chandlery from AZA workshop in NE corner of the harbour.
Taps on quays and pontoons but drinking water by the pumps on Dique Sur.
220v AC points on quays and pontoons.
Gasoleo A and petrol.
Shops and supermarkets behind the harbour, more in Farnals 2M inland.

Communications

Bus and rail services (the station is 2M away). Taxi ☎ 961 470 434.

Puerto de Sagunto

39°39'N 0°12'W

Charts

British Admiralty *1458, 1701*
French *7296, 4720*
Spanish *4812, 481, 835, 482*
Navicarte *E09*

Lights

0212·3 **Escollera de Levante head** 39°38'·7N 0°12'·4W Q.G.14m3M Green masonry tower 11m
0214·2 **Spur head** Fl(4)R.11s13m3M Red masonry tower 10m
0214 **Muelle Sur SE corner** Fl.R.5s6m3M Concrete tower 3m
0214·6 **Dársena pesquera breakwater head** Fl(4)G.11s6m1M Truncated tower 4m

To the north

0212·6 **Pantalán de Sierra Menera head** Q(3)10s12m5M ♦ on black post, yellow band on dolphin 6m
0216 **Cabo Canet** 39°40'·5N 0°11'·9W Fl(2)10s33m23M Brick tower on white base with grey lantern 30m

Air radiobeacon

Sagunto/Cabo Canet c/s *SGO* (···/−−·/−−−) 356kHz 50M 39°40'·52N 0°12'·4W

Port communications
VHF Ch 12, 16. *Capitanía* ☎ 963 233 272.

General
An artificial harbour built to serve an industrial and commercial complex capable of handling vessels up to 90,000 tons. There is a small section of the harbour set aside for fishing boats. Approach and entrance are easy but the harbour is open to S. It is not a place for yachtsmen to call (Siles is next-door) except possibly in an emergency. If here, however, a visit might be made to the very old town of Sagunto, 2M away, to see the many ruins and remains from the past including a castle and a Roman amphitheatre.

Construction is underway on a new contradique and enlargement of the Escollera de Levante. Two new east cardinal buoys have been placed well to the south of the harbour and the port hand buoys all moved to the south by some 300 metres with a new starboard hand buoy about ¾M south of the old pierhead. It is recommended to keep well clear of this port while this development is continuing.

Approach
From the south The coast of Valencia is low, flat and sandy, lined with blocks of flats and villas. Sagunto can be spotted by the Pantalán de Sierra Menera stretching 1700m out to sea. Closer in, the entrance walls will be seen.

From the north South of Burriana, 15M up the coast and easy to miss, the coast is flat and sandy with groups and blocks of buildings. The Pantalán de Sierra Menera makes it easy to locate Sagunto but stand at least two miles offshore until it has been rounded.

Anchorage in the approach
Anchor 400m to SW of head of Escollera de Levante in 7m, sand. Depths in and adjacent to this harbour may be less than charted.

Entrance
Approach the entrance on a N course, passing between a red and a green buoy and then between the head of the Escollera de Poniente (Muelle Sur) and another G buoy.

Berths
It is usually possible to find a berth alongside or stern-to a rather dirty quay in the NE corner of the harbour in the small fishing boat harbour.

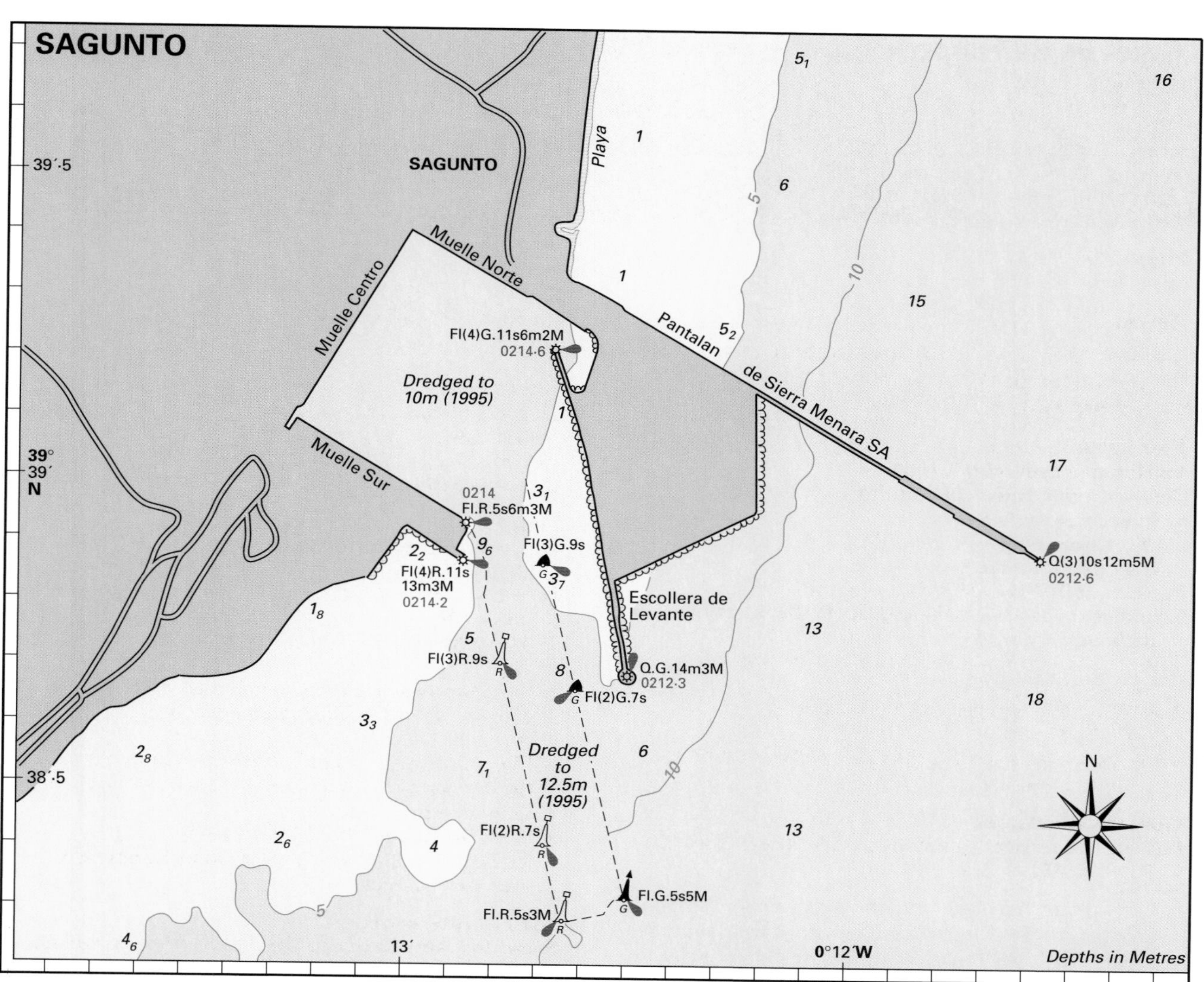

Puerto de Sagunto

Facilities
Water points on Escollera de Levante and at the *lonja*. There are some shops and a market in the village to the N of the harbour and a fair selection of shops in Sagunto.

Communications
Bus service to Sagunto where there is a rail service.

Puerto de Siles (Canet de Berenguer)

39°40'N 0°12'W

Charts
British Admiralty *1701*
French *4720*
Spanish *4812, 481, 835, 482*
Navicarte *E09*

Lights
Approach
0216 **Cabo Canet** 39°40'·5N 0°12'·4W
Fl(2)10s33m23M White 8-sided tower, grey lantern 30m
Harbour
0217 **Dique de Levante head** 39°40'·4N 0°11'·9W
Fl.G.4s7m6M Green truncated tower 3m
0217·2 **Dique de Levante spur** Fl(3)G.9s4m3M Green truncated tower 2m
0217·4 **Contradique S head** Fl.R.4s5m4M Red truncated tower 3m
0217·5 **Contradique N head** Fl(2)R.5s4m3M Red truncated tower 2m
To the north
0218 **Nules** 39°49'·5N 0°06'·5W Oc(2)11s38m14M
Brown square masonry tower 36m

Air radiobeacon
Sagunto/Cabo Canet c/s *SGO* (···/—–·/———) 356kHz 50M 39°40'·52N 0°12'·4W

Port communications
VHF Ch 9. ☎/*Fax* 962 609 223.
Club Marítimo de Regates de Sagunto ☎ 962 678 132.

General
An artificial harbour which may make a good alternative to the Puerto de Sagunto. Disadvantages are that shallows make the entrance dangerous in strong winds or swell from N–NE and the outer berths are subject to swell in winds between E and S. The Río Palencia debouches across the harbour entrance and, like other harbours on this coast, it silts up and is dredged periodically. There are sandy beaches to N and S of the harbour.

The old town of Sagunto is worth visiting to see the old walls, castle and arena. The original town was Iberian, later Greek and then Roman. It put up a famous nine months' defence against Hannibal and his Carthaginian armies. When Rome abandoned them to their fate the citizens built a huge fire and the women, children, sick and old threw themselves into it. The able-bodied men went off to die in the last battle. The result was the complete destruction of the town and its fortifications so that five years later, when the

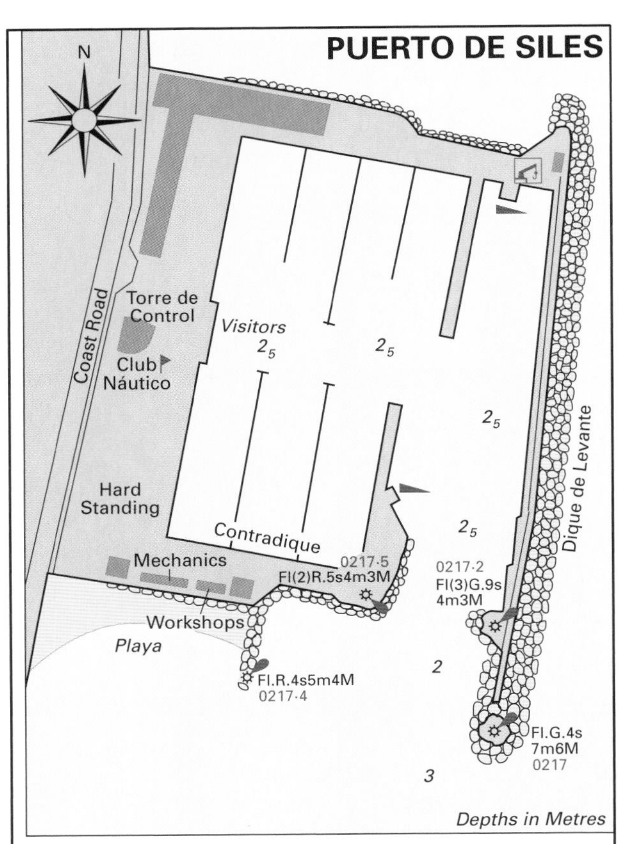

Puerto de Siles

Romans re-occupied it, they called it Muri Veteres, later corrupted to Murviedro, meaning literally Old Walls. The Romans under Scipio Africanus the Elder and later the Moors who called it Murbiter did a lot of rebuilding, making use of the old stones. Traces of these various occupations are to be found everywhere despite further destruction during the French occupation and then during the Spanish Civil War.

Approach

From the south The harbour walls at Puerto de Sagunto, 1 mile to the south of Siles, and the 1·5M long Pantalán de Sierra Menera are easily recognised.

From the north Puerto de Castellón and, to the SW, the petrochemical works, which has two tall chimneys with red and white bands, are conspicuous. Puerto de Burriana can also be recognised.

From either direction Cabo Canet light is immediately behind the harbour and can be seen for miles.

Anchorage in the approach

Anchor in 12m, sand, ½M to SE of the harbour entrance.

Entrance

Depths can vary due to silting and dredging and as of March 2001 the depth was 2m to 2·5m at the entrance. Approach the entrance on a NW course, sounding carefully. Round the head of the Dique de Levante at 15m leaving it to starboard onto a N course and enter between a short spur to starboard and the SE corner of the *contradique* to port.

Berths

The visitors berths are at the second quay to port. Secure and confirm at the office. These outer quays are subject to swell in winds from E through S.

Facilities

Maximum length overall 12m.
Workshop and mechanics on the *contradique*.
Slipway on the *contradique* and one near the root of the Dique de Levante.
A mobile crane (15 tonnes) and a small crane near the root of the Dique de Levante.
Taps on all quays and pontoons.
Points for 220v AC on all quays and pontoons.
Small ice from the Club Marítimo.
Club Marítimo de Regates de Sagunto with bar, lounge, patio, restaurant, WCs, showers and swimming pool.
A supermarket 400m to N of the harbour with cash dispenser. More shops in Puerto de Sagunto 1M to SW.

Communications

Rail and bus services from Sagunto. Taxi ☎ 962 680 999.

Puerto de Burriana

39°51'N 0°04'W

Charts

British Admiralty *1701*
French *7296, 4720*
Spanish *836, 4882, 482*
Navicarte *R5*

Lights

To the south
0216 **Cabo Canet** 39°40'·5N 0°11'·9W
Fl(2)10s33m23M White 8-sided tower, grey lantern 30m
Harbour
0219 **Dique de Levante head** 39°51'·5N 0°04'·0W
Fl(2)G.8s12m5M Green tower 8m
0221·5 **Espigón de Contención Arena** Q(3)10s7m3M ♦ on tower
0221 **Dique de Poniente head** Fl(2)R.8s10m3M Red structure 8m
0220 **Muelle Transversal head** Fl(3)G.10s8m3M Green structure 6m
To the north
0226 **Castellón de la Plana** 39°58'·2N 0°01'·7E
Oc(2+1)10s32m14M White round tower 27m

Port communications

VHF Ch 9.
Club Náutico de Burriana ☎/*Fax* 964 456 073.

General

A small artificial harbour enclosed by two jetties. It is used by fishing craft and yachts. There is a small ship-breaking yard. The local village has limited facilities but more are available at the town some 3km away. The approach is easy but the entrance requires care owing to ever-extending sand bars. Good shelter is obtainable once inside the harbour. Entrance would be difficult with strong winds and swell from E through SW.

The town is worth visiting to see the original walls and gate and an important 16th-century church of Moorish origin. Excellent sandy beach to NE of the harbour.

Approach

From the south The flat, sandy coastal plain continues N from Sagunto for about 8M to Burriana. The town itself is some 2M inland but can seen as can the few blocks of flats near the harbour. In clear weather Pica Espadón (1105m) which lies 15M to WNW of this harbour may be seen. There is a fish farm at 39°50'·2N 0°03'·2E indicated by 4 buoys, Fl.Y.5s with cross topmarks.

From the north The main feature of this low, flat, dull coast are the two conspicuous tall, red and white banded chimneys of Castellón. Burriana itself, located some 2M inland, will be seen in the closer approach.

Anchorage in the approach

Anchor 200m to SW of the head of Dique de Levante in 6m, sand. Careful sounding is advisable.

Entrance

From a position 400m to SW of the head of Dique de Levante approach the entrance on a course of 30°. Pass some 15m to E of the head of Dique de Poniente. The approach to this harbour is tending

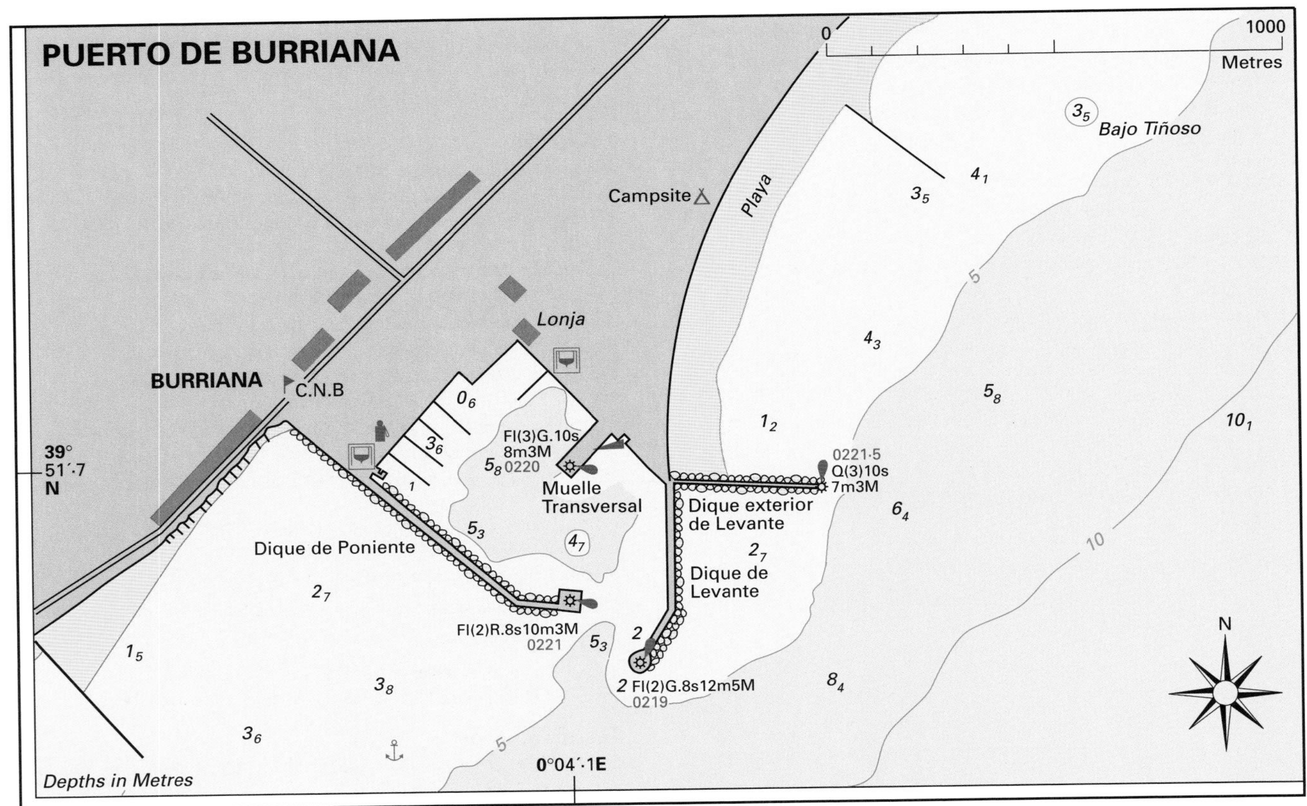

Puerto de Burriana

to shoal and the sandbank that lies to the S of the head of the Dique de Levante is extending southwards.

Berths

Inquire at the *club náutico.*

Anchorage

Anchor NE of the Dique de Poniente, clear of any moorings off the *club náutico* piers, 5m, sand. Use a trip line.

Moorings

Private moorings may be available, apply to the club.

Facilities

Maximum length overall 17m.
Two slipways.
A small crane at the root of the Dique de Levante (5 tonnes) and a number of mobile cranes of greater power. A large one of unknown capacity on the Muelle Transversal.
Mechanic available.
Water from either end of the sheds on the Dique de Levante, from the *club náutico* and pontoons. Sample before filling tanks.
220v AC supplies from the *club náutico* and pontoons.
Gasoleo A.
Ice is available at the *club náutico.*
The Club Náutico de Burriana has a bar, lounge, terrace, restaurant and showers.
Only a few shops near the harbour but many in the town where there is also a good market.

Communications

Bus service and rail service some 4M away. Taxi ☎ 964 511 011.

Puerto de Castellón de la Plana (Castelló)

39°58'N 0°01'E

Charts

British Admiralty *1458, 1701*
French *7296, 4720*
Spanish *4821, 836, 482*
Navicarte *R5*

Lights

To the southwest: Oil Terminal

26700(S) **Safewater Buoy** 39°56'·2N 0°03'·7E LFl.10s3M Red and White Spherical
0224 **Oil Fuelling Berth** 39°56'·7N 0°01'·6E Oc(2)Y.14s13m4M Horn Mo(U) Yellow metal column 6m
0224·2 **120m W** Oc(2)Y.14s9m1M Yellow post on dolphin
0224·4 **150m E** Oc(2)Y.14s9m1M Yellow post on dolphin

Harbour

0226 Faro 39°58'·2N 0°01'·7E Oc(2+1)10s32m14M White round tower 27m Flare 1·8M SW
0226·1 Dique de Levante head Fl.G.13m5M Green round tower
26690(S) **Buoy** 39°58'·1N 0°01'·2W Fl.R.5s4M 40m from Dique de Poniente head
0226·2 **Muelle Transversal head SE corner** Fl(2)G.7s6m3M Green tower 4m
0226·4 **Muelle Transversal head NW corner** Fl(3)G.9s6m3M Green tower 3m
0229·2 **Muelle Pesquero head** Fl(2+1)R.12s5m3M Red tower, green bands 3m
0229·3 **S head** Oc.G.5s5m2M Green truncated pyramidal tower
0229·4 **Muelle Pesquero slipway** Fl(2)R.5s4m3M Red tower 3m
26944(S) **Channel buoy** Q.3M port hand buoy
26946(S) **Channel buoy** Fl.R.5s2M port hand buoy

To the northeast

0230 **Cabo Oropesa** 40°04'·9N 0°09'·0E Fl(3)15s24m21M White tower and house 13m

Radiobeacon

Castellón c/s *AS* (·–/···) 310·5kHz 50M 39°58'·17N 0°01'·23E

Port communications
Oil terminal and pilots. VHF Ch 16, 12, 13.
Harbour ☎ 964 282 352.
Club Náutico de Castellón VHF Ch 9 ☎ 964 282 520 *Fax* 964 283 905.

General
A large commercial and fishing harbour with an easy entrance and good shelter within. It is not laid out for yachts but facilities are adequate. There is an oil terminal off shore with room to pass between it and the shore-line.

The beach about a mile northeast of the harbour is good but approached along a noisy main road. The pleasant town some 2M inland was established by Jaime I of Aragón. It became the capital of the area and prospered as the centre of a fertile region, famous for its oranges and *azulejo* tiles.

Approach
From the south The harbours of Sagunto and Burriana are the only conspicuous features on this low, flat sandy coast. The two tall red and white banded chimneys just S of Castellón de la Plana (which are in line from this direction) are conspicuous as is the oil refinery flare (75m). A pipeline stretches out from the refinery ending about 2½M ESE where tankers anchor; the mooring is marked by a safewater buoy and has 5 mooring buoys (Fl(4)Y.10s). Along the line of the pipeline and a mile offshore is a floating fuelling berth with light and two lit dolphins. Navigation is prohibited between the safewater buoy and the floating berth but small craft may pass between the floating berth and shore. The lighthouse on the Dique de Levante should then be easy to spot as will the group of tall flats located just behind the harbour.

From the north The high Los Colls (420m) feature which extends to the sea at Cabo Oropesa is recognisable. The coast to the S is low, flat and sandy with a line of apartment blocks and houses. The features mentioned above at Castellón de la Plana are also easily seen from this direction.

Anchorage in the approach
Anchor 100m to E of head of Dique de Levante light in 11m, sand.

Entrance
Approach the entrance from S, giving the head of the Dique de Levante an offing of at least 30m and leaving the 3 red buoys to port. Pass some 50m to E of the head of Dique de Poniente, watching for fishing craft leaving the Darsena Pesquero, and enter the Darsena Comercial and make way to the W corner.

Berths
Floating pontoons at the *club náutico*. Get in wherever possible and then ask. Alternatively, find space alongside in the Dársena Comercial and ask.

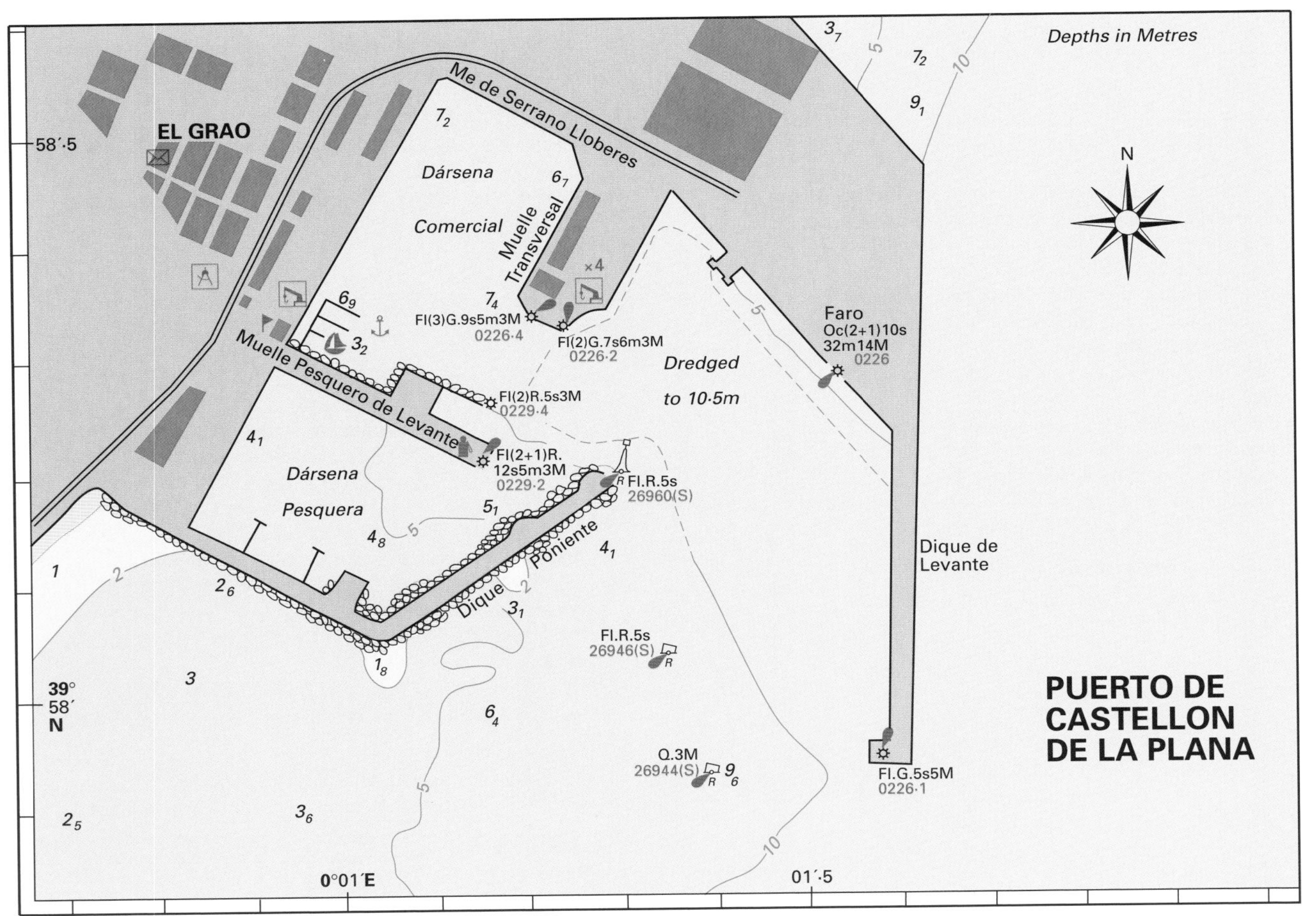

Puerto de Castellon de la Plana

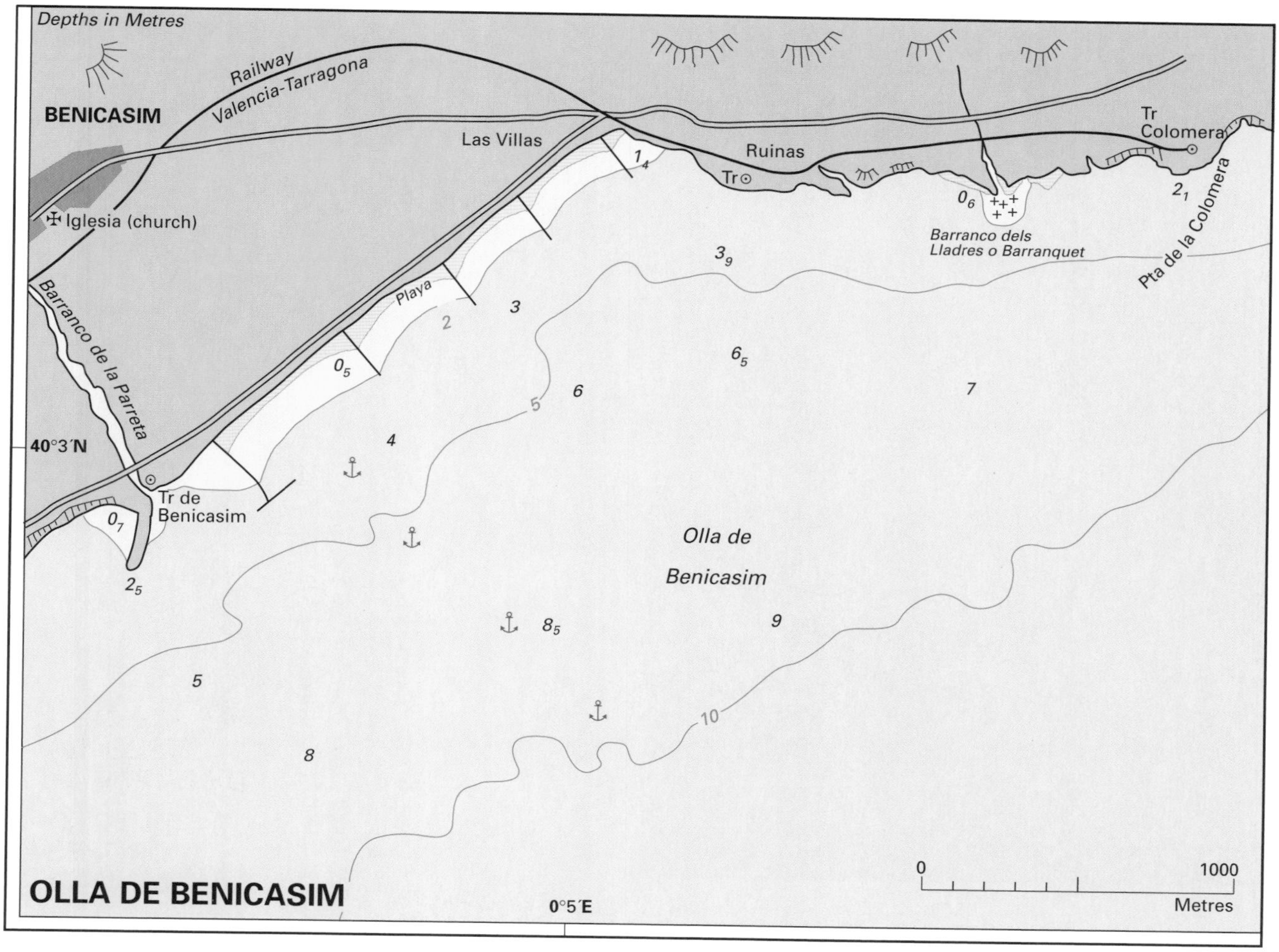

Depths in Metres

BENICASIM

Railway Valencia-Tarragona

Las Villas

Ruinas

Tr

Tr Colomera

Iglesia (church)

Barranco de la Parreta

Playa

Barranco dels Lladres o Barranquet

Pta de la Colomera

40°3′N

Tr de Benicasim

Olla de Benicasim

0 1000 Metres

OLLA DE BENICASIM

0°5′E

Note that swell tends to bounce round the harbour and it has been reported that some berths can be rolly.

Anchorages
As is common with most harbours on this coast at present, it is forbidden to anchor in the commercial harbour.

Facilities
Maximum length overall 20m.
A shipyard on the N side of the Muelle Pesquero where hull repairs can be carried out. Engine mechanics are also available.
Small slipway is located beside the *club náutico*, larger ones in the Dársena Pesquero.
32-tonne travel-lift.
2·5-tonne crane at the *club náutico* and large commercial cranes in Dársena Comercial.
Chandlery shop to the NW of the harbour.
Water from *club náutico*, its pontoons and the quays.
Electricity 220v AC available from the *club náutico* pontoons and the quays.
Gasoleo A and petrol at the fuel quay by the yacht club
Ice from the fuel quay.
The Club Náutico de Castellón clubhouse is in the W corner of the Dársena Comercial. It has a bar, lounge, terrace, restaurant, showers and a repair workshop.
A number of shops including a small supermarket near the harbour. Many more shops and a market in the town 2M away.
Launderette in the town.

Communications
Frequent bus service to the town where there is a rail service. Taxi ☎ 964 237 474.

⚓ Olla de Benicasim
Open between NE and SE and to swell from the S. Daily requirements from shops serving the beach blocks or in the town of Bencasim.

Olla de Benicasim

⚓ S of Cabo Oropesa
A small anchorage tucked away under the cape open to SE. Use with care because of rocky patches. Anchor off sandy beach in 2m, sand. Houses and apartments ashore with road to the village of Oropesa on top of the hill (24m) where everyday supplies are available.

Puerto Oropesa de Mar (Puerto Copfre)

40°04'N 0°08'E

Charts
British Admiralty *1701*
French *4720*
Spanish *836, 482*
Navicarte *R5*

Lights
To the south
0226 **Faro** 39°58'·2N 0°01'·7E Oc(2+1)10s32m14M White round tower 27m
Harbour
0229·7 **Dique de Abrigo head** 40°04'·5N 0°08'·1E Fl(3)G.9s8m5M Green tower 3m
0229·8 **Contradique head** Fl(3)R.9s6m3M Red tower 2m

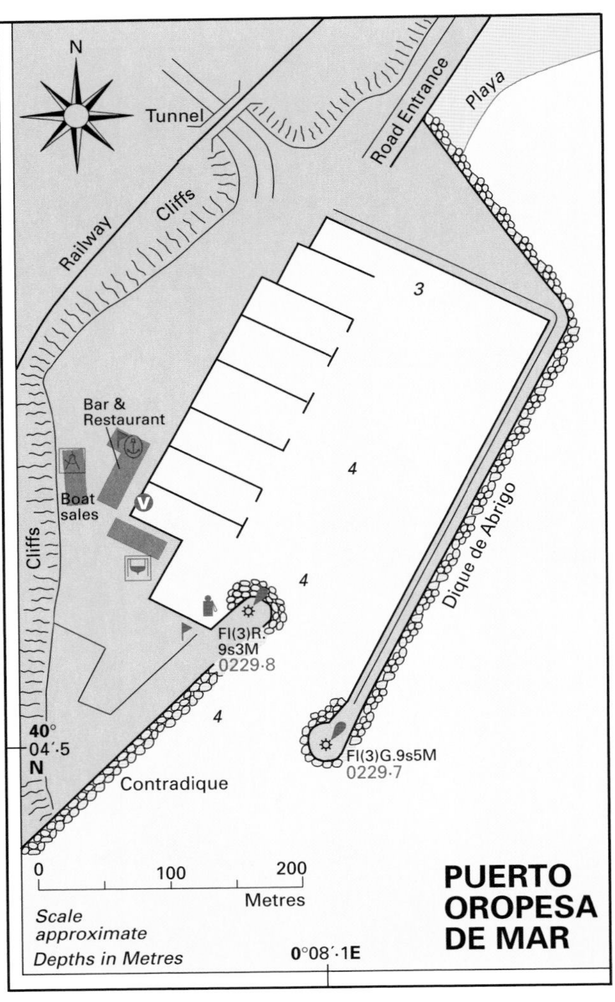

0230 **Cabo Oropesa** 40°04'·9N 0°09'·0E
Fl(3)15s24m21M White round tower and house 13m

Port communications
VHF Ch 9. ☎ 964 313 055 *Fax* 964 310 000.

General
A useful harbour, easy to enter in bad weather and near to a busy seaside resort. It offers good protection though swell may enter the harbour from SE winds. Good facilities for laying up and so forth but there are no local shops. The main line railway is a bit noisy. A climb to the top of Cabo Oropesa is worthwhile for the coastal view. A small sand beach at the N side of the harbour, with a large beach at Oropesa del Mar.

Approach
From the south The huge petrochemical plant just to S of Puerto de Castellón which has two tall red and white banded chimneys is easily recognised as is Puerto de Castellón itself. The low, flat sandy coast is lined with apartment blocks. Cabo Oropesa (21m) is not prominent but the lighthouse and an old tower on its crest can be identified. The harbour is on the N side of the cape.

From the north Puerto de las Fuentes can be recognised by a small sail-shaped building. The shore to S is low flat and sandy. There are towers at Capicorp and the mouth of the Río Cuevas. This harbour is just beyond the collection of high-rise buildings at Oropesa del Mar.

Anchorage in the approach
The water is deep off this harbour. Anchor to S of Cabo Oropesa or in the Olla de Benicasim.

Entrance
Approach the head of the Dique de Levante on a NW course and round it, leaving it 15m to starboard onto a N course in to the harbour.

Berths
Secure on the SW side of the harbour and ask at the *torre de control.*

Facilities
Maximum length overall 15m.
Hard-standing.
35-tonne travel-lift and 10-tonne crane.
Engine mechanic, painting, carpentry, sailmaking.
Chandlery.
Water taps on quays and pontoons.
Gasoleo A and petrol.
220v AC outlets on quays and pontoons.
Small ice from *club náutico.*
Club náutico with bar.
Stock up in Oropesa del Mar.

Communications
Bus and rail services at Oropesa del Mar. Taxi ☎ 964 310 616.

Puerto Oropesa de Mar

Puerto de las Fuentes (Alcocebre)

40°15'N 0°17'E

Charts
British Admiralty *1701*
French *4720*
Spanish *836*
Navicarte *R5*

Lights
To the south
0230 **Cabo Oropesa** 40°04'·9N 0°09'·0E
Fl(3)15s24m21M White round tower and house 13m
Harbour
0231 **Dique de Levante** 40°14'·8N 0°17'·2E
Oc.G.4s6m4M Green concrete column 2m
0231·2 **Contradique** Fl(4)R.14s5m3M Red concrete column 2m
Heads of pontoons and quays F.R and F.G – see plan.
To the north
0232 **Castillo del Papa Luna** 40°21'·6N 0°24'·6E
Fl(2+1)15s56m23M White 8-sided tower and house 11m 184°-vis-040°
0231·6 **Cabo de Irta** 40°15'·8N 0°18'·2E
Fl(4)18s33m14M Square tower on white building 28m

Port communications
VHF Ch 9. ☎ 964 412 084 *Fax* 964 414 657.

General
A pleasant medium-sized yacht harbour near a busy resort. Approach and entrance is not difficult except with strong SSE winds. Fine view from the church, San Benito, 2½M to W. Good but crowded sandy beach to N of harbour and rocky, stony one to S.

Approach
From the south Cabo Oropesa, though high (420m), is not prominent but can be easily recognised by its white round lighthouse and the old Torre del Rey alongside it. The coast is low, flat and marshy and can be closed to ½M. At Capicorp there are two *torres* and the mouth of Río Cuevas, 2½M further N lies the harbour with a number of apartment blocks behind it. The sail-like building of the *torre de control* is unique on this part of the coast and is easily recognised. Careful watch should be kept for floating cages 'Alcocebre' in approximate position 40°13'·9N 0°18'E with 4 yellow buoys (Fl.Y.5s).

From the north Peñíscola, surmounted by the Castillo del Papa Luna, is unmistakable. The coast to S is of low rocky cliffs and small sandy beaches at the mouths of the numerous small streams which descend from the Sierra San Benet (573m) a range of hills located 2M inland and lying parallel to the coast. The coast can be followed at ½M.

The harbour lies near the S end of this hill feature.

Puerto de las Fuentes

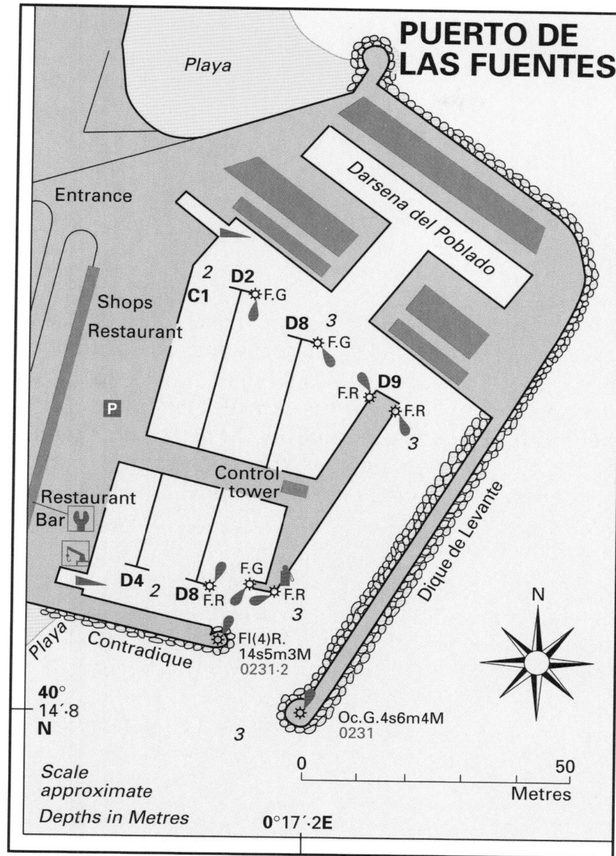

The low breakwater and a number of apartment blocks are a short distance west of a conspicuous white tower and will be seen when close-to. The unique *torre de control* is not so obvious from this direction.

Anchorage in the approach

Anchor 500m to E of the harbour in 8m, sand, or closer in, if weather is suitable, in 5m, sand.

Entrance

Straightforward.

Berths

Secure to the wide quay near the *torre de control*, a sail-like building, for allocation of a berth.

Facilities

Maximum length overall 20m.
Two slipways.
8-tonne crane.
Engine mechanics.
Water taps on pontoons and quays.
220v AC from points on quays and pontoons.
Gasoleo A and petrol.
Some shops in the harbour, better in the village.
Small ice from the bar at SW corner of the harbour.

Communications

Bus service, rail 3M inland. Taxi ☎ 964 410 152.

Puerto de Peñíscola

40°21'N 0°24'E

Charts

British Admiralty *1701*
French *7296, 4720*
Spanish *4841, 837*
Navicarte *E01*

Lights

0232 **Castillo del Papa Luna** 40°21'·6N 0°24'·6E
Fl(2+1)15s56m23M White 8-sided tower and house 11m 184°-vis-040°

Harbour

0234 **Dique de Levante head** 40°21'·3N 0°24'·2E
Fl.G.4s15m4M Green column 4m
0234·4 **Espigón head** F.R.7m3M Red column 6m

General

An attractive bay, buoyed off in summer for the use of swimmers, with a fishing harbour on its east side which has very limited accommodation for yachts. It is overlooked by a Knights Templars castle, one of the more frequently visited sites on the east coast of Spain. The approach and entrance are easy but the bay is open to SE and winds from this direction make it uncomfortable.

A good beach on the N side of the isthmus and another in the bay itself which is often crowded. A holiday, the Fiesta of La Virgen de la Ermitana, is held 8–9 September.

The Phoenicians called the harbour Tyriche, because of its resemblance to Tyre. The Greeks renamed it Chersonesos. Carthaginians and Romans followed and later the Moors. The Moors were driven out by Jaime I who gave the site to the Knights Templars. The castle was completed by the Montesianos in the 14th century. Pope Benedict XIII (often referred to as Papa Luna), the last of the schismatic Popes, retired here from Avignon in 1417 and remained until his death in 1423 at the age of 90. After a spell as part of the Holy See it reverted to the crown of Aragón, withstanding an 11-day siege by the French during the Peninsular War.

Approach by day

From the south After Cabo Oropesa, the coast is low and flat. 10M north, Sierra Benet, a long line of rocky hills, stretches as far as the harbour. From a distance the castle at Peñíscola appears as an off-lying island. Care should be taken to avoid a new artificial reef in position 40°19'·6N 0°24'·8E.

From the north The harbours of Vinaroz and Benicarló with their conspicuous harbour works are easily identified on an otherwise featureless coast. The castle at Peñíscola appears as an island.

The head of the Dique de Levante extends underwater some 25m beyond the above-water visible head and should be rounded at 50m.

Anchorage in the approach

The bay may be marked as reserved for swimmers by a line of buoys between the Muelle de Poniente and the elbow of the *contradique*. If not, anchor

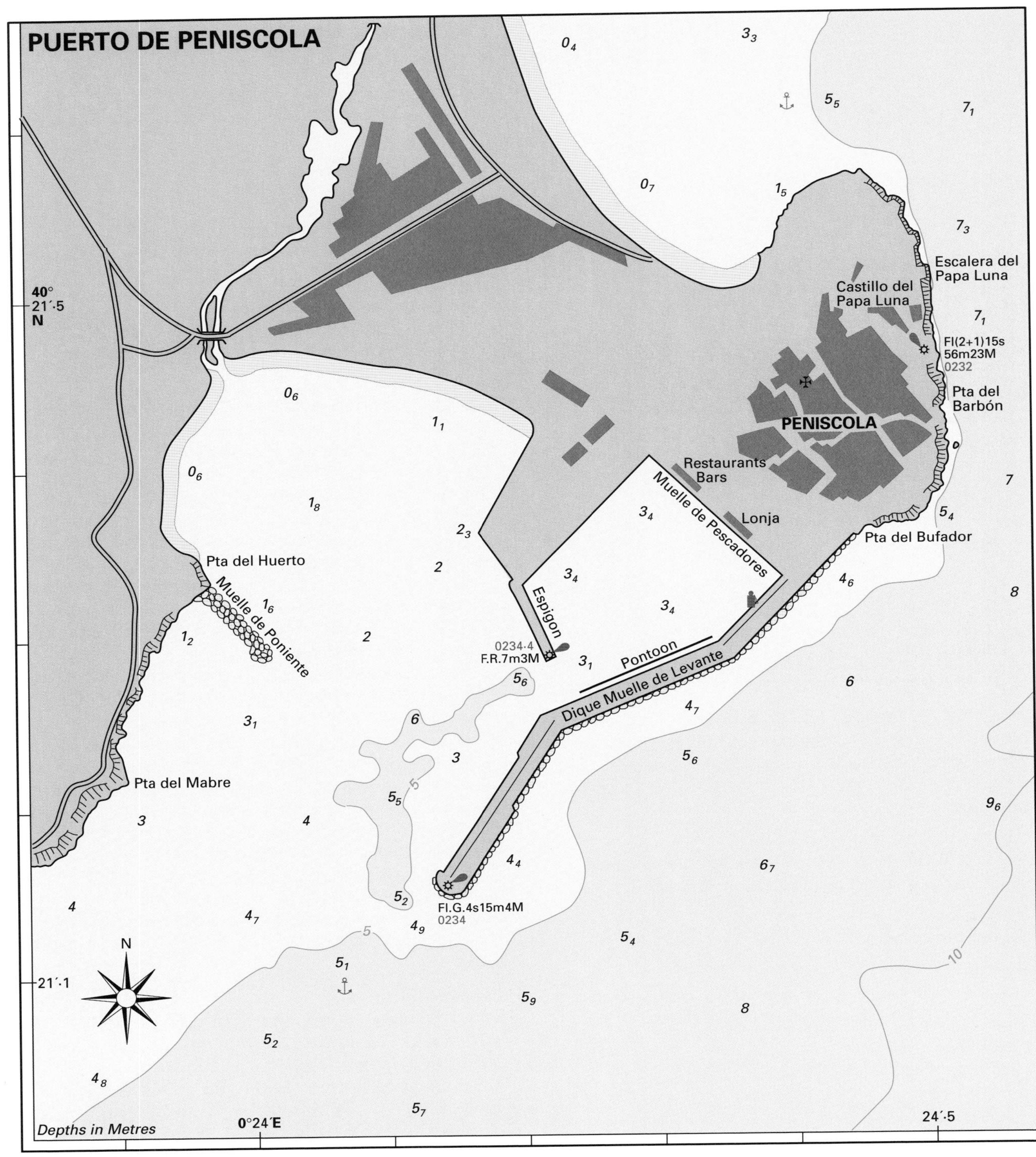

300m to SW of the head of the Dique de Levante in 5m, sand. If so, the options are to anchor near the line of the buoys, out of the fairway on the Muelle de Poniente side, or outside altogether either in the harbour approaches or north of Papa Luna (see below).

Entrance

Straightforward but beware of fishing craft. During strong S winds in early 2002 the entrance silted badly. It was due to be dredged in March 2002 to its original 3 to 4m depth but care should be taken on entering as the silting could recur at any time.

Berths

By day it may be possible to find a berth within the fishing harbour near the head of the *contradique* or alongside pontoons lying parallel to the Muelle de Levante. However, the fishing fleet which returns en masse at about 1700 hours usually requires all available berths.

Puerto de Peñiscola

Charges
Moderate charges in the harbour.

Facilities
Chandlery shop near the root of the jetty.
Water from the Lonja de Pescadores.
Ice available from the Lonja de Pescadores.
A number of small shops scattered around the village.

Communications
Buses.

⚓ N of Peninsula de Peñíscola

Anchorage to N of Peninsula de Peñíscola. The anchorage is to the right of the photograph.

Puerto de Benicarló

40°25'N 0°26'E

Charts
British Admiralty *1701*
French *7296, 4720*
Spanish *4841, 837*
Navicarte *R5*

Lights
To the south
0232 **Castillo del Papa Luna** 40°21'·6N 0°24'·6E
Fl(2+1)15s56m23M White 8-sided tower and house 11m 184°-vis-040°
Harbour
0238 **Dique de Levante head** 40°24'·6N 0°26'·2E
Fl(2)G.5s13m5M Green tower 5m
0239·4 **Espigón head** Fl(2+1)G.15s7m3M Green round tower 3m
0238.5 **External Espigon head** 40°24'·7N 0°26'·1E
Fl(2)R.6s8m3M Red tower 5m
0239 **Dique Sur head** Fl(3)R.s8m3M Red octagonal tower 4m

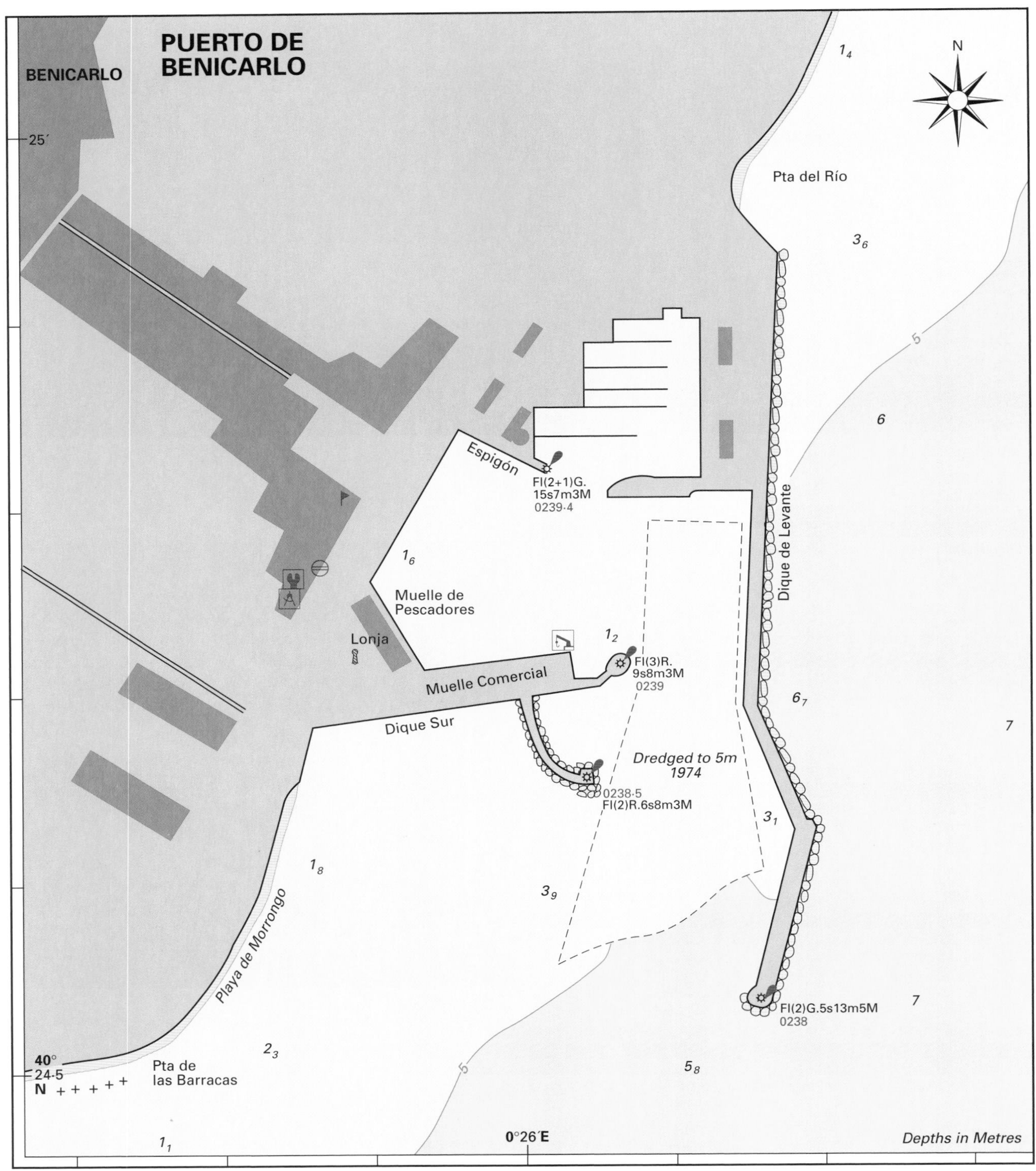

Puerto de Benicarló – note works are in progress in the northern part of the harbour

To the north

0370 **Punta de la Baña** 40°33'·6N 0°39'·7E
Fl(2)WR.12s27m12/8M White round tower, black bands 26m 199·4°-R-232·6°-W-199·4°

Port communications

VHF Ch 9. Marina Benicarló ☎ 964 462 330 *Fax* 964 481 620

General

An artificial fishing harbour sheltered by two breakwaters with an on-going development (March 2001) of a 250-berth marina in the northern part of the harbour. This space has been dredged and most quay space has been made. It is hoped to have the pontoons in place by summer 2001 and full facilities are planned for the 2002 season.

The old church of San Bartolomé is of interest with a baroque façade and an octagonal tower. The remains of the old town wall are visible. Excellent sandy beaches on either side of the harbour and a *parador* close by.

Approach by day

From the south Having passed the conspicuous castle on the island-like feature at Peñíscola, the town and harbour breakwaters of Benicarló will be seen in the distance. The church in particular is easily seen.

From the north From the harbour and town of Vinaroz the coast consists of low broken rocky cliffs. The town, church and harbour walls of Benicarló are conspicuous from this direction. In heavy weather avoid rocky shallows, Piedras de la Barbada (6·4m), lying ½M to NE of the harbour entrance.

Anchorage in the approach

Anchor 200m to W of the head of Dique Sur in 3·5m, sand, or 400m further S, but sound carefully due to silting.

Entrance

Round the head of Dique de Levante, leaving it 50m to starboard as there are underwater obstructions extending some 25m W of the head. Depths may not be as charted due to silting and periodic dredging so sound. Leave the head of Dique Sur 50m to port. Leave the Dique Sur 50m to port and head for the conspicuous marina tower turning to starboard to enter the marina (waiting quay to be specified).

Berths

Until the marina is ready for business in (late) summer 2001 it is advised to keep clear of Benicarló. The works have taken up all the usual places for visiting yachts and even the locals are finding it difficult to moor at present. As usual anchoring is not permitted in the harbour. However when the marina is completed (for the 2002 season) Benicarló will be a very nice harbour to visit.

Charges
Medium to high.

Facilities
In 2002 full water, electricity, chandlery, repair and stores will be on pontoons/site.

A few shops near the harbour but many in the town about 1M away where there is also a market.

Puerto de Vinaroz

40°27'·5N 0°28'·6E

Charts
British Admiralty *1458, 1701*
French *7296, 4720*
Spanish *4842, 485, 837*
Navicarte *R5*

Lights
0244 **Dique de Levante head** 40°27'·5N 0°28'·6E Fl.G.5s14m8M Green round tower 10m
0244·5 **Knuckle** Fl(2)G.7s6m3M Green octagonal tower 3m
0246 **Dique de Poniente head** Fl.R.5s7m4M Red octagonal tower 3m
0248 **Muelle Transversal head** Fl(3)G.9s8m3M Green round tower 6m
0370 **Punta de la Bana** 40°33'·6N 0°39'·7E Fl(2)WR.12s27m12/8M White tower, black bands 26m 199·4°-R-232·6°-W-199·4°

Storm signals
Shown from the root of Dique de Levante.

Port communications
VHF Ch 9. *Capitanía* ☎ 964 451 705.

General
A large artificial commercial fishing and yachting harbour, easy to approach and enter. It is periodically dredged and depths vary from time to time. South to southwest swell may come in but otherwise there is good protection.

The pleasant old town has good shops and a church with a baroque portal. There are sand and pebble beaches to the N of the harbour.

Approach
There are a number of fish farms off Vinaroz (both N and S) and another artificial reef is being set up at 40°27'·8N 0°31'·7E.

From the south Having passed the conspicuous castle at Puerto de Peñíscola and the harbour of Benicarló, which can be recognised by its harbour walls and town standing a little distance inland, the coast from here on is of low sand-coloured cliffs. The harbour walls of Vinaroz, some modern high-rise buildings, a tall chimney and a tall crane will be visible in the closer approach.

From the north The high range of hills, the Sierra de Montsia, which backs the flat delta of the Río Ebro, is easily recognised. Vinaroz lies in the flat plain to the S of this feature. The blocks of flats, chimney and crane are also visible from this direction.

Anchorage in the approach
Anchor 300m to NW of the head of the Dique de Levante in 7m, sand, or 400m to E of this head in 11m, sand.

Entrance
Round the head of the Dique de Levante at 50m, head between the knuckle and the head of Dique de Poniente. When through, leave the head of the Dique Transversal 50m to starboard. There are three black mooring buoys on NE side of Dique de

Puerto de Vinaroz

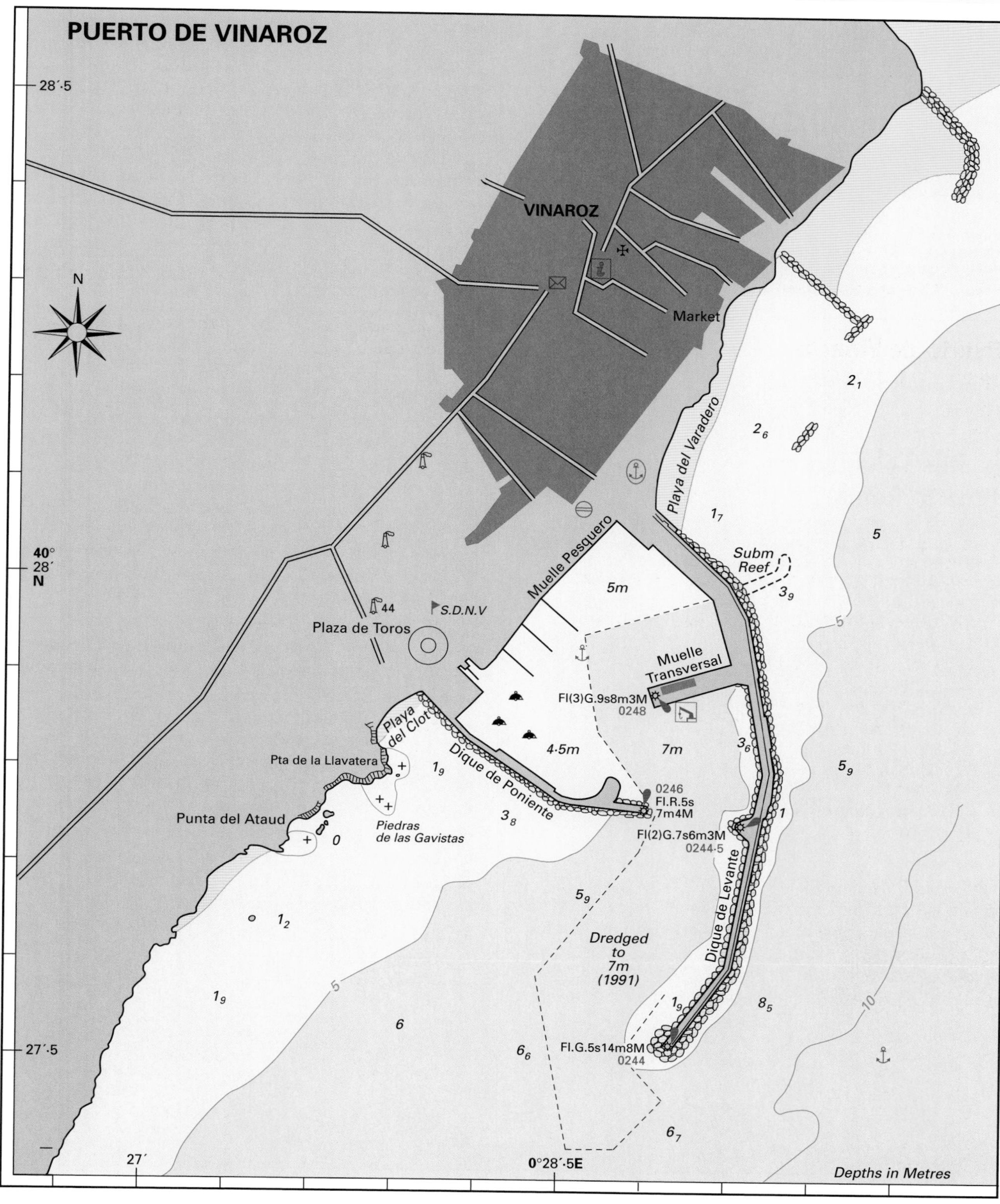

Poniente – not for yachts.

Berths
Secure to a vacant berth on the pontoons in the W corner of the harbour.

Moorings
There are a few private moorings on the NW side of the inner harbour and some may be available; contact the *club náutico*.

Anchorage
Anchor near the centre of the inner harbour, clear of the moorings in 3m, sand. Use an anchor trip-line and hoist the anchor signal.

Facilities
Hull repairs involving metal or woodwork can be carried

out by the shipyards.
An engine workshop at the NW side of the harbour.
One small and two large slipways, one of 100-tonne capacity.
Two small cranes are on the NE side of the harbour. A powerful crane is located on the Dique Transversal where there are a number of mobile cranes.
Chandlery shop near the harbour.
Water points on the pontoon and taps at the *lonja*, at the yacht club and on the Muelle Transversal.
220v AC on pontoons and quays.
Gasoleo A.
Ice available from the *lonja*.
The Sociedad Deportiva Náutica has a small clubhouse to the W of the harbour with restaurant, bar, lounge, terrace and showers.
A good range of shops and a market in the town.

Communications
Buses.

Islotes Columbretes (Puerto Tofiño)
39°52'N 0°40'E

Charts
British Admiralty *1701*
French *4033, 4720*
Spanish *836, 483A, 4831*
Navicarte *R5*

Lights
Columbrete Grande
0222 **Monte Colibri** 39°53'·9N 0°41'·2E Fl(3+1)22s85m21M White conical tower and dwelling 20m Racon
0222·2 **Punta Michorn** Fl.G.5s49m4M White 8-sided tower 6m
0222·4 **Punta Norte** Fl(2)R.9s67m4M White 8-sided tower 6m

General
Don't go without Spanish Chart *483A*.

Four isolated and barren groups of volcanic islets with outlying submerged rocks and shoals, Islotes Columbretes lie some 27M off the coast and opposite Castellón de la Plana. The four groups lie roughly N–S with an isolated shoal patch some 7M to WSW. The most northerly is Islote Columbrete Grande, 65m high, ½M in diameter, with high points to the N and S. This islet has the only lights. The next, Islote la Ferrera, a saddle-shaped island 44m high and 300m long, with a group of six smaller islets and shoal patches. Further S is Islote La Horadada, 55m high and 250m long, and a rough pyramid shape. It has two smaller rocky islets in its group and off-lying shoals. The most southern group consists of Islote El Bergantin 32m high and only 100m wide. It is the core of an old volcano. This group has at least eight smaller islets and several shoal patches. The area around these islands was renowned as one of the best fishing areas in the Mediterranean. Parts are now a marine reserve, interspersed with a rocket range and a target area for the air force.

The islets are inaccessible with the exception of the largest, Islote Columbrete Grande, which has a small military garrison. The islet is horseshoe-shaped and offers limited shelter in Puerto Tofiño where there is a mooring buoy but otherwise no facilities whatsoever. It is open to winds from N through to E and can be dangerous in these conditions. A walk over the arid island to the lighthouse is rewarding on a clear day with a view of the distant mainland.

Approach by day
Avoid Place de la Barra Alta, the shoal area some 7M WSW of the main group, a rocket range in an area W of Isla Columbrete Grande and the area 10M around Islote Bergantin, which is used for aerial exercises. Head for a position N to NE of Islote Columbrete Grande. It is possible to take the passages between the various groups of islets but streams are unpredictable and it can be rough.

Entrance
Approach the NE point of Islote Columbrete Grande on a SW course and follow this coast around at 150m into the anchorage.

Moorings
If free use the mooring buoy.

Islotes Columbretes Looking N at 3M

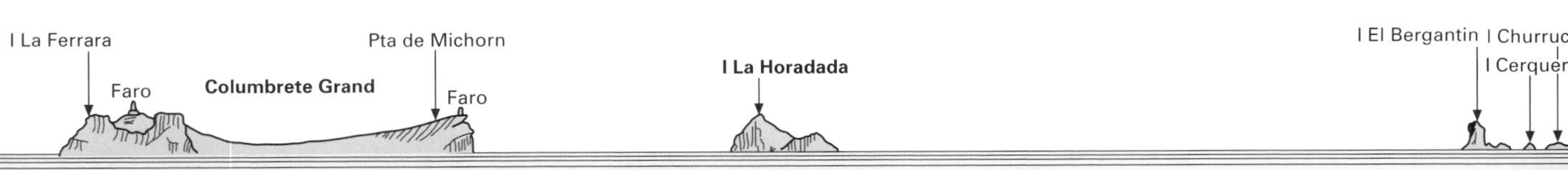

Islotes Columbretes Looking ENE at 7M

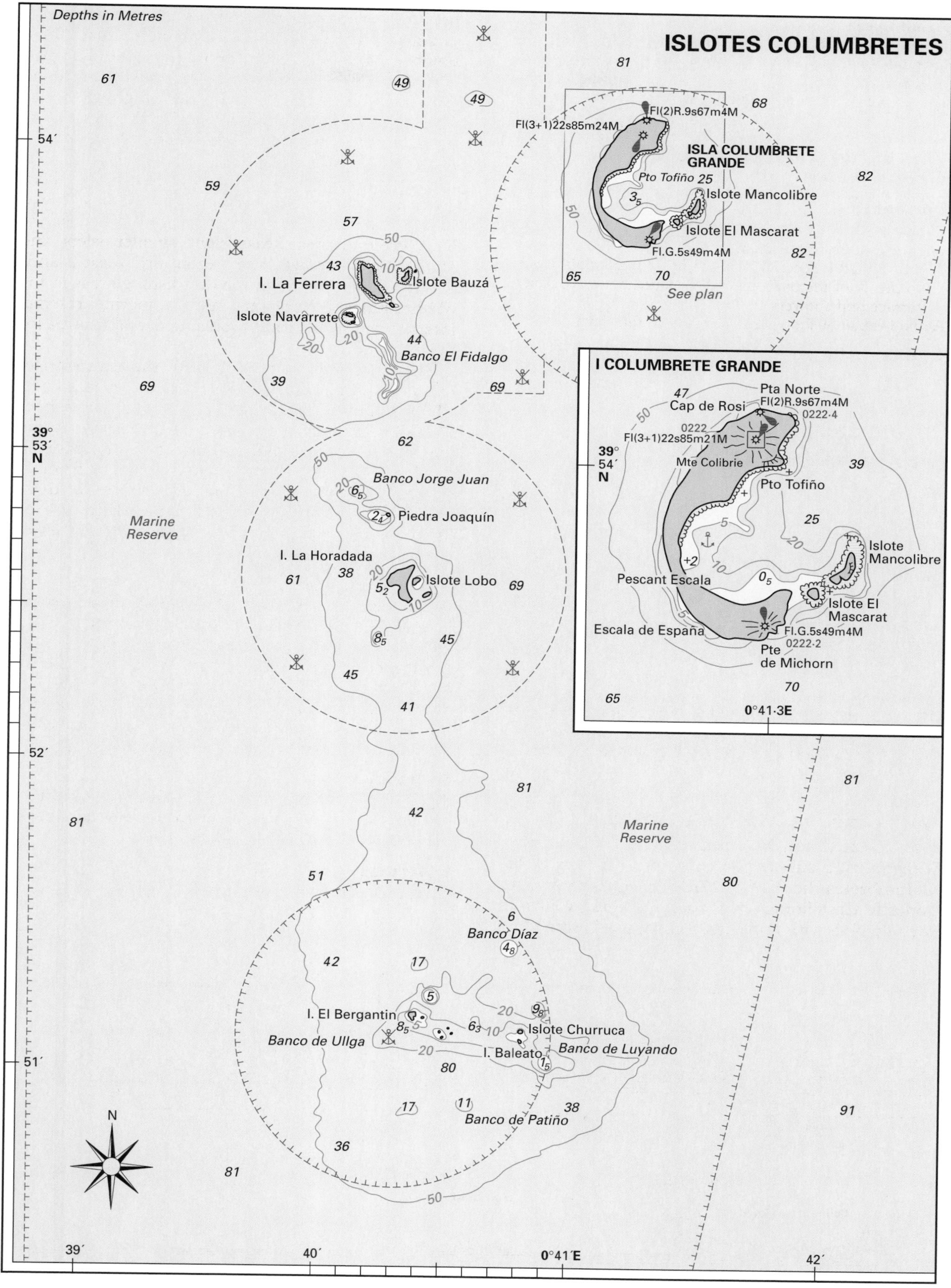
Depths in Metres
ISLOTES COLUMBRETES
ISLA COLUMBRETE GRANDE
Fl(2)R.9s67m4M
Fl(3+1)22s85m24M
Pto Tofiño
Islote Mancolibre
Islote El Mascarat
Fl.G.5s49m4M
See plan
I. La Ferrera
Islote Bauzá
Islote Navarrete
Banco El Fidalgo
Banco Jorge Juan
Piedra Joaquín
I. La Horadada
Islote Lobo
Marine Reserve
Banco Díaz
I. El Bergantin
Islote Churruca
Banco de Ullga
I. Baleato
Banco de Luyando
Banco de Patiño
I COLUMBRETE GRANDE
Pta Norte
Cap de Rosi
Fl(3+1)22s85m21M
Mte Colibrie
Pto Tofiño
Islote Mancolibre
Pescant Escala
Islote El Mascarat
Escala de España
Fl.G.5s49m4M
Pte de Michorn
0°41·3E
39° 54′ N
39° 53′ N
54′
52′
51′
39′
40′
0°41′E
42′
N

Anchorage
Anchor 150m from the W side of the harbour in 5m on rock and stone. An anchor trip-line is advisable. The holding is not good and should only be used in fair weather.

Landings
There are places to land at the head of the bay where the coast is lower.

Formalities
Check with the army on arrival.

Facilities
The island is barren and has no supply of water. Supplies are not available from the garrison except in an emergency.

Costa Dorada

Introduction

General description

The Costa Dorada (Golden Coast) is so called because of the golden sandy beaches between the mouths of the two large rivers, Ebro and Tordera. The 140 miles of coast varies considerably. At the south is the huge flat muddy delta of the Río Ebro which projects well out to sea. It is surrounded by extensive and dangerous shoals and should be given a wide berth. On either side of this delta are high ranges of hills leading down to broken rocky cliffs on the coast. Flat plains and low hills alternate along the coast from just S of Cabo Salou to beyond the delta of the Río Llobregat, backed by higher hills further inland. N of the Río Llobregat these higher hills follow the coastline with a narrow band of low-lying ground along the coast itself as far as the delta of the Río Tordera. In general the coastline is comparatively straight, broken only by the major promontory of the delta of the Río Ebro, Cabo Salou, Cabo Gros and the deltas of Ríos Llobregat and Tordera. Regular soundings follow the coast and with the exception of the areas around the river deltas, there is deep water close inshore. There are no outlying dangers except for a shallow bank, Banco de Santa Susana, parallel to the coast near Pineda and about ½ mile offshore.

Les Cases, at the start of this section, is the southernmost port of Catalunya. The province has some of the largest concentrations of industry in Spain which has resulted locally in some bad pollution of both air and sea. The sandy beaches are attractive to holiday-makers and there has been considerable development along the coastline for both Spanish and foreign tourists.

Visits

Apart from places mentioned in the harbour descriptions, the following sites are interesting but some distance inland. They can be reached by public transport or taxi.

Tortosa, an old Roman and Moorish city with many interesting buildings.

Monasterio de Escornalou, in the Sierra Montsant behind Cambrils with a superb view.

Monasterio de Sants Creus, behind Tarragona, a 12th-century building.

Tamarit, a 12th-century castle and museum.

Arca de Bará, a Roman arch astride the old Via Maxima near Torredembarra.

Castelldefels, a 15th-century tower, the Torre del Homenaje.

Montserrat, an extraordinary saw-shaped mountain ridge behind Barcelona, has a fine view and an interesting monastery dating from the 1st century.

Monasterio de Sant Cugat del Valles, another very old monastery on the site of the Roman Castrum Octavianum located behind Barcelona.

Sierra del Montseny, a number of places with tremendous panoramas located inland from Arenys de Mar.

Pilotage and navigation

Shoaling

The deltas along this coast are constantly altering and their off-lying shoals steadily extend further out to sea. Allowance must be made for the possibility of changes when rounding such promontories – keep well off and sound.

Restricted anchorages

There is a small area near the atomic power station that is located between L'Ametlla and Cambrils, a large area just to the N of Barcelona, and a smaller area to the S, where anchoring is forbidden.

Prohibited areas

Oil wells and exploration drilling platforms are located in an area 15M E of Cabo Tortosa, each platform carrying a light Mo(U)15s+Fl.R. Additional sites may be occupied nearby. Navigation is prohibited within the areas concerned.

Harbours of refuge

Only the main ports of Tarragona and Barcelona offer refuge in really bad storms with onshore winds. In certain conditions one or the other side of the Río Ebro delta may provide shelter and, with offshore winds, the smaller harbours of L'Hospitalet, Castelldefels (Ginesta), Mataró, Cambrils, Vilanova i la Geltrú and Arenys de Mar could be entered.

Magnetic Variation

1°00'W (2002). Decreasing by 7' annually.

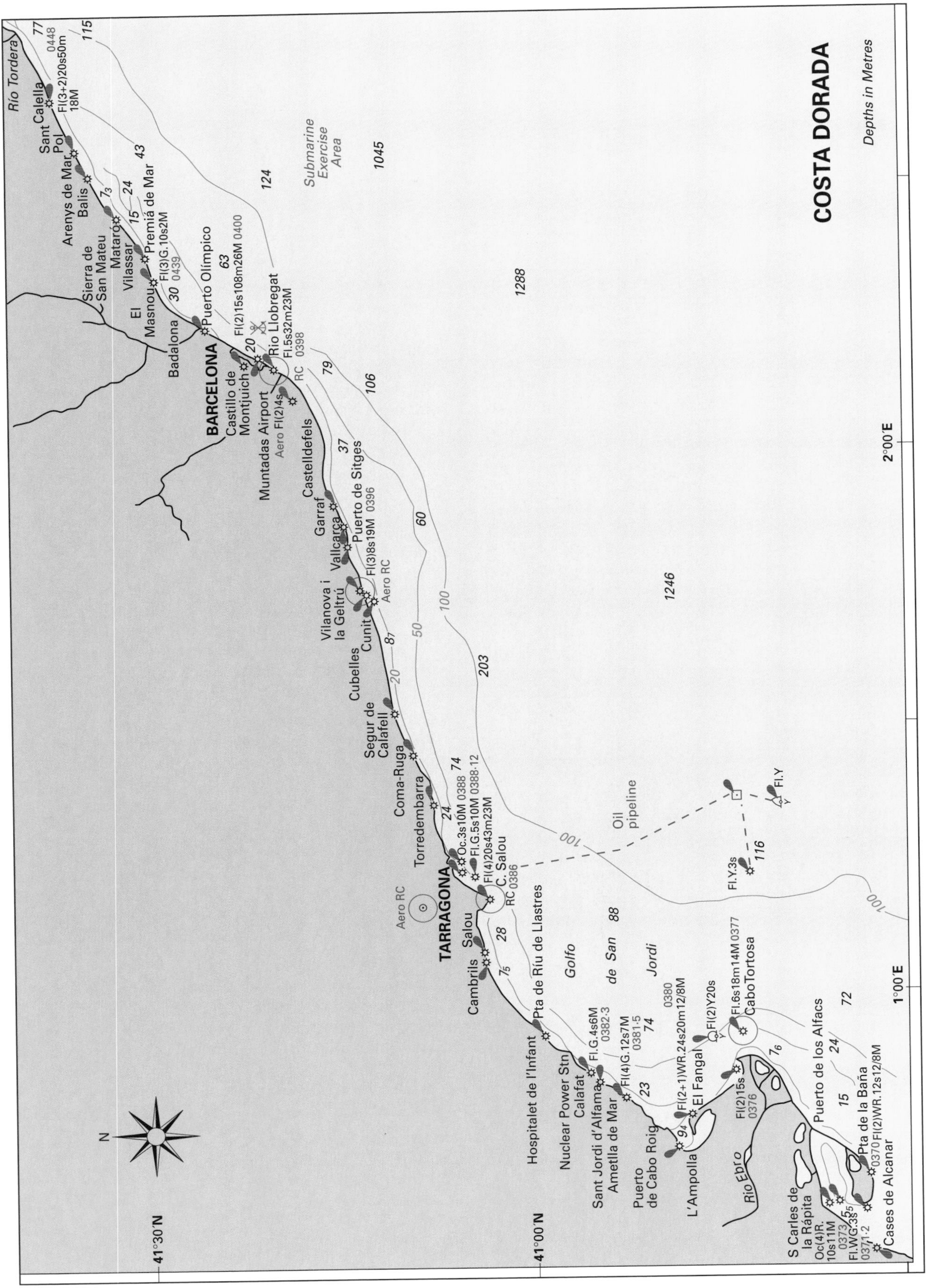

COSTA DORADA
Depths in Metres
Submarine Exercise Area
Rio Tordera
Calella
Sant Pol
Arenys de Mar
Balis
Premiá de Mar
Sierra de San Mateu
Mataró
Vilassar
El Masnou
Badalona
Puerto Olímpico
BARCELONA
Castillo de Montjuich
Rio Llobregat
Muntadas Airport
Castelldefels
Garraf
Vallcarca
Puerto de Sitges
Vilanova i la Geltrú
Cunit
Cubelles
Segur de Calafell
Coma-Ruga
Torredembarra
TARRAGONA
C. Salou
Salou
Cambrils
Pta de Ríu de Llastres
Golfo de San Jordi
Oil pipeline
Hospitalet de l'Infant
Nuclear Power Stn
Calafat
Sant Jordi d'Alfama
Ametlla de Mar
Puerto de Cabo Roig
L'Ampolla
El Fangal
Cabo Tortosa
Rio Ebro
Puerto de los Alfacs
Pta de la Baña
S Carles de la Rápita
Cases de Alcanar
41°30'N
41°00'N
2°00'E
1°00'E
N

Planning Guide (Costa Dorada)

Distance (miles)	*Harbours & Anchorages*	*Headlands*
	Puerto de les Cases d'Alcanar (page 61)	
2M		Punta Paloma
	Puerto de Alcanar (page 64)	
4M		
	Puerto de Sant Carles de la Rápita (page 65)	
20M	⚓ *Bahia de Alfacs*	
		Punta de la Bana
	Delta & Ports of Río Ebro (page 67)	
10M	⚓ *Puerto del Fangar*	Cabo Tortosa
	⚓ *Ensenada de Cartapacio*	
	Puerto l'Ampolla (page 70)	
	⚓ *Cala Montero*	
6M	⚓ *Playa de Roig*	Cabo Roig
	⚓ *Cala del Aguila*	Punta Figuera
	⚓ *Estany Podrit*	Punta de l'Aguila del Islote
	Puerto de l'Estany Gras (page 71)	
	⚓ *Cala Bon Capo*	
1M	⚓ *Cala bon Caponet*	
	⚓ *Cala de Arangaret*	
	Puerto de l'Ametlla de Mar (page 72)	
2M		Cabo de Sant Jordi
	Puerto Sant Jordi d'Alfama (page 74)	
2M		
	Puerto de Calafat (page 74)	
5M		Cabo de Terme
	Puerto de Hospitalet de l'Infant (page 76)	
8M		Punta de la Pixerota
	Puerto de Cambrils (page 78)	
4M	⚓ *Embarcadero de Reus Club de Mar*	Pta de la Riera de Riudoms
	Puerto de Salou (page 80)	
	⚓ *S of Salou*	
	⚓ *Cala de la Torre Nova*	Punta del Porroc
	⚓ *Cala Pinatel*	
	⚓ *N of Punta de Peny Tallada*	
6M	⚓ *Cala de la Font*	
	⚓ *Cala del Cranc*	Punta Grosa
	⚓ *Cala Morisca*	Cabo Salou
	⚓ *Playa de Reco*	
	⚓ *Oiling pier Pantalan Empetrol*	
	Puerto de Tarragona (page 82)	
	⚓ *Playa de Rabassada*	
	⚓ *E of Rabassada*	
	⚓ *Cala de la Jovera*	Punta de la Jovera
7M	⚓ *Altafulla*	
	⚓ *Reco de Fortin*	
	⚓ *Cala de Canadel*	
		Punta de la Galera
	Puerto de Torredembarra (page 88)	
3M	**Port Daurat** (page 90)	
3M	**Puerto de Coma-Ruga** (page 90)	
	⚓ *Sant Salvador*	
3M	⚓ *Calafell*	
	Puerto de Segur de Calafell (page 92)	
4M	⚓ *Cunit*	
	Puerto del Foix (page 93)	
	⚓ *Cubelles*	
3M		Punta Grossa
	Puerto de Vilanova i la Geltru (page 95)	
3M		
	Puerto de Sitges (page 98)	
2M		
	Puerto de Vallcarca (page 99)	
2M		
	Puerto de Garraf (page 100)	

Distance	Harbour / anchorage	Feature
2M		
	Port Ginesta (page 102)	
13M	⚓ *Gava*	
		Río Llobregat
	Puerto de Barcelona (page 104)	
4M		
	Puerto Olímpico (page 109)	
		Río Besos
7M	⚓ *Badalona*	
		Punta del Besos
	⚓ *Mangat*	
	Puerto de El Masnou (page 110)	
2M		
	Puerto de Premia de Mar (page 112)	
5M	⚓ *Vilasser de Mar*	
	Puerto de Mataro (page 114)	
3M		
	Puerto Balis (page 115)	
2M	**Puerto de Arenys de Mar** (page 116)	
	⚓ *Punta Morrell*	
12M	⚓ *Calella*	
	⚓ *Pineda de Mar*	
	Puerto de Blanes (page 124)	Río Tordera

Puerto de les Cases d'Alcanar (Casas de Alcanar)

40°33'N 0°32'E

Charts

British Admiralty *1458, 1701, 1704*
French *7048, 4720*
Spanish *485, 837*
Navicarte *R5*

Lights

0370·3 **Fishing marina S pier head** 40°33'·0N 0°32'·0E Fl(2)R.10s8m4M Red pyramidal tower 4m
0370·35 **Dique de Levante head** Fl.G.4s7m3M Green pyramidal tower 3m

To the south

0370 **Punta de la Baña** Fl(2)WR.12s27m12/8M Round white tower black bands 26m 199°·4-R-232°·6-W-199°·4

Port communications

VHF Ch 9. *Club náutico* ☎ 977 735 001 (office, mornings only), 977 735 014 (club house and bar)

General

A pleasant small artificial yachting and fishing harbour; there is not much depth alongside in the yacht harbour. The area has not been highly developed and the harbour is useful for a vessel on passage wanting to stop before rounding Cabo Tortosa without diverting to Puerto de Sant Carles de la Rápita but space for visitors is limited to two berths. Entrance could be difficult with high winds and seas between NE and SE. In 1998 a new club house was built and a pump for *Gasoleo A* installed.

The town was an important staging place on the N–S coast road from pre-Roman days. Remains from this period are still being found. There are several Roman remains and many from the time of the Moorish occupation. The town suffered many attacks by sea pirates in the Middle Ages and also suffered during the War of the Succession in the 18th century. The Seven Years War and the Civil War also affected the town.

There are several interesting buildings, including the church in Alcanar and the remains of a Roman bridge. Fine views from the Sierra Montsiá. Details from the information office beside the harbour. Excellent sandy beach to S of the harbour. Local holidays include the *Remedio* in the second two weeks of October, in honour of the town's patroness.

Approach

There may be several oil rigs and oil wells located about 10M offshore in this area. They come and go as oil is found or used up. The areas are well marked by lights. Sometimes a tanker is kept moored to one of these wells.

From the SW The coast from Vinaroz is flat with low sandy cliffs as far as this harbour where rocky cliffs commence, backed by the mountain range Sierra

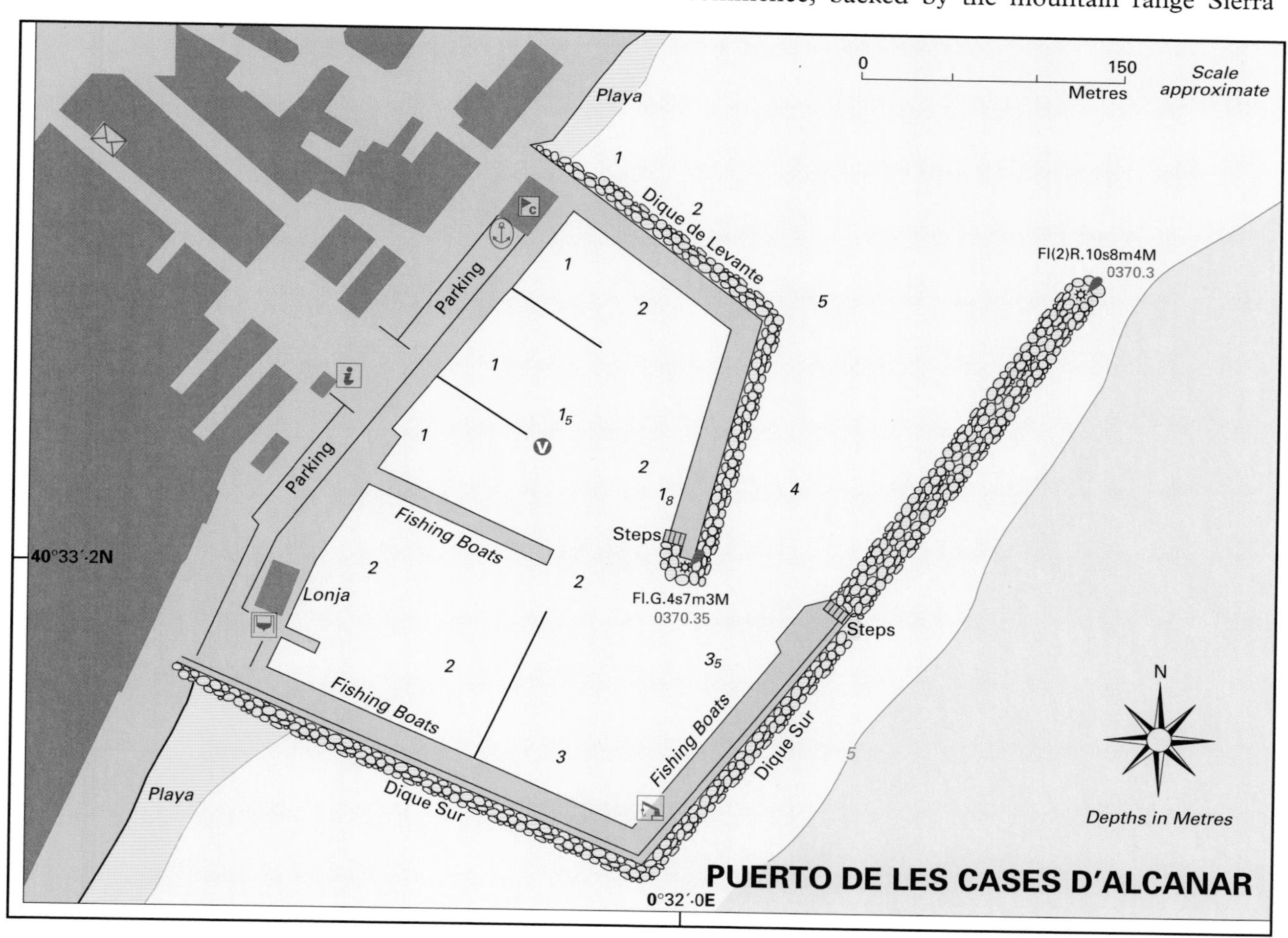

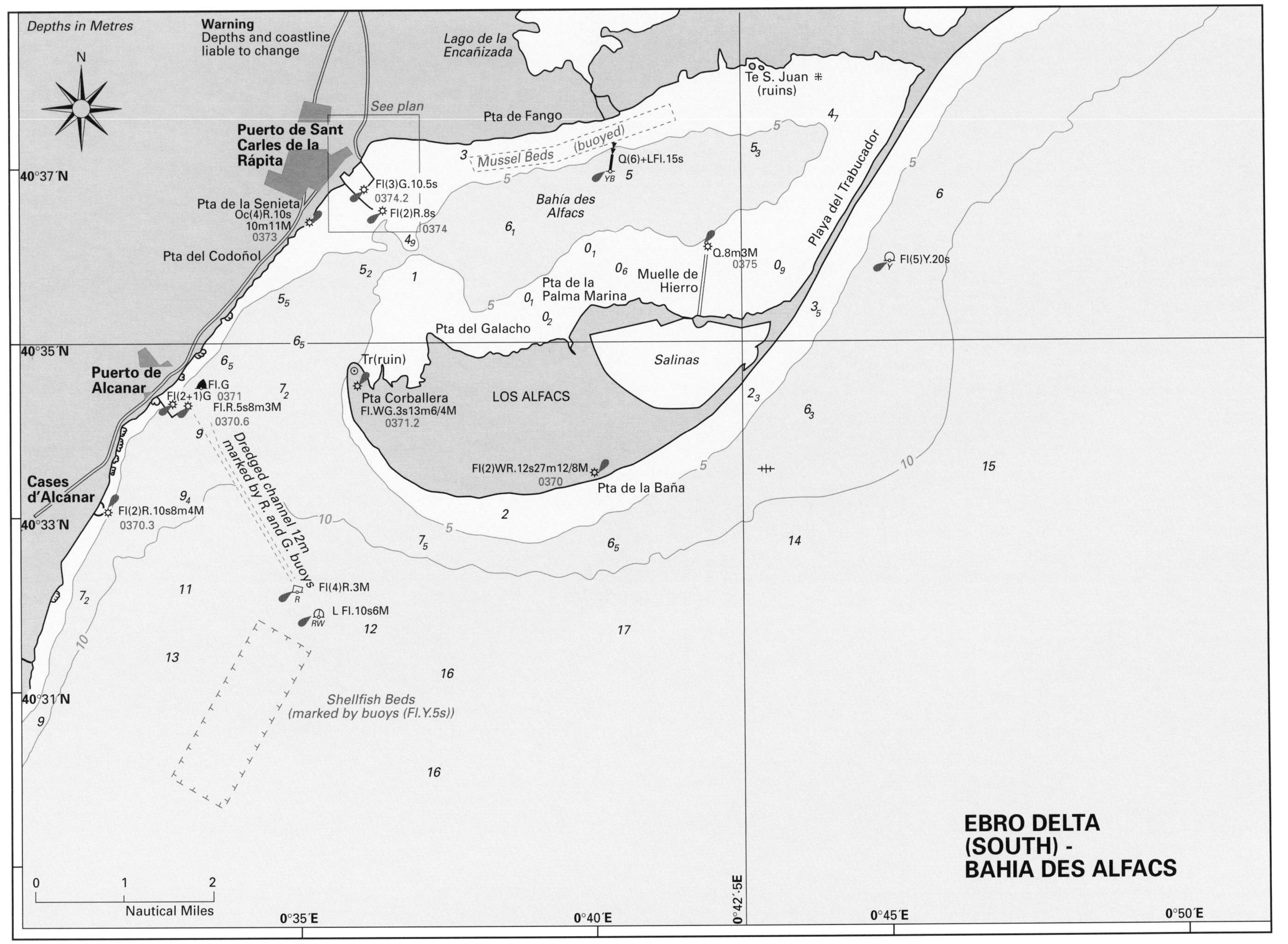
Depths in Metres
Warning
Depths and coastline liable to change
N
Lago de la Encañizada
Te S. Juan (ruins)
See plan
Pta de Fango
Puerto de Sant Carles de la Rápita
Mussel Beds (buoyed)
Q(6)+LFl.15s
40°37'N
Fl(3)G.10.5s
0374.2
Fl(2)R.8s
0374
Pta de la Senieta
Oc(4)R.10s 10m11M
0373
Bahía des Alfacs
Playa del Trabucador
Pta del Codoñol
Q.8m3M
0375
Fl(5)Y.20s
Muelle de Hierro
Pta de la Palma Marina
Pta del Galacho
40°35'N
Salinas
Tr(ruin)
Puerto de Alcanar
Fl.G
Fl(2+1)G 0371
Fl.R.5s8m3M
0370.6
Pta Corballera
Fl.WG.3s13m6/4M
0371.2
LOS ALFACS
Fl(2)WR.12s27m12/8M
0370
Pta de la Baña
Cases d'Alcanar
Fl(2)R.10s8m4M
0370.3
40°33'N
Dredged channel 12m marked by R. and G. buoys
Fl(4)R.3M
L Fl.10s6M
40°31'N
Shellfish Beds (marked by buoys (Fl.Y.5s))
EBRO DELTA (SOUTH) - BAHIA DES ALFACS
0
1
2
Nautical Miles
0°35'E
0°40'E
0°42'.5E
0°45'E
0°50'E

Puerto de les Cases d'Alcanar

Montsiá. The tower Sol de Riv at the mouth of a small river can be identified. The group of houses and apartment blocks behind this harbour can be seen from afar.

From the NE Round the large delta of the Río Ebro as far as Punta de la Baña which can be identified by its lighthouse. Approach the harbour on a W course and cross the line of 22 light buoys which mark a dredged channel leading to Puerto d'Alcanar (La Martinenca), 3M NW(except for the first and last buoys they are in pairs, red can and green conical). The buildings behind the harbour will now be seen.

Anchorage in the approach
Anchor in 5m, sand, 200m to S of the harbour.

Entrance
Approach the harbour on a W course and identify the head of Dique Sur. Note that the head of Dique Levante is well inside the head of Dique Sur. Give them both a 15m berth and enter.

Berths
Secure near head of fuel jetty and apply to *club nautico* for a berth.

Charges
High.

Facilities
Maximum length overall 15m.
Simple repairs only; mechanic in the town.
6-tonne crane and hard-standing on Dique Sur.
A slipway in W corner of the harbour.
Water taps on quays and pontoons.
220v AC points on quays and pontoons.
Ice from café/bars.
Club Náutico Cases d'Alcanar has a clubhouse at the N corner of the harbour.
Several shops in the area near the harbour and many in the town of Alcanar 2M inland where there is a market.

Communications
Bus service. Car Hire.

Puerto de Alcanar (La Martinenca)

40°34'N 0°33'E

Charts

British Admiralty *1701, 1704*
French *7048, 4720*
Spanish *3713, 485, 837*
Navicarte *R5*

Lights

0370·6 **Muelle Exterior head** 40°34'·4N 0°33'·4E
Fl.R.5s8m3M Square tower 2m
0371 **Muelle Interior head** Fl(2+1)G.14s8m3M
Square tower, red and green top 3m

Port communications

Pilots Sant Carles Rápita Prácticos VHF Ch 11, 12, 14, 16. Continuous service.

General

A commercial harbour which is a part of a large cement works. Not normally used by yachts but could be used as a shelter in the event of bad weather. The approach and entrance are easy and good shelter is obtained, though with N to NE winds it can be uncomfortable despite the shelter provided by the Ebro delta. Facilities for yachtsmen are very limited as might be expected from a purely commercial harbour but there are excellent sandy beaches on either side of the harbour.

Approach

From the south The flat coast with low sandy cliffs suddenly gives way to the high range of mountains, the Sierra Montsiá. At the foot of these mountains and close to the coast are the tall cement factory buildings usually with clouds of effluent pouring out from them. The harbour is located nearby. Close-to the dredged channel lightbuoys will be seen.

From the north Round the Ebro delta giving Cabo Tortosa a good berth and follow the low flat coast at 3M in a SW direction. Round Punta de la Baña onto a WNW course. The cement factory by the harbour will be seen from afar and the dredged channel lightbuoys will appear when closer in.

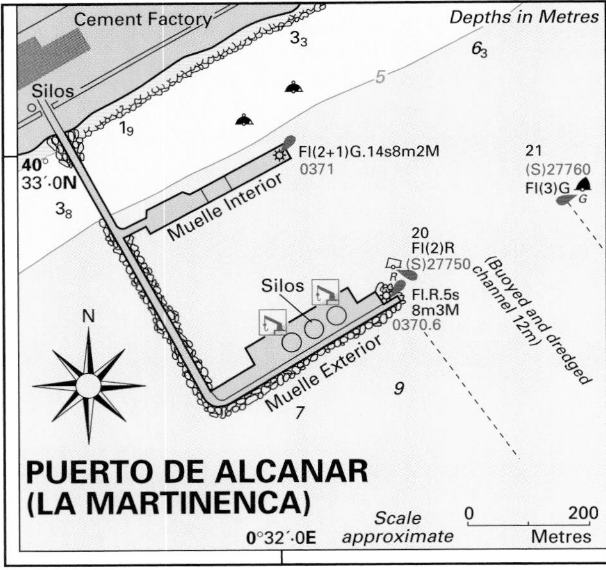

Puerto de Alcanar

Approach channel
The approach channel 330° (dredged to 12m) has on its SE extremity a safewater buoy (Boya de Recalada 40°32'·0N 0°35'·4E LFl.10s6M) nearly 3M distant from the port. The NW end is marked by a green starboard-hand lateral buoy (Boya No.21 Fl.G.3s3M) about 400m NE of the harbour. Between these buoys lie ten pairs of R and G lightbuoys. A fish farm has been established about a mile SW of No.8 buoy.

Anchorage

Anchor with trip-line attached in 3m on sand about halfway between the shore and the Muelle Interior.

Entrance

Approach the head of the Muelle Exterior, round a red can lightbuoy (Fl(3)R) off it and then the head of the Muelle Interior at 25m.

Berths

Temporary berth alongside the quay on the land side of either Muelle.

Moorings

Temporary mooring available on the large mooring buoys in the inner harbour.

Formalities

Report to harbour officials on arrival and ask permission to stay while the bad weather lasts.

Facilities

Provisions from the town some 3M to SW.

Puerto de Sant Carles (San Carlos) de la Rápita

40°36'N 0°36'E

Charts

British Admiralty *1458, 1701, 1704*
French *7296, 7048, 4720*
Spanish *3713, 485, 837*
Navicarte *R5*

Lights

To the south by east

0371·2 **Punta Corballera** 40°34'·7N 0°35'·8E Fl.WG.3s13m6/4M Black round tower 12m 000°-G-180°-W-360°

To the west

0373 **Punta de la Senieta** Oc(4)R.10s10m11M White round tower 7m

Harbour

0374 **Dique de Abrigo head** 40°36'·4N 0°36'·3E Fl(2)R.8s8m6M Red tower on white base 4m

0374·2 **Dique de Levante head** Fl(3)G.10·5s6m4M Green tower 4m

0374·4 **Muelle de Poniente head** Oc.R.4s5m2M Red truncated pyramidal tower 4m.

Cardinal lights mark shellfish beds between 0·65M and 3M ENE

Port communications

Pilots Sant Carles Rápita Prácticos VHF Ch 11, 12, 14, 16. Hours various.

Port ☎ 977 741 103.

Club Náutico de Sant Carles VHF Ch 9. ☎/*Fax* 977 741 103. If this does not work, call the *club náutico* at Ampolla.

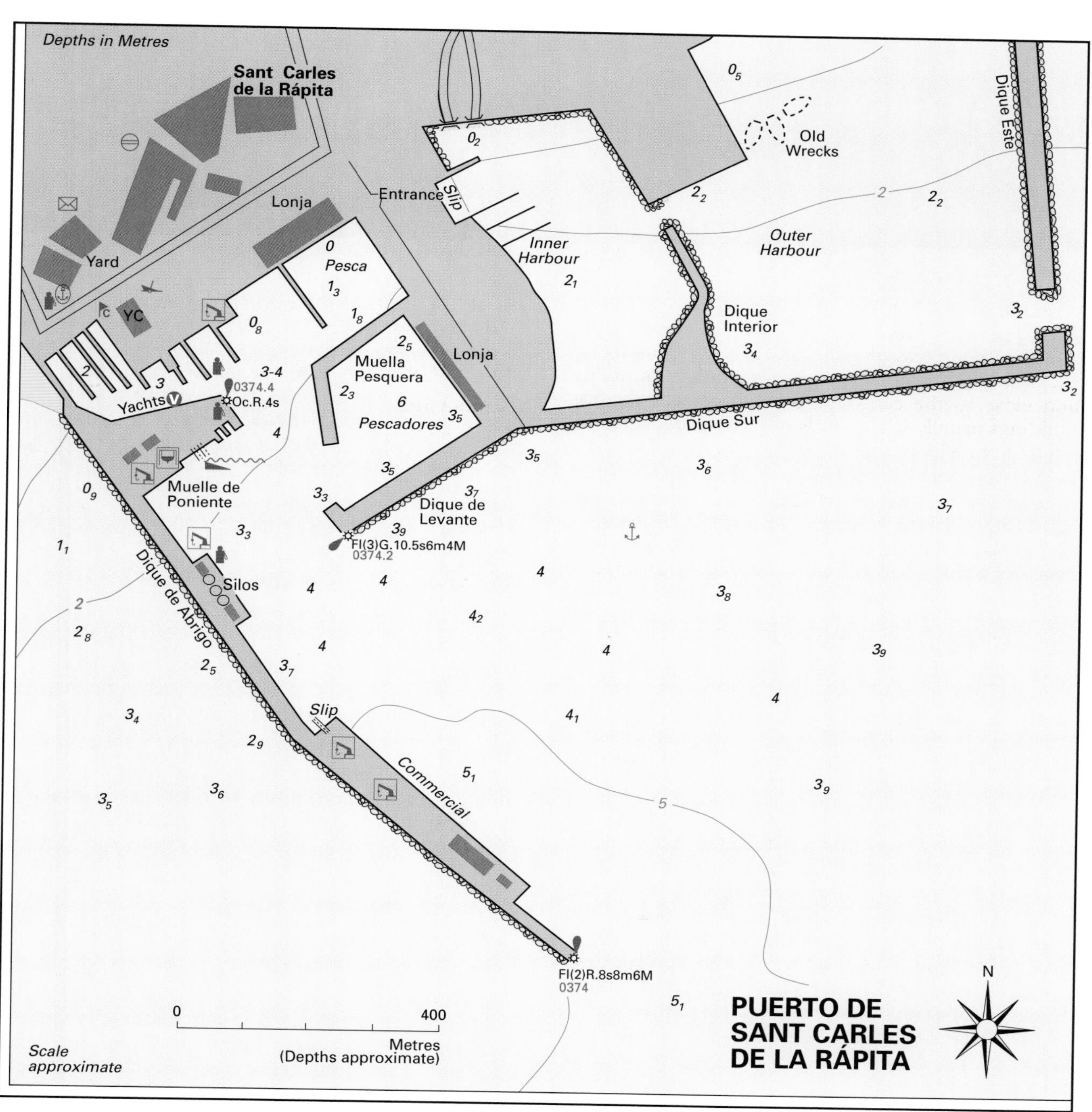

Puerto de Sant Carles de la Rápita

General
A large fishing and commercial harbour with a yachting section. It is well protected from winds and easy to approach (once round the Ebro delta, if coming from the north). The facilities are fair and the area is attractive in a wild and unexploited way.

There are two sets of harbours. The older, to the southwest, has the yacht harbour, a commercial basin and a fishing harbour. The newer harbour to the northeast has an inner and outer basin and was developed for small fishing craft and yachts. This harbour is a good launching place for those who trail their yachts and wish to visit the enclosed sea area to the east, Puerto de los Alfacs.

The original harbour was founded by Carlos III with the intention of making it into a large trading port but this scheme never prospered and the grandiose Plaza Carlos III is the sole reminder of it. The Cerro de la Guardiola which lies behind the town has a fine view.

Approach
From the south Pass the conspicuous harbours of Benicarló and Vinaroz where the coastal plain is low and flat. Further to N the high range of the Sierra Montsiá (764m) leads to this harbour. Follow the coast at 1M or less passing through the line of red and green lightbuoys leading to the conspicuous cement works at Alcanar (La Martinenca). This course passes W of the shallows off the low and inconspicuous Punta Corballera and Punta del Galacho. The harbour breakwaters will be seen in the closer approach.

From the north round the large delta of the Río Ebro and follow the S side round, keeping outside the 10m soundings. Careful navigation is necessary due to the lack of identifiable features and the low flat coast. When S of Punta Corballera cross over towards the mainland shore and follow this in a NE direction at 1M distance.

Anchorage in the approach
Possible location for yachts is 600m to E of the entrance in 4m, mud.

The southwest harbours
This is the old harbour area.

Entrance
Round the head of the Dique de Abrigo leaving it 50m to port onto a NW course and approach the entrance following the Dique de Abrigo at 50m.

Berths
Go to the visitors berth on the N side of the Muelle de Poniente or moor at the fuel berth and arrange a berth at the newly enlarged club nautico. All berths have lazy lines running out from the quays/pontoons.

Harbour charges
Low.

The northeast harbours

Entrance
Although there has been much talk of developing this harbour as a large marina, nothing has been done to date and there are no plans for the

forseeable future. There is some infilling going on in the NW corner of the outer harbour and the depths shown on the chartlet on page 61 should be taken as optimistic. For those who wish to anchor enter by following the low Dique Sud at 50m and when the entrance opens up enter, sounding carefully, and anchor in the southern portion of the outer harbour in 2m mud.

Anchorages

No anchoring is permitted in the old harbour. Anchoring is allowed in the NE harbour close to the Dique Sud.

Facilities in the southwest harbour

Maximum length overall 15m.
Shipyard to the NW of the harbour and an engine repair workshop nearby.
Several slipways in the complex.
Cranes up to 8 tonnes and a large mobile crane.
Several chandlery shops in town and near the harbour.
Water from the pontoons and the *lonja* and from the *club náutico*.
220v AC on the pontoons and at the *club náutico*.
Gasoleo A and petrol.
Ice from the *lonja* and *club náutico*.
Club Náutico de Sant Carles has a new clubhouse to the NW of the harbour with bar, lounge, terrace, showers and pontoon.
Shops of all kinds, supermarket, in the town nearby. A few shops near the harbour.
Launderette in town.

Communications

Rail and bus service. Taxi ☎ 977 741 317.

Bahía des Alfacs

40°36'N 0°40E

Charts

British Admiralty *1704, 1458*
French *7048, 4720*
Spanish *485, 837*
Navicarte *R5*

Lights

0375 **Muelle de Hierro head** 40°36'·2N 0°41'·4E Q.8m3M N card pole 082°-vis- 229°(this light is well inside the bahía)
S card lights mark shellfish beds on the north side of the *bahía*

General

This *bahía* is an inland lake blocked off to seaward by a spit formed from the wash-out of the Río Ebro (Ebre). It is some 6M long and 2M wide. The entrance, which has Sant Carles de la Rápita on its N side, is about 1M wide and is shoal on the S side. Depths within range from 6m to 0m, the shallows being on the S side; the sea level tends to increase with winds between NE and SE and decrease with winds from other directions. The area offers considerable scope for larger boats to anchor out of the swell of the open sea for smaller boats wishing to sail in sheltered waters.

Apart from two small villages with a road inland from the N coast, there is little activity in the area. There are many rice fields, *salinas* (saltpans) and a few factories dealing with the salt. One such factory on the S side has a long metal jetty, the Muelle de Hierro, extending 1M out from the shore. The N side of the area has a long line of mussel beds, marked by three S cardinal buoys. Keep clear of them. The surrounding area, largely marsh, is low and flat; squalls can descend without warning from the Sierra Montsiá.

Approach

Go up to and pass ½M off Sant Carles de la Rápita.

Anchorage

Anchorage is possible virtually anywhere in the Bahía des Alfacs in mud in depth to suit draught. Use an anchor light.

Delta and Ports of the Río Ebro

Alfacs de Tortosa

40°43'N 0°54'E

General

The Ebro is the largest river in Spain depositing vast amounts of silt, building the delta out to sea. In some places the shore is advancing by 10m a year, sometimes leaving inland what were once coastal marks. In other places currents have washed away the shore and similar features have been left standing in water. Away from the sea, the delta consists of many small islands separated by canals, saltpans, pools, marshes and mud, all subject to flooding; it is hovercraft terrain. For some, and for fauna, it has its attractions. A large part of the delta on the NE side is a nature reserve and park.

The shore line of the delta is probably the most dangerous section of this coast. It is featureless, very low-lying, it extends over 12M seawards from the general line of the coast and has unmarked, shifting, off-lying shoals. A peculiarity is that in good visibility, buildings etc. which are located some distance inland appear to be situated on the coast. A branch of the *tramontana* NW gale can come down the Ebro valley with considerable force and little warning. Altogether, from the point of view of the navigator, it is a place to be avoided.

Entry

It is possible for shallow draught vessels to enter and leave the river but very dangerous without a pilot (*práctico*) with up-to-date knowledge of the channels at the bar. The bar is itself dangerous if there is any sea running at the time.

The River

There are two main ports on the lower section of the Río Ebro, Amposta 16M upstream from the river mouth and Tortosa a further 9M. Yachts with draught of 1·5m or less can ascend the river to Tortosa and for some miles more but again, a pilot (*práctico*) is essential. There are high tension wires, 13m or less above the water, just downstream of Isla Gracia, well before Amposta. Yachts with masts over 10m high will not be able to go beyond the three road bridges at Amposta. There are also rail and road bridges at Tortosa.

Amposta

Amposta is a small old town with narrow streets and with 14,650 inhabitants. There is an old narrow road bridge and a series of quays alongside the river on the right (SW) bank. Below the town is a new wide bypass road bridge and above it is the new motor route bridge. There are a fair number of shops in town and everyday requirements can be met.

The Club Náutico de Amposta has a base with a pontoon and a small crane on the right bank of the Río Ebro just below the old road bridge. ☎ 977 701 824. There are showers, WCs and bar. A mechanic is available.

Tortosa

A very old town of 31,200 inhabitants with quays on the left bank, many interesting places and ruins to visit. This town had the first and only road bridge over the lower part of the Río Ebro and it was an important place from the point of view of commerce and defence. The Romans established the town and called it Dertosa Julia Augusta but they lost it to the Visigoths. They in turn lost it to the Moors in 714 who built the castle, now in ruins. It was then re-conquered by the Catalan, Ramon Bereguer IV, and for several centuries Catalans, Moors, Jews and others lived here together in peace. In 1938 there was a terrible battle here on the right (W) bank of the river between the Republicans and the Nationalists who triumphed; 150,000 died. A memorial stands in the middle of the river.

Rounding the Delta

Charts

British Admiralty *1701, 1704*
French *7048, 4720*
Spanish *485*
Navicarte *R5*

Lights

0371·2 **Punta Corballera** 40°34'·7N 0°35'·8E Fl.WG.3s13m6/4M Black round tower 12m 000°-G-180°-W-360°

0370 **Punta de la Baña** 40°33°·6N 0°39'·7E Fl(2)WR.12s27m12/8M White round tower, black bands 26m 199·4°-R-232·6°-W-199·4°

0376 **Río Ebro N Bank (Margen N)** 40°43'·5N 0°51'·6E Fl(2)15s13m3M White metal tower, black bands 11m

0377 **Cabo Tortosa** 40°43'·0N 0°55'·8E Fl.6s18m14M Black metal framework tower and platform, aluminium top 18m Racon (in the sea about 2M E of the *cabo*)

0380 **El Fangal** 40°47'·5N 0°46'·2E Fl(2+1)WR.24s20m12/8M Round tower, red and white bands 18m 019·4°-W-301·6°-R-019·4° Fl.2·5s Lts mark mussel beds 1·8M WSW

Buoys

In 1996 there were wave measuring buoys at 40°36'·4N 0°45'·2E (Fl(5)Y.20s) and 40°43'·4N 0°59'·1E (Fl(5)Y.20s)

General

Identifiable features on this low coast are few and far between. The coastline is constantly changing, as are the off-lying shoals. Navigational marks are not always on the coast and may be inland or out to sea. Sea levels tend to increase with winds between NE and SE and decrease with those from other directions. There is usually southerly current off the cabo.

From the S

From the area of Vinaroz set course for Punta de la Baña if necessary using the features on Sierra Montsi to keep a navigational fix. The industry at Alcanar (La Martinenca) may also be identified by the dust from the cement works. In the closer approach the lighthouse Punta de la Baña will be seen. Keeping about 1½M from the coast and outside the 10m contour, follow the coast in a NNE direction. The features marked on the plan will be seen in clear weather but in poor visibility little that can be identified will be seen. Do not cut the corner at Cabo Tortosa and keep at least 1M outside any visible land. The old lighthouse may be seen about a mile inland from the *cabo*. Continue outside the 10m contour which is about ½M off the coast.

Rounding the Ebro Delta from the N

It is normal to set course from the area of L'Ametlla de Mar direct for Cabo Tortosa. The houses at Ampolla and the lighthouse at Faro del Fangar will provide a position. The old lighthouse which lies about a mile inland to the W of Cabo Tortosa is difficult to spot even in good visibility. Do not approach the shore closer than the 10m contour. Do not attempt to round Cabo Tortosa within a mile of any visible land. Having rounded the *cabo* follow the coast about 1½M offshore, outside the 10m contour. If going up to Sant Carles, get into mid-channel between Alcanar and Punta Corballera.

Puerto del Fangar (Fangal)

Charts
British Admiralty *1701, 1704*
French *7048, 4720*
Spanish *485*
Navicarte *R5*

Lights
0380 **El Fangal** 40°47'·5N 0°42'·8E
Fl(2+1)WR.24s20m12/8M Round tower, red and white bands 18m 019·4°-W-301·6°-R-019·4° Fl.2·5s
Lts mark mussel beds 1·8M WSW

General
Another large stretch of water which is enclosed by the N part of the Río Ebro (Ebre) delta. It is about 1M by 2M with an entrance about 1M but space is limited by *viveros,* fish farms, here raising mussels. It is wide open to the N and with a NE wind a current crosses the entrance. Depths, which ordinarily range from 4m to 0m, may be raised as much as 0·6m by easterly winds and lowered the same amount by

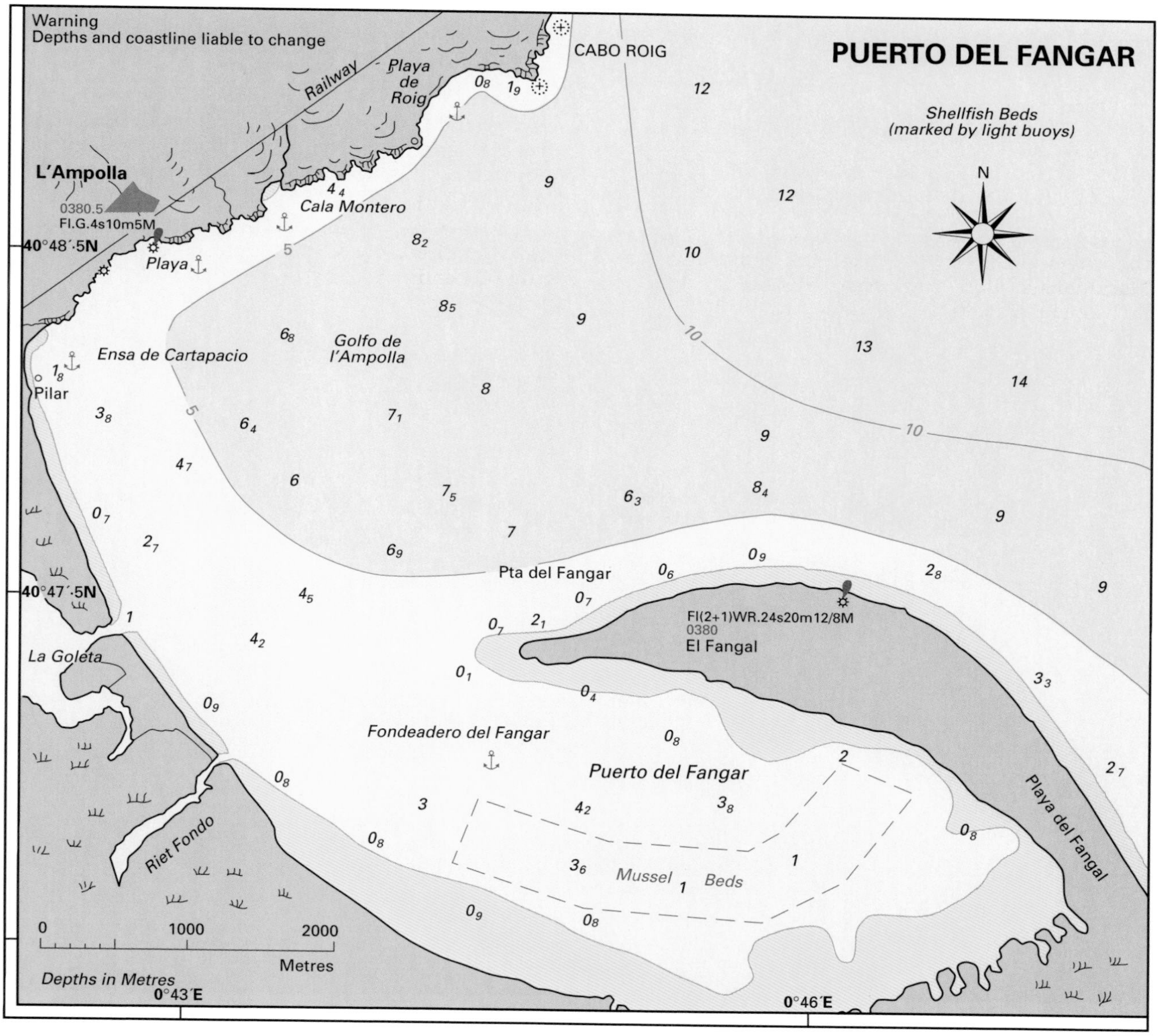

El Fangal lighthouse

PUERTO DEL FANGAR

Warning
Depths and coastline liable to change

CABO ROIG
Railway
Playa de Roig
L'Ampolla
0380.5
Fl.G.4s10m5M
Cala Montero
Playa
40°48'·5N
Shellfish Beds
(marked by light buoys)
N
Ensa de Cartapacio
Golfo de l'Ampolla
Pilar
Pta del Fangar
Fl(2+1)WR.24s20m12/8M
0380
El Fangal
40°47'·5N
La Goleta
Fondeadero del Fangar
Puerto del Fangar
Riet Fondo
Mussel Beds
Playa del Fangal
0 1000 2000
Metres
Depths in Metres
0°43'E
0°46'E

westerlies. The sides are very shallow. It is surrounded by rice fields and *salinas* (saltpans) ashore, together with a few barns and salt factories but no roads or villages.

The *viveros* are all round the bay but there are anchorages to be found, depending on draught. Sound carefully.

⚓ Ensenada de Cartapacio

An anchorage in the W corner of the Golfo de L'Ampolla in 1·8m, sand, open to NE–E. Sandy beach. Road to L'Ampolla.

Puerto L'Ampolla

40°48'N 0°46'E

Charts

British Admiralty *1701*
French *7048, 4720*
Spanish *485, 838*
Navicarte *R5*

Lights

0380·5 **Dique head** 40°48'·5N 0°42'·8E Fl.G.4s10m5M Green pyramidal tower 5m

0380·55 Contradique head Fl.R.5s4m3M Red truncated tower 3m

0380·6 Contradique interior Fl(2)R.7s4m3M Red square tower 3m

28350(S) **New mole (under construction)** Fl(2)G.12s4m1M Green tripod 3m

Port communications

VHF Ch 9. Club Náutico L'Ampolla ☎ 977 460 211 *Fax* 977 593 007.

General

A working fishing port with facilities developed for yachts and apparently a place favoured by Andorrans. The approach and entrance are easy but

Puerto L'Ampolla

could be difficult if not dangerous in strong easterlies. Construction work is going on in the harbour and care should be taken on entering.

Approach

From the south Round the delta of the Río Ebro and from off the Faro del Fangar, go WNW towards the houses of L'Ampolla and look for the *dique.*

From the north Follow the steep rugged and indented coast at 400m. Punta Figuera and Cabo Roig will be identified, the latter having a reddish streak of rock. The houses of L'Ampolla can be seen in the distance and, when close, the *dique.*

There are oyster beds marked by buoys Fl.Y.13s in the approaches to Ampolla.

Anchorage in the approach

Anchor off the Nuevo Contradique according to depth, with a line ashore.

Entrance

Approach the head of the Dique on a W course, round it at 25m.

Berths

Wait at the end of the *contradique* and ask at the *club náutico.*

Charges

High-ish but include showers, water, electricity and security.

Facilities

Maximum length overall 15m.
30-tonne travel-lift.
10- and 5-tonne cranes.
Slipway (but shallow approach).
Engine mechanics.
A small chandlery shop in the village.
Water from the *lonja* and taps on pontoons.
220v AC on piers, 380v AC on slipway.
Ice from the *club náutico* and the *lonja.*
Club Náutico L'Ampolla with terrace, swimming pool, showers and WCs.
Shops and supermarket nearby in the village.

Communications

Buses. Rail service to Barcelona. Taxi ☎ 977 490 386.

⚓ Cala Montero

A dry river mouth with rocky sides provides a small anchorage in 2m, mud, open between NE and S, stony beach.

⚓ Cala del Aguila

A small anchorage off the mouth of a dry river open NE to S. The bottom is rocky 1 to 3m deep.

⚓ Estany Podrit

An open anchorage off the mouth of a dry river open to NE to S. The bottom is 1 to 3·5m, weed, rocks and sand. A peak, Montaña del Aquila (159m), lies 1M to W.

⚓ Playa de Roig

Playa de Roig (beyond the first headland): the S half of the bay is better than the N half where the bottom is mostly rock.

Puerto de L'Estany Gras

40°52'N 0°47'E

Chart

British Admiralty *1701, 1704*
French *4720*
Spanish *838*
Navicarte *E01*

Lights

0381 **North Point** 40°52'·4N 0°47'·7E
Fl(3)G.10s14m3M Green pyramidal tower 5m
0381·2 **Jetty** Fl(4)R.12s6m3M Red pyramidal tower 3m
Offshore, opposite entrance
There are a number of fish farms off the harbour which must be avoided when entering.

General

A small, most attractive, old natural harbour, now virtually deserted, which is located in a narrow deep rocky *cala.* A fish farm has been established opposite the entrance, about two miles out. The approach is easy but the entrance should not be attempted with onshore winds or swell. Facilities are limited to a broken quay. All supplies have to be obtained from L'Ametlla about 1M away to NE.

Approach

From the south Round the delta of the Río Ebro and set a NW course from off Cabo Tortosa. The town of L'Ametlla will be seen on approaching the mainland coast and the harbour lies 1M to the SW of this town. In the closer approach the two small lighthouses, 6m and 4m, will be seen.

From the north Follow the rocky broken coast in a SW direction past a conspicuous nuclear electric generating station near Cabo del Terme and the town of L'Ametlla. This harbour lies about 1M to SW of L'Ametlla. The two small lighthouses, 6m and 4m high, will be seen beside the entrance.

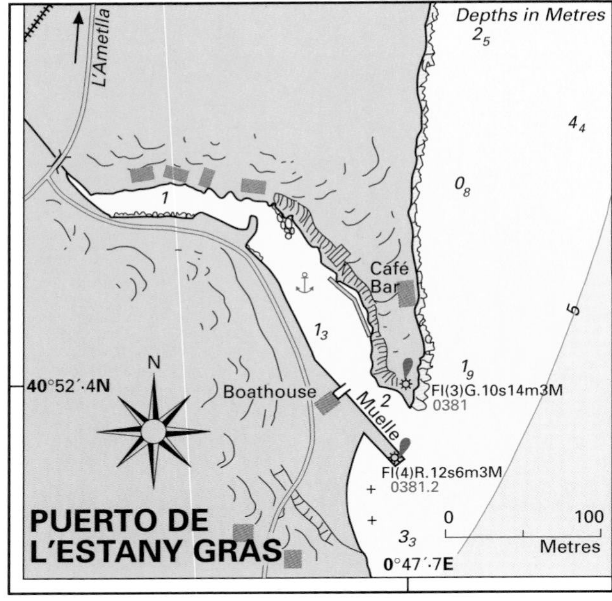

Entrance
Very tight. Approach on a NW heading and enter with care, towards the W side.

Anchorage
Depth off the quay is only 0·4m and ashlars and other underwater obstructions stick out from it. Anchor near the centre of the harbour in 1·5m, weed and rock, using an anchor trip-line. Lines can be taken ashore if others do not wish to get by.

Communications
A country road runs to L'Ametlla about 1M away where most requirements can be met.

⚓ Cala Bon Capo and Cala Bon Caponet

Bon Capo: two small *calas* either side of this small promontory. 1·8–2·5m, rock, sand and weed, open between NE and SE.

Puerto de L'Estany Gras

⚓ Cala de Arangaret

A very small anchorage in 1·5m, sand, 400m to SW of Puerto de L'Ametlla de Mar. Open between NE, S and SE.

Note There are many small coves between Puerto de L'Ametlla and Cabo de Sant Jordi that may be used with care and prudence as day anchorages.

Puerto de L'Ametlla de Mar

40°53'N 0°48'1E

Charts

British Admiralty *1701, 1704*
French *4720*
Spanish *838*
Navicarte *R5*

Lights

0381·5 **Dique de Levante head** 40°52'·7N 0°48'·2E Fl(4)G.12s17m7M White post, green top 10m
0381·6 **Dique de Poniente head** Fl(2)R.7s9m4M Red truncated tower 4m
0381·7 **Contradique head** Fl(3)R.9s8m2M Red truncated tower 4m

Port communications

VHF Ch 9. *Capitania* ☎ 977 456 007. *Club náutico* 977 457 240.

General

An active fishing harbour with an area in the south developed for yachts. The yacht quays are all new and well equipped with water and electricity but are some way from the old part of town which is well

Puerto de L'Ametlla de Mar – note that there is a new club house and *capitanía* at the SW corner of the port and extra pontoons extending S from the central jetty

worth a visit. There are a number of small beaches in *calas* near the harbour.

Approach

From the south To the N of the Ebro delta the mainland coast is of reddish rock and is of very broken low cliffs with high ground further inland. Punta Figuera with a red and white beacon on it is easily recognisable but Punta del Aguila is not conspicuous. The wide Cala de Santa Cruz and the deep Puerto de L'Estany Gras, which has two small lighthouse towers can be identified. The town of L'Ametlla can be seen from afar.

From the north From the conspicuous promontory Cabo de Salou the coast is low until Punta Llastres where the high Sierra de Balaguer range reaches the sea. The grey blocks of two nuclear power stations just to the N of Cabo Terme are conspicuous; off shore there are two buoys, one an E cardinal. The town of L'Ametlla will be seen from afar.

Entrance

Straighforward but give the Dique de Levante a reasonable (25m) berth as its foundations slope out into the water. Make for the head of the Dique de Poniente and turn to port around its head into the yacht basin.

Berths

The *capitanía* should be called (Ch 9 or phone) before entering to obtain berthing instructions. Failing this pick up a vacant berth (all berths have lines from the quay) and go ashore to the *capitanía* for further instructions. The inner harbour is now totally taken over by fishing vessels and a yacht should not proceed past the fuelling berth – and, as usual, no anchoring is permitted in the harbour.

Charges

Medium.

Facilities

Full repair facilities with slipway and 20-tonne crane.
Chandlery in NW corner.
Water and electricity on quays and pontoons.
Fuel and ice.
Club nautico has new building with WCs, showers, bar, restaurant and office.
Many shops near harbour and in town.

Communications

Rail and bus service.

Puerto Sant Jordi d'Alfama

Sant Jordi was once a small attractive private harbour but the whole development of houses and harbour appears to have run out of steam (and/or money) about 3 years ago. All lights have been withdrawn and the entrance has silted up to about 0·5m depth. It is sad to see the derelict walkways etc. but this harbour is totally closed and entry should not be attempted.

Puerto de Calafat

40°56'N 0°51'E

Charts

British Admiralty *1701, 1704*
French *4720*
Spanish *838*
Navicarte *R5*

Lights

Harbour

0382·3 **Dique de Abrigo head** 40°55'·7N 0°51'·3E Fl.G.4s9m6M Green tower 6m
0382·4 **Contradique** Fl(2)R.10s5m4M Red tower 4m

To the northwest

0386 **Cabo Salou** 41°03'·4N 1°10' 4E Fl(4)20s43m23M White tower with red bands, white building 11m

Radiobeacon

Cabo Salou c/s *UD* (··–/–··) 288·5kHz 50M 41°03'·42N 1°10'·38E

Port communications

VHF Ch 9. *Capitanía* ☎/*Fax* 977 486 184, *email* calafat@teleline.es

General

A medium-sized yacht harbour built as part of a large residential development. Easy to approach and enter except in a gale in the south quadrant when the entrance is difficult and the harbour uncomfortable. Limited supplies. Sandy beach at NE side of the harbour.

Approach

From the south From Cabo Tortosa head NNW towards the two peaks of Es Frares (470m) and La Mamelleta (713m) which lie behind the harbour. The grey concrete buildings of the nuclear power

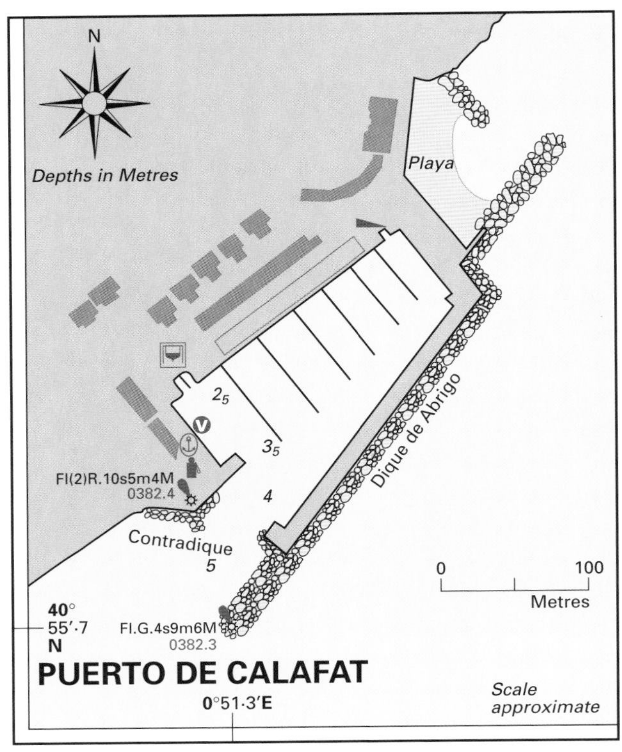

Puerto de Calafat

station are about a mile beyond the harbour.

In the closer approach Cabo de Sant Jordi, with a ruined fort, and its near-by port may be seen, then the housing estate in the trees behind the harbour and its breakwaters will be recognised.

From the north from Cabo de Salou (79m) the coast to SW is of low rocky cliffs with concentrations of houses. Puerto de Cambrils has some tall apartment blocks and a long rocky breakwater which are easily recognised.

Puerto de Hospitalet de L'Infant can likewise be recognised by the high-rise buildings and the harbour breakwater. Punta de Ríu de Llastres is a low promontory and has shallow water off its point. The two large concrete buildings of the nuclear reactors can be seen from afar. In the close approach the housing estate and the harbour breakwaters will be seen.

Anchorage in the approach
Anchor ¼M to S of the harbour in 10m sand.

Entrance
Straightforward but if entering with a strong following wind, be prepared for some sharp manoeuvring once inside.

Berths
Secure to quay at port side of the entrance and ask. If no-one around, inquire at the *torre de control.*

Facilities
Maximum length overall 20m.
40-tonne travel-hoist.
5-tonne crane.
Limited hard-standing near travel-hoist.
Slipway.
Water from taps on quays and pontoons.
Gasoleo A and petrol.
Some shops and a small supermarket near the harbour; probably better to go to Ametlla.

Communications
Bus and rail. Car hire. Taxi ☎ 977 456 468.

Puerto de Hospitalet de L'Infant

40°59'N 0°56'E

Charts

British Admiralty *1701, 1704*
French *4720*
Spanish *838*
Navicarte *R5*

Lights

0382·5 **Dique SE head** 40°59'·3N 0°55'·7E Fl(4)G.10s10m5M Green truncated tower
0382·6 **Contradique head** Fl.R.2s5m2M Red truncated tower
28530(S) **Buoy** 40°59'·3N 0°55'·6E Fl(4)R.17s2M Port hand can topmark

To the northwest

0386 **Cabo Salou** 41°03'·4N 1°10'·4E Fl(4)20s43m23M White tower with red bands, white building 11m

Radiobeacon

Cabo Salou c/s *UD* (··–/–··) 288·5kHz 50M 41°03'·42N 1°10'·38E

Port communications

VHF Ch 9. ☎ 977 823 004/977 823 187 *Fax* 977 823 005.

General

An artificial yacht harbour of medium size controlled by the Club Náutico de L'Hospitalet-Vandellós. Entry is usually easy but difficult in S

Cabo del Terme

Two nuclear power stations, one inside a large square concrete building with no windows, the other inside a round tower-shaped building, are located 1 to 1½M respectively to NE of this *cabo* and are very conspicuous. A special spar light buoy lies 600m off the coast to NE and a S cardinal lightbuoy lies to SW marking water intakes.

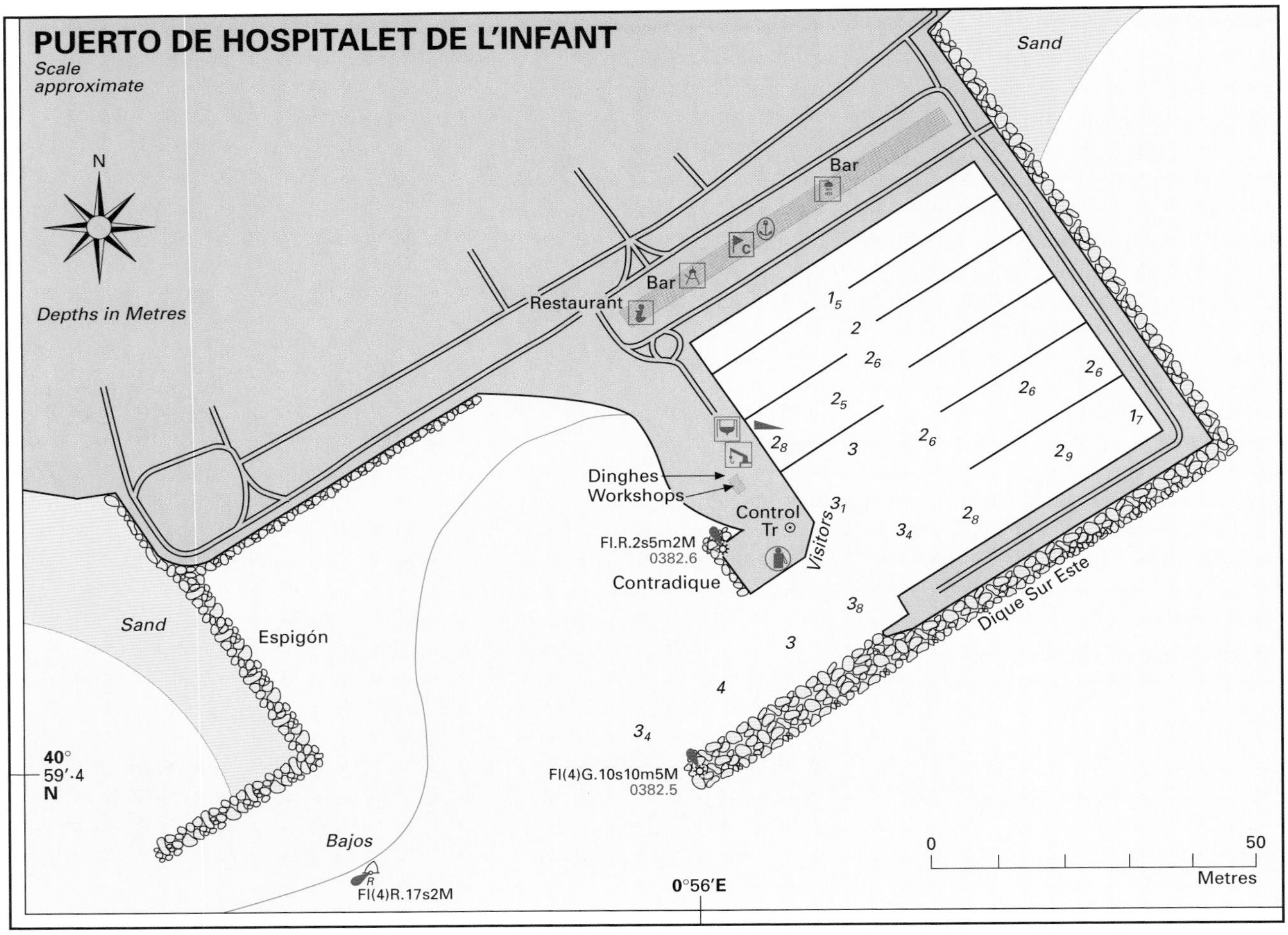

PUERTO DE HOSPITALET DE L'INFANT
Scale approximate
N
Depths in Metres
Sand
Bar
Bar
Restaurant
Dinghes
Workshops
Control Tr
Visitors
Fl.R.2s5m2M
0382.6
Contradique
Dique Sur Este
Sand
Espigón
Fl(4)G.10s10m5M
0382.5
40° 59'·4 N
Bajos
Fl(4)R.17s2M
0°56'E
0 50
Metres

gales when swell enters the harbour. This is a tourist area and there are many apartment blocks and hotels. Quite a lot of walking to be done to get anywhere. Good large sandy beach to SW. A hospice was founded here in 1314. Its ruins and a tower can still be seen.

Approach

From the south The harbour is due N from Cabo Tortosa. As the coast is approached Vandellós nuclear power station, with two large grey concrete buildings 3M SW of the harbour, should be seen. The group of high-rise buildings behind the harbour and its breakwaters will appear in the close approach.

From the north From Cabo Salou, a prominent and easily recognised feature, the low rocky cliffs and sandy beaches stretch SW. The houses, breakwater and tower of Puerto de Cambrils will be recognised as will the high-rise buildings of L'Hospitalet and its harbour breakwaters in the close approach.

Anchorage in the approach

Anchor in 8m, sand, ¼M to S of the harbour entrance.

Entrance

Approach on a N course, round Dique Sud Este and go to the waiting quay on the *contradique*, by the fuel pumps. Do not stray inshore on the west side of the *contradique*.

Berths

If no-one comes, ask at the *torre de control*. Berths have posts instead of mooring buoys or lines for securing the bow of the yacht. Berths for smaller yachts on pontoons have floating spurs.

Harbour charges

Medium.

Facilities

Maximum length overall 18m.
8-tonne crane.
Limited hard-standing.
Slipway.
Two chandlers beside the harbour.
Water on quays and pontoons.
Electricity 220v AC on quays and pontoons.
Small ice from the club and bars.
Gasoleo A and petrol.
Club Náutico de L'Hospitalet-Vandellós has a clubhouse on the NW side of the harbour with bar, showers, WCs etc. The club controls the harbour.
Food shops etc. in the village.

Communications

Road and rail. Taxi ☎ 977 810 363.

Puerto de Hospitalet de L'Infant (Vandellós)

Puerto de Cambrils

41°04'N 1°04'E

Charts
British Admiralty *1701, 1704*
French *4720*
Spanish *838*
Navicarte *R5*

Lights
0383 **Dique de Levante head** 41°03'·7N 1°03'·7E Fl.G.4s15m5M Green pyramidal tower 11m
0384 **Dique de Poniente head** Fl(2)R.8s13m5M Red tower 9m
0383·4 **Malecón Dársena Deportiva head** Fl(2)G.7s6m2M Green pyramidal tower 4m
To the west
0386 **Cabo Salou** 41° 03'·4N 1°10'·4E Fl(4)20s43m23M White tower with red bands, white building 11m

Radiobeacon
Cabo Salou *UD* (··–/–··) 288·5kHz 50M 41°03'·42N 1°10'·38E

Port communications
VH Ch 9. *Club náutico* ☎ 977 360 531 *Fax* 977 362 654.

General
An artificial fishing harbour with a yacht enclave. It is easy to approach and enter and has good shelter. The area caters for a large number of tourists in the season and a number of ferries use the harbour for day trips. Facilities and the shops are good.

The Monasterio de Escornalou some 5M inland has a spectacular view. The Roman 'Oleaster', a fortified church tower in the front of the town is of interest. Good sandy beaches on either side of the harbour, the better being to SW.

Approach
From the south The reddish rocky cliffs where the Sierra de Balaguer lies alongside the coast end at Punta de Ríu de Llastres and the coast becomes low, flat and sandy. The houses and harbour works at Cambrils can be seen from afar.

From the north Having rounded the rocky-cliffed promontory of Cabo de Salou, which is covered with large private houses and some high-rise buildings, the coast becomes low, flat and sandy. The houses, flats and light-coloured rocky breakwater of this harbour can be seen from afar.

Anchorage in the approach
Anchor some 400m to W of the entrance in 5m on sand.

Entrance
Round the head of the Dique de Levante, leaving it 25–30m to starboard and enter nearer to the head of

Puerto de Cambrils

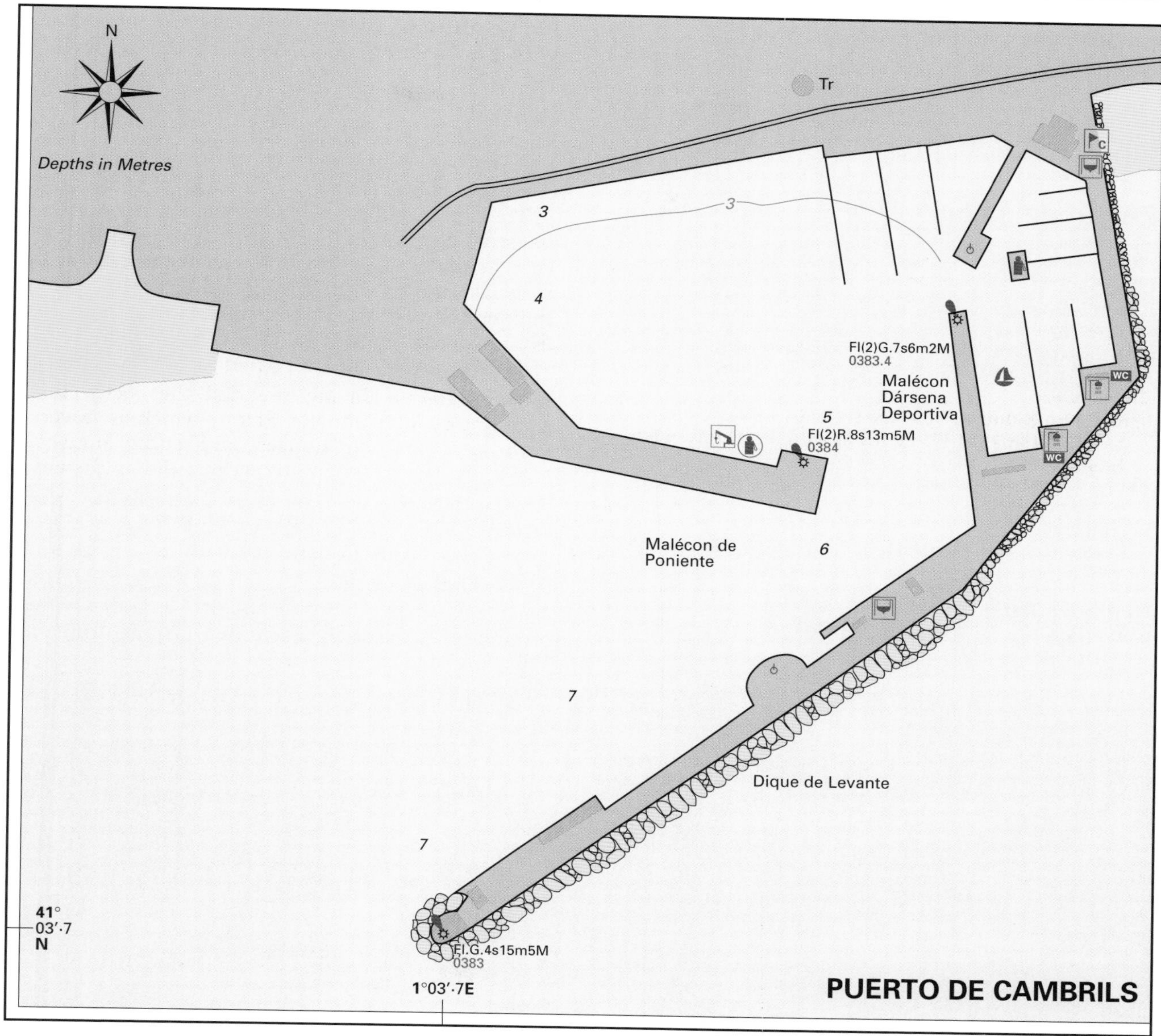

the Dique de Poniente which can be rounded at 15m. Go across the harbour and round the head of the Malecón Darsena Deportiva at about 15m.

Berths
Berth stern-to the pontoons with mooring buoy from the bow in the E side of the yacht harbour and check at the reception centre.

Harbour Charges
Low.

Moorings
A few private moorings are available in the main harbour.

Facilities
Maximum length overall 20m.
Limited repairs are possible and there are a number of engine mechanics in town.
140-tonne travel-lift and 12-tonne crane in port.
7·5-tonne crane.
Two slipways.
A chandlery shop in the town.
Water on the pontoons in the yacht harbour or from the *lonja*.
110v and 220v AC from the *club náutico,* pontoons and quay.
Gasoleo A and petrol.
Ice factory near the *lonja.*
Club Náutico de Cambrils with restaurant, bar, terrace, showers.
A number of shops alongside the harbour but many more in the town itself which is about ½M inland.
Launderette in the town.

Communications
Rail and bus service. Air services from Tarragona-Reus about 10M away. Taxi ☎ 977 362 622.

Embarcadero de Reus Club de Mar

A jetty 100m long projecting from the shore ¾M to E of Puerto de Salou. Roads, railway and houses ashore. Can be used as a landing. Anchor in 2m, sand, to S of head of pier.

Puerto de Salou

41°07'N 1°07'E

Charts

British Admiralty *1701, 1704*
French *4720, 4827*
Spanish *4861, 487A, 838*
Navicarte *E06*

Lights

0385 **Dique de Levante head** 41°04'·3N 1°07'·7E Fl(2)G.8s7m5M Green post 4m
0385·5 **Dique de Poniente head** Fl(2)R.8s4m3M Red metal post 2m
To the west
0386 **Cabo Salou** 41°03'·4N 1°10'·4E Fl(4)20s43m23M White tower with red bands, white building

Radiobeacon

Cabo Salou Lt *UD* (··–/–··) 288·5kHz 50M 41°03'·42N 1°10'·38E

Port communications

VHF Ch 9. ☎ 977 382 166/977 382 167 *Fax* 977 384 454.

General

Salou has been a fishing port since Roman times when it was called Salauris; from it Jaime I (El Conquistador) set forth to conquer Mallorca in 1229. It is now one of the more popular summer resorts and the town is primarily concerned with the mass tourist trade. It has an expensive, small artificial harbour with very limited space for visitors and limited facilities. The approach and entrance are not difficult but would be dangerous in strong winds and swell from SW. There are excellent sandy beaches on each side of the harbour.

Approach

From the south The high Sierra de Balaguer gives way to flat, sandy coasts at Punta de Ríu de Llastres. The houses, flats and breakwater at Cambrils are easily identified. The many high-rise buildings at Salou can be seen from afar and the harbour will be seen when closer in.

From the north Cabo de Salou, a rocky-cliffed promontory, is easily identified. Apart from its

Puerto de Salou

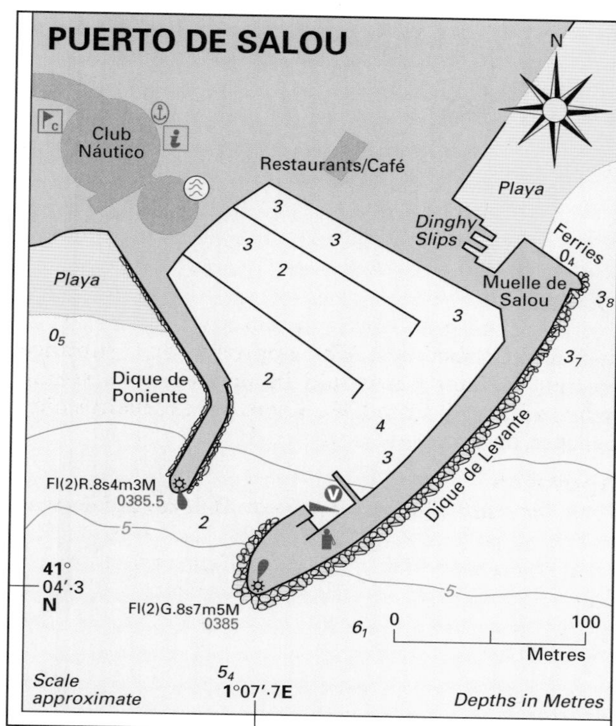

lighthouse it has a number of high-rise buildings and large houses on it. Once rounded, the buildings of Salou will be seen about 4M further on. In the close approach the harbour will be seen.

Anchorage in the approach
Anchor 300m to W of the head of the Dique de Levante in 3m, sand.

Entrance
Straightforward but the visitors berth is immediately inside the entrance to starboard.

Charges
High.

Facilities
Engine mechanics.
10-tonne crane and a mobile 5-tonne crane.
Two slipways and dinghy slips.
Water points on the quays and pontoons.
220v and 380v AC on the quays and pontoons.
Ice from the *club náutico.*
Gasoleo A and petrol.
Club Náutico de Salou clubhouse has good facilities.
Supermarket and many shops in the town nearby.
Launderette in town.

Communications
Bus and rail. Tarragona airport 7M. Taxi ☎ 977 380 034.

⚓ S of Salou
A big ship anchorage ½M to S of Puerto de Salou in 11m, sand and weed. Open to SE through to W.

⚓ Cala de la Torre Nova (or del Lazareto)

Cala de la Torre Nova (or del Lazareto): an anchorage in 2m, sand, open SE through to W. Sandy beach and high-rise buildings.)

⚓ Cala Pinatel (or Gran)
An open anchorage off a large sandy beach the Playa de Pinatell in 2m, sand. Open to SE through to W.

⚓ N of Punta de Peny Tallada
A small bay open between S and W; anchor in 2m, sand.

⚓ Cala de la Font
A small anchorage off a beach with a projecting rock. Open to S through to NW. Anchor in 2m, sand.

⚓ Cala del Cranc
A narrow bay with small beach and an isolated rock 0·5m deep in its mouth. Anchor in 2m, sand. Open between S and SW.

Cabo Salou

A built up and prominent headland with conspicuous lighthouse tower (11m) and a second tower (120m) NE of it on the top of the headland.

⚓ Cala Morisca
A small bay open to NE through to S. Anchor in 2m, sand.

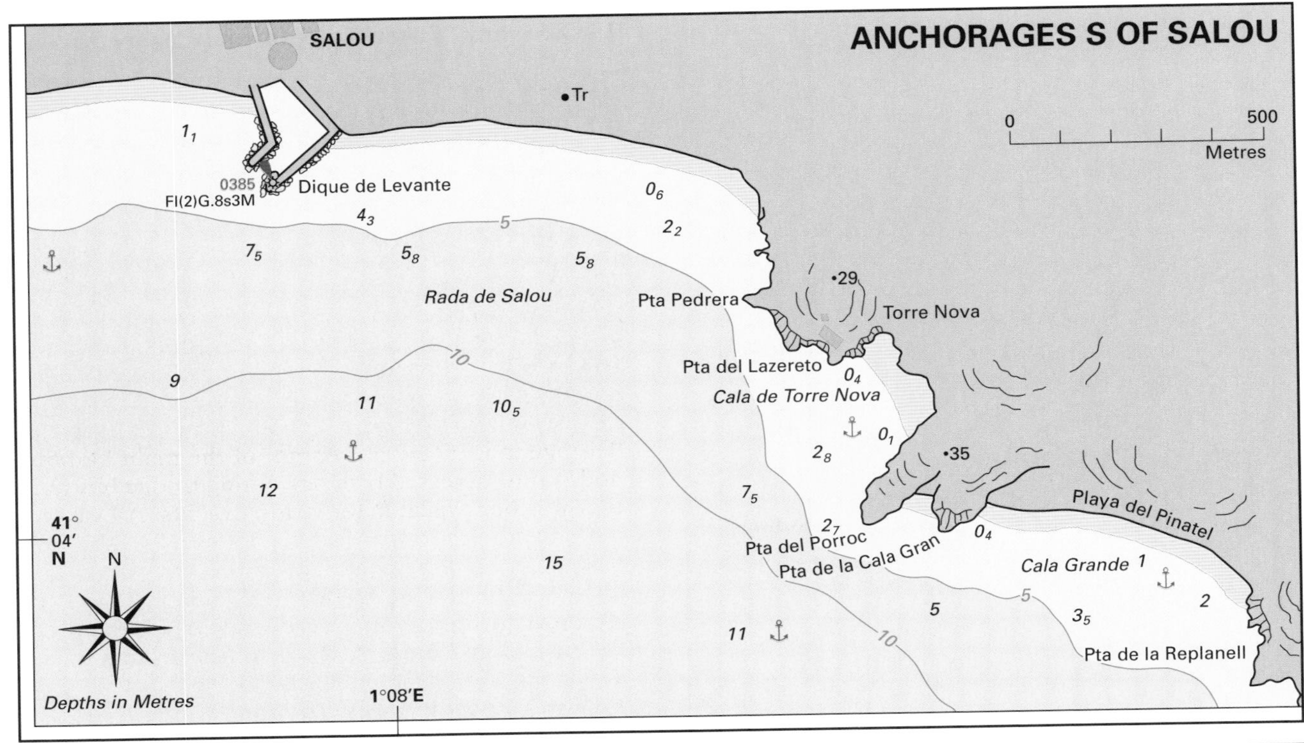

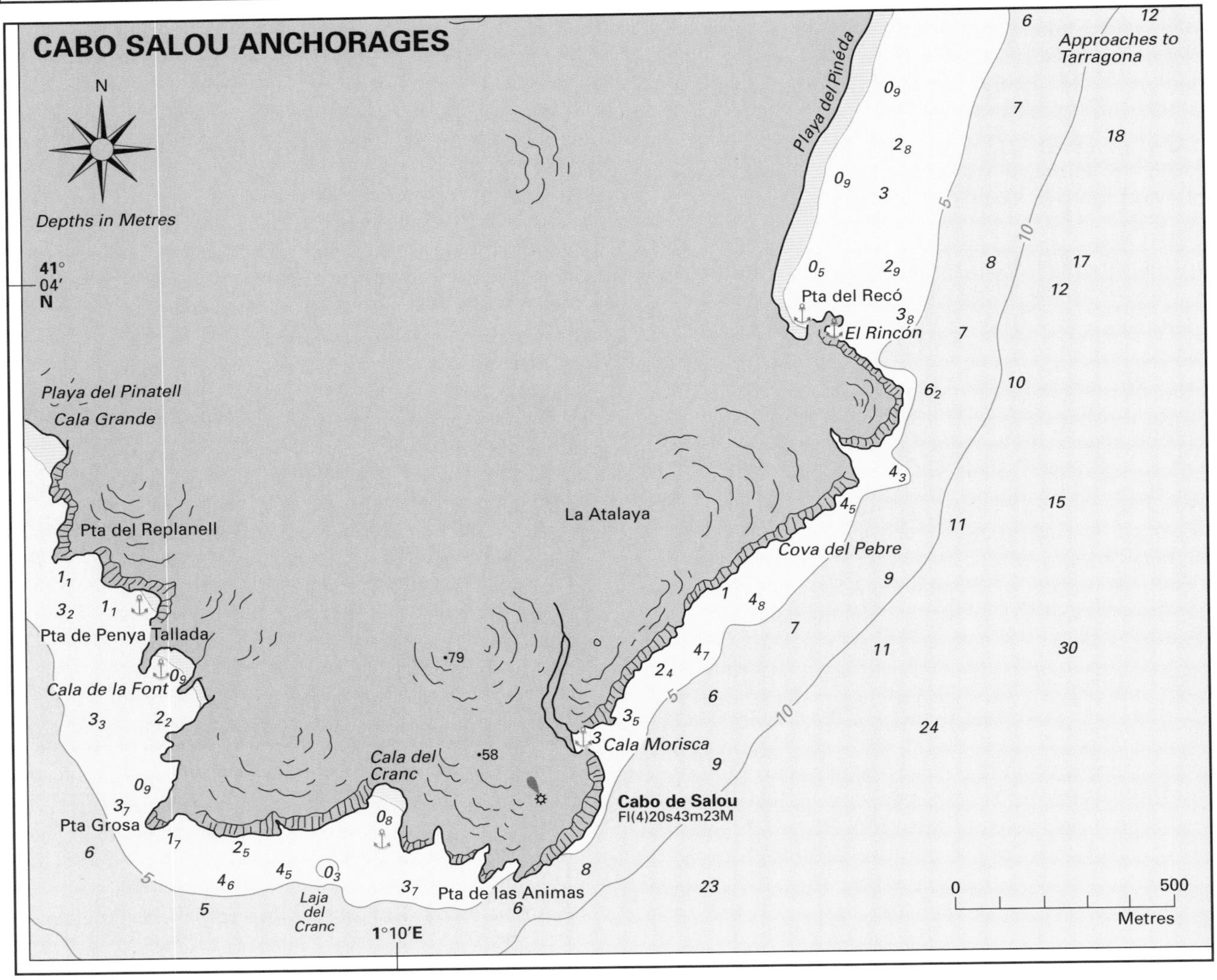

CABO SALOU ANCHORAGES

N

Depths in Metres

41°
04′
N

Approaches to Tarragona

Playa del Pinéda

Pta del Recó

El Rincón

Playa del Pinatell

Cala Grande

La Atalaya

Pta del Replanell

Cova del Pebre

Pta de Penya Tallada

Cala de la Font

79

Cala Morisca

Cala del Cranc

58

Cabo de Salou
Fl(4)20s43m23M

Pta Grosa

Laja del Cranc

Pta de las Animas

1°10′E

0 500
Metres

⚓ El Recó

A small bay open between N and E; anchor in 2m, sand. Two small rocky islets one each side of the bay.

⚓ Playa del Recó

An open anchorage off a long sandy beach. Anchor to suit draught, sandy bottom. Open between NE and S. Note pipeline on chart.

Oiling pier Pantalán Empetrol

A ¾M-long pier runs out into the bay between Cabo Salou and the Puerto de Tarragona.

Puerto de Tarragona

41°05'N 1°13'E

Note The old harbour is normally forbidden to yachts but might be used in stress of weather. In normal circumstances go to the Port Esportiou (Puerto Deportivo).

Charts

British Admiralty *1193, 1701, 1704*
French *7047, 4720, 4827*
Spanish *4871, 487A, 838*
Navicarte *E06*

Lights

To the south

0386 **Cabo Salou** 41°03'·4N 1°10'·4E Fl(4)20s43m23M White tower with red bands, white building

Approach and entry – main harbour

28750(S) **Repsol Pipeline Buoy** 41°04'·1N 1°13'·3E Fl(4)Y.20s5M Spar with topmark

0388·12 **Dique de Levante head** 41°05'·1N 1°13'·3E Fl.G.5s22m10M Green mast 11m

0386·6 **Pantalán Repsol head** Fl.R.2·5s11m5M Post on red 6-sided base 3m

0388 Dique de Levante Faro de la Banya Oc.3s27m10M 6-sided hut on piles 18m

0392·1 **Lifting bridge W side S head** Fl(3)R.9s4m1M Red mast 2m Traffic signals on bridge

0392·105 **Centre** Fl(4)R.11s4m1M Red mast 2m

0392·11 **N head** Fl(3)R.9s5m1M Red post 1m

0392·12 **E side S head** Fl(4)G.11s4m1M Green mast 2m

0392·125 **Centre** Fl.G.5s4m1M Green mast 2m

0392·13 **N head** Fl(4)G.11s5m1M Green mast 1M

Puert Esportiou

0392·3 **Dique de Abrigo** 41°06'·4N 1°15'·1E Fl(2)G.10s7m3M Green post 3m

0392·33 **Dique de Abrigo corner** Q(3)10s5m3M BYB post ♦ card top

0392·37 **Interior arm** Fl(3)G.10s3m1M Green post 1m

0392·4 **Contradique head** Fl(2)R.10s4m3M Red post 1m

To the north

0393·6 **Altafulla Beach breakwater** 41°07'·8N 1°22'·2E Q(6)+LFl.15s5m5M ⧗ on black beacon, yellow top 4m

Marine radiobeacon

Cabo Salou c/s *UD* (··–/–··) 288·5kHz 50M 41°03'·42N 1°10'·38E

Port communications

Tarragona Pilots – VHF Ch 9, 12, 14, 16.
Capitanía ☎ 977 226 611.
Club Náutico de Tarragona ☎/*Fax* 977 240 360.
Port Esportiou VHF Ch 9. ☎ 977 213 100 *Fax* 977 212 702.

Storm signals

Flown from a flagstaff on the Muelle de Pescadores.

General

The very old port of a city with a fascinating history with a new yacht marina alongside. The old commercial and fishing port, greatly enlarged by the addition of huge breakwaters has an easy all weather approach and entrance. The Club Náutico de Tarragona is in the NE corner of the main harbour and is now accessed by a new lifting bridge but note that it is not available for visiting yachts. All visiting yachts and pleasure craft should proceed to the Port Esportiou outside the Dique de Levante. However entry there may be difficult in strong S to SW winds in which case go to the old harbour. Apart from berthing, facilities in the old harbour are good. The Port Esportiou was established in 1996 and is now fully developed.

Originally the Iberian stronghold of Cosse, Tarragona has been an important place since the Carthaginians built a fortress here called Tarchon in the 3rd century BC. Some of the walls can still be seen. Known under the Romans as Callipolis, Terraco, Togata and later Colonia Julia Victrix Triumphans, the city flourished, only to be occupied by the Goths and later razed by the Moors in 714. It was subsequently rebuilt but damaged again by the French and later the British during Sir John Murray's retreat in the face of Soult's advance in 1813. There are so many interesting places to visit in Tarragona and the surrounding area that if a green *Michelin* or a *Guide Bleu* is not aboard, it is worth getting a guide from the local tourist board. Apart from all the historic monuments, there are good sandy beaches on either side of the harbour.

Approach

Commercial craft have right of way in the harbour and its approaches.

A special yellow pillar lightbuoy Fl(4)Y.20s marks the extremity of a pipeline about 1M SE of the harbour, with floating hose lines marked by buoys Fl.Y.

From the south The low, flat, sandy coast extends to the rocky-cliffed promontory of Cabo de Salou which is easily recognised by its conspicuous lighthouse, houses and some high-rise buildings. Once these are rounded the city of Tarragona on its hill, the large petrochemical works and factories to its W will be seen. In the closer approach the port breakwater, cranes and silos will become apparent. The entrance to the Port Esportiou lies outside the Dique de Levante, about 2M from its head.

From the north The long, flat, sandy beaches backed by low ranges of hills are only broken by the low yellow cliffs of Cabo Gros and Punta Mora. The city

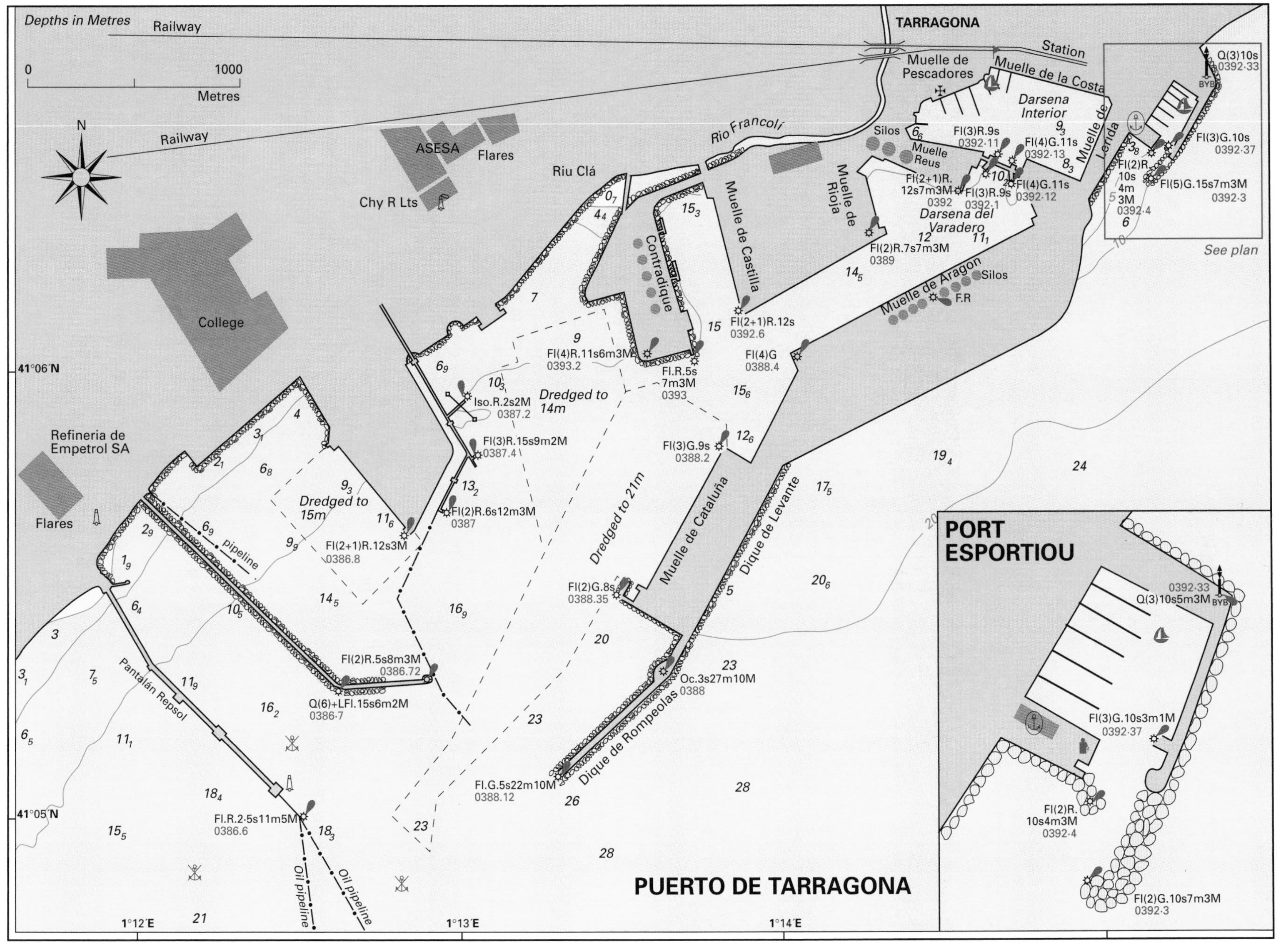
PUERTO DE TARRAGONA
PORT ESPORTIOU
TARRAGONA
Depths in Metres
0
1000
Metres
Railway
Railway
Station
Muelle de la Costa
Darsena Interior
Muelle de Lerida
Muelle de Pescadores
Muelle Reus
Darsena del Varadero
Muelle de Aragon
Silos
Silos
Muelle de Rioja
Muelle de Castilla
Rio Francolí
Contradique
Riu Clá
Dique de Levante
Muelle de Cataluña
Dique de Rompeolas
Dredged to 21m
Dredged to 14m
Dredged to 15m
Flares
Flares
ASESA
Chy R Lts
College
Refineria de Empetrol SA
Pantalán Repsol
Oil pipeline
Oil pipeline
pipeline
See plan
Q(3)10s 0392·33
Fl(3)G.10s 0392·37
Fl(5)G.15s7m3M 0392·3
Fl(2)R. 10s 4m 3M 0392·4
Fl(3)R.9s 0392·11
Fl(4)G.11s 0392·13
Fl(4)G.11s 0392·12
Fl(2+1)R. 12s7m3M 0392
Fl(3)R.9s 0392·1
Fl(2)R.7s7m3M 0389
F.R
Fl(2+1)R.12s 0392.6
Fl(4)G 0388.4
Fl.R.5s 7m3M 0393
Fl(4)R.11s6m3M 0393.2
Fl(3)G.9s 0388.2
Oc.3s27m10M 0388
Fl(2)G.8s 0388.35
Fl.G.5s22m10M 0388.12
Iso.R.2s2M 0387.2
Fl(3)R.15s9m2M 0387.4
Fl(2)R.6s12m3M 0387
Fl(2+1)R.12s3M 0386.8
Fl(2)R.5s8m3M 0386.72
Q(6)+LFl.15s6m2M 0386·7
Fl.R.2·5s11m5M 0386.6
0392·33 Q(3)10s5m3M
BYB
Fl(3)G.10s3m1M 0392·37
Fl(2)R. 10s4m3M 0392·4
Fl(2)G.10s7m3M 0392·3
41°06′N
41°05′N
1°12′E
1°13′E
1°14′E

Puerto de Tarragona. The Port Esportiou is at the extreme right of the photograph

of Tarragona on its hill will be seen from afar, probably before passing Altafulla Beach breakwater marked by a S cardinal light. In the closer approach the yellow rocky harbour breakwater will be seen together with the smoke and flares from the factories beyond the port. The Port Esportiu lies on the way to the old harbour entrance, outside the harbour walls, just southwest of the point where the city buildings turn inland to skirt the harbour.

Anchorage in the approach
Anchor ½M to NE of the head of the Dique de Levante in 26m, sand, or about 200m to W of the *contradique* in 6 to 10m sand. Beware oil pipelines which run across the harbour from the entrance to the various terminals.

Entrance
Main harbour Round the head of the Dique de Levante, giving it a berth of at least 400m to starboard. Follow the NW side of this *dique* at 100m into the Dársena de Varadero which should be crossed on a NE course, entering the Dársena Interior between the heads of the two *muelles*. The *muelle* to starboard may be marked by a buoy.

Port Esportiou Straightforward but awkward and possibly dangerous in strong southerlies. There may be backwash from the harbour wall if there is a sea running.

Berths
Main harbour Visiting pleasure craft are not welcome in the main harbour but in severe weather or other emergency situations one may be allowed to moor in the Darsena Interior.

Port Esportiou Inquire on Ch 9; if no response, go alongside wherever possible and inquire ashore.

Charges
High.

Facilities
Main harbour
One of the best yacht yards on the coast is located in the W corner of the Dársena Interior. There are a number of engine repair workshops and one which repairs electronic equipment.
A small crane at the *club náutico* but 20 tonnes and floating 60 tonnes cranes are available.
Three slipways.
Many chandlery shops near the port.
Water taps on quay and at *club náutico* pontoons, and a public tap just to N of the club. It is necessary to approach the port officials for the keys to the water points on the quay.
Public showers are located on Muelle de la Costa.

Port Esportiou at Tarragona

220v AC at the *club náutico.*

Ice factory is located three streets behind the Muelle de Pescadores.

Club Náutico de Tarragona has bars, lounges, restaurant, terrace, showers and pontoons. The latter are usually fully occupied by members' yachts. The clubhouse has been established many years.

Many small shops near the port. Most shops and a large market in the city a short bus ride away.

Launderette in the city near the market.

Port Esportiu

Maximum length overall 20m.

Engineering services arranged from the old harbour.

7-tonne crane.

Water, electricity on the piers.

Gasoleo A and petrol.

Laundry.

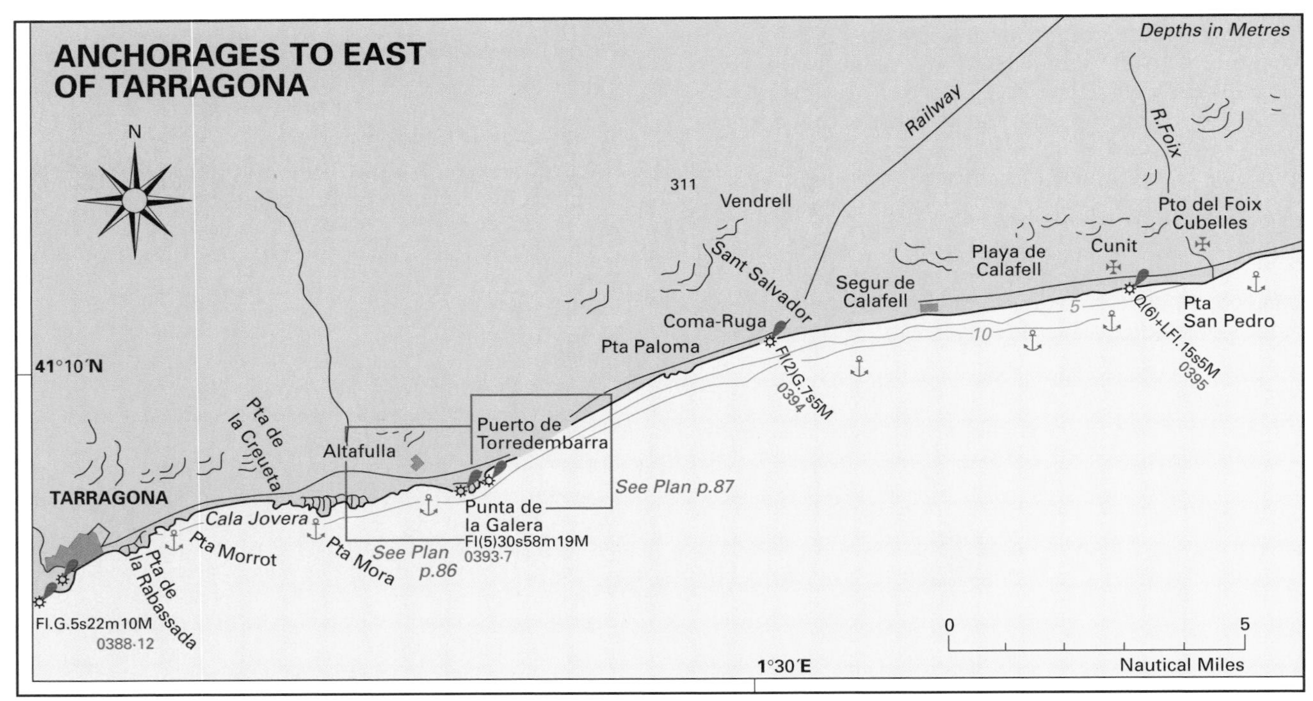

Communications

Bus and rail service. Airport at Reus, 7M. Limited bus service to mountainous parts inland. Taxi ☎ 977 221 414.

British Consul: Calle Real 33 1°1a 43004 Tarragona ☎ 977 220 813 *Fax* 977 218 469.

⚓ Playa de la Rabassada

Playa de la Rabassada: anchor off the beach in 4m. Open between E and SW. The 9m high Torre del Escipions nearby, 2nd century BC, is thought by some to be a memorial to the brothers Scipio (d.212 BC)

⚓ Anchorage E of Rabassada

Anchorage E of Rabassada: anchor to suit draught. Open between E and SW.

⚓ Cala de la Jovera

A very small anchorage in 1·8m, sand, tucked away at the foot of the 12–13th-century castle of Tamarit which has three towers. Only for use by small yachts with care, open to E to S

⚓ Altafulla

A deep-water anchorage ½M offshore to S of the town of Altafulla in sand open from E through S to W. Yacht club for dinghies ashore. Ruins of a Roman city. Sandy beach.

⚓ Recó del Fortin

An anchorage backed by holiday flats located where sandy Playa de Selmar meets the rocky mass of Cabo Gros. Anchor in 2m, sand. Open from S to W.

⚓ Cala del Canadel

An anchorage in front of a small sandy beach surrounded by low rocky cliffs in 2m, sand, open to SE through W.

Punta de la Galera

A prominent rocky headland (20m) with a tall new lighthouse Fl(5)30s58m19M on its tip. The point has rocky cliffs with some houses on top.

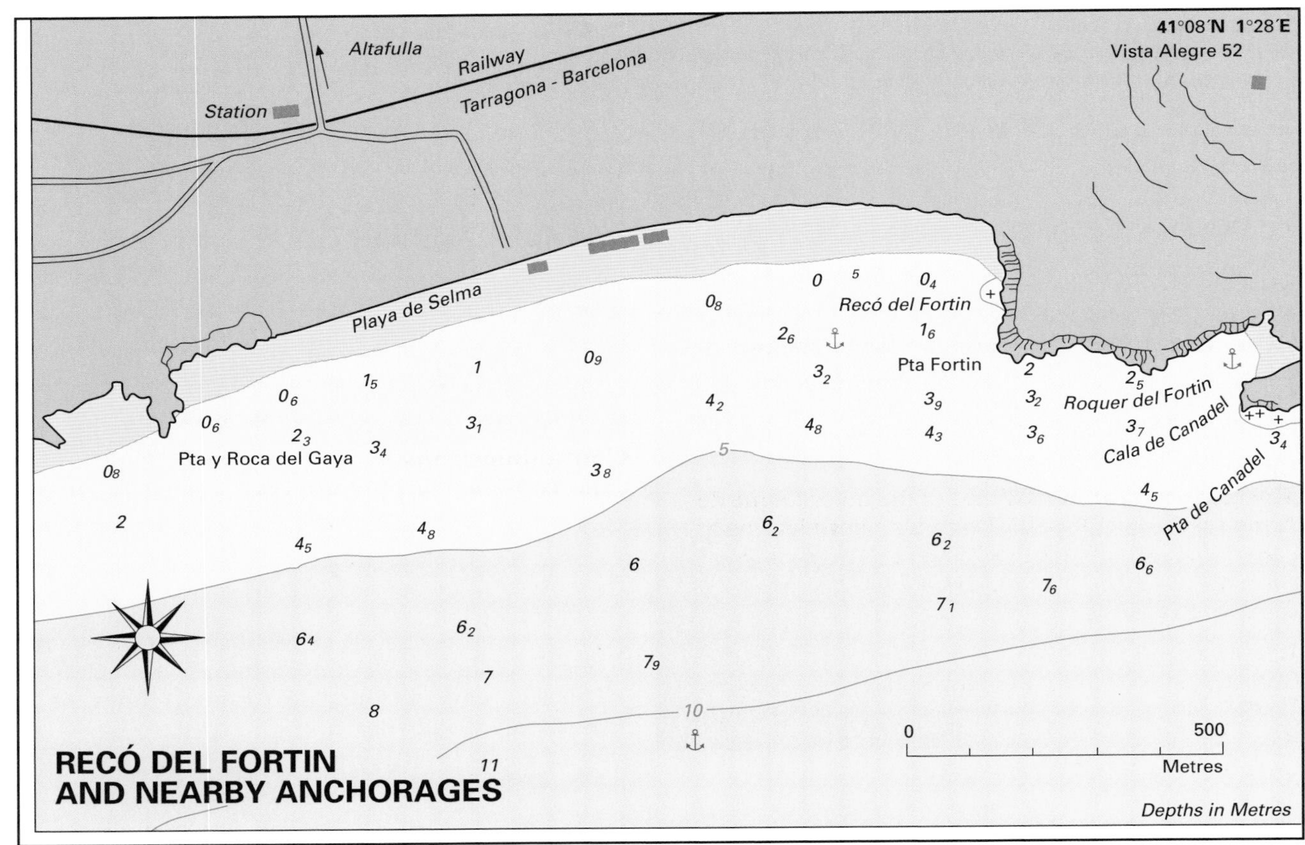

⚓ **W of Punta de la Galera (Roquer)**

A very small anchorage surrounded by rocky cliffs in 2m, sand, open to SE through W.

Puerto de Torredembarra

41°07'N 1°24'E

Charts

British Admiralty *1701, 1704*
French *4720, 4827*
Spanish *838, 487A*
Navicarte *E06*

Lights

0393·7 **Punta de la Galera** 41°08'·0N 1°23'·8E Fl(5)30s58m19M Octagonal white tower, coppery top 38m
0393·8 **Dique de Abrigo head** 41°07'·9N 1°24'·0E Q(4)G.10s10m5M Green post 5m
0393·82 **Inner Spur** Fl.G.5s4m1M Green post 2m
0393·83·**Contradique corner** Q(4)R.10s4m3M Red post 0·5m
0393·84 **Contradique head** Fl.R.5s4m3M Red post 2m on short *espigón* jutting out of *contradique*
0393·85 **Dique de Abrigo corner** Q(3)10s9m3M BYB post ♦ E card topmark 3m

Port communications

VHF Ch 9. *Capitanía* ☎ 977 643 234 *Fax* 977 643 236.

General

Now Torredembarra has been completed, it is a first class marina with excellent shelter, all facilities but lacking only stores and provisioning which can be obtained in the town nearby. The marina has some 'twee' shops but good chandlers, bars and restaurants.

Approach

From the south Cabo de Salou and the huge breakwater of Puerto de Tarragona are easily recognised. The old castle and towers at Tamarit near Punta de la Mora will be seen if close in, also the rocky-footed Punta de la Galera with its conspicuous 38m tall lighthouse at its tip. Torredembarra town may be visible inland.

From the north Pass the modern harbour at Aiguadolç with its old houses and new housing developments plus the large Puerto de Vilanova i la Geltrú close to SW. There is a tall white chimney at Cubello and a yellow generating station with breakwaters at Cunit. Puerto de Coma-Ruga which has a tall tower inland behind it may also be seen.

Entrance

The entrance is at the SW end of the outer Dique de Abrigo and runs SW–NE. Round the head leaving at least 20m clear and proceed towards the head of the contradique. Note the light at its head is situated on a short *espigón* jutting SE.

Berths

Call the *capitanía* on Ch 9 (or phone) to arrange a berth before entering – otherwise go alongside the fuel berth and ask. All berths have lazy lines to the quay and anchoring is not permitted.

Anchorage in the approach

Anchor off the Playa de Torremdebarra NE of the harbour wall in a depth to suit.

Facilities

Maximum length overall 20m.
Full repair facilities including engine, welding, painting.
New *club náutico* has restaurant and bar.
45-tonne travel-lift.
6-tonne crane.
Chandlery.
Water on quays.
Showers.
220v AC on quays.
Gasoleo A and petrol.
Ice at the bar and at the petrol station.

Communications

Taxis ☎ 977 641 147/977 640 266.

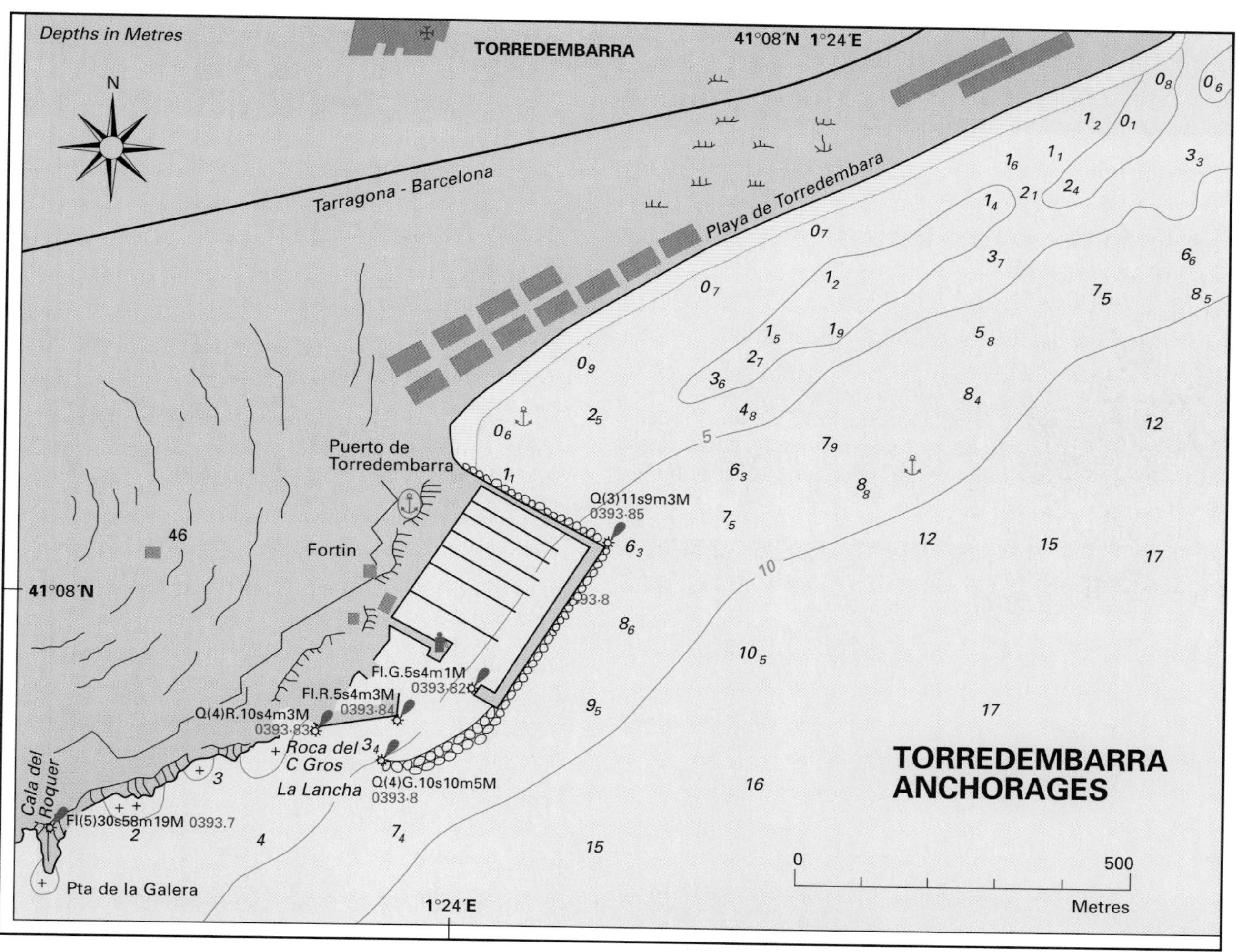

Puerto de Torredembarra

Roda de Bara (Port Daurat)

41°10'·0N 1°28'·5E

General

Construction has just started (October 2000) on a new 500-berth marina. Breakwaters are due to be finished shortly and the completion is due in 2004 but berths may be available in late 2002. Plans include all repair, fuel, water and electricity facilities laid on as well as the usual shoreside shops and stores.

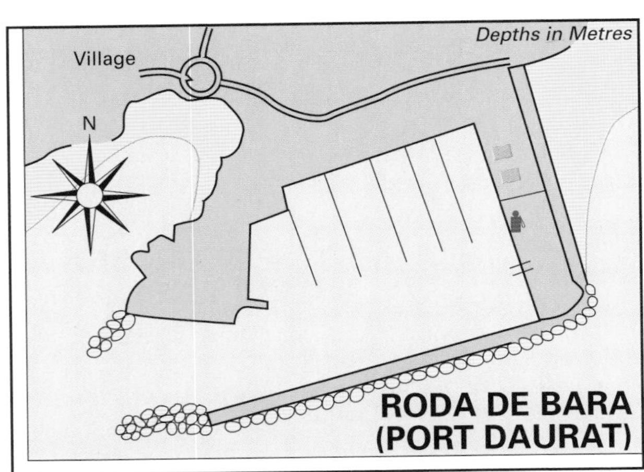

Puerto de Coma-Ruga

41°11'N 1°31'E

Charts

British Admiralty *1701, 1704*
French *4827*
Spanish *838*
Navicarte *E06*

Lights

0394 **Dique Oeste head** 41°10'·7N 1°31'·0E
Fl(2)G.7s7m5M Green post 2m
0394·2 **Muelle Transversal W corner**
Q(6)+LFl.15s9m3M ⯯ on yellow tower, black base 4m
0394·4 **E corner** VQ(6)+LFl.10s9m3M ⯯ on yellow tower black base 4m
0394·6 **Dique Este head** Fl.R.5s7m5M Red post 2m
Heads of pontoons F.G or F.R

Port communications

VHF Ch 9. *Capitanía* ☎ 977 680 120 *Fax* 977 681 753.

General

An extraordinary harbour for small craft built at the end of a 300m elevated road reaching out into deep water. It has two entrances, one open to the East, the other to the West. The water is shallow on either side and the harbour is kept open by dredging.

Puerto de Coma-Ruga

Facilities are limited but everyday requirements can be met in the town.

The Arco Roman de Bará, a 2nd-century Roman arch 1½M to SW of the town, is worth a visit and for those interested in the 'cello, there is a Casals museum. Excellent sandy beaches on either side of the harbour.

Approach

From the south After the huge breakwaters of Tarragona the old castle and towers at Tamarit near Punta de la Mora will be seen if close in, as will the rocky footed Punta de la Galera with its conspicuous lighthouse. Torredembarra marina just N of Punta de la Galera and the its inland town may be seen. Puerto Coma-Ruga itself appears to be well out to sea.

From the north The modern harbour at Aiguadolç with its old houses and new housing developments plus the large Puerto de Vilanova i la Geltrú close to SW are easily seen. The power station and chimney at Foix are conspicuous, followed by the Puerto de Segur de Calafell which, like Coma-Ruga, is built out to sea.

Anchorage in the approach

Anchor ¼M to SE of the harbour in 10m, sand and mud, or closer in during good weather.

Entrance

Approach the E side of the harbour from the SE, follow the Dique Este shorewards and enter by rounding its head at 15m leaving it to port. Do not use the entrance on the W side unless directed to do so or to fill up with fuel. Sound as you go. The entrance usually has about 2·5m but can be much less.

Berths

Secure to the inner side of the Dique Este and ask at the *torre de control* for a berth.

Facilities

Maximum length overall 15m.
Engineer on other side of the coast road.
A 10-tonne crane on the Dique Oeste.
A small slipway at the head of the Dique Oeste.
Chandlery in the town.
Water taps on quays and pontoons.
Showers and WCs at SW corner of the harbour.

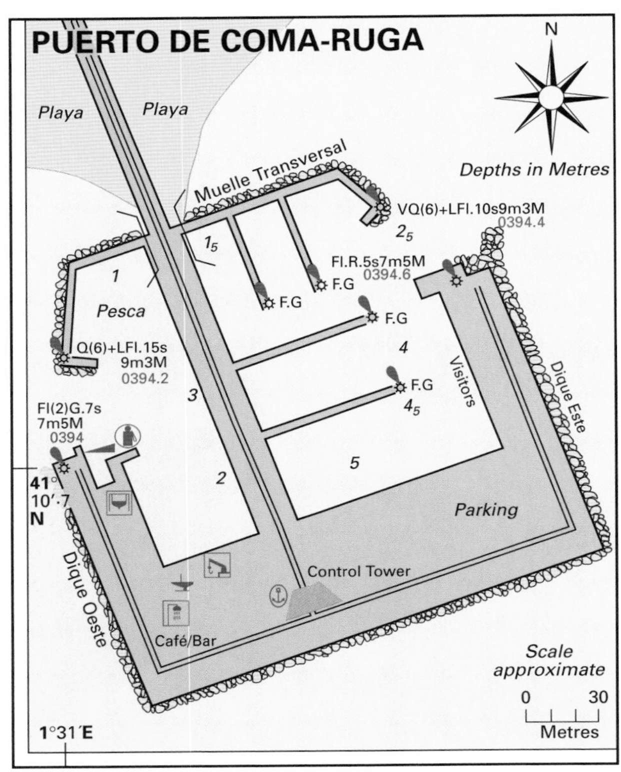

220v AC from points on quays and pontoons.
Gasoleo A and petrol from pumps at the head of the Dique Oeste.
Small ice from the bar.
Club Náutico de Coma-Ruga has a temporary clubhouse at the junction of the harbour road with coast road.
Many shops including supermarkets in the town.

Communications
Bus and train services. Taxi ☎ 977 641 147.

⚓ Sant Salvadór
An anchorage with 4 to 10m, sand, open from E to SW with a sandy beach ashore. There is a basic *club náutico* ashore for dinghies. A small town of 2000 inhabitants (approx) several hotels and some shops.

⚓ Calafell
An open anchorage in 4 to 10m, sand, off a sandy beach. Some houses ashore on the coast but the town of Calafell (4500 inhabitants) is 1½M inland, where there is a 12th-century castle. Two hotels, shops etc. There is a *club náutico* ☎ 977 69 03 37 which is a dinghy club with bar, restaurant, showers, WCs and a slipway. Not an attractive area. The anchorage is open between E and SW.

Puerto de Segur de Calafell
41°11'N 1°36'E

Charts
British Admiralty *1704*
French *4827*
Spanish *871*
Navicarte *E06*

Lights
0394·7 **S breakwater SE corner** 41°11'·2N 1°36'·3E VQ(6)+LFl.10s7m3M on metal tripod

Port communications
Ch 9, 27. *Capitanía* ☎ 977 690 502/977 693 550/977 622 323.

General
A small artificial yacht harbour built offshore and connected by a causeway to the coast road. The entrance to dredged harbour silts continuously and is dangerous in strong winds between west and south.

Facilities are limited but everyday requirements are available in the town. There is a 12th-century castle at Calafell 2M inland. Good sandy beaches on either side of the harbour.

Approach
From the south North of Tarragona the coast has sandy beaches broken by the rocky Punta de la Galera just south of Torredembara. Puerto de Coma-Ruga which, like this harbour, is joined to the coast by a causeway is easily seen as is this harbour in the closer approach.

From the north From the easily recognised Puerto de Vilanova i la Geltrú the sandy beach stretches past the power station at Foix to this harbour which is easily seen in the closer approach.

Anchorage in the approach
Anchor ½M to S of the harbour in 10m, sand and mud.

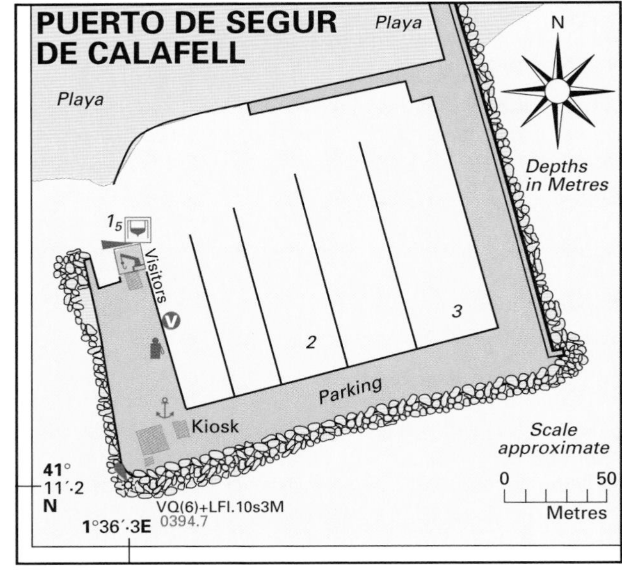

Puerto de Segur de Calafell

Entrance
The entrance is very close to the shore and of uncertain depth. Sound carefully and approach the W side of the harbour on a N course. Leave the length of the breakwater 20m to starboard and round its head at 10m onto an E course.

Note that entrance is only allowed during daylight hours and the *capitanía* must be contacted before entering.

Berths
Secure inside the entrance by the crane and apply at the *capitanía* for a berth.

Facilities
Engine mechanic available.
6-tonne crane.
A slipway at the head of the breakwater.
Chandlery in the town.
Water taps on quays and pontoons.
Points for 220v AC on quays and pontoons.
Petrol.
Shops in the town on the other side of the coast road.

Communications
Bus and rail services.

⚓ Cunit
An anchorage open between E and SW off a sandy beach with T-shaped groynes. Anchor in 4 to 10m, sand. Ashore is a small town of some 1000 inhabitants and a small *club náutico* for dinghies.

Puerto del Foix (Cubelles)

41°12'N 1°39'E

Charts
British Admiralty *1704*
French *4827*
Spanish *871, 487*
Navicarte *E06*

Lights
0395 **Dique de Abrigo E end** 41°11'·6N 1°39'·4E
Q(6)+LFl.15s5m5M Black ⧗ on yellow concrete post, black base 3m
F.R on conspicuous chimney 0·5M WNW

General
The harbour was built to service the Central Termica del Foix, a conspicuous power station with a very tall chimney. The outer part of the harbour forms a useful passage anchorage but the inner part should only be used in emergency. The harbour silts and is occasionally dredged; depths are unreliable. The entrance is dangerous in strong on-shore winds.

Approach
From the south Cabo de Salou and the large harbour of Tarragona are easily recognised. The coast eastwards is low and flat and lined with houses and summer apartment blocks. The small harbours of Coma-Ruga and Segur de Calafell jutting out into the sea are significant and the tall chimney and power station of Central Termica del Foix are conspicuous.

From the north The harbours of Aiguadolç and Vilanova i la Geltrú stand out and the Central Termica del Foix with its tall chimney will be seen from afar.

Entrance
The entrance to the outer harbour and anchorage is through a gap between the W head of the Dique de Abrigo which has a small post beacon and notice board and the E end of a groyne. The groyne and the Dique de Abrigo have recognisable regular crenellations.

The entrance to the inner harbour and quays lies to the E of the outer harbour behind and to N of the Dique de Abrigo.

Berths
Secure with care alongside one of the quays. There are some underwater projecting rocks and very few securing bollards. Keep well away from power station water intake at the NE corner of the harbour.

Anchorage
In the outer harbour near the centre of the bay about 2m, sand.

Facilities
None.

⚓ Cubelles
Anchorage behind two breakwaters in a sandy-edged pool about 1·5m, but sound carefully because the depth can vary. Club Marítimo de Cubelles, a dinghy club, has a building ashore with restaurant, bar, patio and showers. Road and rail ashore.

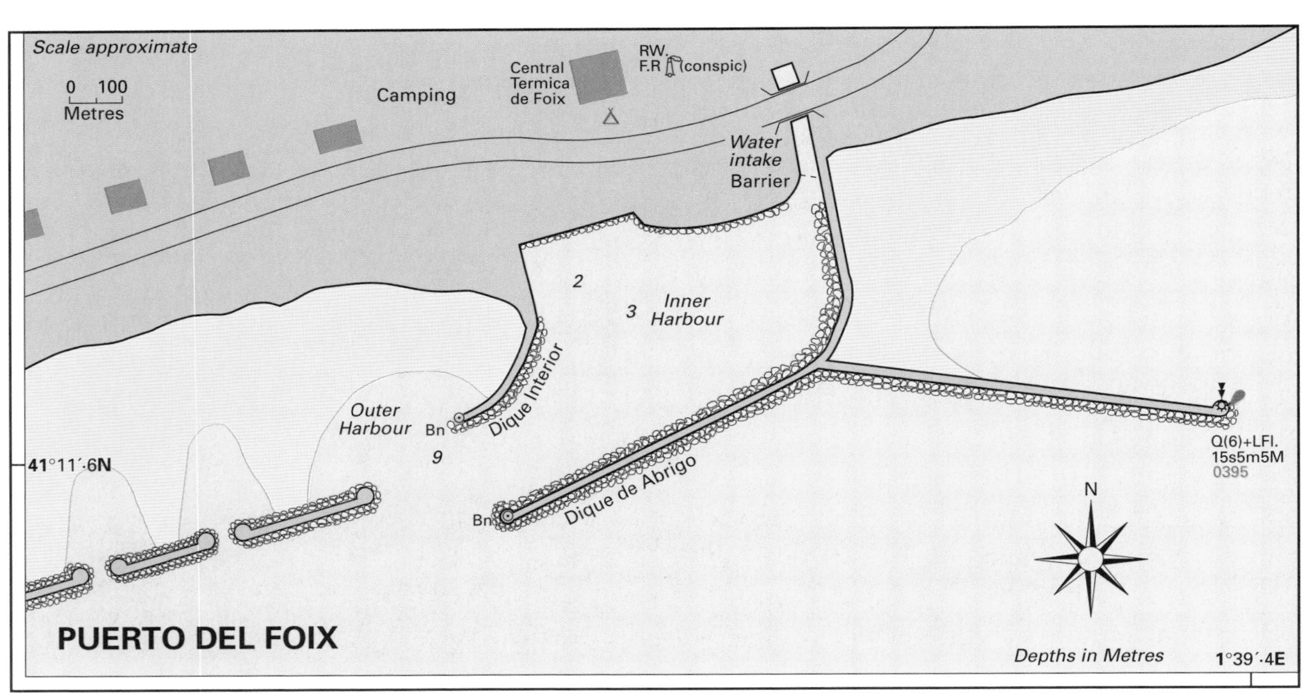

Puerto de Vilanova i la Geltrú (Villanueva y Geltrú)

41°13'N 1°44'E

Charts

British Admiralty *1704*
French *4827, 7298*
Spanish *871, 488A, 4881*
Navicarte *E06*

Lights

0396 **Punta San Cristobál** 41°13'·1N 1°44'·3E Fl(3)8s27m19M Truncated conical stone tower, aluminium cupola, white house 21m 265°-vis-070°
0396·2 **Dique de Levante S head** 41°12'·3N 1°43'·7E Fl(2)G.10s18m5M Green tower on white base 10m
0396·12 **Nuevo Contradique head** Fl(2)R.10s15m3M Red pyramidal tower 5m
0396·14 **Dique de Poniente head** Fl(3)R.12·5s9m2M Red pyramidal tower 3m 122°-vis-032°
0396·3 **Dique de Levante N head** Fl(3)G.10·5s5m2M Green pyramidal tower 3m
0396·5 **Espigón Transversal head** Fl(2+1)R.12s9m2M Red pyramidal tower, green band 3m
0396·52 **Espigón de la Pesca head** Fl(4)R.11s9m2M Red pyramidal tower 3m
0396·53 **Espigón head** Fl(4)G.11s5m1M Green post

Air radiobeacon

Villanueva c/s *VNV* (···–/–·/···–) 380kHz 75M 41°12'·59N 1°42'·29E

Port communications

VHF Port Ch 16. Marina Ch 9. ☎ 938 150 267 *Fax* 938 156 469.

General

A large artificial fishing, commercial, ship-breaking and yachting harbour, easy to enter and with good protection. There are good facilities for yachtsmen and hotels, restaurants and good shops ashore.

Villanueva developed rapidly from a small fishing village in the 18th century when the Basque families who had been engaged in plundering the West Indies since the 16th century returned to Spain with their fortunes. They built large houses, set up some industries and are still occasionally referred to as *Los Indianos*.

The 10th-century castle and the two museums are worth a visit. Excellent sandy beaches on either side of the harbour.

Approach

From the south From Tarragona the coast has low cliffs with sandy bays and backed by hills. North of the steep cliffs of Cabo Gros are the three marinas of Torredembara, Coma-Ruga and Segur. The conspicuous power station and chimney at Foix is about 2½M W of Vilanova i la Geltrú. The harbour lies at the edge of a plain and has yellow rocky harbour breakwaters and a backdrop of factory chimneys, blocks of flats and houses.

Puerto Vilanova i la Geltrú

Puerto de Vilanova i la Geltrú

From the north Barcelona is easily identified by the concentration of buildings, harbour works and smoke. The comparatively flat and featureless delta of the Río Llobregat is followed by a range of hills, the Sierra de la Guardia, which reach the sea in broken cliffs and small bays. South of this outcrop the harbour with its yellow rocky breakwater and factories, flats and houses will be seen, backed by a flat plain. A rocky patch lies on the W side of the Dique de Levante.

Anchorage in the approach
Anchor about 100m to W of the elbow of the Nuevo Contradique in 4m, sand.

Entrance
Leave the head of the Dique de Levante 50m to starboard and round it onto a NE course then enter between the head of the Dique de Poniente and the root of the Dique de Levante.

Berths
Secure to pontoon near office of the *capitán de puerto* for allocation of a berth.

Charges
Medium.

Facilities
Maximum length overall 25m.
Repairs to wooden hulls by a local yard.
Mechanics and sailmakers.
30-tonne travel-lift.
25-tonne crane at the *club náutico* and several larger cranes at the ship breaking yard.
Slipway in the NW corner of the harbour, larger ones in the NE corner and the Dársena Comercial.
Three small chandlery shops near the harbour.
Water taps on the pontoons of the *club náutico* and the quays.
220v AC from points on the pontoons and quays.
Gasoleo A and petrol.
Ice at fuel quay or from a factory at the N end of the Dársena de la Pesca.
The Club Náutico de Vilanova i la Geltrú clubhouse, in the NW corner of the harbour, has bars, lounge, terrace, restaurant, showers and a swimming pool.
Good shops of most types in the town, also a market and supermarket.
Launderette at marina.
Weather forecast at *capitanía.*

Communications
Rail and bus services. Taxi ☎ 938 933 241.

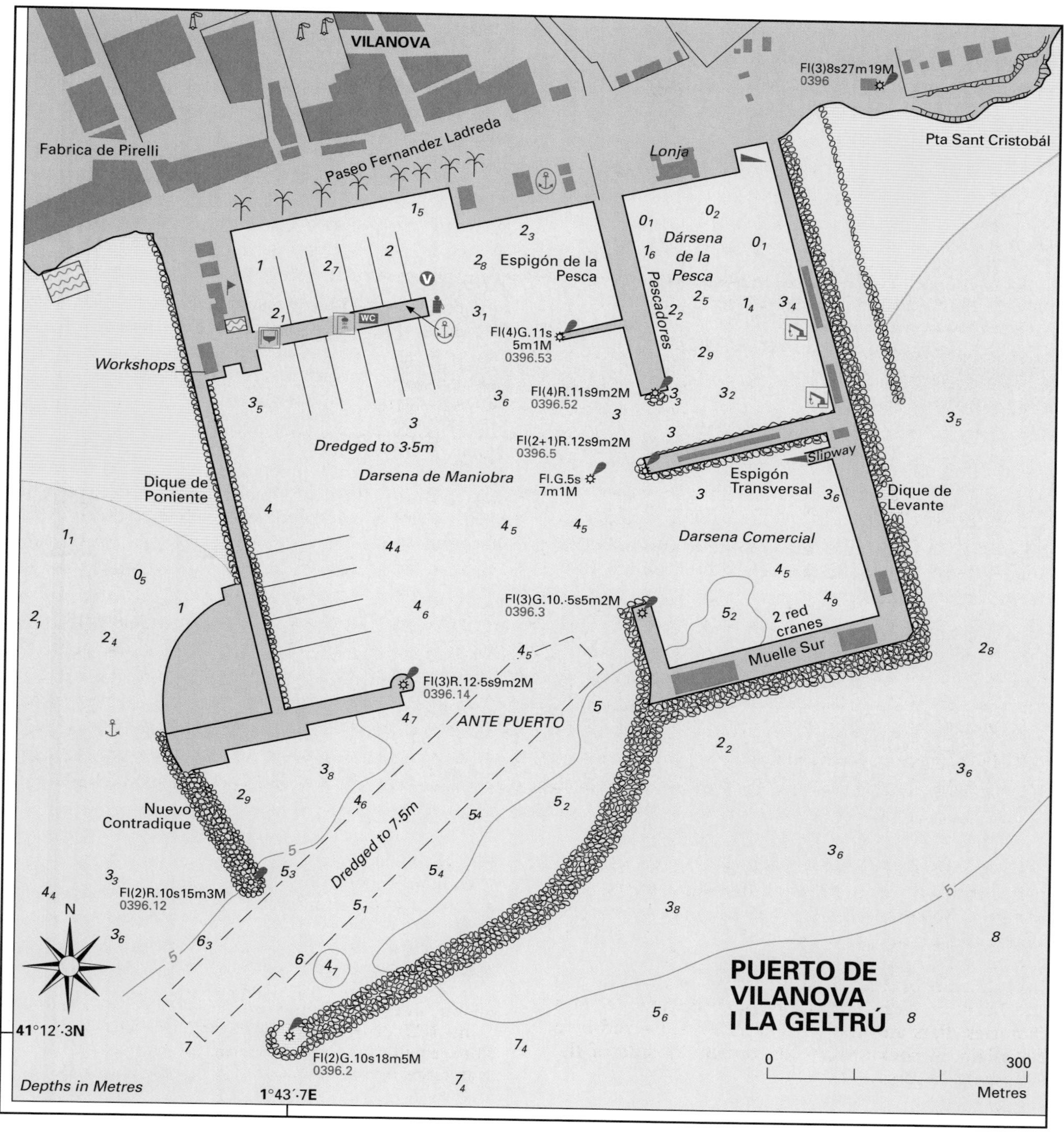
VILANOVA
Fl(3)8s27m19M
0396
Pta Sant Cristobál
Fabrica de Pirelli
Paseo Fernandez Ladreda
Lonja
Espigón de la Pesca
Dársena de la Pesca
Pescadores
Workshops
Fl(4)G.11s 5m1M
0396.53
Fl(4)R.11s9m2M
0396.52
Dredged to 3·5m
Fl(2+1)R.12s9m2M
0396.5
Darsena de Maniobra
Fl.G.5s 7m1M
Espigón Transversal
Slipway
Dique de Poniente
Dique de Levante
Darsena Comercial
Fl(3)G.10.·5s5m2M
0396.3
2 red cranes
Muelle Sur
Fl(3)R.12·5s9m2M
0396.14
ANTE PUERTO
Nuevo Contradique
Dredged to 7·5m
Fl(2)R.10s15m3M
0396.12
N
41°12′·3N
Fl(2)G.10s18m5M
0396.2
Depths in Metres
1°43′·7E
PUERTO DE VILANOVA I LA GELTRÚ
0
300
Metres

Aiguadolç (Puerto de Sitges)

41°14'N 1°49'E

Charts

British Admiralty *1704*
French *4827, 7298*
Spanish *871, 4882, 488A*
Navicarte *E06*

Lights

0396·54 **Dique de Levante head** 41°14'·0N 1°49'·5E Fl.G.5s12m5M Green tower, white base 10m
0396·55 **Dique de Levante Spur** Fl(2)G.13s6m1M Green tower, white base 6m
0396·56 **Contradique head** Fl.R.5s10m3M Red house corner 1m

Port communications

VHF Ch 9. *Capitanía* ☎ 938 942 600 *Fax* 938 942 750, *email* port-de-sitges@bcn.servicom.es. Yacht Club ☎ 938 150 267.

General

An artificial yacht harbour with good facilities. Approach and entrance are easy and good shelter obtained, but with wind from the SW swell will find its way into the harbour.

The town of Sitges nearby is very attractive and provides most facilities for visitors. There are three important museums here, some interesting old buildings and good sandy beaches near the town.

Sitges has been in occupation since Roman times, made popular by its climate. The area is well sheltered from the cold northeast winds. The painters Rusiñol and Utrillo worked here. The town holds a *fiesta* in the form of a flower show in late May or early June, on the first Thursday after Whitsun.

Approach

From the south The town and harbour of Vilanova i la Geltrú are easily recognised. The coast is low and flat as far as Sitges which has a small hill feature a little distance inland. Its concentration of flats and houses has a conspicuous church at its E end and the harbour lies 500m to the E.

From the north The rocky broken coast where the Sierra de la Guardia meets the coast gives way to the flat coastal plain near this harbour. A conspicuous cement works is located some 1·5M to the E of the harbour.

Aiguadolç (Puerto de Sitges)

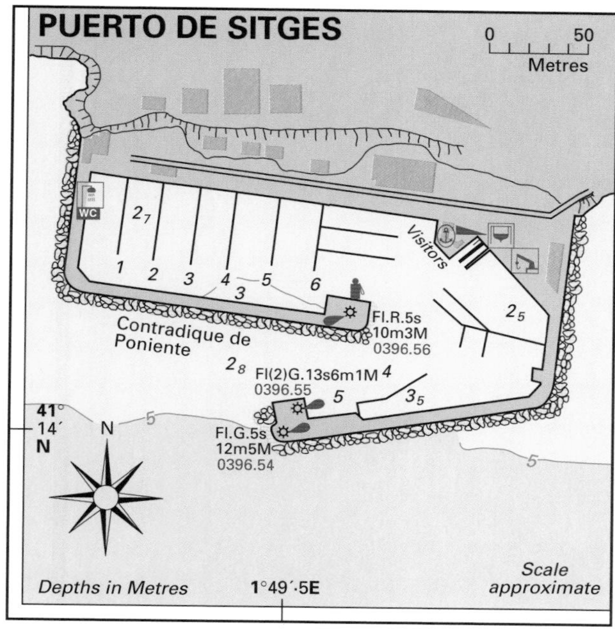

Anchorages in the approach

Anchor 200m to the S of the entrance in 8m, sand.

Entrance

Approach the entrance on a NE course and enter between the two *diques* and in mid-channel. Then round the head of the Contradique de Poniente leaving it 25m to port, secure to the quay by the *torre* and ask for a berth.

Facilities

Maximum length overall 26m.
A shipyard on the NE side of the harbour with two workshops and an engineer.
23-tonne travel-lift.
2-tonne mobile crane.
Slipway on the NE side of the harbour.
A hard-standing area for yachts to NE of the harbour.
Two chandlers at the harbour.
Water from taps on the pontoons.
Showers on W side of the harbour.
220v AC supply points on the pontoons.
Gasoleo A and petrol from the head of the Espigón Nord.
Ice available from bars and fuel berth.
Many shops in the town, also a market and supermarket. Shops also around the harbour.
Launderette in the town and one to be established at the harbour.
Weather forecasts posted at the *torre* daily.

Communications

Bus and rail services. Taxi ☎ 938 943 594/938 941 329. Car Hire ☎ – Hertz 938 945 750, Avis 938 949 926.

Puerto de Vallcarca

41°14'N 1°52'E

Charts

British Admiralty *1704*
French *4827, 7298*
Spanish *871, 488*
Navicarte *E06*

Lights

0396·6 **Muelle head** 41°14'·3N 1°52'·0E
Fl(4)G.13s10m4M Green tower, white base 5m

General

A private harbour belonging to a huge cement works. It might be used in emergency but not when wind and swell are between W and S as it is wide open to that quarter. There are no facilities for yachtsmen other than water and a beach restaurant. The noise and dust created by the Fradera SA cement works which is in operation day and night makes it an unpleasant place to stay.

Approach

From the south The flat plains around the harbours at Vilanova i la Geltrú and Aiguadolç give way to the high mountainous feature, the Sierra de la Guardia, which reaches to the coast near this harbour. The cement works, two white silos on the harbour wall and the clouds of dust are all conspicuous.

From the north From Barcelona the coast is low and flat until the rocky cliffs where the Sierra de la Guardia meets the coast beyond the delta of the Río Llobregat. The cement works, two white silos and the dust near this harbour are also conspicuous from this direction.

Entrance

Round the head of the Muelle de Atraque leaving it 50m to starboard and follow this *muelle* in a NE direction.

Puerto de Vallcarca

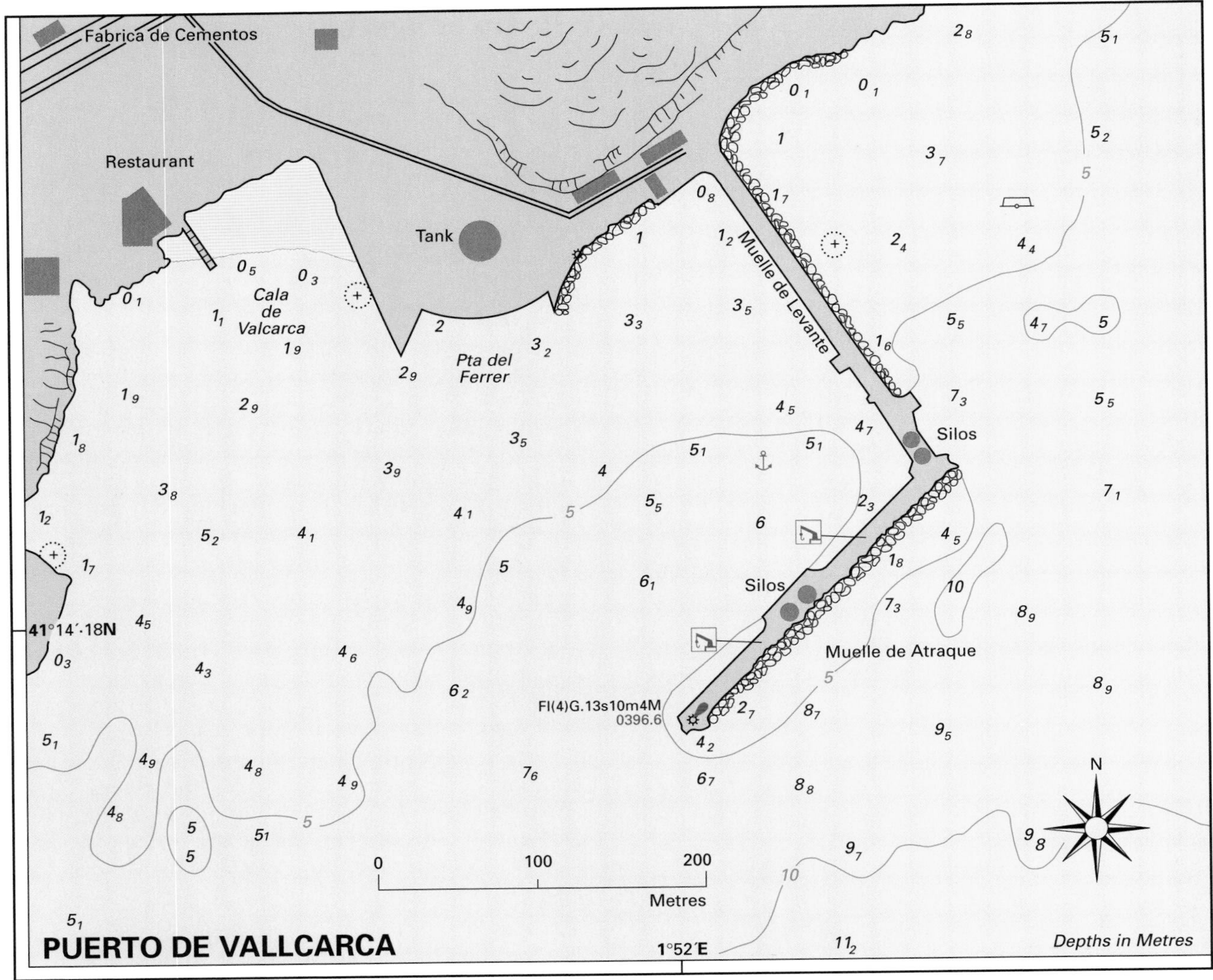

Berths

In calm weather, temporary berths may be available alongside the Muelle de Levante if not in use by commercial shipping.

Anchorage

Anchorage on a temporary basis is possible in the E corner of the harbour and also outside the harbour to the NE if the swell is entering the harbour itself.

Mooring

Temporary moorings to one of the hauling off buoys might be possible if they are not in use.

Facilities

Water from a tap near root of *muelle*.
Small beach restaurant.

Communications

Bus and rail service.

Puerto de Garraf

41°15'N 1°54'E

Chart

British Admiralty *1704*
French *4827, 7298*
Spanish *871, 488A*
Navicarte *E06*

Lights

0396·62 **Dique de Levante head** 41°15'·0N 1°54'·0E Fl(3)G.9s7m5M Green tower 3m
0396·64 **Dique de Poniente head** Fl(3)R.9s4m3M Red tower 3m

Port communications

VHF Ch 9 *capitanía* ☎ 936 320 013 *Fax* 936 320 126 *email* info@clubnauticgarraf.com

General

A large marina but unaccompanied by the trappings (and traps) which surround most of the marinas along the coast. A few bars and restaurants can conveniently be reached by foot. Repair facilities are very limited but many are available at Port Ginesta, next door.

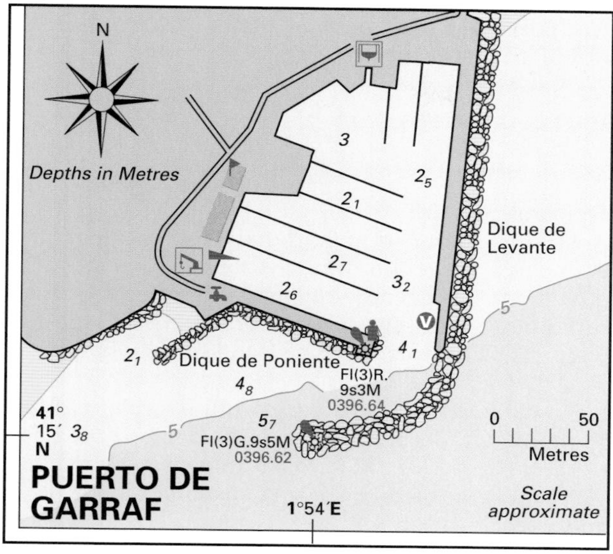

Approach

From the south After passing the flat coast around Vilanova i la Geltrú the coast becomes rocky and broken where the high Sierra de la Guardia reaches the sea. The harbour is located on this section of coast 1·7M beyond a conspicuous cement works and harbour at Vallcarca.

From the north South of the wide flat delta of the Río Llobregat, where Barcelona airport is located, is the rocky broken coast of the Sierra de la Guardia. Port Ginesta is the first along that stretch, Garraf the second, in sight of the conspicuous Vallarca cement works.

Entrance

During a March 2001 visit there was a sand bank of 0·7m depth extending from the centre of the fuelling jetty in an arc to the shore to the west. This severely restricted the width of the entrance channel but the bank was marked with a string of small red buoys.

Enquiries at the *club náutico* revealed that after Easter a dredger would be employed to shift the sand bank so that full access would be available by end of May. Further enquiries revealed that this bank can return after a few days of strong winds. Therefore, although the entrance is straightforward, it is advised to round the Dique de Levante close to and follow it along keeping 10m or so from it, sounding carefully. Go right into the port and then turn to come alongside the fuelling pier from the NE and berth starboard side to. Sort out a berth with the torre de control in the *club náutico* building.

Facilities

Workshop outside the marina with mechanic.
20-tonne travel-hoist.

Puerto de Garraf

6-tonne crane.
Hard-standing.
Water on the quays.
Gasoleo A and petrol.
Showers and ice at the *club náutico*.
220v AC on the quays.
Laundry in marina, limited shops in the town.

Communications
Bus and rail services. Taxi ☎ 936 653 557.

Port Ginesta (Puerto de Castelldefels)

41°15'N 1°55'E

Charts
British Admiralty *1704*
French *4827*
Spanish *871, 488*
Navicarte *E06*

Lights
0396·8 **Dique de Abrigo head** 41°15'·5N 1°55'·4E Fl(2)G.10s8m5M Green tower 3m
0396·85 **Contradique head** Fl(2)R.10s5m3M Red tower 3m
0396·9 **Espigón de Levante** Q(6)+LFl.15s5m3M ♦ on black beacon, yellow top 3m
To the north
0398 **Río Llobregat** 41°19'·6N 2°09'·2E Fl.5s32m23M Tower on building 31m 240°-vis-030°

Radiobeacon
Punta de Llobregat Lt RC c/s *OR* (---/·-·) 303·5kHz 50M 41°19'·6N 2°09'·2E

Port communications
VHF Ch 9. *Capitanía* ☎ 936 643 661 *Fax* 936 650 166 *email* ginesta@chi.es

General
A large modern yacht harbour, easy to enter and with good protection. There is a wide range of yacht repair and brokerage facilities besides chemist, restaurant, bars etc. and a crafts market at the weekend. The port is popular and usually full; book ahead.

Castelldefels (originally Castrum de Fels) has fair shopping and its Romanesque church and the keep of the castle (AD1211) are worth a visit. Barcelona, 12M away, is within striking distance. There is a good beach to NE.

Approach
From the south Aiguadolç and the cement works at Puerto de Vallcarca are conspicuous followed by Puerto de Garraf. Ginesta is at the end of the coastal cliffs.

From the north Barcelona is unmistakable, after which the delta of the Río Llobregat is low and flat with its light and radio antenna as features. Follow the sandy coast at ½M in 10m, sounding. The harbour is where the sandy beach stops and coastal cliffs commence.

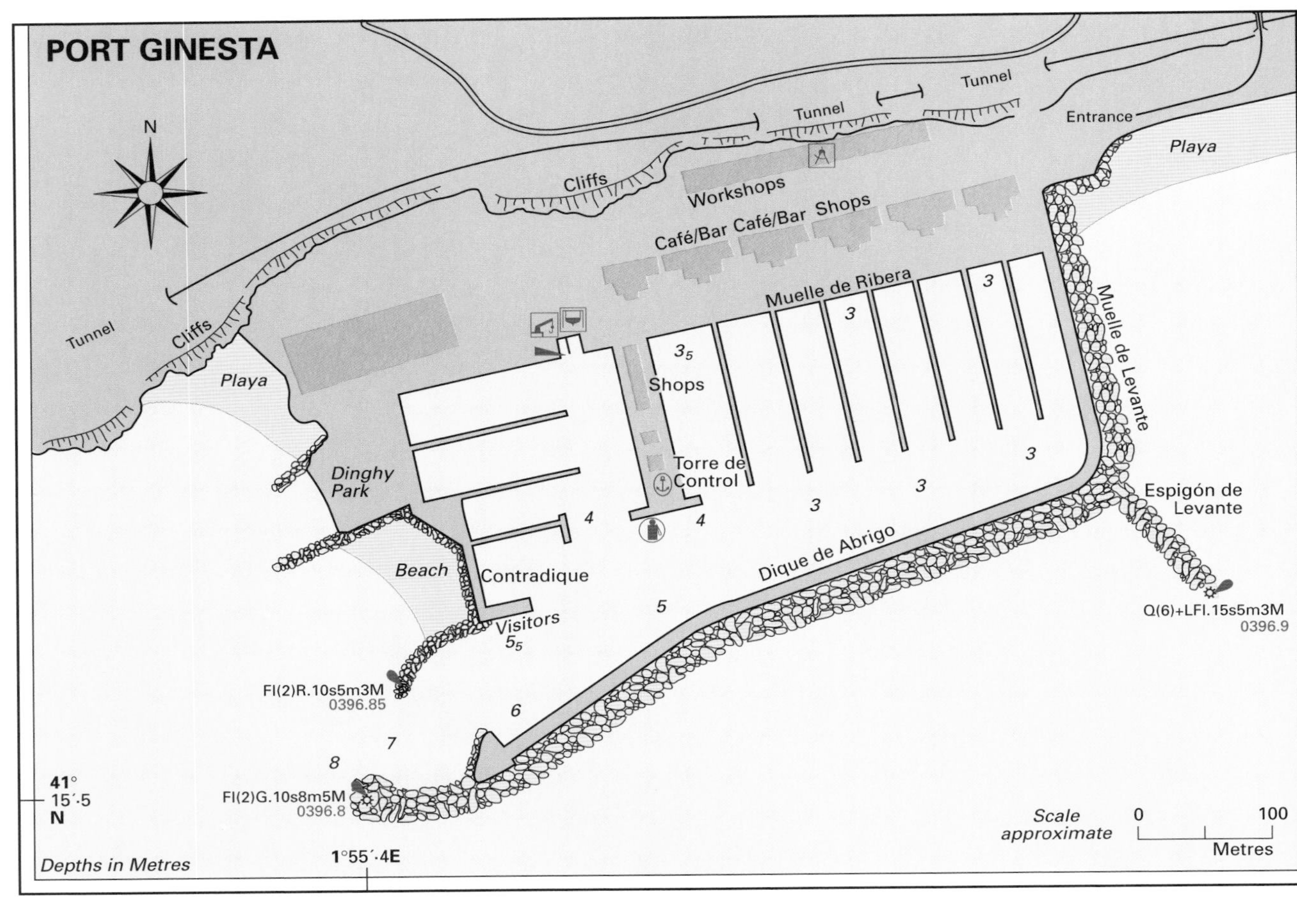

Port Ginesta (Puerto de Castelldefels)

Anchorage in the approach
Anchor 400m to S of the entrance to the harbour in 10m sand and mud. Not recommended in heavy weather because of undertow.

Entry
Approach the area where there is a large quarry in the background. The entrance between the breakwaters is straightforward. However the entrance is prone to silting and during a March 2001 visit there was a small red buoy just 20m from the Dique de Abrigo light which marked a 1m patch in the centre of the fairway with less than 2m to the north of it. There was also a dredger at work pumping the sand on to a nearby *cala*. Watch for this on entry, sound carefully and tend to keep closer to the Dique de Abrigo than one usually would. If a berth has not been previously arranged by phone/VHF, secure at the fuelling berth and ask at the *torre de control* for a berth.

Facilities
Maximum length overall 30m.
Workshops with mechanics to NW of the harbour.
GRP, joinery, paintwork, sailmaking.
Slipway at NW side of the harbour (6m).
50-tonne travel-lift.
8-tonne crane.
Hard-standing for yachts at N side of the harbour.
Shops selling chandlery to N side of the harbour.
Water taps on quays and pontoons.
Showers and WCs in the *torre de control* complex.
220v AC points on quays and pontoons.
Gasoleo A and petrol.
Small ice from the café/bars and fuel station.
Some shops around the harbour, many more in the town 3M away.
Laundry in town.
Weather forecasts posted daily at the *torre de control.*

Communications
Bus and rail service. Barcelona International Airport 5M Taxi ☎ 936 635 537.

⚓ Gava

An open anchorage off a sandy beach about 1M to WSW of the airport, wide open to the S. Dinghy yacht club ashore. Coast road and road to Gava.

Barcelona

During 1999 the port of Barcelona started an enormous reconstruction programme, which is due to complete in 2010. The initial phase was to build a half-mile long Dique de Abrigo outside and at the root of the Dique del Este and to build a bridge, Puerta de Europa, joining Dique del Este and the Muelle de Poniente. Infill was poured to join the Dique de Abrigo to the Dique del Este and there is now a brand new harbour for the Barcelona fishing fleet at the root and outside the Dique del Este.

The next phase is to break through the Dique del Este just outside the new fishing harbour entrance (planned for mid 2002) and this will then become the only entrance for pleasure craft wishing to go to Port Vell or the repair facilities inside the old harbour.

Meanwhile at the southwest end of the harbour even more extensive works are in progress. The mouth of the Río Llobregat is being moved about a mile to the SW much infilling is taking place and the Dique del Este is being extended by nearly a mile with a new Dique Sur being built to make a new port to the SW of the present one.

With all this construction work in progress it is difficult to give timely advice on the changes that are happening almost daily. At present mid 2002 all pleasure craft must keep well clear of the construction work going on SW of the present entrance. Craft wishing to go to Port Vell should pass close to the Dique del Este head and proceed under the Puerta de Europa (18·5m clearance) – but it is highly recommended to use the Puerto Olimpico, if at all possible. Later in 2002 it is probable that the only entrance for pleasure craft will be through the new entrance just S of the fishing harbour and when this comes into operation no pleasure craft should approach the construction works at the SW end of the port where there will be a number of buoys laid to indicate work in progress.

Puerto de Barcelona

41°20'N 2°10'E

Charts

British Admiralty *1704, 1196, 1180*
French *4827, 7046*
Spanish *873, 489A, 4891*
Navicarte *E06, E05*

Lights

Approach – to the south
0398 **Río Llobregat** 41°19'·6N 2°09'·2E Fl.5s32m23M Tower on building 31m 240°-vis-030°
Approach – central
0400 **Montjuich** 41°21'·7N 2°10'·0E Fl(2)15s108m26M Tower on red brick building 13m 240·5°-vis-066·5°
Note Montjuich light is well within the harbour.
Harbour
0401 **Dique del Este S head** 41°20'·2N 2°10'·4E Fl.G.5s17m6M Green tower on concrete base 7m
0402 **Dique del Este W head** Fl(2)G.7s9m3M Green tower on concrete base 5m

Puerto de Barcelona - a bridge 'Puerta de Europa' now spans the gap between the pier at the centre of the photo and the breakwater on the right. A new fishing complex has been constructed outside the breakwater and work is ongoing to make a new entrance for pleasure craft in the centre of the breakwater's 'S' bend.

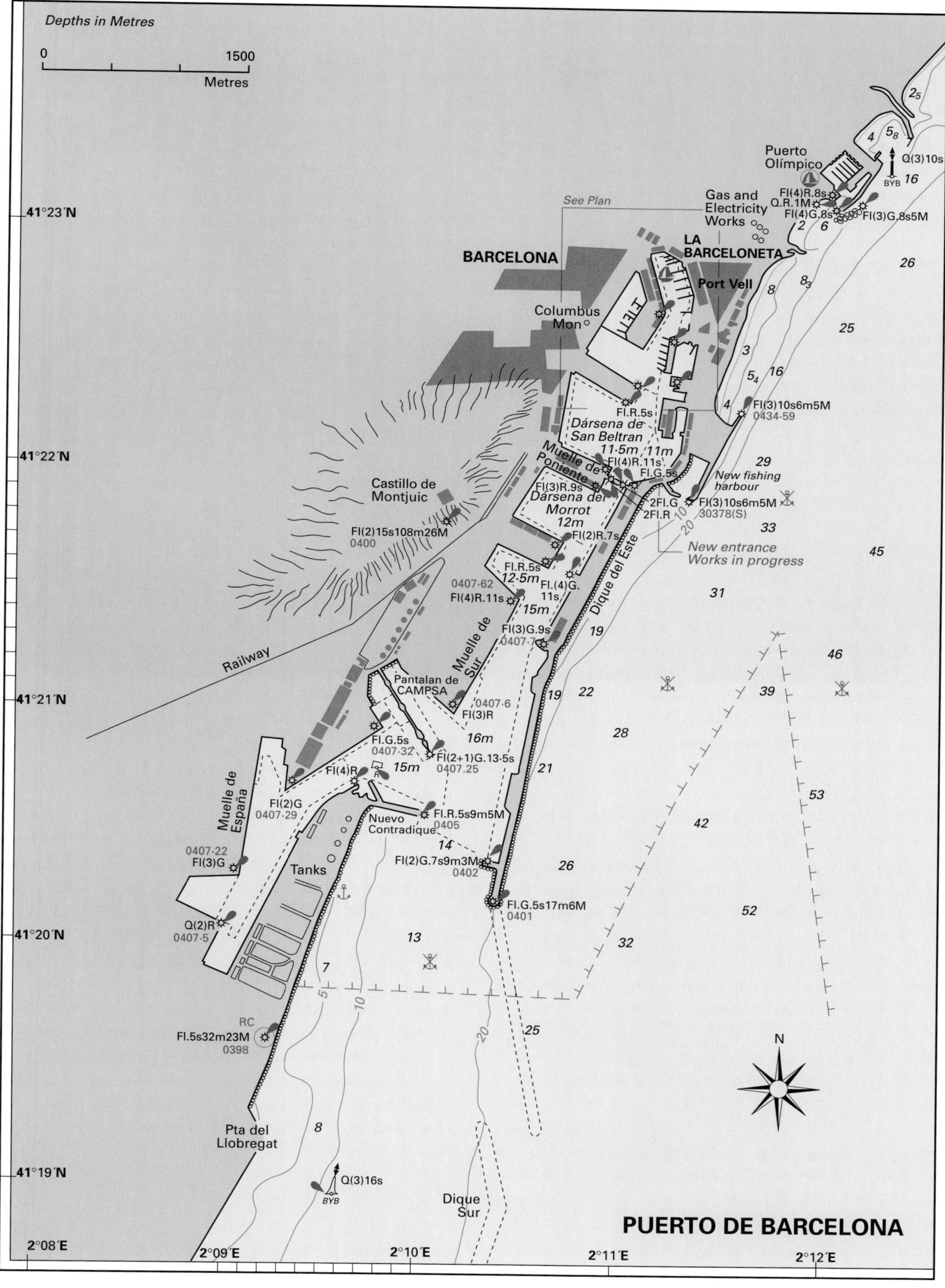
Depths in Metres
0
1500
Metres
Puerto Olímpico
Q(3)10s
BYB
Fl(4)R.8s
Q.R.1M
Fl(4)G.8s
Fl(3)G.8s5M
Gas and Electricity Works
See Plan
BARCELONA
LA BARCELONETA
Port Vell
Columbus Mon
Dársena de San Beltran
Fl.R.5s
Fl(3)10s6m5M
0434·59
Muelle de Poniente
Fl(4)R.11s
Fl.G.5s
New fishing harbour
Fl(3)R.9s
Dársena del Morrot
2Fl.G
2Fl.R
Fl(3)10s6m5M
30378(S)
Castillo de Montjuic
Fl(2)15s108m26M
0400
Fl(2)R.7s
New entrance Works in progress
Fl.R.5s
Fl.(4)G. 11s
0407·62
Fl(4)R.11s
Dique del Este
Fl(3)G.9s
0407·7
Muelle de Sur
Railway
Pantalan de CAMPSA
0407·6
Fl(3)R
Fl.G.5s
0407·32
Fl(2+1)G.13·5s
0407.25
Fl(4)R
Muelle de España
Fl(2)G
0407·29
Fl.R.5s9m5M
0405
Nuevo Contradique
Fl(2)G.7s9m3M
0402
0407·22
Fl(3)G
Tanks
Fl.G.5s17m6M
0401
Q(2)R
0407·5
RC
Fl.5s32m23M
0398
Pta del Llobregat
Q(3)16s
BYB
Dique Sur
N
PUERTO DE BARCELONA
41°23′N
41°22′N
41°21′N
41°20′N
41°19′N
2°08′E
2°09′E
2°10′E
2°11′E
2°12′E

Puerto de Barcelona. Looking into Port Vell. The new fishing harbour and entrance are being built in the framed area

0405 **Nuevo Contradique head** Fl.R.5s9m5M Red round tower, white band at base 4m
0406 **Dique de Alba head** Fl(2)R.7s3m1M Dolphin 2m
0407·25 **Muelle Evaristo Fernandez pontoon head** Fl(2+1)G.13·5s6m3M Green post on concrete base 3m
Note The numerous lights between Evaristo Fernandez and Occidental are shown on the chartlets but not listed here. All are red on the west side and green on the east side.
0418·5 **Muelle Occidental SW elbow** Fl(2)G.7s6m2M Green metal post on concrete base 3m
0420 **Muelle de Barcelona SW corner** Fl.R.5s6m2M Red metal post on concrete base 3m
0418·6 **Muelle de Cataluña S corner** Fl(3)G.9s6m2M Green metal post on concrete base 3m
0418·62 **Muelle de Cataluña N corner** Fl(4)G.11s6m2M Green metal post on concrete base 3m
0422·2 **Muelle de Barcelona NE corner** Fl(2)R.7s6m2M Red metal post on concrete base 3m
0434 **Muelle de las Baleares SW corner** Fl(2+1)G.13·5s6m2M Green post, red band, on concrete base 3m
0424 **Muelle de España E end** Fl(2+1)G.13·5s6m2M Green post, red bands
0434·2 **Muelle de las Baleares N corner** Fl(4)G.11s6m2M Green post on concrete base
0424·4 **Muelle de España N end** Fl(3)R.9s6m2M Red metal post on concrete base
0434·59 **Dique de Abrigo N head** 41°22'·2N 2°11'·5E Fl(3)10s6m5M Card E post
30378a(S) **Dique de Abrigo S head** 41°21'·7N 2°11'·2E Fl(3)10s6m5M Card E post

Radiobeacon

Punta de Llobregat Lt RC c/s *OR* (−−−/·−·) 303·5kHz 50M 24hrs 41°19'·57N 2°09'·20E

Port communications

Pilots VHF Ch 11, 12, 14, 16 (hours various).
Port VHF Ch 12, 14, 16 24hrs. ☎ 933 177 500.
Real Club Marítimo (RCM) VHF Ch 9 (hours various). ☎ 933 150 007/933 170 197.
Real Club Náutico de Barcelona ☎ 932 216 521.
Marina Port Vell VHF Ch 68 ☎ 934 842 300 *Fax* 934 842 333 *email* info@marinaportvell.com *Web* www.marinaportvell.com

General

Barcelona is the capital of Cataluña and the largest city and port on this coast. The port of Barcelona itself (as distinct from Puerto Olímpico which is outside the main harbour walls) is easy to approach and enter in any weather, though winds may funnel at the entrance (but see opening paragraphs on page 104). There is good protection inside. Commercial traffic must be given right of way near and inside the port. Facilities for yachts and their crews are excellent and there are many attractions in the city

Puerto de Barcelona - Port Vell

and surrounding area. The marina at Port Vell is close to Las Ramblas and the city centre.

There are scores of places to see, such as 38 museums, 26 art galleries besides permanent trade fairs and exhibitions. To mention but three, visit Gaudi's cathedral, the Picasso Museum and walk along Las Ramblas at the hour of the *paseo*.

Though the area was probably occupied by the Iberians and later the Phoenicians, the first recorded history is of its occupation by the Carthaginian Hamilcar Barca in 230BC when it was called Barcino. The Romans took over in about 200BC and later called it Colonia Julia Augustus Pia Faventia. The town was destroyed by the Barbarians in AD263 but was later retaken by the Romans who fortified it with a great wall. The Visigoths made it their capital of Gothalania in AD415, from which name the province of Cataluña is thought to have originated. The town surrendered to the Moors in AD713; they were in turn driven out in AD801, only to return in AD985 for a short period during which the town was burnt. For the next 600 years, while still asserting her independence and rights, the town was ruled by the various royal and noble houses as their fortunes changed. An event of note was the royal reception of Columbus in June 1493 on his return from his discovery of America. In 1714 the city was sacked by the French because the inhabitants supported the cause of Archduke Charles against the French nomination of Philip V for the crown. The French also occupied the city from 1808 to 1813. From then until the Civil War the city was often the centre of agitation and revolt against the established order, insisting on its own rights and customs. In the 19th century the industrial revolution created a situation which caused the vast development of the city and its surroundings into one of the largest and most prosperous in Spain. It was the centre of Republican activity during the civil war and was badly bombed; the fall of Barcelona in January 1939 virtually marked the end of the war.

Approach

From the south The high feature and broken rocky cliffs of the Sierra de la Guardia suddenly give way to the flat low delta of the Río Llobregat which has the airport and a lighthouse. On a clear day the high hill immediately behind the harbour (Montaña de Montjuic), the harbour installations and the mass of buildings of the city will be seen from afar. The two towers of the aerial railway are also conspicuous.

From the north The coastline is backed by a series of hills consisting of the Sierras del Corredó, de Sant Mateu and de Matas, which fall back inland in the area of Barcelona, leaving the isolated feature of

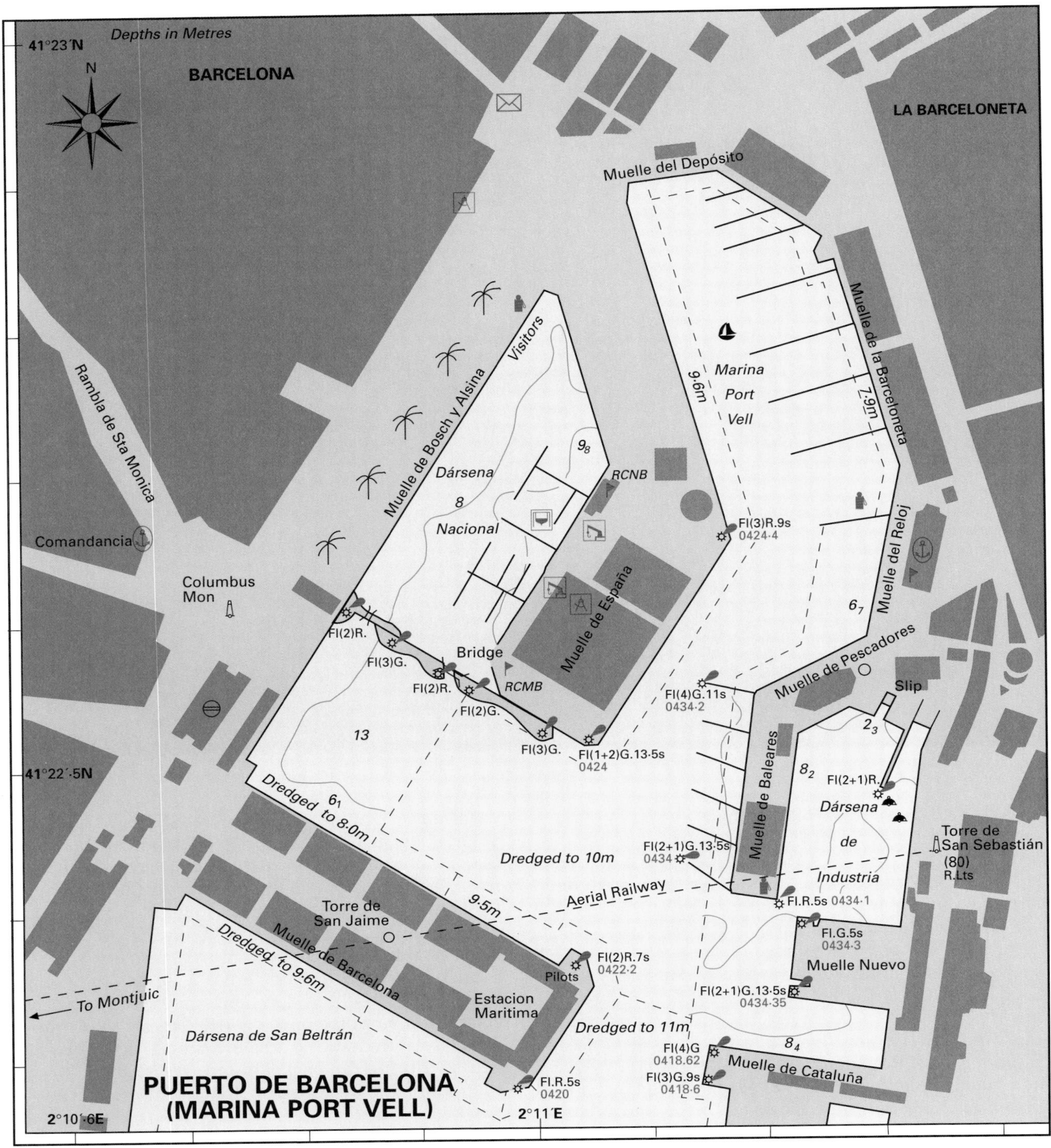

Montaña de Montjuic easily located. The coast is lined with concentrations of houses and high-rise buildings which extend across the delta of the Río Bésós. The bridge over this river will be seen. The concentration of buildings and harbour works continues past Montaña de Montjuic, silos and the two towers of the aerial railway. In clear conditions the jagged peaks of Montaña de Montserrat some 20M inland can be seen from.

Entrance
Leave the Dique del Este and its spur 150M to starboard and go north up the harbour to the end. At night there is one green light to be left to port, Muelle Evaristo Fernandez pontoon head; after that, keep red to port and green to starboard. For Port Vell, after passing under the new bridge, Puerta de Europa with 18·5m clearance and between Muelle de Cataluña and Muelle de Barcelona, ignore Muelle Nuevo and the Dársena de la Industria, head for Muelle de las Baleares (SW corner) and enter Marina Port Vell between Muelles Baleares and España.

Later in 2002 there will be a new entrance for pleasure craft just south of the new fishing harbour at the root of Dique del Este. From the south follow outside the Dique del Este for narly 2 miles until the entrance opens up.

Berths

The visitors berths are at Port Vell. Call for a berth on Ch 68 or at the fuel quay. The Real Club Marítima may accept visitors by arrangement; the Real Club Náutico de Barcelona is for members only. An alternative is to go to Puerto Olímpico but this has less character and is further out of town.

Harbour charges

High.

Facilities

Barcelona can support all repairs, in or out of the water. Many are close to Port Vell. Consult a marina or club official if help is needed.
Chandlery shops near the port, one 200m SW of the main post office and another between the two *clubs náutico*.
Chart agent in Avenida Marques de l'Argentana.
At Port Vell
Maximum length overall 70m.
Water taps on the pontoons.
220v and 380v AC on the pontoons.
Gasoleo A and petrol.
Ice, ask at the fuelling berth.
In town:
Supermarket at 100m.
Thousands of shops of all kinds and a large market in the city, many in the narrow streets near the port.
Launderette in the second road back from the NW side of the Dársena Nacional, many others elsewhere in the city.

Communications

International and national bus, rail and air services, car hire etc. Shipping to most parts of the world. Taxi ☎ 933 912 222.
British Consulate-General: Edificio Torre de Barcelona Avineda Diagonal 477, 13th Floor, 08036 Barcelona ☎ 934 199 044 *Fax* 934 052 411.

Puerto Olímpico

Puerto Olímpico

41°23'N 2°12'E

Charts

British Admiralty *1704, 1196, 1180*
French *4827, 7046*
Spanish *873, 489A, 4891*
Navicarte *E06, E05*

Lights

0434·7 **Puerto Olímpico Dique de Abrigo head** 41°23'·1N 2°12'·0E Fl(4)G.8s9m1M Green post 6m
0434·75 **Contradique head** Fl(4)R.8s3m1M Red post 2m
0434·6 **Outer breakwater head** Q.R.3m1M Red post
Submerged breakwater
0434·71 Fl(3)R.8s6m3M Red post
0434·72 Fl(3)G.8s6m5M Green post
0434·73 Q(3)10s6m5M ♦ on black tower, yellow band
0434·74 Q(3)10s6m5M ♦ on black tower, yellow band (¾M NW of 0434·73)

Port communications

VHF Ch 9. ☎ 932 210 106/932 210 191 *Fax* 932 210 594.

General

This yacht harbour was built for the 1992 Olympic Games. The area of the city behind it formed the Olympic village. The metro is 10–15 minutes walk and the harbour is less convenient for shopping than Port Vell. But the place is tidy, secure and well sheltered.

Approach

From the south The low, flat delta of the Río Llobregat and the long breakwater of the Puerto de Barcelona are easily identified. Puerto Olímpico lies under a couple of skyscrapers (one marked MAPFRE) some 4M N of the S end of the outer

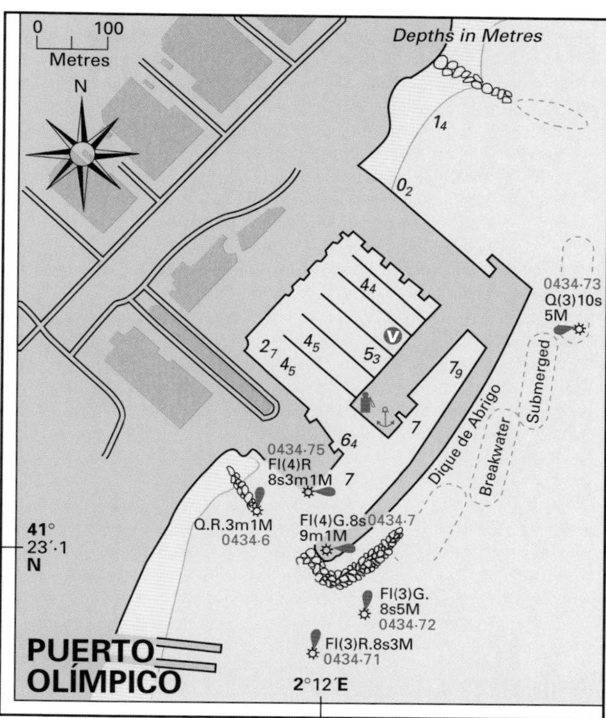

breakwater of the old harbour.

From the north The harbour at El Masnou and the mouth of the Río Besós which has power and gas stations with tall chimneys either side of its mouth are easy to recognise. The harbour can be located by the two skyscrapers (one marked MAPFRE) immediately behind it.

Entrance
Approach the S end of the harbour passing between red and green beacon poles. Continue in towards the beach until the rocky extension at the head of the Dique de Abrigo can be rounded. A fairly sharp turn to starboard is needed to avoid running up on the beach.

Berths
Moor at fuel berth and obtain berth from *capitanía*.

Harbour charges
Low.

Facilities
Maximum length overall 30m.
Some maintenance facilities.
Travel-lift 50 tonnes.
Crane 6 tonnes.
Large hard-standing.
Gasoleo A and petrol.
Water on the quays.
Showers.
220v and 380v AC on the quays.
Shopping mall in basement of eastern skyscraper.
Tourist bus stop on main road N of marina.

Communications
Metro, buses. Taxi ☎ 933 581 111.

Besós
More extensive construction work is going on at Besós where a huge development of marina, hotels, convention centre etc is being built. To seaward two buoys have been laid to indicate the limit of the work. Keep clear of the area until 2004.
30394a(S) Buoy 41°24'·2N 2°13'·8E Q(3)10s5M E card
30396a(S) buoy 41°25'·1N 2°14'·4E Q(3)10S5M E card

⚓ Badalona
An open anchorage off the long sandy Playa de Badalona open between NE and S. Yacht club ashore with good facilities. Originally the Roman city of Betulo it is now a highly industrial area. Some shops.

⚓ Mangat (Mongat)
Another open anchorage similar to Badalona.

Puerto de El Masnou
41°28'N 2°18'E

Charts
British Admiralty *1704*
French *4827*
Spanish *873, 4892, 489*
Navicarte *E05*

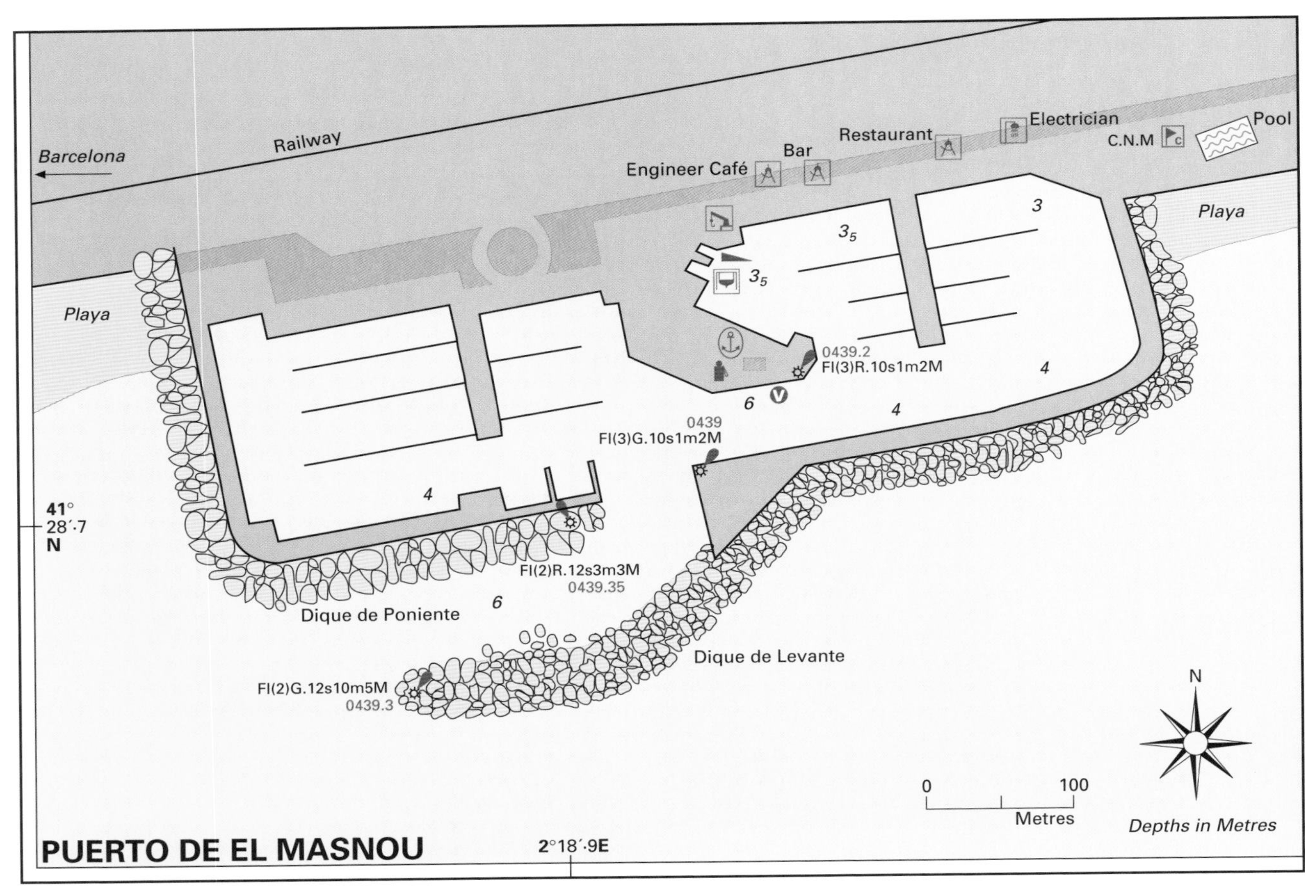

Puerto de El Masnou (note the *capitania* is not in the tower on the far jetty but in a new building on the fuel jetty and the *dique* on the right has been extended)

Lights

0439·3 **Dique de Levante head** 41°28'·4N 2°18'·7E Fl(2)G.12s10m5M Green tower 7m

0439·35 **Dique de Poniente head** Fl(2)R.12s3m3M Red post 2m

0439 **Dique de Levante corner** Fl(3)G.10s2m2M Square green tower 1m

0439·2 **Fuel jetty corner** Fl(3)R.10s1m2M Square red tower 1m

Port communications

VHF Ch 9. *Capitanía* ☎ 935 403 000 *Fax* 935 403 004.

email portmasnou@chi.es

Club Náutico de El Masnou ☎ 935 550 605.

General

A pleasant yacht harbour which has all facilities. Easy to approach and enter with excellent protection from even SW winds as the Dique de Levante has recently (Nov 2000) been lengthened by 70m. The modern seaside town has shops and restaurants and there are fine sandy beaches either side of this harbour.

Approach

From the south The mass of houses, harbour works and installations of Barcelona are unmistakable. Further N, and either side of the mouth of the Río Bésós, lie power stations with five tall chimneys and a jetty. The town of Badalona and many houses and flats line the coast, which is flat and sandy, backed by ranges of hills. The church at El Masnou and a tower, the Turó de Moná, on an isolated hill 1M inland are recognisable.

From the north The cliffs on either side of Arenys de Mar and its harbour can be recognised. Southwards the coast is flat and sandy with ranges of hills inland. The concentration of buildings at Mataró and its harbour can be identified, after which come the tower and church at El Masnou.

Anchorage in the approach

Anchor 200m to SW of the entrance in 5m, sand.

Entrance

The entrance is nearly at the west end of the harbour and runs ENE–WSW between the breakwaters. The gap won't be obvious until it bears about NE. Pass between the piers and proceed to the fuel quay by the new *torre de control.*

Berths
Ask at the *torre de control* for allocation of a berth.

Charges
Low off season, medium in high season.

Facilities
Maximum length overall 22m.
Practically all repair facilities including sailmaking.
50-tonne travel-lift.
4-tonne crane.
Two slips.
Three chandlery shops beside the harbour.
Water on the pontoons and quays.
Showers.
220v AC on the pontoons and quays.
Gasoleo A and petrol.
Camping Gaz.
Club Náutico de El Masnou has a clubhouse to the NE of the harbour with bar, terrace, showers and a pool. It is separate from the harbour. Ask the secretary.
Supermarket, shops in the town nearby and hypermarket at Mataró.
Laundry collects from the marina.

Communications
Bus and rail services. Taxi ☎ 935 402 492.

Puerto de Premiá de Mar

41°29N 2°21'E

Charts
British Admiralty *1704*
French *4827*
Spanish *873, 489*
Navicarte *E05*

Lights
0439·5 **Dique de Abrigo head** 41°29'·4N 2°22'·0E Fl.G.3s6m5M Green post 3m
0439·52 **Contradique head** Fl.R.3s3m3M Red lantern on hut

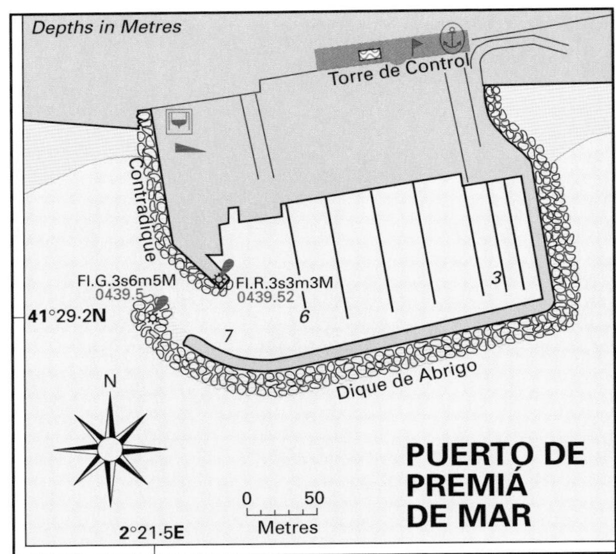

Puerto de Premiá de Mar

Port communications
VHF Ch 9. *Capitanía* ☎ 937 511 458/937 524 111 *Fax* 937 523 711.
Club Náutico de Premiá ☎ 937 523 098.

General
An off-shore marina with man-made breakwaters, it will eventually have more than 700 berths. In early 2001 the marina looked just like the photo but there had been a fresh injection of money and work had started on completion of the original project which is due for the 2002 season when full facilities should be available. The town, well known for its carnations which are sent all over Spain, has good supplies but is on the other side of the railway track, a bit of a hike. Entrance to the marina is simple but could be dangerous in strong SW winds. There are long sandy beaches on both sides of the harbour.

Approach
From the south After Barcelona there are two large power stations either side of the Río Besós. 2M further north east is Port Masnou; then the large white *torre de control* behind Premiá de Mar should be spotted.

From the north Puerto de Arenys de Mar and the smaller ports of El Balís and Mataró are easily recognised. The very small landing at Vilassar may also be seen. The white control tower of Puerto de Premiá is easily identified from this direction.

Anchorage in the approach
Anchor in 10m, sand, ½M to S of this harbour.

Entrance
The entrance is straightforward. However, the old harbour mouth, which was further inshore, used to silt up and the new one may do the same. Sound carefully both on the approach and inside the harbour.

Berths
Secure to end of central jetty and report to *torre* for allocation of berth.

Facilities
Mechanic with workshop.
A slipway on the NW side of the harbour.
A 1·5-tonne in the E corner.
Chandlery in town on road to Calvo Sotelo.
Water on quays and pontoons.
220v and 380v AC on slipway.
Ice at the bar.
Club Náutico de Premiá has a large clubhouse with restaurant, bar, terrace, lounge, swimming pool, showers and WCs.
A few local shops with many more in Badalona 5M and Mataró 5M.
Weather forecasts posted at *torre de control.*

Communications
Bus and rail services. Taxi ☎ 937 522 532.

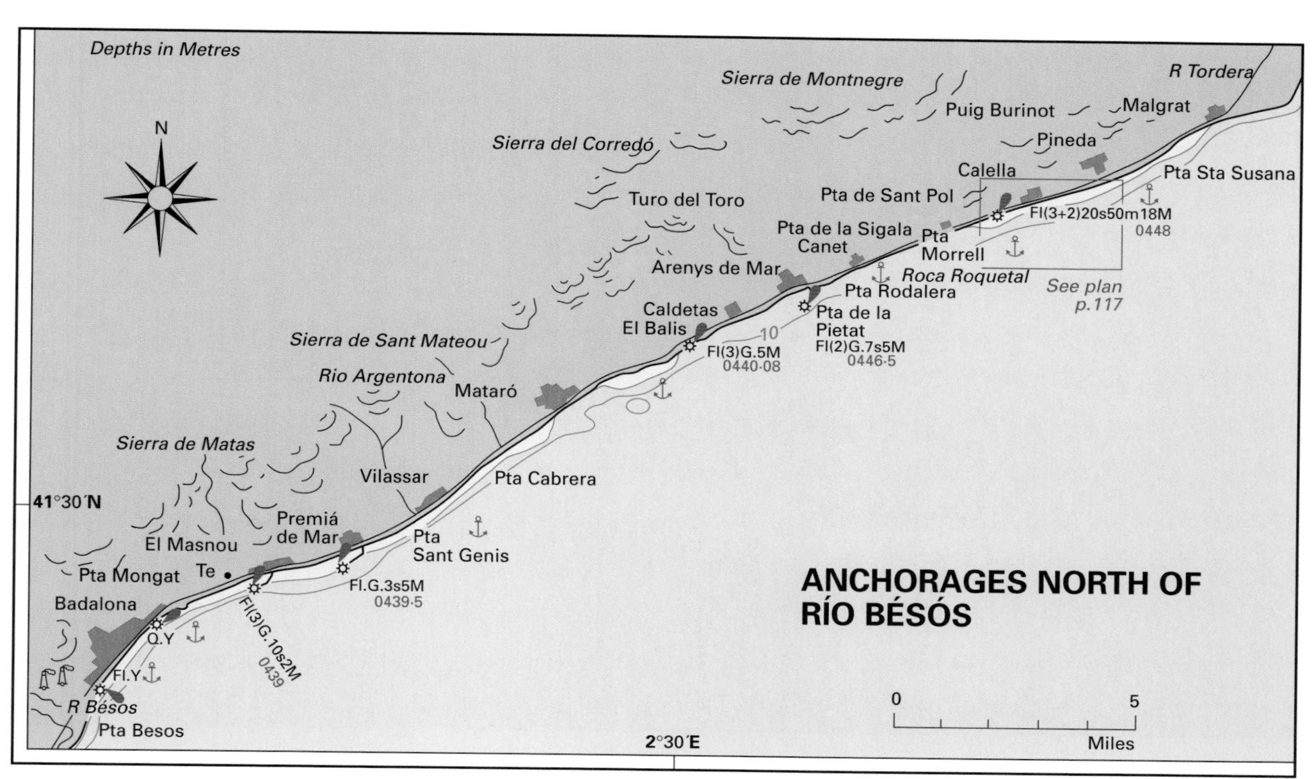

⚓ Vilassar de Mar

Anchorage off sandy beach in 3m, sand, with a conspicuous yacht club and slipway enclosed by two rocky breakwaters with many small fishing boats on the hard. The Club Náutico de Vilassar de Mar has a restaurant, bar, water, showers, WCs and swimming pool. The village of 9,000 has many restaurants, café/bars, a chandler, post office, two hotels, bus and rail services and at 1½M the well preserved Castle Barbara and a flower-growing centre. Open between NE and SW.

Puerto de Mataró

41°31'N 2°26'E

Charts

British Admiralty *1704*
French *4827*
Spanish *873, 489, 301A*
Navicarte *E05*

Lights

0439·8 **Dique de Abrigo head** 41°31'·6N 2°26'·7E
Fl(4)G.12s15m5M Green tower
0439·85 **Contradique head** Fl(4)R.8s5m4M Red tower

Port communications

VHF Ch 9. *Capitanía* ☎ 937 550 961 *Fax* 937 902 942.

General

A large artificial yacht harbour cut off from the dreary town by the main road and railway. It is a useful stop-over, handy for Barcelona (20 minutes by train).

Mataró is the ancient Roman town of Iluro and many remains of that period have been discovered including the important Villa Torre Llauder. There are also Moorish relics. The first railway in Spain was laid from here to Barcelona in 1848. The town expanded and became well known for its shipbuilding. It is now equally well known for growing and marketing carnations.

The church and the ruined castle of St Vincente de Burriach, both 15th century, and the walled medieval town of Argentona should be visited. There are sandy beaches on both sides of the harbour.

Puerto de Mataró

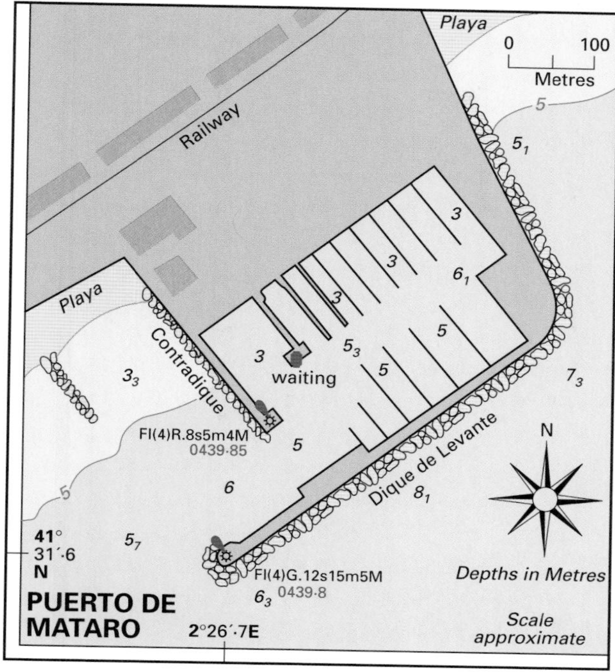

Approach

From the south Northeast of Barcelona the coast is flat with a long sandy beach with a series of towns and villages. The chimneys of the power stations at the mouth of the Río Besós, the yacht harbours of El Masnou and Premiá de Mar and the mouth of the Río Argentona are easy to see. The town of Mataró and the harbour breakwaters are large and easily recognised.

From the north Blanes and the mouth of the Río Tordera can be identified. The coast is low and flat with a long sandy beach, lined with small villages and towns including Puerto de Arenys de Mar and Puerto de El Balís. The town and breakwaters of Mataró are conspicuous.

Anchorage in the approach

Anchor in 7m, sand, 50m to SE of the Dique de Levante.

Entrance

Approach the head of the Dique de Levante on a course between W and N and round the head at 20m.

Berth

Pass the *contradique* close to port and make for the waiting quay under the *torre de control,* next to the fuelling point, at the end of the first jetty to port. Moor and arrange a berth with the *capitanía* in the *torre*.

Charges

Lowish, no variation between high and low season.

Facilities

Maximum length overall 20m.
Almost all repair services.
100-tonne travel-lift.
12-tonne crane.
Two chandlers on the coast road.
Water on pontoons and quays.
Showers.
220v and 380v AC on pontoons and quays.
Gasoleo A and petrol.
Ice on fuel quay.
Shops, bars.
Supermarket and a weekly market in the town.
Laundry.

Communications

Bus and rail services. Taxi ☎ 937 986 060.

Port Balís

41°33'N 2°30'E

Charts

British Admiralty *1704*
French *4827*
Spanish *873, 489*
Navicarte *E05*

Lights

0440 **Dique de Levante head** 41°33'·5N 2°30'·5E Fl(4)G.12s4m2M Green column 2m
0440·08 **Espigón head** Fl(3)G.10s10m5M Green tower 6m
0440·2 **Dique de Poniente head** Fl(3)R.10s6m2M Red column
0440·4 **Contradique interior head** Fl(4)R.12s3m2M Red post 1m

Port communications

VHF Ch 6. *Capitanía* ☎ 937 926 451/937 926 475 *Fax* 937 927 261.

General

A pleasant yacht harbour, easy to enter and offering good protection though the swell from SW gales can enter the harbour. Facilities are good.

The nearby town of Caldetas with its hot springs and 13th-century church, and Mataró, the ancient Iluro, a walled town with many Moorish remains, can be visited. There are fine sandy beaches on either side of the harbour.

Approach

From the south The chimneys of the power stations at the mouth of the Río Besós, the yacht harbours of El

Port Balís

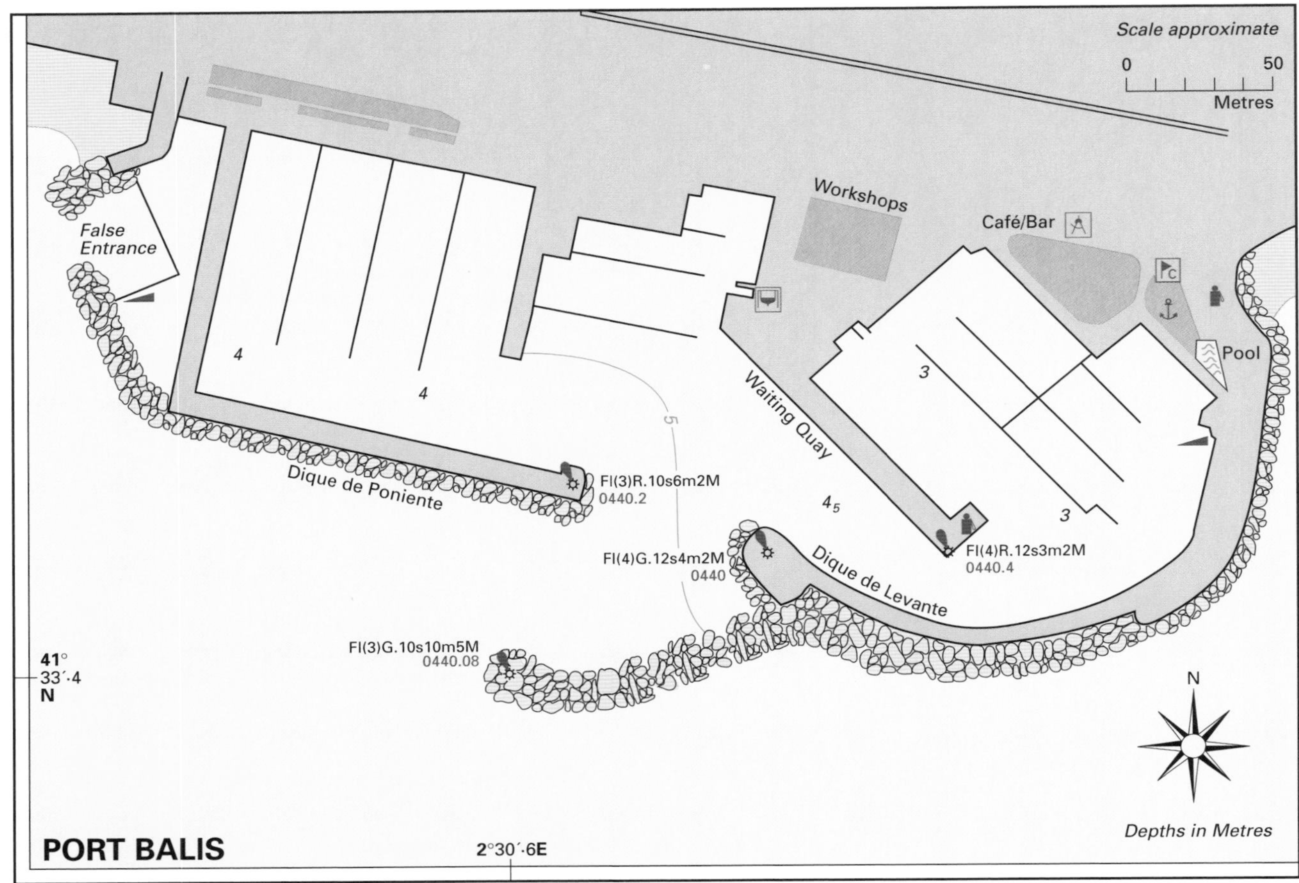

Masnou and Premiá de Mar and the mouth of the Río Argentona are easy to see. The town of Mataró and the harbour breakwaters are large and easily recognised. The harbour walls of El Balís will be visible in the closer approach.

From the north From the flat, low delta of the Río Tordera the coast has sandy beaches backed by ranges of hills with several small towns. A pair of towers near Calella and the harbour breakwater at Arenys de Mar will be seen.

Anchorage in the approach

Anchor 200m to SW of the entrance in 10m, sand and mud.

Entrance

Approach the head of the Dique de Levante on a N course and round it at 25m.

Berths

Secure to the fuel quay for allocation of a berth.

Facilities

Maximum length overall 25m.
50-tonne travel-lift.
5-tonne crane.
There is a slipway in the N corner of the harbour and on the beach outside the entrance.
A chandlery shop at the N of the harbour.
Water on pontoons and quays.
220v AC on pontoons and quays.
Gasoleo A and petrol.
Ice on the fuel quay.
Club Náutico El Balís is on the N side of the harbour and has bars, restaurant, lounge, terrace, swimming pool, showers etc.
Shops in the town nearby and some around the harbour.

Communications

Bus and rail services. Taxi ☎ 937 958 390.

Puerto de Arenys de Mar

41°34'N 2°33'E

Charts

British Admiralty *1704*
French *4827, 7298*
Spanish *873, 489, 4911*
Navicarte *E05*

Lights

0446·5 **Dique de Portiñol head** 41°34'·5N 2°33'·5E Fl(2)G.7s9m5M Green tower on white base 5m
0446 **Dique del Calvario head** Fl(2+1)R.15s5m2M Red tower, green band 3m
0446·2 **Dique de Portiñol elbow** Fl(3)G.10s7m2M Green tower 3m 025°-vis-185°
0446·3 **Contradique de Poniente head** Fl(2)R.7s8m3M Red tower 3m

To the northeast

0448 **Calella** 41°36'·4N 2°38'·7E Fl(3+2)20s50m18M White tower on building 10m (Aeromarine)

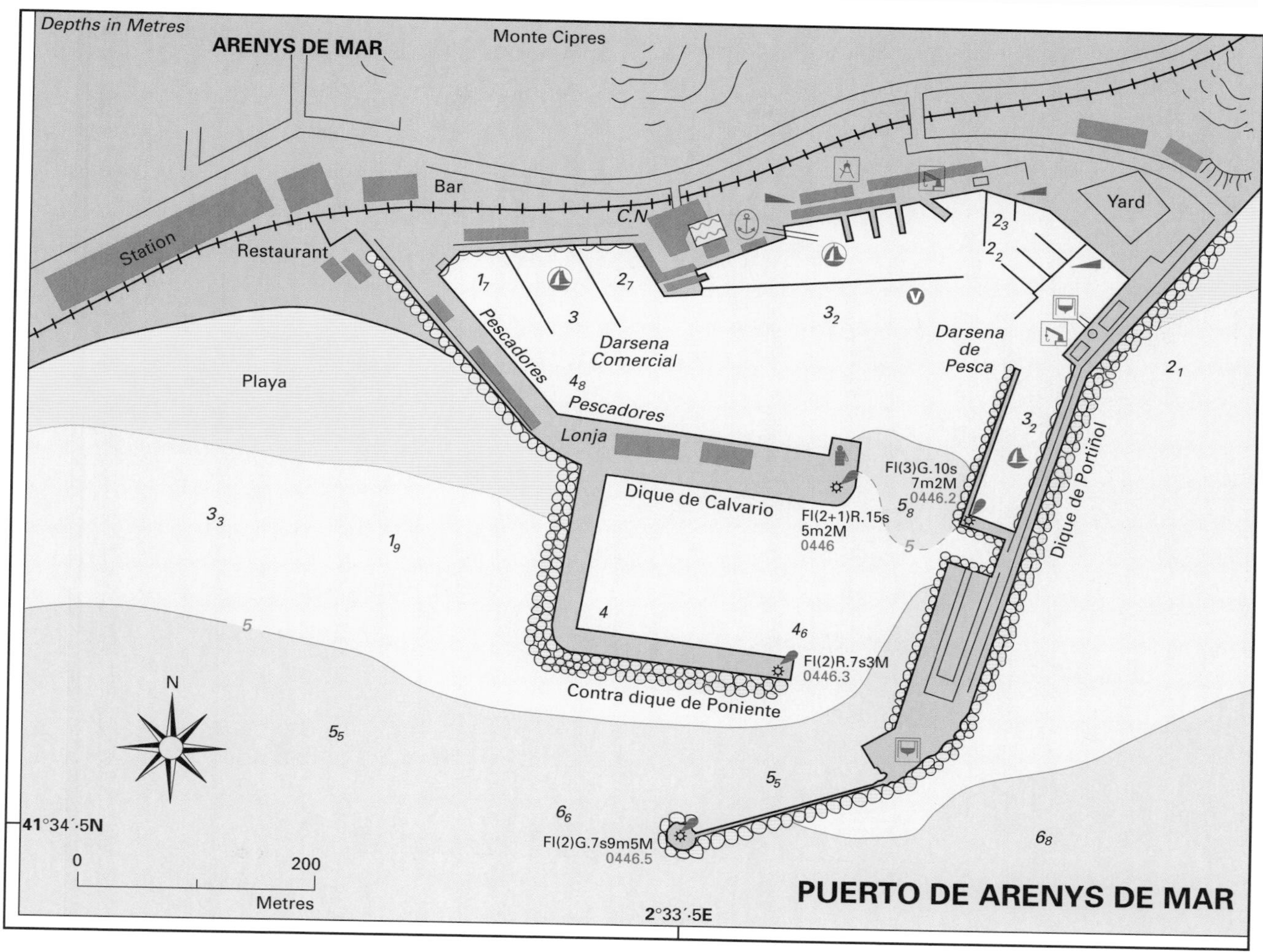

Port communications
VHF Ch 9. ☎ 937 920 896/937 920 980 *Fax* 937 920 744.

General
A major fishing harbour now accommodating a large number of yachts in addition to the fishing fleet. Popular with French yachts, it becomes crowded in summer so book ahead. It is easy to approach and enter. Inside, protection is good though SW winds send in some swell.

Those interested in history might visit the Torre del Encantate, built on the site of a pre-Roman town, and a 16th-century church. The beaches on either side of the harbour are good but have coarse sand.

Approach
From the south The low and sandy coast is lined with towns and, a short distance inland, ranges of hills. El Masnou, the harbour at Mataró and a conspicuous tower just inland from Caldetas will be recognised. The cliffs either side of Arenys de Mar and the tall blocks of flats can be seen from afar and the harbour walls show up on the approach.

From the north After the low, flat delta of the Río Tordera the sandy coast is backed by ranges of hills and lined with a number of small towns. A breakwater (in ruins) at Malgrat and two towers at Calella may be seen. Arenys de Mar will be recognised by cliffs either side of the town, blocks of flats and, in the closer approach, by the harbour breakwaters.

Anchorage in the approach
There is no good anchorage. A pipe-line runs out to sea W of the Dique de Calvario.

Entrance
Approach the head of the Dique de Portinol on a N course and round it at 50m.

Berths
Berth stern-to pontoons with bows-to mooring buoy as directed by the club officials. Vacant berths have a red plaque around the bollard on the pontoons.

Charges
High.

Facilities
Maximum length overall 18m.
A yard to the N of the harbour and another larger one in the NE corner. Engine repair shops to the N of the harbour where there is also an electronic workshop.
Travel-lift in NE corner and two more, one of 100 tonnes near harbour entrance.

Puerto de Arenys de Mar

Two slipways in the NE corner and another on the N side of the harbour.
10-tonne crane at the NE side and another on the N side of the harbour.
Two chandlers in the road to the N of the harbour.
Water on the pontoons and at the *lonja*.
220v AC on the pontoons 380v AC in the workshops.
Gasoleo A and petrol.
Ice from a factory to the N of the harbour or from the *lonja*.
Club Náutico de Arenys de Mar has bars, lounges, terrace, restaurant, showers and a swimming pool.
The shops in the nearby town can supply most normal requirements.
Launderette in the town.

Communications
Bus and rail services. Taxi ☎ 937 958 390.

⚓ Sant Pol de Mar

An offshore anchorage, open NE through S to W, in 5m, sand. The usual undistinguished high-rise conglomeration behind the beach with its usual undistinguished facilities. Railway and road.

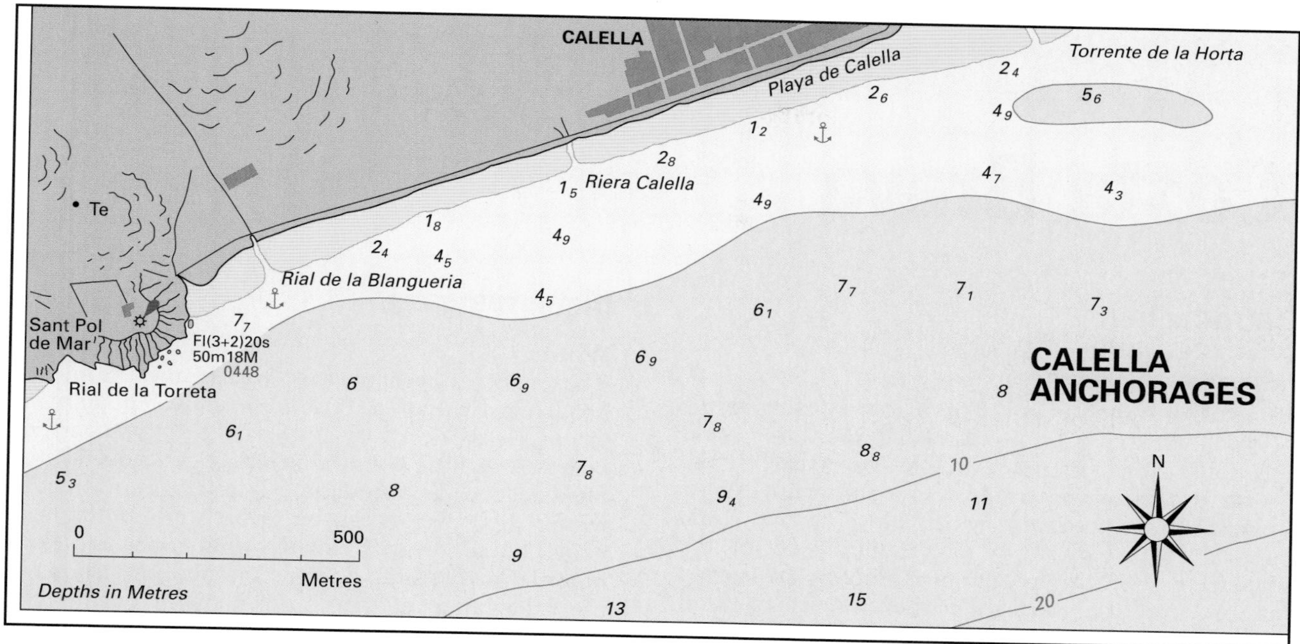

⚓ Punta Morrell

A small anchorage in 4m, sand, protected by an L-shaped breakwater, open between E and SW with a sandy beach ashore and a large *club náutico*. Behind the coast road and railway line is the town of San Pol de Mar.

⚓ Calella

Another open anchorage off a sandy beach in 3m, sand, with another deep-water anchorage ½M to SE of the town in 32m, sand, open between NE and SW. A yacht club ashore for dinghies. A large town backs up a variety of food shops. It is a centre of the hosiery trade. Rail and road connections.

⚓ Pineda de Mar

Again an offshore anchorage in 3m, sand, in front of a conglomeration with some facilities and a good sandy beach. Rail and road connections.

Río Tordera

This small river is the boundary between Barcelona and Girona and also marks the junction between Costa Dorada and Costa Brava.

Costa Brava

Introduction

General description

The 67M stretch of coast from Río Tordera to the French border is more dramatic than the other sections. *Brava* means wild, savage. Much of the coast is broken with steep rocky cliffs and can be scoured by *tramontanas* which blow up with little notice. It is backed by the eastern end of the Pyrénées. The scenery, the proximity of the rugged shores and the deep *calas* beneath steep-sided promontories make this the most attractive of all the *Costas* of Mediterranean Spain for cruising yachtsmen.

The rugged coast runs from Blanes to the wide, flat flood plain of the Río Ter. The hills and cliffs rise again at L'Estartit and continue for 5M as far as the second flood plain of the Ríos Fluviá and Muga. From Roses onwards to France the coast is even less hospitable with high mountains quite close to the sea.

Offshore are the two groups of islands, Islas Formigues and Islas Médes. There are also some islands off Cabo Creus and several groups of rocks close inshore. In general the coast is steep-to and can be approached to within 100m with care. The exceptions are the shallow waters at river-mouths which may extend 300–400m off-shore.

There are numerous attractive anchorages but all are open to the sea one way or another; none have all-round shelter and if the wind is from the wrong quarter, the swell comes rolling in. Often the sheltered places are occupied by moorings. Many of the better known anchorages are mentioned and, for some, details are given. For more adequate shelter, there are harbours and an increasing number of marinas.

Though tourism has been established for some time, development along the Costa Brava is not so raw and ugly as that along the coastline to the southwest. Moreover, there are no really large towns and very little industry. The price is paid in more literal terms. Prices for holiday properties increase along the coast of Spain from south west to north east: harbour dues in the Costa Brava are about double those in the Costa del Sol. Proximity to France adds to the demand on yachting facilities and it is more important to arrange a berth in advance of arrival on the Costa Brava than it is on the other coasts.

Meteorological

Winds

The main danger in this area comes from the sudden arrival of a NW *tramontana* (*tramuntana mestral*, *mistral*), a very strong cold dry wind which arrives with little warning from a clear blue sky and often reaches gale force in a quarter of an hour. In winter these winds can be severe and contingency plans should always be made when at sea and extra mooring or berthing lines used when in harbour in the expectation of their sudden onset. Many *calas* that offer good protection from this wind on an otherwise barren coast have been included and advice as to the best place to secure inside harbours under these conditions has been given where applicable.

On occasion this wind can blow from the N and also to a lesser extent the NE wind and the E *levanter (llevant)* may be experienced. These latter winds are usually preceded by a heavy swell and clouds with rain and poor visibility accompanying them. They rarely reach gale force but their seas can be dangerous.

Harbours of refuge

The following harbours can be entered with strong winds and gales from seaward although with some difficulty:

Puerto de Sant Feliu de Guíxols
Puerto de Palamós
Puerto de Port de la Selva
Puerto de Roses

Magnetic variation

0°40'W (2002). Decreasing 7' annually.

Tides

The maximum spring range is under 0·5m and its effects are small.

Currents

There is a permanent S-going current of 1–2 knots. It is stronger off promontories and especially off Cabo Creus. Winds from N and E quarters tend to increase the flow and those from the S and W tend to reduce it.

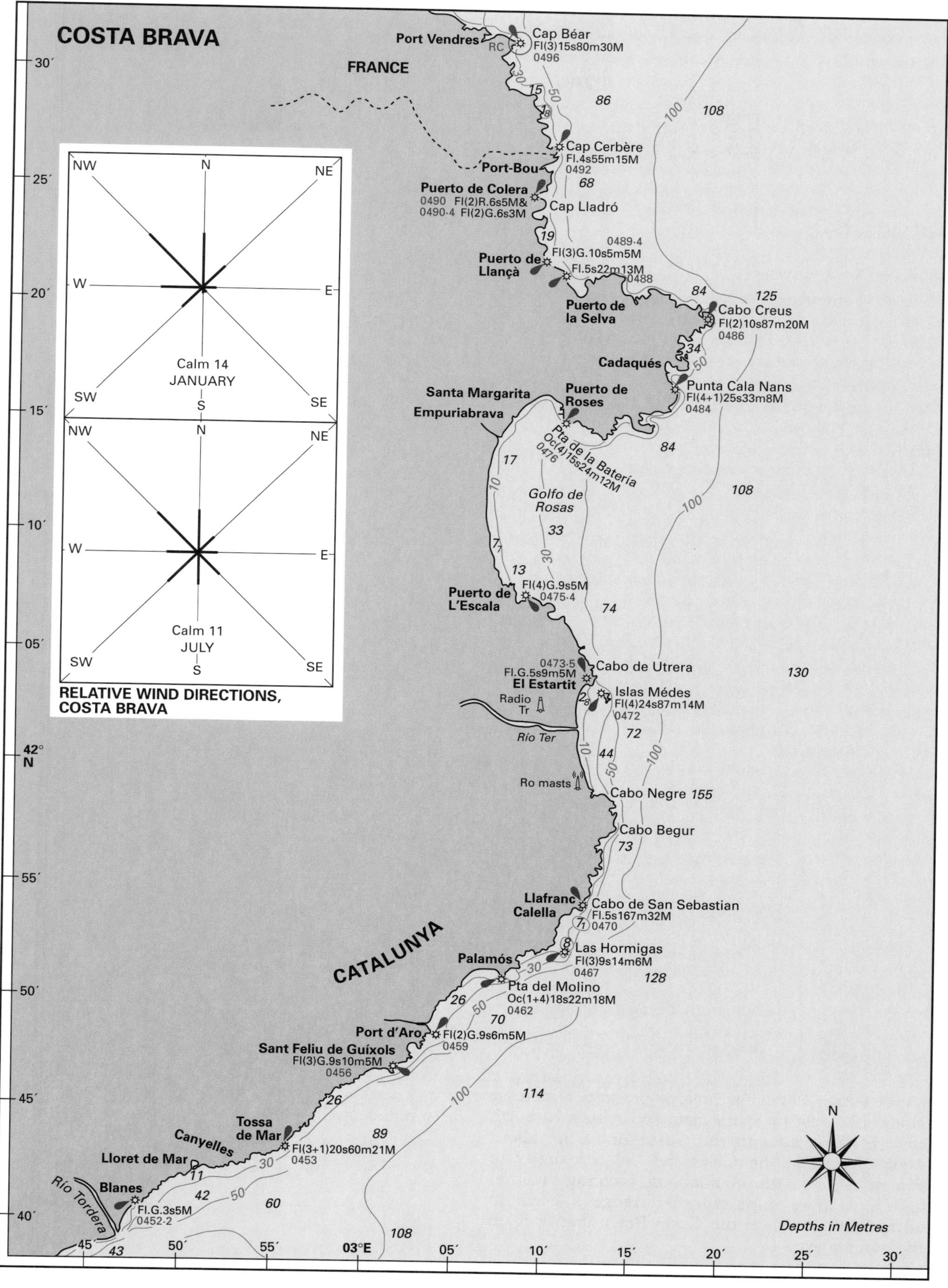
COSTA BRAVA
FRANCE
Port Vendres
Cap Béar
Fl(3)15s80m30M
0496
Cap Cerbère
Fl.4s55m15M
0492
Port-Bou
Puerto de Colera
0490 Fl(2)R.6s5M&
0490·4 Fl(2)G.6s3M
Cap Lladró
0489·4
Fl(3)G.10s5m5M
Puerto de Llançà
Fl.5s22m13M
0488
Puerto de la Selva
Cabo Creus
Fl(2)10s87m20M
0486
Cadaqués
Punta Cala Nans
Fl(4+1)25s33m8M
0484
Santa Margarita
Empuriabrava
Puerto de Roses
Pta de la Batería
Oc(4)15s24m12M
0476
Golfo de Rosas
Puerto de L'Escala
Fl(4)G.9s5M
0475·4
Cabo de Utrera
0473·5
Fl.G.5s9m5M
El Estartit
Islas Médes
Fl(4)24s87m14M
0472
Radio Tr
Río Ter
Ro masts
Cabo Negre
Cabo Begur
Llafranc
Calella
Cabo de San Sebastian
Fl.5s167m32M
0470
Las Hormigas
Fl(3)9s14m6M
0467
CATALUNYA
Palamós
Pta del Molino
Oc(1+4)18s22m18M
0462
Port d'Aro
Fl(2)G.9s6m5M
0459
Sant Feliu de Guíxols
Fl(3)G.9s10m5M
0456
Tossa de Mar
Fl(3+1)20s60m21M
0453
Canyelles
Lloret de Mar
Blanes
Fl.G.3s5M
0452·2
Río Tordera
Depths in Metres
N
42° N
03°E
RELATIVE WIND DIRECTIONS, COSTA BRAVA
Calm 14
JANUARY
Calm 11
JULY

Planning Guide (Costa Brava)

Distance (miles)	*Harbours & Anchorages*	*Headlands*
	⚓ *El Portell*	Río Tordera
	Puerto de Blanes (page 124)	
	⚓ *La Falconera*	Punta de Santa Anna
	⚓ *L'Illa*	
	⚓ *Cala Bona*	
	⚓ *Cala La Llapizada*	
	⚓ *Playa Treumal*	Piedra Aguilla
	⚓ *Playa de Sta Cristina*	
4·5M	⚓ *Playa de la Buadella*	Punta de Sta Cristina
	⚓ *Playa de Fanals*	Punta d'en Sureda
	⚓ *NE of Punta Banys*	Punta de Banys
	⚓ *Playa de Lloret de Mar*	Punta d'en Rusaris
	⚓ *La Caleta*	
	⚓ *Calas E of Punta Roja*	Punta de Calafats
	⚓ *Cala de la Tortuga*	Punta de Capdells
		Punta de Sta Goita
	Puerto de Cala Canyelles (page 129)	
	⚓ *Cala Morisca*	
	⚓ *Playa de Llorell*	
3M	⚓ *N of Els Cars*	Punta Roquera
	⚓ *Cala Es Codolar*	
		Cabo de Tossa
	Puerto de Tossa de Mar (page 131)	
	⚓ *Playa de la Palma*	
	⚓ *N of Punta de la Palma*	Isla de la Palma
	⚓ *Cala Bona*	
	⚓ *Cala Pola*	Punta de Pola
	⚓ *Cala Giverola*	
	⚓ *Cala Futadera*	Punta Salions
6M	⚓ *Cala S of Punta d'en Bosch*	
	⚓ *Calas de Canyet & Els Canyerets*	Punta d'en Bosch
	⚓ *Cala del Uigueta*	
	⚓ *Cala de Port Salvi*	
	⚓ *Cala S of Pta. de los Pianetes*	Punta de Garbi
	⚓ *Cala de Tetuan*	
	⚓ **Puerto de Sant Feliu de Guíxols** (page 135)	
	⚓ *Anchorages E of Sant Feliu*	
	⚓ *Cala de Sant Pol (S'Agaro)*	Punta del Mula
2·5M	⚓ *Calas Pedrosa, de la Font, Vaques, Conca*	Punta del Pinell
	Port d'Aro (page 139)	
	⚓ *Playa (Platja) d'Aro*	
	⚓ *Playa de la Cova*	
	⚓ *Playas de Cap Roig & Belladona*	Cabo Roig
4M	⚓ *Cala Canyers*	
	⚓ *Playa de San Antonio*	Punta de Rocas Planas
	⚓ *Playa de Palamos*	
	Puerto de Palamós (page 143)	
		Punta del Molino
	Marina Palamos (page 145)	
	Islas Hormigas (Formigues) (page 147)	
		Cabo Gros
	⚓ *Cala Fosca*	
	⚓ *Cala S'Alguer*	
	⚓ *Cala Castell*	
4M	⚓ *Cala Cobertera o Coves*	Punta Castell
	⚓ *Cala Senia*	
	⚓ *Cala N of Punta Canyes*	
	⚓ *Calas Estreta, Remendon, Roco Bona & Planas*	
	⚓ *Cala Fumorisca*	Cap de Planas
	⚓ *Playa de la Cadena*	
	⚓ *Cala d'en Massoni*	

Distance	Harbours and anchorages	Headlands
	⚓ *Cala Golfet*	
	⚓ *Cala del Aigua Dolca*	Cabo Roig
		Punta Forcat
	Calella de Palafrugell (page 150)	
1M		Punta d'els Canons
	⚓ *Cala del Canadell*	
	Puerto de Llafranc (page 151)	
	⚓ *Cala de Gens*	Cabo San Sebastian
	⚓ *Cala Pedrosa*	
	⚓ *Cala Tamariu*	
3M		
	⚓ *Cala Aigua Xelida*	
	⚓ *Cova del Bisbe & Port d'Esclanya*	
		Punta del Mut
	Calas de Aiguablava y Fornells (page 156)	
	⚓ *Cala d'el Pins*	
2M		
		Cabo Begur
	Calas de Sa Tuna y Aiguafreda (page 158)	
	⚓ *Cala de Sa Riera*	
4M		
	⚓ *Playa de Pals*	Cabo Negre
	Puerto de L'Estarit (page 162)	
	Las Islas Médes (page 165)	
	⚓ *N of Punta Salines*	
	⚓ *Ensenada del Rossinyol*	Cabo d'Utrera
5M		
	⚓ *Golfo de la Morisca*	
	⚓ *Cala Ferriola*	
	⚓ *Cala de Montgo*	
		Punta Trenca Bracos
	Puerto de L'Escala (page 168)	
	⚓ *Calas de L'Escala*	
7M		
	⚓ *Las calas de Empuries*	
	Puerto de Empuriabrava (page 172)	
1M		
	Puerto de Santa Margarida (page 174)	
	⚓ *Bahia de Roses*	
1M		
	Puerto de Roses (Rosas) (page 176)	
	⚓ *Cala de Canyelles Petites*	Punta de la Bateria
	⚓ *Cala de Canyelles Grosses*	
	⚓ *Cala Llaurador*	Punta Falconera (Cabo Falco)
	⚓ *Cala Murtra*	
	⚓ *Cala Rustella*	
8M		
	⚓ *Cala de Montjoi*	
	⚓ *Cala Pelosa*	
	⚓ *Cala de Joncols (Jontulls)*	Punta de la Creu
	⚓ *Cala Nans*	
	⚓ *Cala Conca*	
	Puerto de Cadaqués (page 183)	
	⚓ *Playa del Ros*	
2M		
		Isla Arenella
	Cala de Port Lligat (page 186)	
	⚓ *Playa d'en Ballesta & Playa de l'Alqueria*	Isletas Massina
	⚓ *Cala Guillola & Cala Jonquet*	
	⚓ *Cala Bona*	Punta d'en Cudera
2M		
	⚓ *Cala d'Illes*	
	⚓ *Cala Jugadora*	
	⚓ *Cala Fredosa (Cova del Infern)*	
	Cabo Creus y Freus (page 190)	Cabo Creus
	⚓ *Cala Culip*	
	⚓ *Cala Portalo*	
	⚓ *Cala de Galladera*	
	⚓ *Cala de Mula*	
	⚓ *Cala Portitxo*	Punta d'els Farallons

Visits

Details of interesting local places to visit are listed with the harbour concerned. There are a number of places worth visiting located some distance inland which can be reached by public transport or taxi. These include:

Caldas de Malavella, a small place inland from Tossa with ruins of old Roman baths and an old church.

Romany a de la Selva where there is a Megalithic tomb. The village is located behind San Feliu de Guíxols.

Girona, the largest and most important town in the area, originally a Roman settlement where many old churches can be seen, together with old buildings and walls dating from the time of the Moors. There is a cathedral, several museums and a castle.

Ullastret, not far from L'Estartit which has some Iberian and Greek remains and an 11th-century church.

Figueres, a major town lying behind the Golfo de Roses, founded by the Romans on their Via Augusta. It has a castle almost intact, a museum and a monastery.

Empuries, on the coast near L'Escala, is the most important archaeological site on the Costa Brava. It represents a microcosm of the history of this coast. The two Greek settlements of Paleopolis and Neapolis, sometimes called Emporion (c.500BC) were taken over in 209BC by the Romans and renamed Empuries. It co-existed with the nearby settlements of Iberian natives until it was first over-run by the Barbarians, then destroyed by the Moors and later ravaged by Norman pirates. The ruins were covered by sand and silt and in part built over by the small village of Sant Martí only to be rediscovered some 1000 years later. These ruins are well worth a visit.

⚓ El Portell

El Portell: anchor off the beach according to draught.

Puerto de Blanes

41°40'N 2°47'E

Charts

British Admiralty *1704*
French *4827, 7298*
Spanish *873, 4913, 491*
Navicarte *E05*

Lights

0452 **Dique de Abrigo** 41°40'·4N 2°47'·9E Fl.G.3s7m5M White post, green top 3m
0452·2 **Espigon head** Fl.G.3s7m5M White post, green top 3m
0452·1 **Dique Interna head** Fl(2)R.6s6m2M Red post 4m

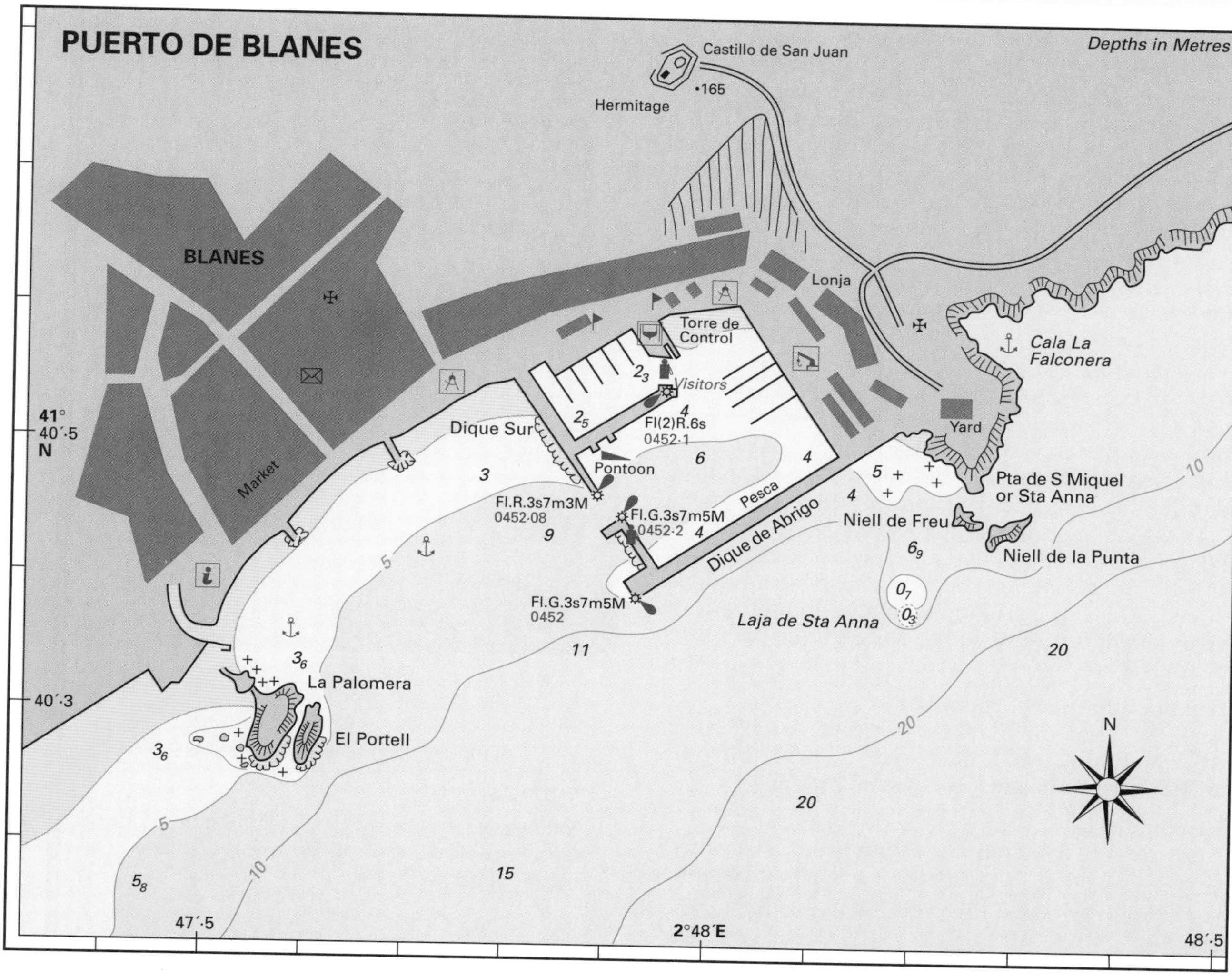

0452·08 **Dique Interna Spur** Fl.R.3s7m3M White post on white block, red top 3m

To the north

0453 **Cabo Tossa** 41°42'·9N 2°56'·0E Fl(3+1)20s60m21M White tower 11m 229·7°-vis - 064·2°

Port communications

VHF Ch 9. *Capitanía* ☎ 972 330 552 *Fax* 972 331 498, *email* club@cvblanes.es http://www.cvblanes.es

General

A fishing and yachting harbour based on an old port and improved by breakwaters, quays and pontoons. The harbour is easy to approach and enter but heavy winds between SE and S may send swell into the harbour. The surrounding area is attractive and the town is pleasant. The harbour is crowded in summer.

The botanical garden and the 14th-century church and ruined palace are interesting. The view from Castillo de San Juan on the top of the hill behind the harbour is worth the climb. There is a fine sandy beach to the W of the harbour and to the northeast are a number of attractive small *calas* that can be visited by boat.

Originally a Roman port called Blanda, it once rivalled Barcelona and Tarragona but little remains of that era. The port did not develop at the same rate as its rivals and remained under the Counts of Cabrera whose ruined palace is beside the church.

Puerto de Blanes

Approach

From the south A narrow coastal plain backed by ranges of mountains gives way to the deep flat delta of the Río Tordera which projects about ½M out to sea and must be given a berth of at least ¼M because of shoals. The isolated conical hill topped by the Castillo de San Juan which lies just behind this harbour can be seen from afar. The small low rocky Islets de la Palomera and El Portell lie very close inshore just before this harbour is reached, they have deep water to seaward of them but are shoal either side.

From the north Cabo Tossa, a rocky-cliffed peninsula with a conspicuous lighthouse and castle with towers, is easily recognised. The coast remains broken and rocky-cliffed with a number of *calas* and small bays. The conical hill topped by Castillo de San Juan is conspicuous from this direction.

Punta de Santa Anna (or San Miquel) just to the NE of this harbour has outlying rocky islets and shoals. It should not be approached nearer than 300m and the harbour entrance should not be approached until the head of the Dique de Abrigo bears NW.

Anchorage in the approach

Anchor 300m to W of the head of the Dique de Abrigo in 6m, sand and weed. There are other anchorages in the area, see harbour plan.

Entrance

Approach the Dique de Abrigo on a northerly course, leaving it 50m to starboard and turn slowly to starboard to enter between the pier heads.

Berths

There are 2 mooring areas – one on the NE of the harbour with 4 pontoons for small (<8m) craft administered by the commune and seemingly controlled by a man who lives in a white house in the N corner of the harbour. The *club náutico* controls the pontoons in the NW side of the harbour. It is advised to go round the end of the internal quay and moor to the fuelling berth for berthing instructions if it has not been possible to contact the *capitanía* previously.

Charges

High.

Facilities

Maximum length overall 15m.
A shipyard in the E corner of the harbour. Here or elsewhere in the harbour repairs to wood and GRP hulls, engines and sails.
50-tonne travel-lift.
3-tonne crane.
A slip in N corner of the harbour.
Chandlery on the front near the harbour and another beside the harbour.
Water on the quays and pontoons.
220v on the pontoons.
Gasoleo A and petrol.
Ice is delivered daily to a store behind the *lonja*.
Club de Vela de Blanes has a clubhouse beside the inner harbour with bar, lounge, restaurant, terrace, showers, etc.
Many shops and supermarkets in the town and a market every day except Sunday.
Launderette in the town.

Communications

Bus and rail service. Taxi ☎ 972 330 037.

⚓ La Falconera

An anchorage in a rocky-cliffed bay open between NE and SE. Small stoney beach, crowded in season. Road and houses ashore.

⚓ L'Illa

Anchorage on S side of a hooked promontory in sand and stone with off-lying islets, open between E and S, road ashore.

⚓ Cala Bona

Cala Bona: anchor off the beach in sand. Open between NE and SE.

⚓ Cala La Llapizada

A rocky sided *cala*. Anchor in N corner under headland with house on its point and off-lying islet,

⚓ Playa Treumal

Playa Treumal: anchor off either beach. Open between NE and SE.

Piedra Agulla, to its E. Anchor in sand and stone – open between E and S. Road ashore.

⚓ Playa de Sta Cristina

Anchorage off a wide sandy beach in sand, open between E and SE. Beach café/bar, pleasure boats.

⚓ Playa de la Buadella

Sandy beach between two rocky headlands. Anchor in sand off beach, open between E and S. Beach café/bar.

⚓ NE of Punta de Banys

A rocky-cliffed *cala*, anchor near centre in sand and stone, track ashore.

⚓ La Caleta

A small *cala* at the E end of the Playa de Lloret de Mar below a castle with a small beach, usually crowded. Anchor in sand near the centre. Open between S and SW.

For the preceeding anchorages, see plans on page 128.

⚓ Playa de Fanals

Playa de Fanals: anchor according to draught in sand. Open between NE and SE with some shelter at each end. Beach café/bars, showers.

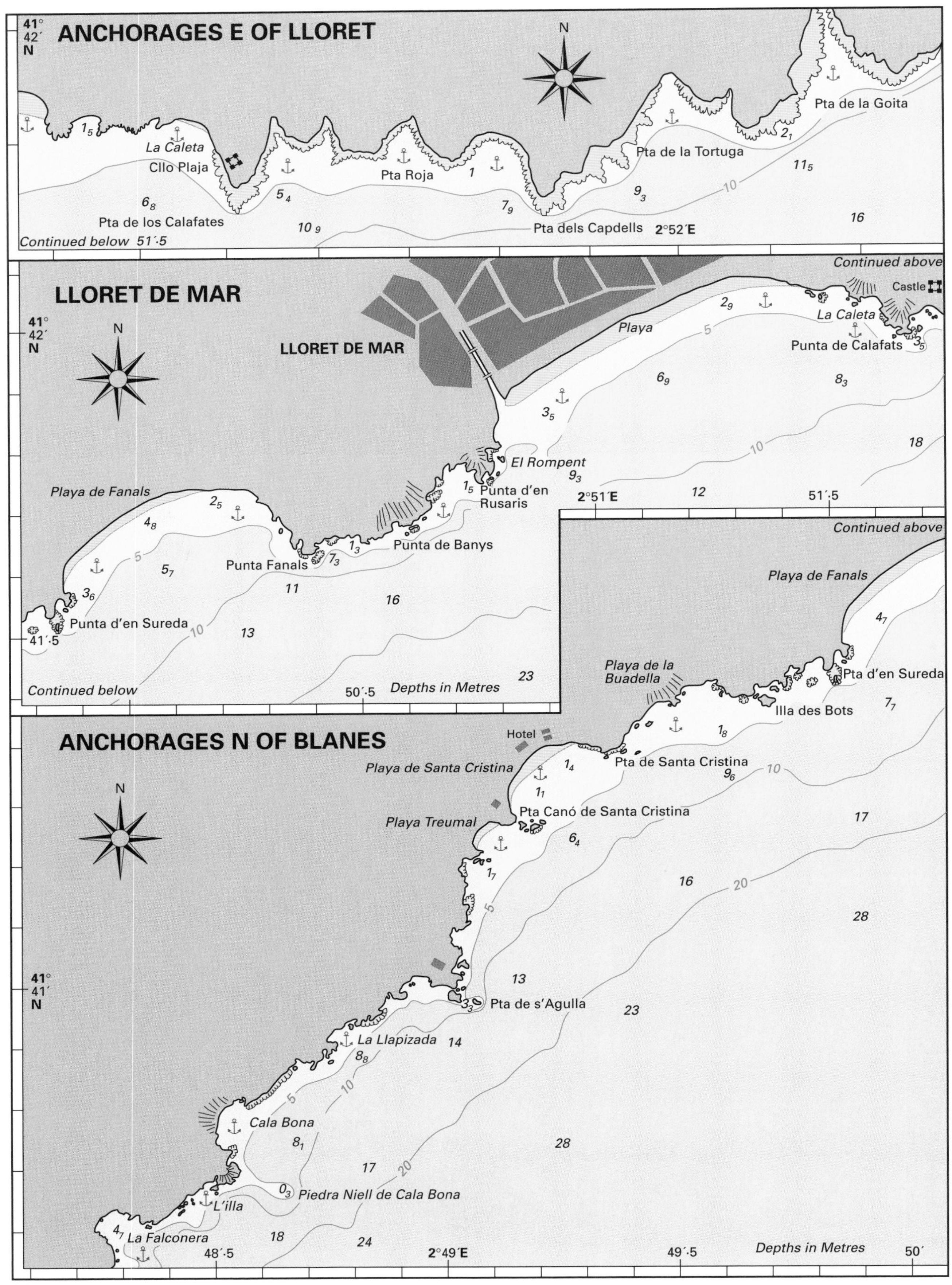
ANCHORAGES E OF LLORET
La Caleta
Cllo Plaja
Pta de los Calafates
Pta Roja
Pta dels Capdells
Pta de la Tortuga
Pta de la Goita
2°52´E
Continued below 51´·5
LLORET DE MAR
LLORET DE MAR
Playa
Continued above
Castle
La Caleta
Punta de Calafats
El Rompent
Punta d'en Rusaris
2°51´E
51´·5
Playa de Fanals
Punta de Banys
Punta Fanals
Punta d'en Sureda
41´·5
Continued below
50´·5
Depths in Metres
ANCHORAGES N OF BLANES
Continued above
Playa de Fanals
Pta d'en Sureda
Playa de la Buadella
Illa des Bots
Hotel
Playa de Santa Cristina
Pta de Santa Cristina
Pta Canó de Santa Cristina
Playa Treumal
Pta de s'Agulla
La Llapizada
Cala Bona
Piedra Niell de Cala Bona
L'illa
La Falconera
48´·5
2°49´E
49´·5
Depths in Metres
50´

⚓ Playa de Lloret de Mar

Playa de Lloret de Mar: open between E and SW with some shelter at either end. Very crowded ashore in summer.

⚓ Calas to E of Punta Roja

A series of rocky-edged small *calas* with a pair of islets – take extra care. Low rocky cliffs with roads and houses ashore. Anchor in sand and stone. Open between SE and SW.

⚓ Cala de la Tortuga

A V-shaped *cala* with stony beach at its head, road and houses ashore. Anchor in sand and stone, open between SE and SW. A similar *cala* lies to E on the other side of the Punta de Santa Goita.

⚓ Punta de Santa Goita

An inconspicuous point lying just to W of Cala Canyelles, rocky-cliffed and tree-covered with some houses. 10m depths near the point.

Puerto de Cala Canyelles (Cañelles)

41°42'N 2°53'E

Charts
British Admiralty *1704*
French *4827*
Spanish *873, 492*
Navicarte *E05*

Lights
0452·7 **Dique de Abrigo head** 41°42'·3N 2°52'·9E
Fl(4)G.11s5m5M Green tower 3m
To the north
0453 **Cabo Tossa** 41°42'·9N 2°56'·0E
Fl(3+1)20s60m21M White tower 11m 229·7°-vis-064·2°

Port communications
VHF Ch 9. *Capitanía* ☎ 972 368 818.

General
A yacht harbour for smaller yachts (8m max) and fishing boats. Built into the W end of a beach at the side of an attractive *cala*. Entrance is normally easy but could be difficult with strong winds between E and SW. The swell from these winds also makes it

Puerto de Cala Canyelles

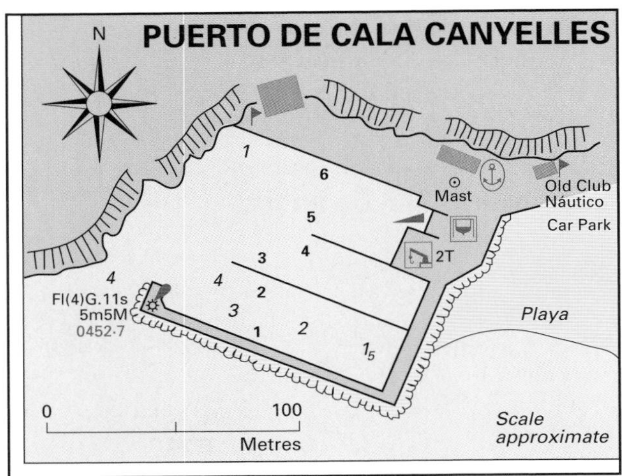

uncomfortable inside the harbour. Facilities are limited, provisions are available from shops in the nearby village.

The area around has been built over with large private houses and the beach of fine sand to the E of the harbour is crowded in summer with day-trippers.

Approach

From the south Puerto de Blanes is unmistakable with Castillo de San Juan on a hill behind it. Further NE there are some eight *calas*, most with sandy beaches at their head, the largest being the Playa de Fanals and the Playa de Lloret which has the town of Lloret de Mar behind it with a conspicuous church tower. There are a few small *calas* to E of the Playa de Lloret de Mar but the next large *cala* has a sandy beach with the harbour at its west end.

From the north Puerto Sant Feliu de Guíxols is easily recognised by its long breakwater and the prominent Punta de Garbí on the W side. Broken rocky cliffs with small *calas* extend 5·5M to Cabo Tossa which has a conspicuous lighthouse and tower on its summit. The harbour lies 2¼M to SW of Cabo Tossa. Do not mistake the large *cala* of Playa de Lloret (no connection with the Playa de Lloret de Mar which lies opposite the town of the same name which is only 1·5M from Cabo de Tossa). This stretch of coast has broken rocky cliffs with many small *calas*. The sandy beach and harbour of Cala de Canyelles are easily seen when S of the *cala*.

Anchorage in the approach

300m to S of the sandy beach of Cala de Canyelles in 10m, sand and stone.

Entrance

The entrance, which is only 12m wide, lies to the W side of the harbour between the head of the Dique de Abrigo and the red rocky cliffs.

Approach the head of the Dique de Abrigo and enter, keeping close to the head, at slow speed with a bow lookout because the channel is narrow.

Berths

Secure to a vacant berth and ask the *capitanía* for a berth.

⚓ Cala Es Codolar

Cala Es Codolar: open between SE and SW. A pre-Roman anchorage and harbour. See plan of Tossa, page 132.

Facilities
Maximum length overall 8m.
Mechanic for simple repairs.
2-tonne crane.
A small slip in NE corner of the harbour.
Small hard-standing.
Water on the quays.
Provisions from the village up the hill or in Lloret de Mar 3M away.
Club Náutico de Cala Canyelles now operates from a porta-cabin in low season and the restaurant/bar may now belong to a private concern.

Communications
Bus service on coast road 0·5M inland.

⚓ Cala Morisca
A small V-shaped *cala* with stony beach at its head, anchor in mid-*cala* in rock and sand, open between SE–S–SW.

⚓ Playa de Llorell
Anchor off sand and pebble beach in sand open between SE and SW. Beach café/bar, road, some houses and apartment blocks.

⚓ N of Els Cars
A small bay open between E and S with rocky coast and cliffs. Anchor in sand and rock in middle.

Puerto de Tossa de Mar
41°43'N 2°56'E

Charts
British Admiralty *1704*
French *4827, 7505*
Spanish *873, 876, 491*
Navicarte *E04, E05*

Lights
0453 **Cabo Tossa** 41°42'·9N 2°56'·0E
Fl(3+1)20s60m21M White tower 11m 229·7°-vis-064·2°

General
Not actually a harbour but an important and very attractive anchorage. Under Tossa it is well sheltered from the prevailing winds though open between NE and SE; further north up the bay the anchorages are more exposed to the south. In the season the bay is crowded with tourists.

Tossa is a very old harbour and town that has been in occupation since pre-Roman times. The Romans called it Turissa. It was, like the rest of the towns on this coast, destroyed by the Vandals and rebuilt only to be destroyed again. In the 10th century the Castrum de Tursia, as it was then called, was given by the Count of Barcelona to the monks of Ripoll. Between the two world wars this town was discovered by foreign tourists and became a popular resort. There are many interesting places to visit including a Roman villa, the old town (Villa Vella), a Baroque church and a museum. The view from the lighthouse is worth the climb.

Puerto de Tossa de Mar

Approach
From the south The coast from Blanes, which can be recognised by the conical hill topped by a small castle, is very broken and rocky-cliffed with many *calas*. The concentration of houses and flats at Lloret de Mar where there is a long sandy beach is easy to identify. The lighthouse and tower on Cabo de Tossa can be seen from afar.

From the north From Punta de Garbí the coast is likewise very broken with rocky cliffs and ranges of hills inland. The lighthouse and tower at Cabo Tossa is also conspicuous from this direction.

Entrance
The easiest entrance is on a NW course towards the river mouth where there is a gap in the line of buildings.

From the northeast, the passage between Punta de la Palma and Isla de la Palma should only be attempted in good conditions with caution and then only at the N side of the passage between Punta de la Palma and the 0·3m shallows of Pedras del Freu. Use in a NE–SW direction; minimum depth 3·0m. When through, beware the unmarked rocky shoal Llosa de la Palma, 2m, in the N half of the bay.

Anchorage
Anchor where indicated on the chart to suit prevailing wind in 4m, sand. The nearest alternatives are Es Codolar to the south or Playa de la Palma to the north.

Landings
On the sandy beach where and when swell allows.

Facilities
Many shops of all kinds in the town.

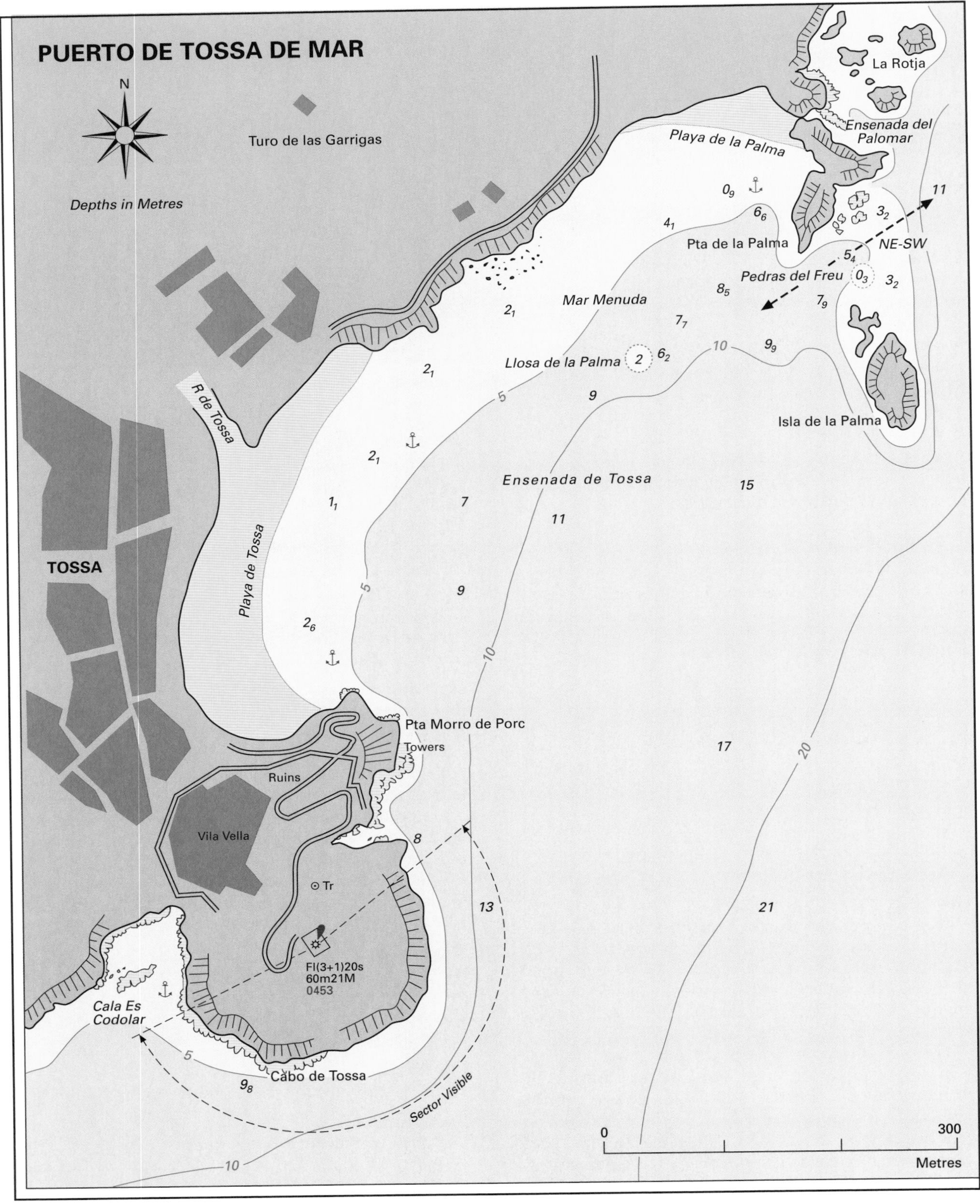
PUERTO DE TOSSA DE MAR
N
Turo de las Garrigas
Depths in Metres
TOSSA
R de Tossa
Playa de Tossa
Playa de la Palma
Ensenada del Palomar
La Rotja
Pta de la Palma
NE-SW
Pedras del Freu
Mar Menuda
Llosa de la Palma
Isla de la Palma
Ensenada de Tossa
Pta Morro de Porc
Towers
Ruins
Vila Vella
Tr
Fl(3+1)20s
60m21M
0453
Cala Es Codolar
Cabo de Tossa
Sector Visible
0
300
Metres

⚓ Playa de la Palma

Playa de la Palma: anchor in 5m, sand, stone and weed. Open to S. See plan page 132.

⚓ N of Punta de la Palma

A wide rocky bay with three small *calas*. Anchor in 5m sand, stone and weed in mid-bay, open between E and S.

⚓ Cala Bona

A long narrow *cala* open between E and SE with rocky tree-covered sides and sandy beach at its head, with a beach café/bar. Anchor in mid-*cala*, sand and rock.

Punta de Pola

A rocky-cliffed, tree-covered headland with high ground inland, ending in a conspicuous hump. Dangerous rocks off the point but 5m depths nearby.

⚓ Cala Pola

Cala Pola: 300m NE of Cala Bona. Open between SE and S.

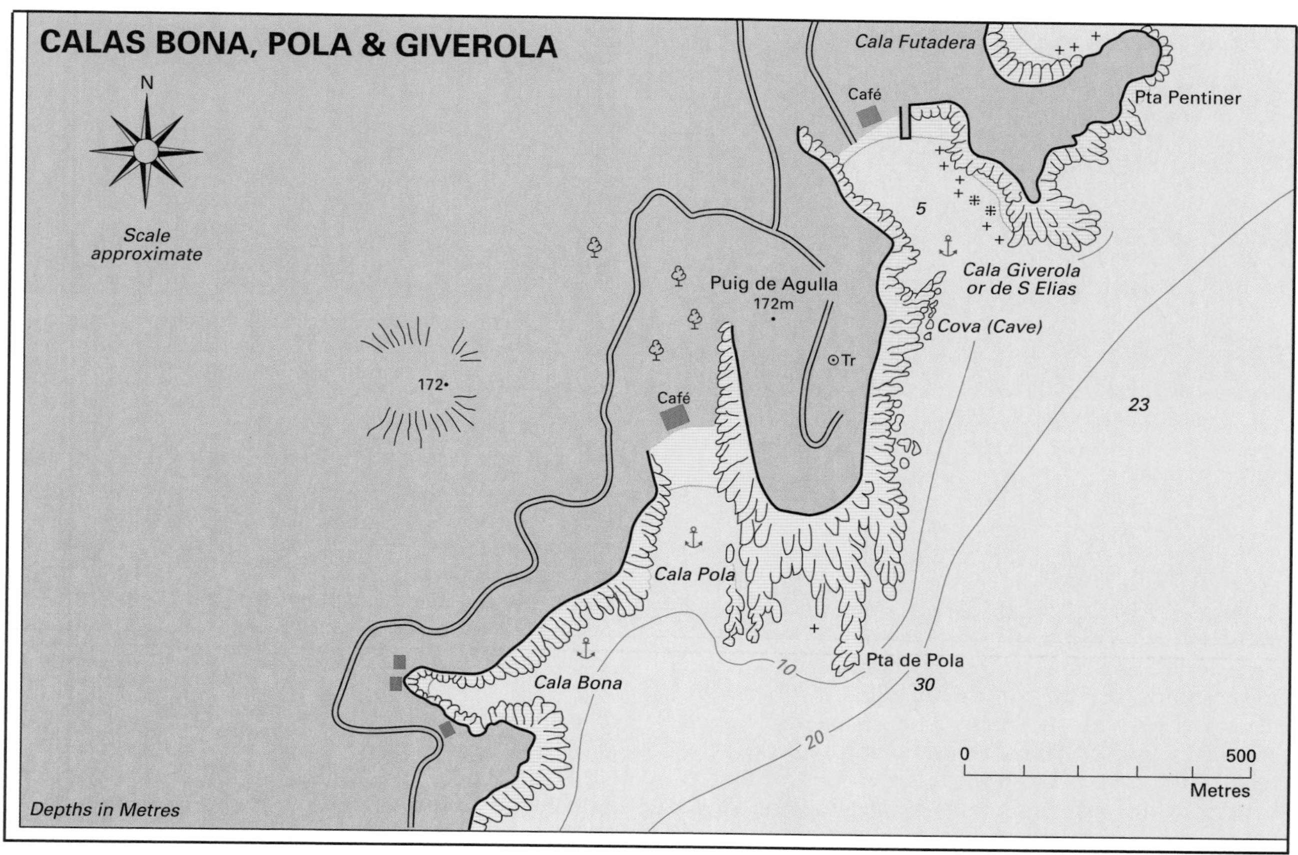

⚓ Cala to S of Punta d'en Bosch

Punta d'en Bosch: this *cala* south of en Bosch does not welcome yachts in summer.

⚓ Cala Giverola (or de St Elias)

Cala Giverola (or de St Elias): in summer reserved for swimmers. Open between E and S. A cave on the W side can be entered by dinghy.

⚓ Cala del Uigueta

A large *cala* with rocky-cliffed sides and inshore rocks, small sand and stone beach at its head. Ermita de Sant Elm (100m) a church with a small spire stands on top of the headland. There are several very small sub-*calas*. The main *cala* is open between S and W. Anchor in sand and rock near the head of the *cala*. It has been reported (2000) that in easterly winds effluent builds up around the small jetty in this *cala*.

⚓ Cala Futadera

Cala Futadera: anchor in the middle, sand and rock. Open between NE and SE.

⚓ Cala de Port Salvi

A small *cala* on the SE point of Punta de Garbí open between E and S. Unfortunately, throughout the summer season, a diving mark (Flag 'A' on yellow inflatable) is moored permanently in the middle of the *cala* and diving training by the Eden Roc Diving Centre takes place most days. For this reason it is not recommended to anchor in this *cala*. There is a 1·1m shoal 50m to S of the mass of Punta Garbí.

Punta de Garbí

A very prominent and conspicuous high headland with rocky cliffs which has rocky dangers extending 50m to SE and there is a 1·1m shoal 50m to S of point. The Ermita de Sant Elm stands on the crest and there are many houses and apartments.

⚓ Calas de Canyet and Els Canyerets

Calas de Canyet and Els Canyerets: anchor off the beach of Els Canyerets (at the right of the photograph). Open between E and S.

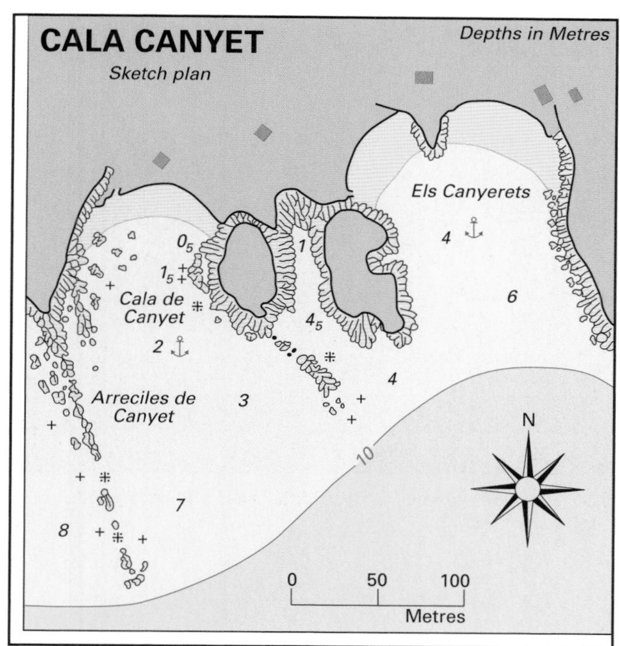

⚓ Cala between Punta de Garbí and Punta de las Planetes

A small *cala* open between NE and E with rocky sides. Anchor in mid-*cala,* rocks and stone.

⚓ Cala de Tetuán

Another small *cala* open between N and E with rocky cliffs around it. Anchor in mid-*cala,* rocks and stone.

See plan on page 137.

Puerto de Sant Feliu de Guíxols

41°46'N 3°01'E

Charts

British Admiralty *1704*
French *4827, 7008, 7505, 7298*
Spanish *876, 4922, 492*
Navicarte *E04*

Lights

0456 **Dique Rompeolas head** 41°46'·7N 3°02'·0E Fl(3)G.9s10m5M White tower, green top 5m
0458 **Anchorage Ldg Lts 343°**
Front Iso.3s7m4M o on white mast, black bands 5m
0458·1 *Rear* 52m from front Oc.3s14m4M o on white mast, black bands 12m

Port communications

VHF Ch 9. *Capitanía* ☎ 972 321 700 *Fax* 972 321 300.

General

A fishing, commercial and yachting harbour improved by the addition of a breakwater, quays and pontoons. The town and area are attractive but considerable tourist development continues apace and many old buildings are being pulled down. Swell from winds between E and S comes into the harbour.

This very old harbour, known to the Romans as Gesoria, came to fame by virtue of its monastery, originally built before the 8th century but then destroyed by the Moors and rebuilt in the 10th and 11th centuries. The abbot was feudal lord of the large area and the town and port prospered, becoming the most important town in the SE of Spain. During the Middle Ages the local people continuously fought against their overlords and

Puerto de Sant Feliu de Guíxols

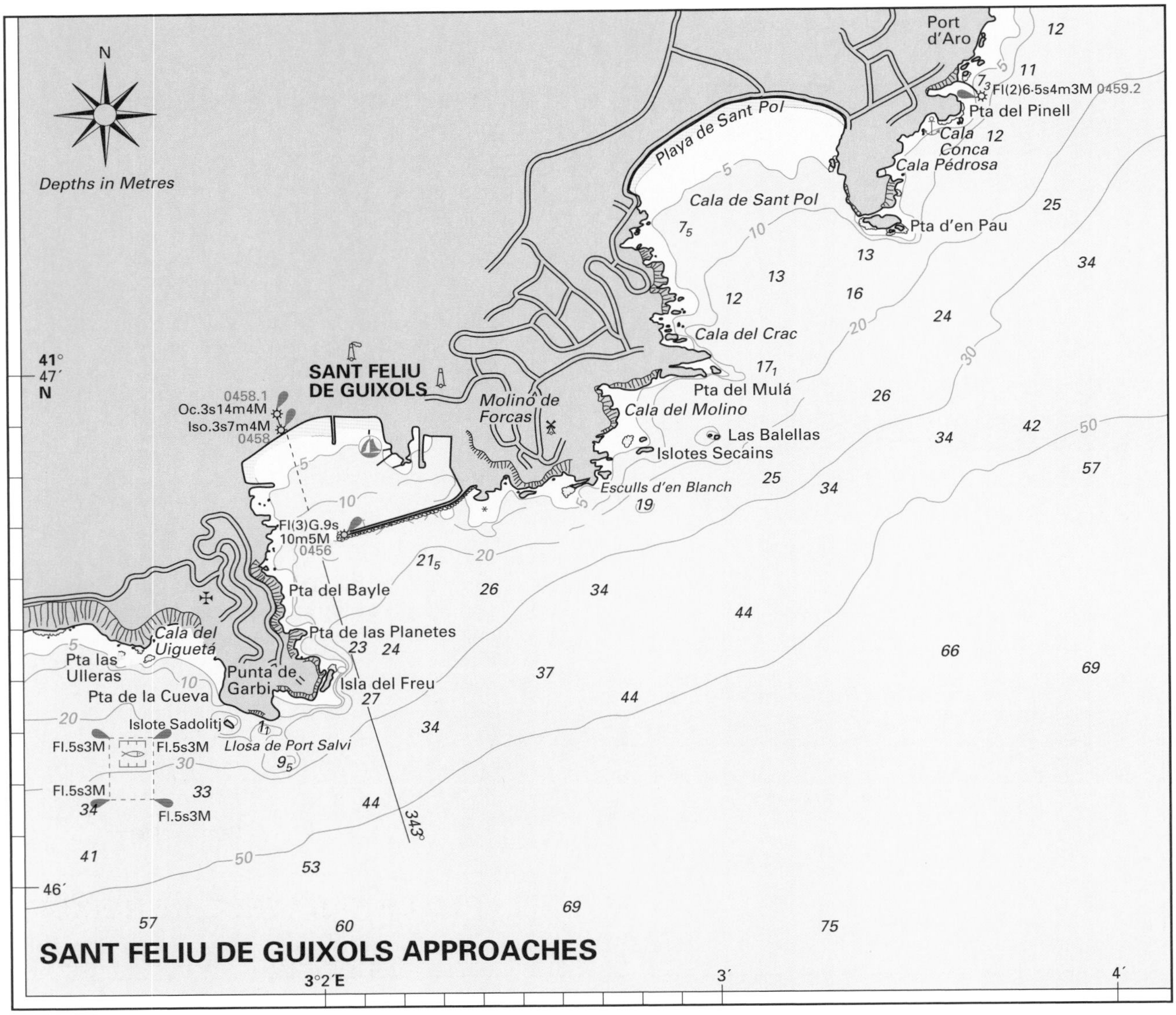

N

Depths in Metres

Port d'Aro

Fl(2)6·5s4m3M 0459.2

Pta del Pinell

Cala Conca

Cala Pédrosa

Playa de Sant Pol

Cala de Sant Pol

Pta d'en Pau

Cala del Crac

Pta del Mulá

Cala del Molino

Las Balellas

Islotes Secains

Esculls d'en Blanch

Molino de Forcas

SANT FELIU DE GUIXOLS

0458.1 Oc.3s14m4M

Iso.3s7m4M 0458

Fl(3)G.9s 10m5M 0456

Pta del Bayle

Pta de las Planetes

Isla del Freu

Cala del Uiguetá

Punta de Garbi

Pta las Ulleras

Pta de la Cueva

Islote Sadolitj

Llosa de Port Salvi

Fl.5s3M

Fl.5s3M

Fl.5s3M

Fl.5s3M

343°

41° 47′ N

46′

3°2′E

3′

4′

SANT FELIU DE GUIXOLS APPROACHES

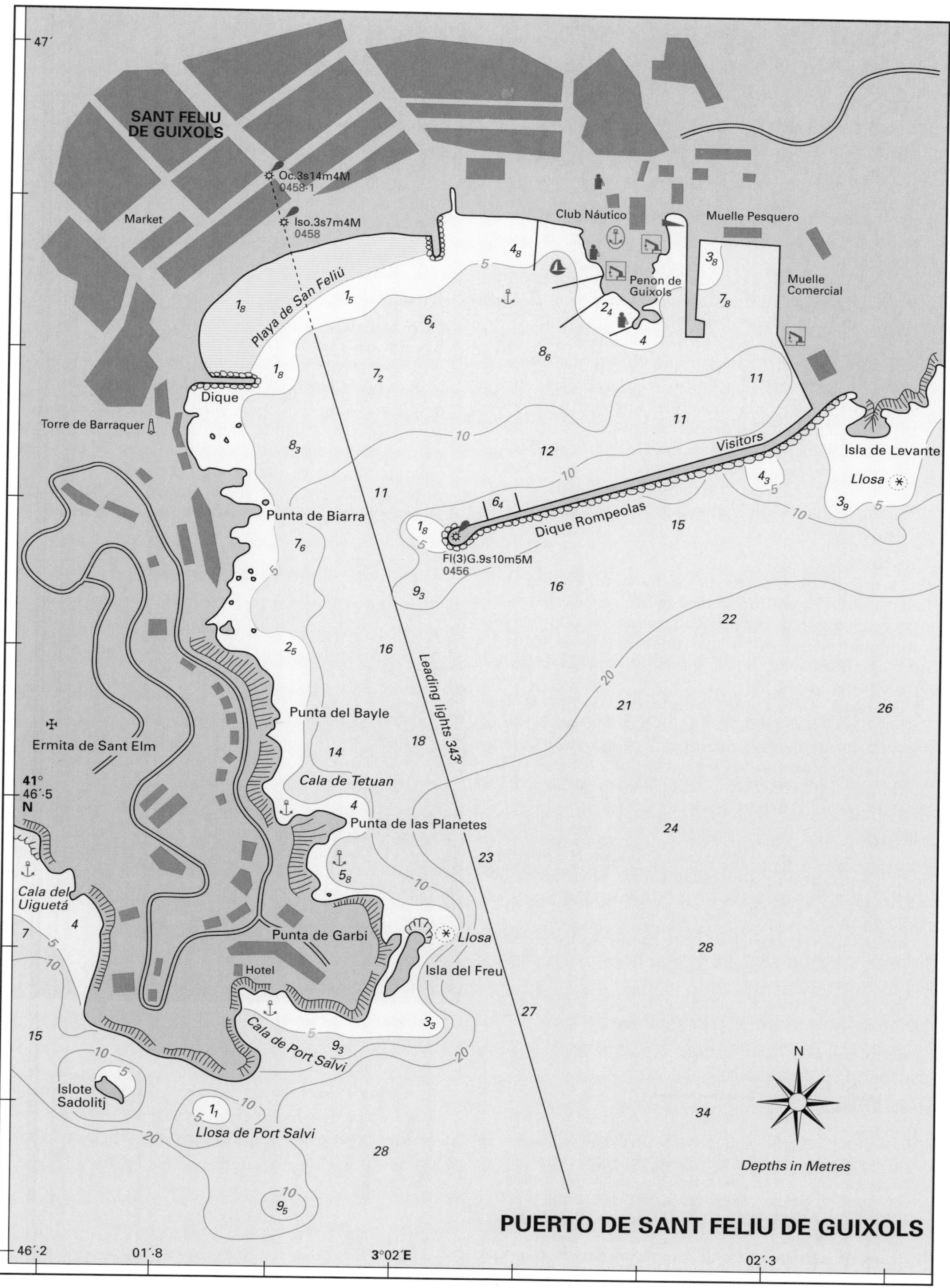
SANT FELIU DE GUIXOLS
Oc.3s14m4M 0458·1
Iso.3s7m4M 0458
Market
Playa de San Feliú
Club Náutico
Muelle Pesquero
Penon de Guixols
Muelle Comercial
Dique
Torre de Barraquer
Visitors
Isla de Levante
Llosa
Punta de Biarra
Dique Rompeolas
Fl(3)G.9s10m5M 0456
Leading lights 343°
Punta del Bayle
Ermita de Sant Elm
Cala de Tetuan
Punta de las Planetes
Cala del Uigueta
Punta de Garbi
Llosa
Isla del Freu
Hotel
Cala de Port Salvi
Islote Sadolitj
Llosa de Port Salvi
Depths in Metres
N
47′
41° 46′·5 N
46′·2
01′·8
3°02′E
02′·3
PUERTO DE SANT FELIU DE GUIXOLS

eventually overthrew them. In the 18th century the cork trade brought further wealth and in recent years the tourist trade developed.

The museum in the old monastery and the 14th-century church can be visited and the view from the Ermita de Sant Elm is worth the climb. There is a pleasant beach ½M to E of harbour; the fine sandy beaches to the NW are very crowded in summer.

Approach

From the south From the conspicuous lighthouse and castle with tower on Cabo Tossa the very broken rocky-cliffed coast continues northeast. Punta de Garbí with the Ermita de Sant Elm is prominent and easily recognised. Round this promontory at 200m or more and the harbour entrance will be seen. Pay attention to a 1·1m rocky shallow, Llosa de Port Salvi, 50m to S of the massif of Punta de Garbí.

From the north From the Bahía de Palamós, which is easily recognised by virtue of its harbour wall and mass of houses and high-rise buildings, the rugged coast is broken by the wide sandy Bahía de Platja d'Aro and an almost square-shaped Cala de Sant Pol. Punta de Garbí is also prominent from this direction. Keep ½M off this section of coast to avoid off-lying shoals.

Entrance

On a course of 343° enter the harbour leaving the head of the Dique Rompeolas 100m to starboard. It may be possible to see the leading marks, two sets of round white discs with black diagonal stripes located on white masts with black bands in the trees in front of the town.

The head of the Dique Rompeolas and that of the small *dique* on the E side of the harbour have been washed away several times and much rubble lies near their heads underwater; give them a berth of at least 30m. When clear of the head turn to a NE course.

Berths

Go bow to the inner side of the Dique Rompeolas with a stern line to a mooring buoy. The outer half of the *dique* is allocated to the *club náutico* and has yellow railings.

In season, secure stern-to the pontoons located on W side of Peñón de Guíxols with bows to a mooring buoy.

In a NW *tramontana* secure in the lee of the Peñón de Guíxols or to the Muelle Pesquero.

Anchorages

Anchoring is forbidden.

Facilities

Maximum length overall 15m.
Minor repairs can be carried out by the shipyard and there are a number of mechanics for engine repair.
50-tonne crane in port, 6-tonne crane at the *club náutico*
Small slips on either side of the Peñón de Guíxols and a slipway on the NE side of the harbour with 2m of water at its foot.
Chandlery: Hipocampo, a shop in the street which is one back from the N side of the harbour. There is another chandler on the Muelle Comercial.
Water from the quays, pontoons, *club náutico* and the *lonja*.
220v AC at the *club náutico* and the Dique Rompeolas.
Gasoleo A and petrol from pumps at the *club náutico* and from service station just to the N of this club.
Ice from the *club náutico*, from a shop behind the market or from an ice factory near the root of the Dique Rompeolas.
Many good shops in the town and a good market which is open on Sundays.
Club Náutico de Sant Feliu de Guíxols has a clubhouse to the W of the Peñón de Guíxols with bar, lounge, terrace, restaurants, showers etc. Visitors using the club berths may use the club.
Launderettes in the town.
A weather forecast is posted daily at the *club náutico*.

Communications

Bus service. Taxi ☎ 972 320 934.

⚓ Anchorages E of Sant Feliu de Guíxols

The ¾M section of coast from the root of the Dique Rompeolas to Cala de Sant Pol is very broken with many small islets, *calas* and passages. It is a most spectacular and attractive area. Explore in a powered dinghy or shallow-draught yacht. Spanish chart 305A and a forward lookout are essential.

⚓ Cala de Sant Pol (S'Agaro)

Cala de Sant Pol (S'Agaro): open between E and S. S'Agaro is ½M to N and Sant Feliu 1M to SW. See plan page 136.

⚓ Calas Pédrosa, de la Font, Vaques, Conca

Four *calas* in a rocky-cliffed coast with large private houses on top of the cliffs. Anchor with care in mid-*cala*, sand, rock and weed. Open between NE and SE.

Port d'Aro

41°48'N 3°02'E

Charts

British Admiralty *1704*
French *4827, 7505*
Spanish *876, 492*
Navicarte *E04*

Lights

0459 **Playa de Aro Espigón head** 41°48'·1N 3°04'·0E Fl(2)G.9s6m5M Green metal column 3m
0459·2 **Contradique** Fl(2)R.6·5s4m3M Red column on pyramidal base 2m

To the northeast

0462 **Punta del Molino** 41°50'·6N 3°07'·8E Oc(1+4)18s22m18M White round tower, grey cupola 8m
0460 **Bajo Pereira (La Llosa de Palamós)** 41°50'·1N 3°07'·2E Fl(2)7s10m5M Red round tower, grey cupola

Port communications

VHF Ch 9. *Capitanía* ☎ 972 818 929 *Fax* 972 825 909.

General

A holiday development with a yacht harbour built on the delta of the Río Ridaura at the S end of the Playa de Platja d'Aro. Approach and entrance is simple but would be difficult and dangerous with strong winds between NE and SE which also send swell into the harbour. There are good facilities and other shops are available at S'Agaró 0·7M (where there is an interesting 14th-century cloister incorporated into a modern church), Castillo d'Aro 1·2M and behind the Playa (Platja) d'Aro. The long sandy beach to the N is very crowded in summer.

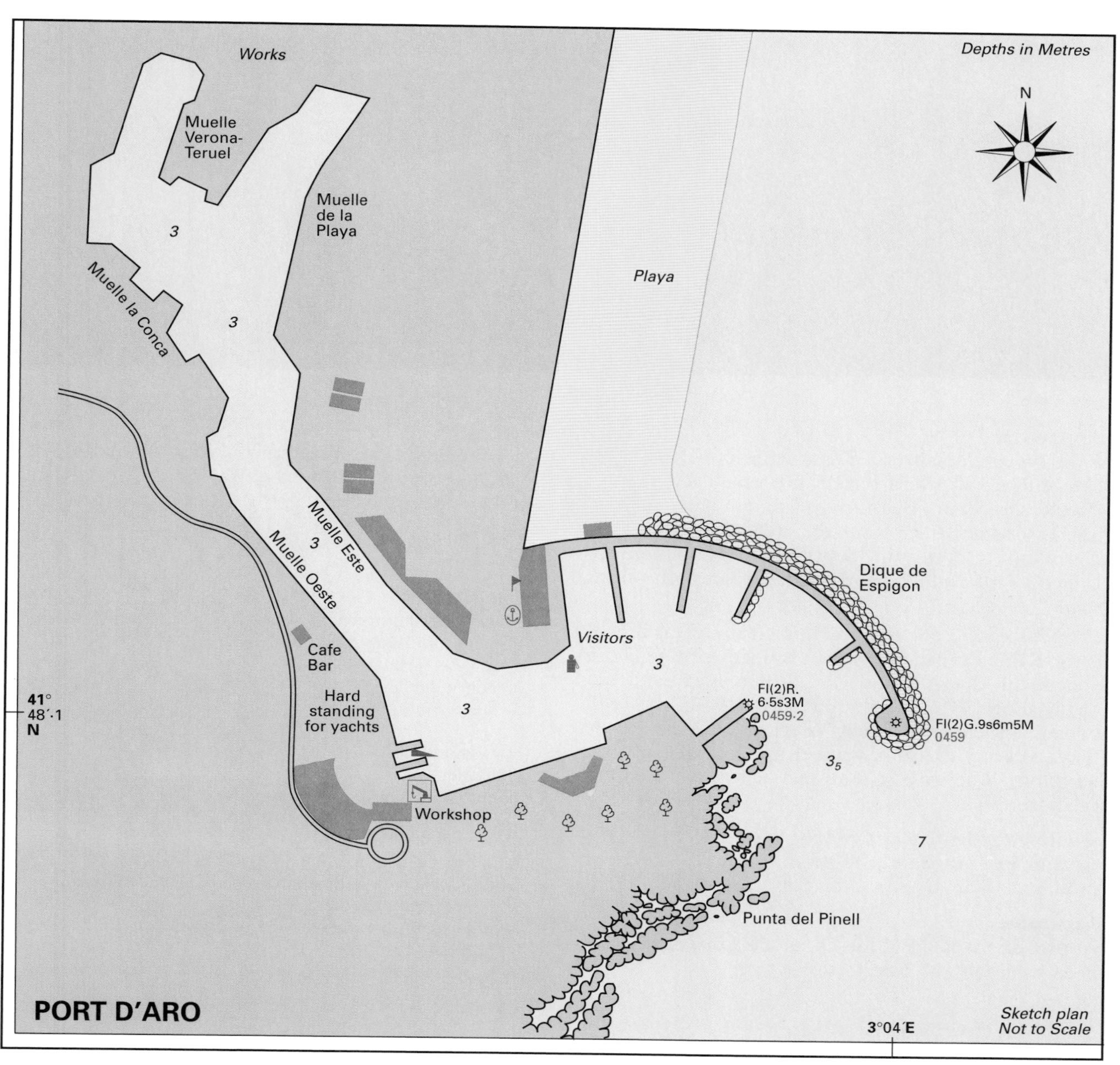

Port d'Aro

Approach

From the south Cabo de Tossa with its conspicuous lighthouse, town and beach, are easily recognised. Puerto de Sant Feliu de Guíxols with a long breakwater and its prominent headland, Punta de Garbi, are also easy to identify as is the wide deep Cala de Sant Pol. The harbour lies 1M to NE of this *cala*.

From the north Puerto de Palamós is unmistakable as is the Bahía de Palamós which is lined with high-rise apartment blocks. Cabo Roig is not prominent but has shallows extending 500m towards SE and with two small exposed rocky islets. The long sandy Playa (Platja) d'Aro is backed by lines of high-rise buildings. The harbour entrance lies at the S end of the beach.

Anchorage in the approach

Anchor in 15m, sand, 300m to NE of the harbour mouth.

Entrance

Approach the head of the Dique de Abrigo on a SW heading leaving it 20m to starboard.

Berths

If not directed by VHF, secure on the NW side of the second of the three spurs within the harbour on the starboard side, then ask. The SE side of the spur is protected by rocks.

Charges

Medium.

Facilities

Maximum length overall 15m.
Repairs to hull and engines possible at the yard in the SW corner.
20-tonne travel-lift.
8-tonne crane.
Slip.
Hard-standing.
Chandlery nearby.
Water on quays and pontoons.
220v AC on quays and pontoons.
Gasoleo A and petrol.
Ice from the *club náutico*.
Club Náutico de Port d'Aro with bar, ice, restaurant, launderette, showers, WCs, etc.
Provisions from S'Agaro ½M or behind the Platja d'Aro about 1M to N.
Weather forecast posted once a day at *oficina de capitán*.

Communications

Taxi ☎ 972 817 032.

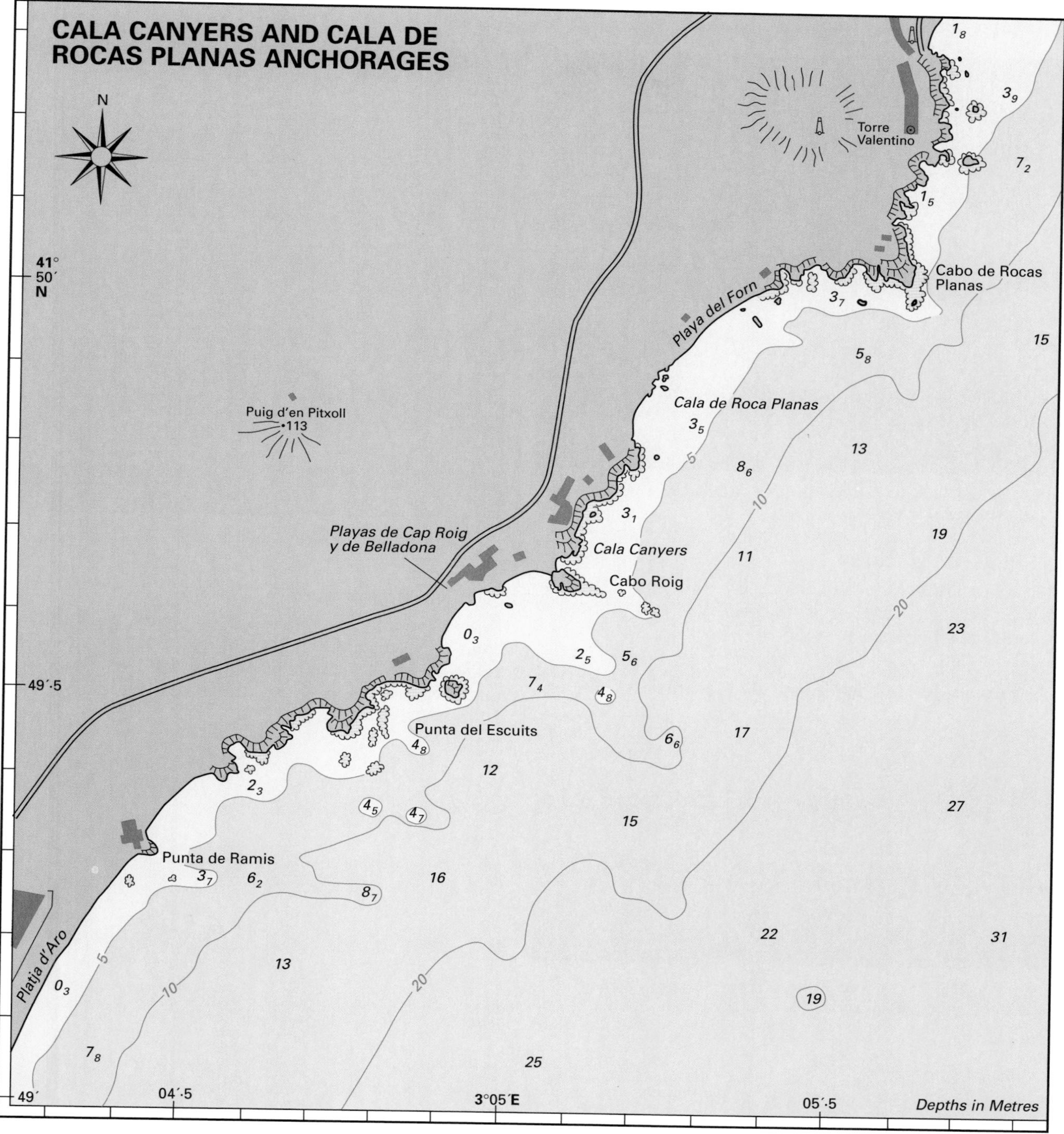
CALA CANYERS AND CALA DE ROCAS PLANAS ANCHORAGES
N
Torre Valentino
Cabo de Rocas Planas
Playa del Forn
Cala de Roca Planas
Puig d'en Pitxoll
113
Playas de Cap Roig y de Belladona
Cala Canyers
Cabo Roig
Punta del Escuits
Punta de Ramis
Platja d'Aro
41° 50′ N
49′·5
49′
04′·5
3°05′E
05′·5
Depths in Metres

⚓ Playa (Platja) d'Aro

Playa (Platja) d'Aro: open between NE and S. A seaside resort with the usual facilities.

⚓ Playa de la Cova

An open anchorage off rocky cliffs with some small sandy beaches. Anchor in mid-*cala* to S of a small islet. Open between E and S.

⚓ Playas de Cap Roig and de Belladona

Playas de Cap Roig and de Belladona: open between E and S with foul ground around.

⚓ Playa de San Antonio

Playa de San Antonio: open between E and SE.

⚓ Playa de Palamós

A long sandy beach backed by roads and lines of high-rise buildings. All facilities of a large seaside holiday town available. Anchor off the beach in sand, open between E and SW. Many stone groynes to trap the sand.

⚓ Cala Canyérs

Cala Canyérs: open between NE and SE. Note the rocks off Cabo Roig.

Puertos de Palamós

41°50'N 3°07'E

Charts

British Admiralty *1704*
French *7298, 4827*
Spanish *4923, 492, 876*
Navicarte *E04*

Lights

0462 **Punta del Molino** 41°50'·6N 3°07'·8E Oc(1+4)18s22m18M White round tower, grey cupola 8m

Commercial Port

0464 **Dique de Abrigo head** 41°50'·6N 3°07'·3E Fl.G.3s9m5M Grey/green metal globe, 4m diameter, with clear top

0465 **Old Commercial mole head** Fl.R.5s5m3M Red column on concrete base 3m

0466 **Spur NW head** Fl(2+1)R.15s7m3M Red column, green stripe 4m

0466·4 **Dársena Pesquera Muelle comercial NE corner** Fl(2)R.6s6m3M White column, red top 4m

0466·6 **Dársena Pesquera Espigón Sur head** Fl(2)G.6s6m3M White column, green top 4m

Marina – Puerto Deportivo

0466·7 **Dique de Abrigo head** 41°50'·7N 3°08'·2E Fl(4)G.10s11m5M Green tower 8m

0466·75 **Contradique head** Fl(4)R.10s4m3M Red tower 2m

0466·8 **Muelle de Levante head** Fl.G.5s2m3M Green tower

To the south

0460 **La Llosa de Palamós (Bajo Pereira)** 41°50'·1N 3°07'·2E Fl(2)7s10m5M Isolated danger tower, topmark of 2 spheres

To the northeast

0467 **Hormiga Grande** 41°51'·7N 3°11'·1E Fl(3)9s14m6M White round tower on hut 6m

0470 **Cabo San Sebastián** 41°53'·7N 3°12'·1E Fl.5s167m32M White round tower on white building, red roof 12m Aeromarine

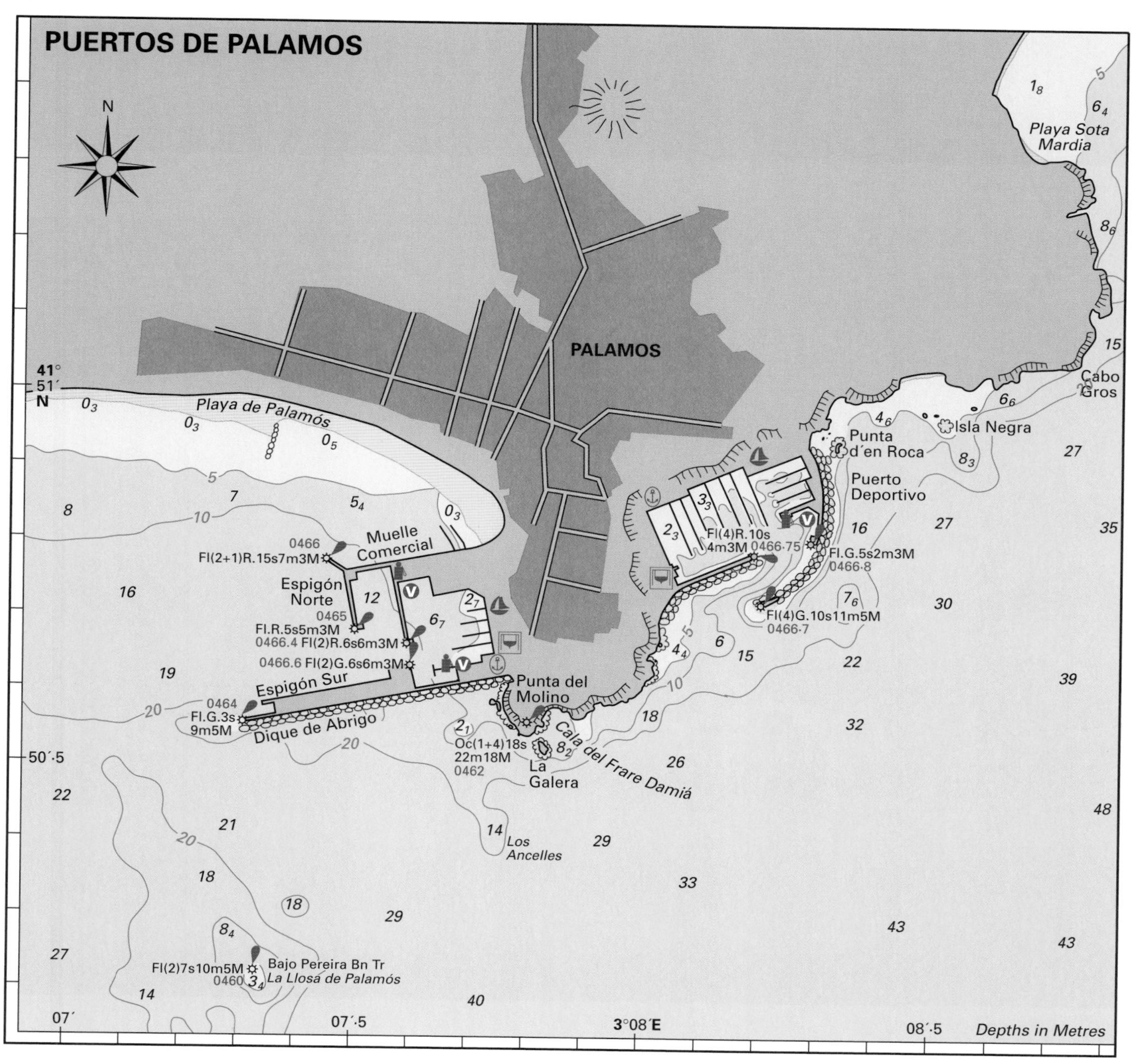

Puerto de Palamós

Punta del Molíno

Marina Palamós

Buoys

A black buoy marks Llosa del Molino, 1·9m, 100m SW of Punta del Molino.

Radiobeacons

Cabo San Sebastián c/s *SN* (···/–·) 291kHz 50M 41°53'·93N 3°12'·17E

Port communications

VHF Ch 8, 9. Club Náutico Costa Brava ☎ 972 314 324.

Puerto Deportivo VHF Ch 9 ☎ 972 601 000 *Fax* 972 602 266.

General

There are two harbours at Palamós, one on either side of the headland, Punta de Molino, which catches the full force of the NW *tramontana* when it blows. The harbour on the west side is used by fishing and commercial craft. It is easy to approach and enter but does not welcome visiting yachts. The Club Náutico Costa Brava is in the old harbour but has no visitors berths. On the east side, the Puerto Deportivo is a private development. It does not have a yacht club (though a noisy disco has been noted). The town serving both is pleasant but in the season is crowded with tourists.

The museum and 14th-century church (much altered in the 16th and 18th centuries) can be visited. There are many attractive *calas* along the coast which can be reached by boat. The ancient villages of Ullastret (12M) and Calonge (1M) are worth a visit. Fine beach to the N of the harbour.

Palamós rose to prominence in the Middle Ages when it won an age-long struggle with Sant Feliu de Guíxols to be the maritime outlet for Girona. In 1334 it became the maritime district of Girona and prospered greatly. In 1534 it was sacked and burnt by Barbarossa with the Turkish Fleet after which it fell on hard times. With the development of the cork industry and agriculture its fortunes revived but it was again heavily damaged during the Civil War. Today it depends largely on the tourist industry.

Approach

From the south The prominent Punta de Garbí with the Ermita de Sant Elm on its summit and the harbour of Sant Feliu de Guíxols are easily recognised as is the deep square-shaped Cala de Sant Pol. The masses of high-rise buildings at Platja d'Aro and Palamós can be seen from afar. There are two high-rise buildings 500m due N of the harbour and in the close approach the grey rocky breakwater will be seen jutting out westwards from the Punta del Molino. Keep an eye out for La Llosa de Palamós. If going round to the Puerto Deportivo, keep ¼M off Punta del Molino and the breakwater will be seen to the E of the point.

From the north From the high prominent Cabo San Sebastián which has a conspicuous lighthouse, the coast is very rocky and broken. The lower wooded Capo de Planas, the small rocky Islas Hormigas should be easily recognised. There is a passage inside the Islas Hormigas (see page 147) but it is simpler to keep to seaward, especially in heavy weather. Later the two high-rise buildings located side by side 500m to N of the harbour at Palamós, should be spotted (they may appear as one). The coast should not be approached closer than ½M

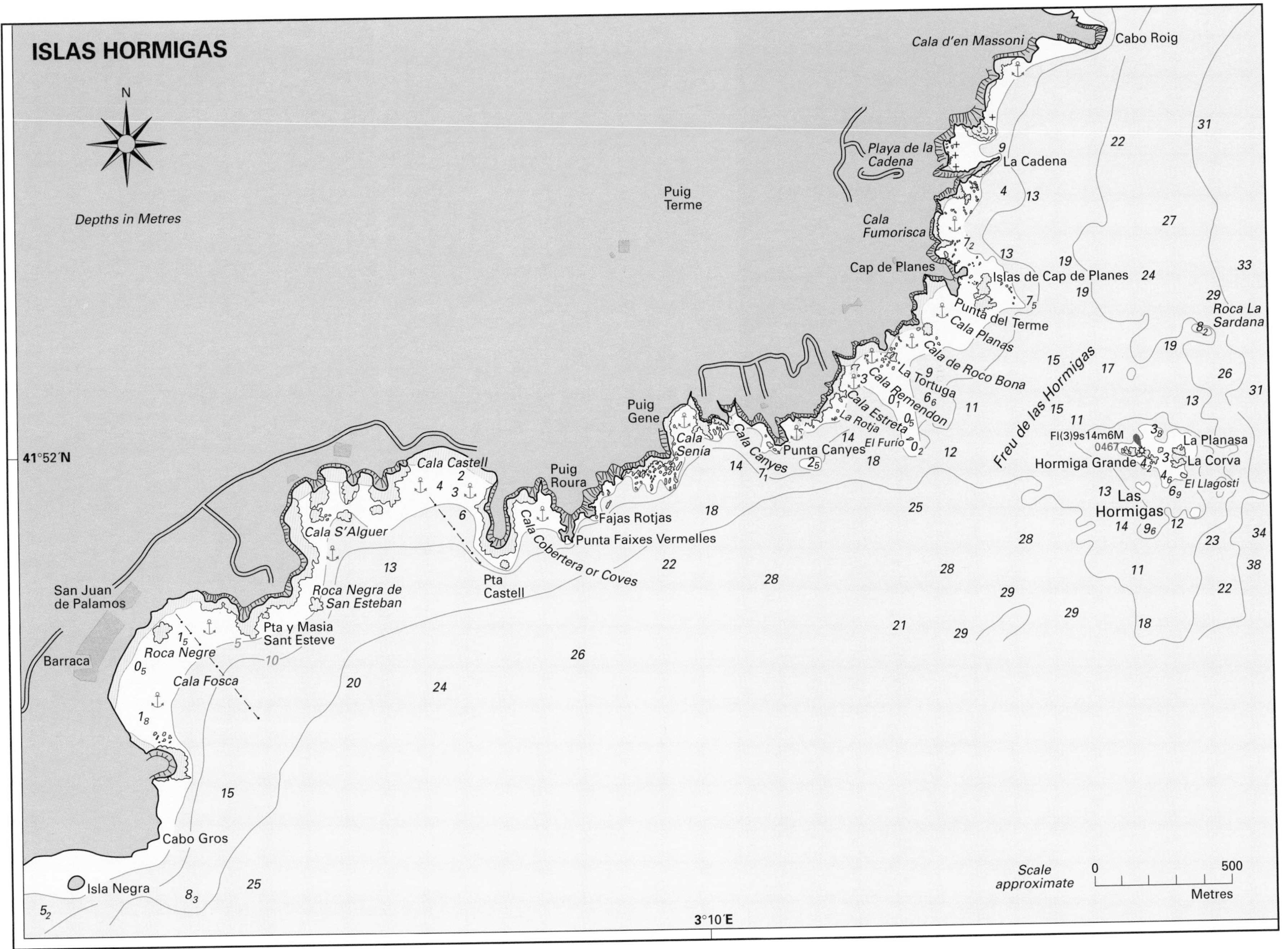
ISLAS HORMIGAS
N
Depths in Metres
41°52'N
3°10'E
Scale approximate
0
500
Metres
Cabo Roig
Cala d'en Massoni
La Cadena
Playa de la Cadena
Puig Terme
Cala Fumorisca
Cap de Planes
Islas de Cap de Planes
Punta del Terme
Cala Planas
Cala de Roco Bona
La Tortuga
Cala Remendon
Cala Estreta
La Rotja
El Furio
Punta Canyes
Cala Canyes
Cala Senía
Puig Gene
Puig Roura
Fajas Rotjas
Punta Faixes Vermelles
Cala Cobertera or Coves
Pta Castell
Cala Castell
Cala S'Alguer
Roca Negra de San Esteban
Pta y Masia Sant Esteve
San Juan de Palamos
Barraca
Roca Negre
Cala Fosca
Cabo Gros
Isla Negra
Freu de las Hormigas
Roca La Sardana
Fl(3)9s14m6M
0467
La Planasa
La Corva
Hormiga Grande
El Llagosti
Las Hormigas

because of outlying dangers. If going to the old harbour, keep at least ¼M off Punta del Molino but beware of La Llosa de Palamós. Punta del Molino lighthouse is not conspicuous.

Outside anchorage
A possible anchorage is north of the Muelle Comercial in 10m or less.

Entrance
Puerto Deportivo Head north to give the head of its Dique de Abrigo an offing of 30m or so, then turn in. The entrance is difficult in a south to southwest wind with swell.

Old Harbour Go alongside the fuel berth and ask for a berth or report to the *capitanía* nearby. Charges are higher than at Puerto Deportivo.

Berths
Puerto Deportivo If not met by a *zodiac*, go to the fuel berth and ask. If no-one there, ask at the office. Charges are high.

Old Harbour The option is to get in wherever possible and ask the *capitán de puerto.* Charges are higher than at the Puerto Deportivo.

Facilities
Puerto Deportivo
Maximum length overall on quays 18m but a vessel up to 25m can be fitted in.
Some repair and maintenance facilities on site.
Chandler.
20-tonne travel-lift.
6-tonne crane.
Water on pontoons.
Showers.
220v AC on pontoons, 380v AC on Contradique.
Gasoleo A and petrol.

Old Harbour
Maximum length overall 17m.
A large yard under the bridge behind the *club náutico* and a smaller one to the N of it. Repairs to hulls can be carried out. Engine shops.
5-tonne crane on the N side of the Muelle Comercial and three cranes, 3 to 10 tonnes, at the *club náutico.*
Large slip on the inner side of the Dique de Abrigo.
Small slipway by the *club náutico.*
A small hard alongside the *club náutico.*
Two chandlers in the town and a large one under the bridge behind the *club náutico.*
Water on the Dique de Abrigo, pontoons, the Muelle Comercial and at the *club náutico* and the *lonja.*
220v AC points on Dique de Abrigo, pontoons and the Muelle Comercial.
Ice from a factory behind the *lonja.*
Club Náutico Costa Brava is located at the root of the Dique de Abrigo with bar, lounge, terrace, restaurant, showers and swimming pool.
Weather forecast posted at *club náutico* once a day.

In town
Supermarket and other shops.
Fish can be bought from a market at the *lonja* in the evening.
Launderettes.

Communications
Bus service. Taxi ☎ 972 310 525.

Islas Hormigas (Formigues)
41°51'N 3°11'E

Charts
British Admiralty *1704*
French *4827, 7008, 7505*
Spanish *876, 4924, 492*
Navicarte *E04*

Lights
To the south
0462 **Punta del Molino** 41°50'·6N 3°07'·8E
Oc(1+4)18s22m18M White round tower, grey cupola 8m

The islands
0467 **Hormiga Grande** 41°51'·7N 3°11'·1E
Fl(3)9s14m6M White tower on hut 6m

To the north
0470 **Cabo San Sebastián** 41°53'·7N 3°12'·1E
Fl.5s167m32M White round tower on white building, red roof 12m

General
The Islas Hormigas (*hormiga* is Spanish for an ant) or Formigues are a group of unoccupied rocky islets which lie some ½M off Cap de Planas between Palamós and Llafranc. The islands are low, bare and

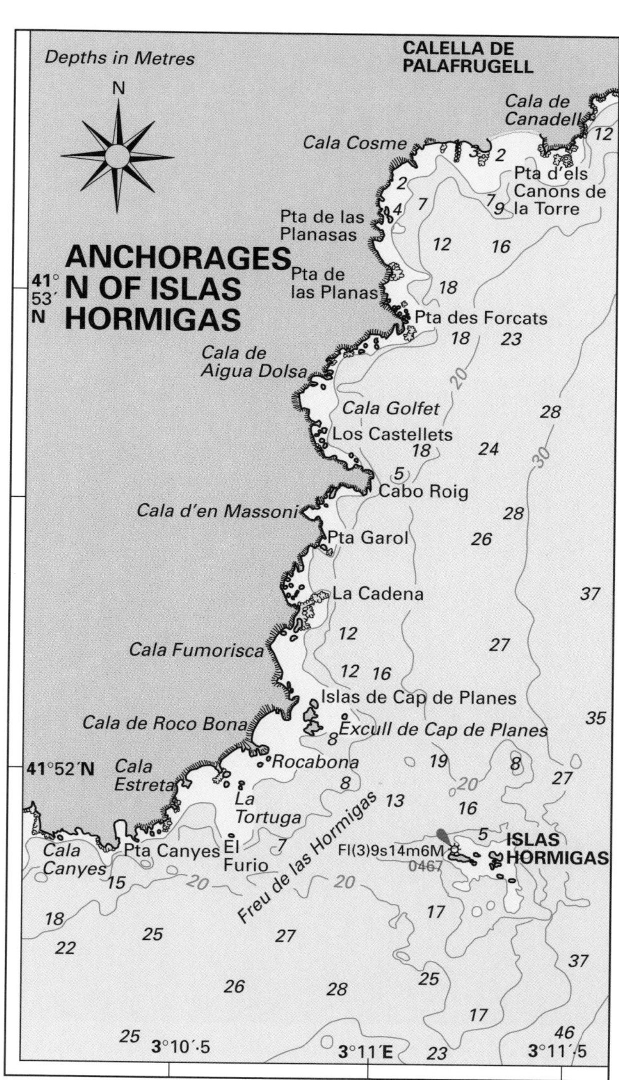

foul. The highest, La Hormiga Grande, is only 12m high and 100m long. The mainland coast is also foul, notably the El Furió shoal and the rocks, Escuits del Cap de Planas, which extend to 400m from the shore. The area is generally foul and should be given a good berth especially in foul weather. However, Freu de las Hormigas, the passage between the islands and the mainland, about 400m wide, can be taken in fair weather.

Passage

From the south Approach the islands on a NE course and when level with Punta Faixes Vermelles bring Cabo San Sebastián onto 030°. This should lead through the Freu de les Hormigas about one third distant from the islands and two thirds from the mainland. Keep on this course until Cap de Planas is well past the beam.

From the north From Cabo San Sebastián make a course towards the islands. About 400m from them bring Punta del Molino on to 240° and pass through the Freu at a distance of about one-third of its width from the islands and two-thirds of its width from the mainland.

Landings

Hormiga Grande can be approached with care from the SW in deep water and landing is possible in calm weather.

⚓ Cala Fosca

Cala Fosca. Open between E and S with foul ground on the south side of the bay. Mind the pipeline shown on the chart.

⚓ Cala S'Alguer

A small bay, the head of which is divided into three rocky beaches with a number of rocks lying off them. Anchor in the middle in 9m, stone, sand and rock. Open between SE and S.

⚓ Cala Senía

A rocky-cliffed bay with a rocky spur on the NE side. Approach on a NW course, enter with care and anchor in the middle in rock and stone. Open between E and S.

⚓ Cala Castell

Cala Castell: closed off for swimmers in summer. Open between SE and W.

Cala Cobertera (or Coves): anchor in the middle, stone and rock. Open between SE and SW.

⚓ Cala Fumorisca

An open *cala* with rocky outcrops and reefs on either side. Open between N and SE. Enter with care on a W course.

⚓ Playa de la Cadena

A medium-sized rocky-cliffed *cala* protected on its SE side by a long thin projection of rock, La Cadena. Open between NE and SE. Anchor in 5m, stone and rock. Rocks off head of *cala*.

⚓ Cala N of Punta Canyes

Cala N of Punta Canyes: enter with care and anchor in the middle. Open between E and S.

⚓ Cala d'en Massoni

A *cala* just to S of Cabo Roig, open between E and SE. Use the N half of the *cala*, the SW side has projecting rocks. Anchor in 3m, stone and rock.

⚓ Cala del Aigua Dolça

A small *cala* with low rocky cliffs and submerged rocks. Open between E and S. Anchor in mid-*cala* in rock and stone.

⚓ Calas Estreta, Remendon, Roco Bona and Planas

Calas Estreta, Remendon, Roco Bona and Planas: divided by rocky outcrops and with sandy beaches at their heads, open between NE and S. Approach with great care and in good weather.

⚓ **Cala Golfet**

Cala Golfet: a wide rocky *cala* with a small pebble beach. Open between NE and SE.

Calella de Palafrugell

41°51'N 3°09'E

Charts

British Admiralty *1704*
French *4827, 7008, 7505*
Spanish *876, 492*
Navicarte *E04*

Lights

To the north

0470 **Cabo San Sebastián** 41°53'·7N 3°12'·1E
Fl.5s167m32M White round tower on white building, red roof 12m Aeromarine

General

A series of delightful little anchorages offering good shelter from all except winds and sea between NE and SE, Callela lies between Punta Forcat and Punta d'els Canons (or de la Torre). Care is necessary in the close approach owing to isolated submerged rocks and the anchorage is full of moorings. The village is most attractive but very crowded in the season. Facilities are reasonable for a large holiday village.

Cap Roig botanic gardens 1M away are worth a visit. On the first Saturday in July, there is a singing festival on the beach, *Cantada de Habaneras*.

The original town of Palafrugell was Roman, possibly Celebandica, and was greatly enlarged when the inhabitants of the coast moved there in the 8th and 9th centuries. It became Palaz Frugell, that is Palace of Fruits, from which its present name is derived. It is an interesting old town and has the remains of its original walls.

Approach

Because of submerged rocks near the coast, approach should be made with care, in calm weather and with a forward lookout.

From the south Pass between the Islas Hormigas (see page 145) and the mainland leaving Cabo Roig and Punta Forcat at least 200m to port. Approach the anchorage with the conspicuous church on a N heading.

From the north Having rounded the high Cabo San Sebastián with its conspicuous lighthouse and

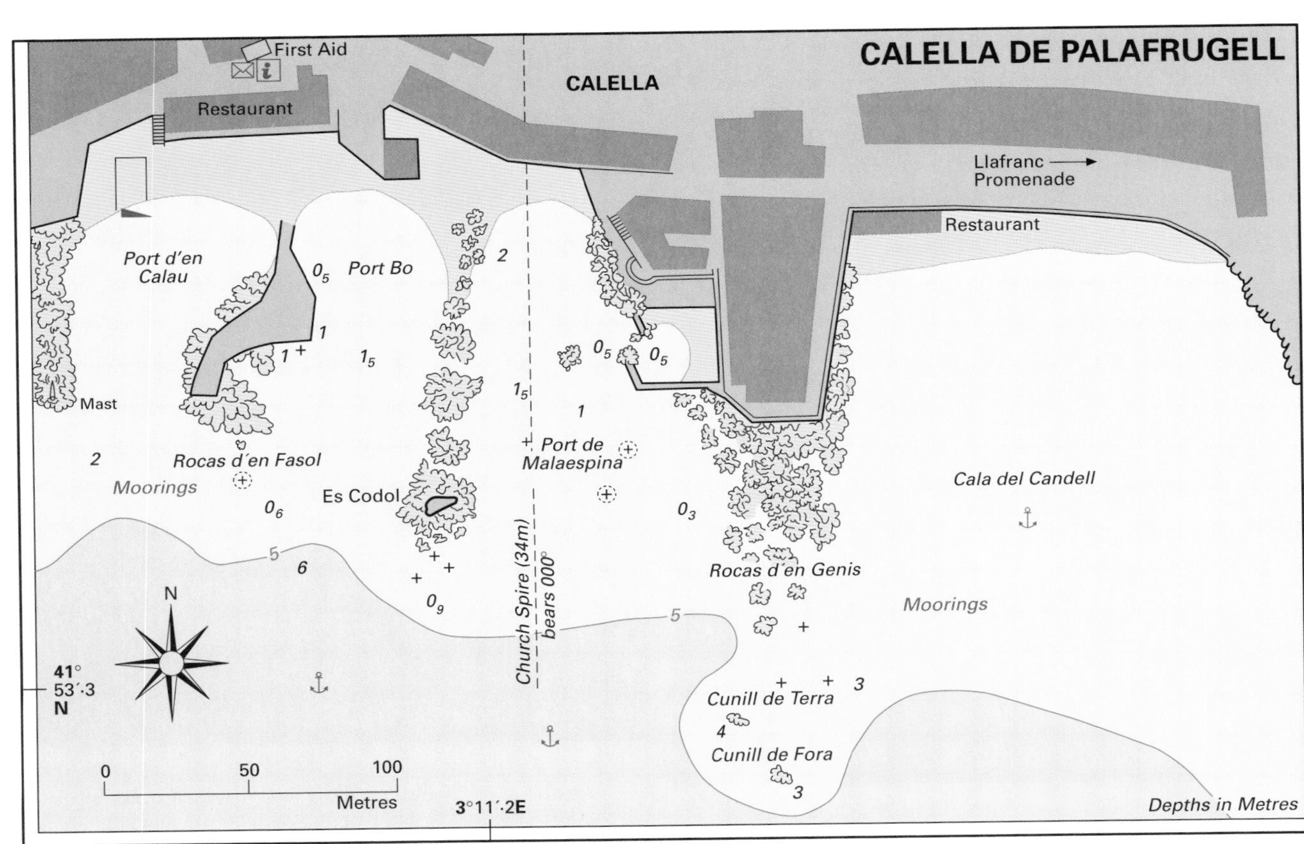

Calella de Palafrugell

restaurant, the Cala de Llafranc with houses on its head will be seen. The Punta d'els Canons, a lowish rocky point with a tower, should be given a berth of at least 200m and the coast followed at this distance. When the conspicuous church at Calella de Palafrugell is due N, approach on that heading.

Anchorage

Anchor W of the very small rocky islet Cunill de Fora, opposite the centre bay but short of the rocky outcrops, in 5m sand, rock and stone (partly weed-covered). The holding ground is very patchy. Use a trip-line. Alternative anchorages exist opposite the other two bays but there are isolated rocks which restrict swinging room. It is also possible to anchor in the Cala del Canadell some 400m to the E but care is necessary.

Quays

There is a small quay on the W side of the centre bay with 1m alongside and another in the form of a miniature harbour on the E side of the E bay with 0·5m alongside.

Facilities

Water available from cafés.
Everyday supplies available from shops in the village and much greater variety from Palafrugell some 2M away.
Club Vela de Calella is a dinghy club with few facilities other than a terrace.

⚓ Cala del Canadell

A wide bay divided by a projecting rocky point near the middle. Anchor on either side in 4m, sand. Open between SE and SW.

Puerto de Llafranc

41°53'N 3°12'E

Charts

British Admiralty *1704*
French *4827, 7008, 7505, 7298*
Spanish *876, 492*
Navicarte *E04*

Lights

To the north

0470 **Cabo San Sebastián** 41°53'·7N 3°12'·1E
Fl.5s167m32M White round tower on white building, red roof 12m Aeromarine

Harbour

0468 **Dique del Sur head** 41°53'·6N 3°11'·8E
Fl(3)G.11s6m5M White metal post, green top 2m

Buoys

Red and white buoys mark the entrance channel, one port-hand buoy has a spar and one has a F.R light.

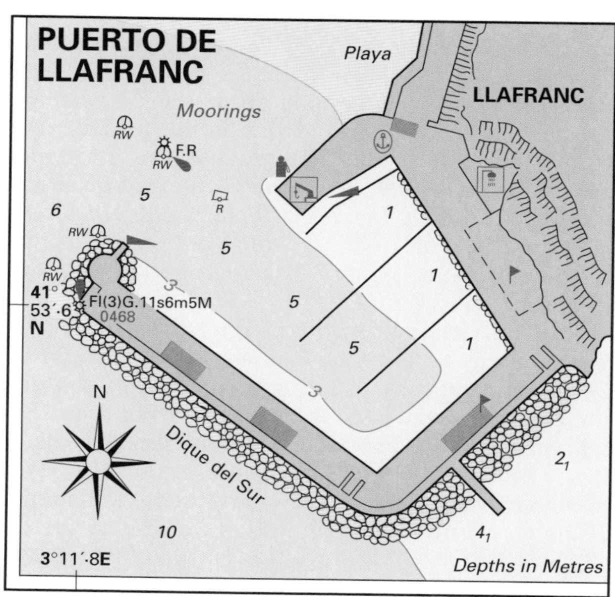

Puerto de Llafranc

Port communications

VHF Ch 8. Club Náutico de Llafranc ☎/*Fax* 972 300 754.

General

Puerto de Llafranc is under the high, steep-sided SW side of Cabo San Sebastián. It is an artificial yacht harbour established in a most attractive *cala* which has been used as a harbour since time immemorial. Approach and entrance need some care but, once inside, there is good protection though heavy swell coming from the SE can be tiresome. The hills around the harbour offer good protection against the NW *tramontana*. Everyday requirements can be met in the village and there are good shops and a market in Palafrugell 2M away. The area becomes very crowded and expensive in the season and, as the *capitanía* remarked, the harbour is always full.

The harbour is probably of Phoenician origin. It was certainly used by the Romans and is thought to be the ancient port of Cypsela. In the 8th century the Normans razed the town to the ground and its inhabitants moved to Palafrugell. In recent years it has been redeveloped as a tourist resort. The excellent sandy beach is crowded in season. There is a fine view from the lighthouse of San Sebastián.

Approach

From the south A tree-covered promontory, Cap de Planas, and the Islas Hormigas, a group of low, jagged rocky islands are readily recognisable. If the weather is fair a passage inside these islands is possible (see page 145). The harbour wall will be seen under Cabo San Sebastián.

From the north Cabo Begur with its conspicuous signal station and the deep *calas* of Aiguafreda, Aiguablava and Tamariú are easily recognised. The high steep-sided Cabo San Sebastián with its lighthouse, restaurant and *ermita* on its summit can be seen from afar and the harbour will be found on its further side.

Anchorage in the approach

Anchor 200m off the centre of the sandy beach in 6m sand. Use a trip-line. In summer there are many moorings and a diving board between the anchorage and the beach.

Entrance

Enter the bay on a NW course and approach the head of the Dique del Sur with care. Round it at 10m leaving it to starboard. Note the head of the *dique* extends some 5m underwater. Leave a line of small red and white buoys to port and two similar buoys close to the head of the *dique* to starboard.

There is little room to manoeuvre once inside the harbour.

Berths

Berth stern-to the inner side of the Dique del Sur with bows-to mooring buoy.

Facilities

6-tonne crane.
Small slip in the NW corner and another at the head of Dique del Sur.
Water from the pontoons and quays.
220v AC on the pontoons and quays.
Gasoleo A and petrol.
Club Náutico de Llafranc has a small office to the NW of the harbour. The clubhouse is on the NE side of the harbour with restaurant, bar, showers and WCs.
A limited number of shops near the harbour for everyday requirements. Many shops in Palafrugell 2M away.
Launderette in Llafranc.

Communications

Bus service.

Cabo San Sebastián (Cap de Sant Sebastián)

A prominent, cliffed headland of reddish rock with a 12m lighthouse on the 167m high rounded summit. A number of houses are located near the summit. The headland is steep-to. There is also a restaurant and *ermita* on top.

⚓ Cala de Gens

A small *cala* ½M to N of Cabo San Sebastián and a useful place if waiting to round the Cape. High rocky cliffs with houses. Anchor in 10m plus, stone and rock bottom. Hut on small stony beach.

⚓ Cala Pedrosa

Cala Pedrosa, S of Punta Tamariú: anchor in 10m, stone and rock. Open between E and S.

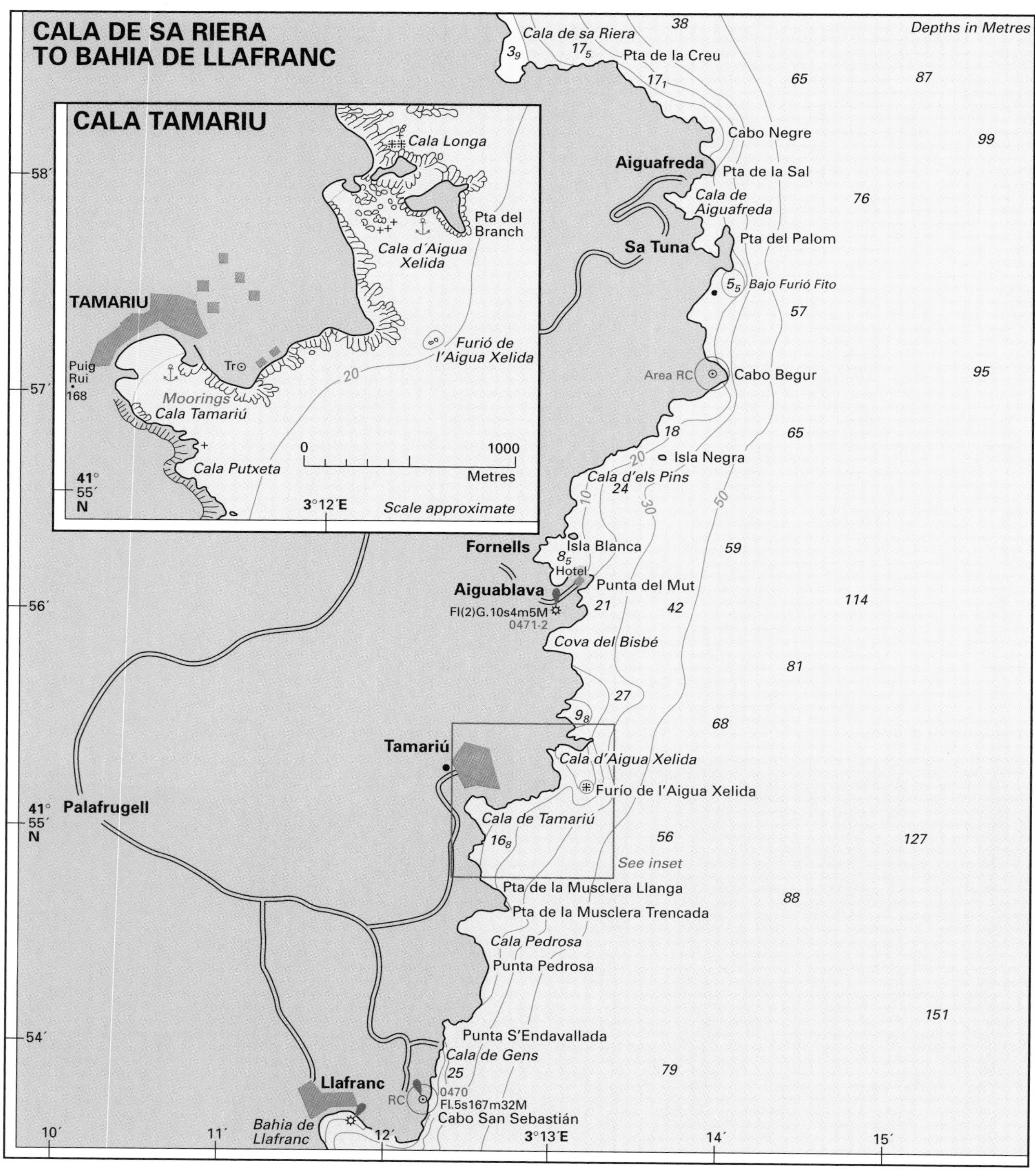
CALA DE SA RIERA
TO BAHIA DE LLAFRANC
Depths in Metres
CALA TAMARIU
Cala Longa
Pta del Branch
Cala d'Aigua Xelida
TAMARIU
Furió de l'Aigua Xelida
Puig Rui 168
Moorings
Cala Tamariú
Cala Putxeta
Metres
Scale approximate
Cala de sa Riera
Pta de la Creu
Cabo Negre
Aiguafreda
Pta de la Sal
Cala de Aiguafreda
Sa Tuna
Pta del Palom
Bajo Furió Fito
Area RC
Cabo Begur
Isla Negra
Cala d'els Pins
Fornells
Isla Blanca
Hotel
Aiguablava
Punta del Mut
Fl(2)G.10s4m5M
0471·2
Cova del Bisbé
Tamariú
Cala d'Aigua Xelida
Furío de l'Aigua Xelida
Palafrugell
Cala de Tamariú
See inset
Pta de la Musclera Llanga
Pta de la Musclera Trencada
Cala Pedrosa
Punta Pedrosa
Punta S'Endavallada
Cala de Gens
Llafranc
0470
Fl.5s167m32M
Cabo San Sebastián
Bahia de Llafranc

⚓ Cala Tamariú

Cala Tamariú: anchor in the middle, 5–10m, sand. Hotels and restaurants ashore. Cala Putxeta, S of the entrance, is a useful day anchorage. To the NE, Aigua Xelida with its rocky islets, promontories and bays is fun to explore by dinghy or other small boat.

Cala Aigua Xelida

See plan opposite.

⚓ Cova del Bisbé and Port d'Esclanya

Two very small square-shaped *calas* 80m apart, open between NE and SE with rocky cliffs. Anchor in 5m, rocks. There is a large cave at Bisbe.

Calas de Aiguablava y Fornells

41°56'N 3°13'E

Charts

British Admiralty *1704, 1705*
French *4827, 7008, 7505*
Spanish *876, 492*
Navicarte *E04*

Lights

To the south

0470 **Cabo San Sebastián** 41°53'·7N 3°12'·1E
Fl.5s167m32M White round tower on white building, red roof 12m Aeromarine

Basin

0471 **Basin entrance port side** 41°56'·0N 3°12'·9E
Fl(2)R.6s2m3M Red lantern

0471·2 **Starboard side** Fl(2)G.10s4m5M Green tower, white base 3m

Port communications

Club Náutico Aiguablava ☎ 972 622 449/972 623 161.

General

A beautiful and sheltered anchorage with a small private harbour with protection from all but strong NE winds. Facilities are very limited and it is crowded in the season with many occupied moorings. Cala de Aiguablava has shelter from the NW *tramontana*.

There are fine sandy beaches. A visit to the old town of Begur is recommended.

Approach

From the south Pass the high prominent Cabo San Sebastián with its conspicuous lighthouse and restaurant and the deep Cala Tamariú with its houses. 1M to the N will be found the Punta del Mut with a large square-shaped hotel, the Parador la Costa Brava, on its summit. Follow the coast around into the anchorage.

From the north Round the prominent Cabo Negre and then Punta de la Sal where there is a very large hotel on the point and then in 1M round Cabo Begur which has a castle and a signal station. 1M to the S lies Punta del Mut with a large square-shaped hotel on its summit. Leave this point to port and the Isla Blanca to starboard and enter the anchorage.

Entrance

Enter the Calas de Aiguablava y Fornells on a W course nearer to the Punta del Mut than to Isla Blanca.

Cala de Aiguablava

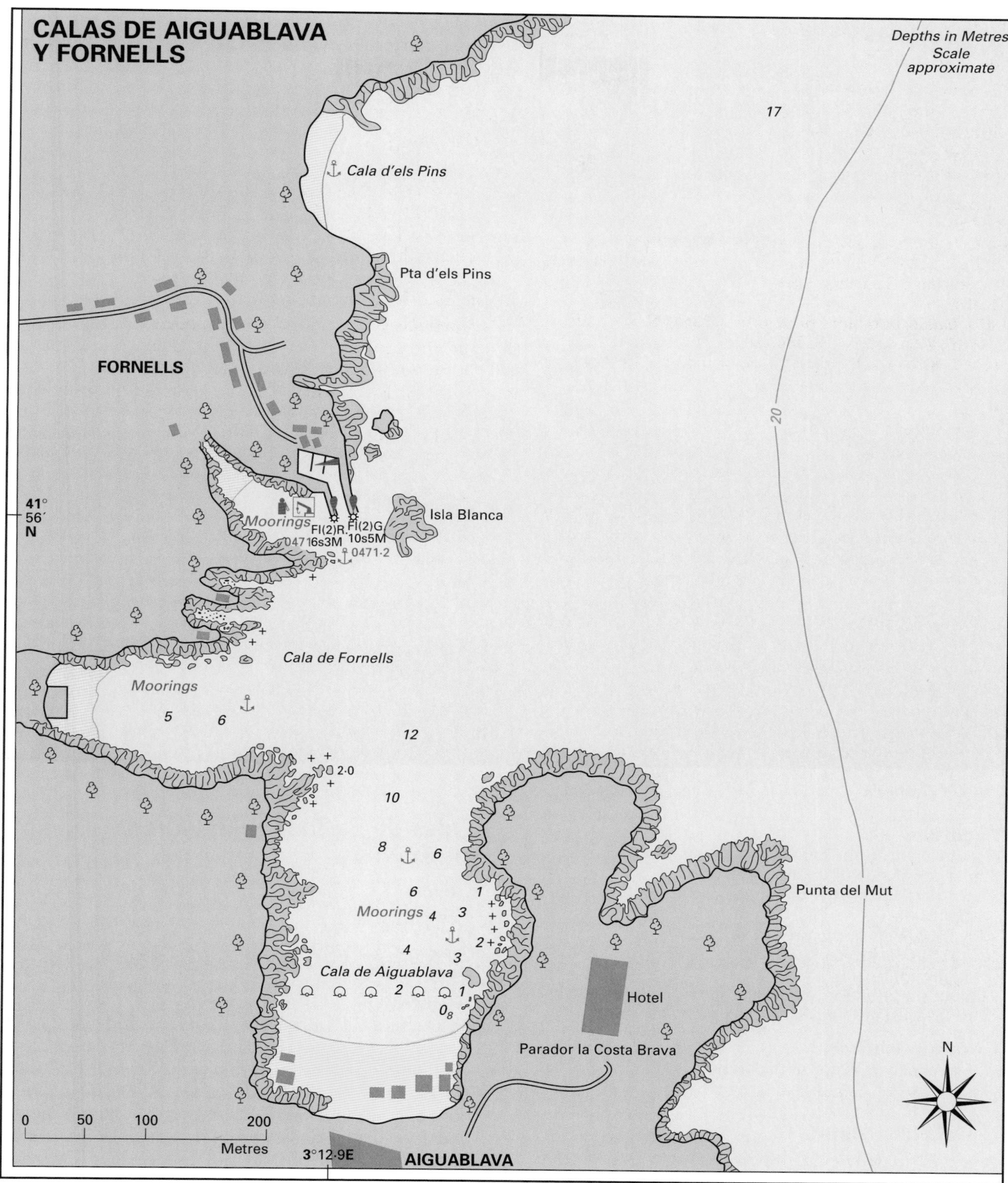

Anchorage

Anchor in 3m, sand and weed, in the E half of Cala de Aiguablava as near to the cliffs as draught will allow. There are ring-bolts on the cliffs and an isolated rock and there are also many moorings. In summer the southern part of Cala de Aiguablava is reserved for bathing.

Alternative anchorages are at the entrance to Cala Fornells and in a smaller *cala* 100m further to N but they do not have as good protection as Aiguablava.

Quays

There is a small stone quay in the SE corner of the Cala de Aiguablava with 0·5m alongside and a small pier in the Cala de Fornells at the entrance to the small private harbour.

Puerto de Fornells

Facilities

4-tonne crane at the entrance to the private harbour.
Slip at the N side of the private harbour.
Water from the beach restaurants and from the private harbour.
220v AC points at the private harbour.
Club náutico is located at the Playa de Fornells and is a dinghy club.
Limited supplies from two small shops at Fornells. More shops exist at Begur some 2M away.

Communications

A bus service to Begur in the season.

⚓ Cala d'els Pins

A small, narrow *cala* open between NE and E, surrounded by rocky cliffs. Anchor in rock and sand.

Cabo Begur (Cabo Bagur)

A large hooked headland, 115m, with rocky cliffs and a conspicuous low yellowish coloured lookout station on its crest. The headland is steep-to.

Calas de Sa Tuna y Aiguafreda

41°58N 3°14'E

Charts

British Admiralty *1704, 1705*
French *4827, 7008, 7505*
Spanish *876, 492*
Navicarte *E04*

General

Two beautiful inlets, easy to enter and with good shelter from all but E wind which sends in a nasty swell; some shelter from this wind behind the Punta del Palom spur. Shelter from the NW *tramontana* is possible but not very effective with winter gales. Facilities are very limited. Though there are many visitors in summer it is not as crowded as some resorts. Many large houses have been built near these *calas* in recent years.

A visit to the ancient town of Begur is recommended. There is a sand and shingle beach at the head of each *cala*.

Approach

From the south Cabo Begur, a rocky headland can be recognised by a signal tower on its summit. Keep 400m from the coast to avoid the Furió Fito rocks.

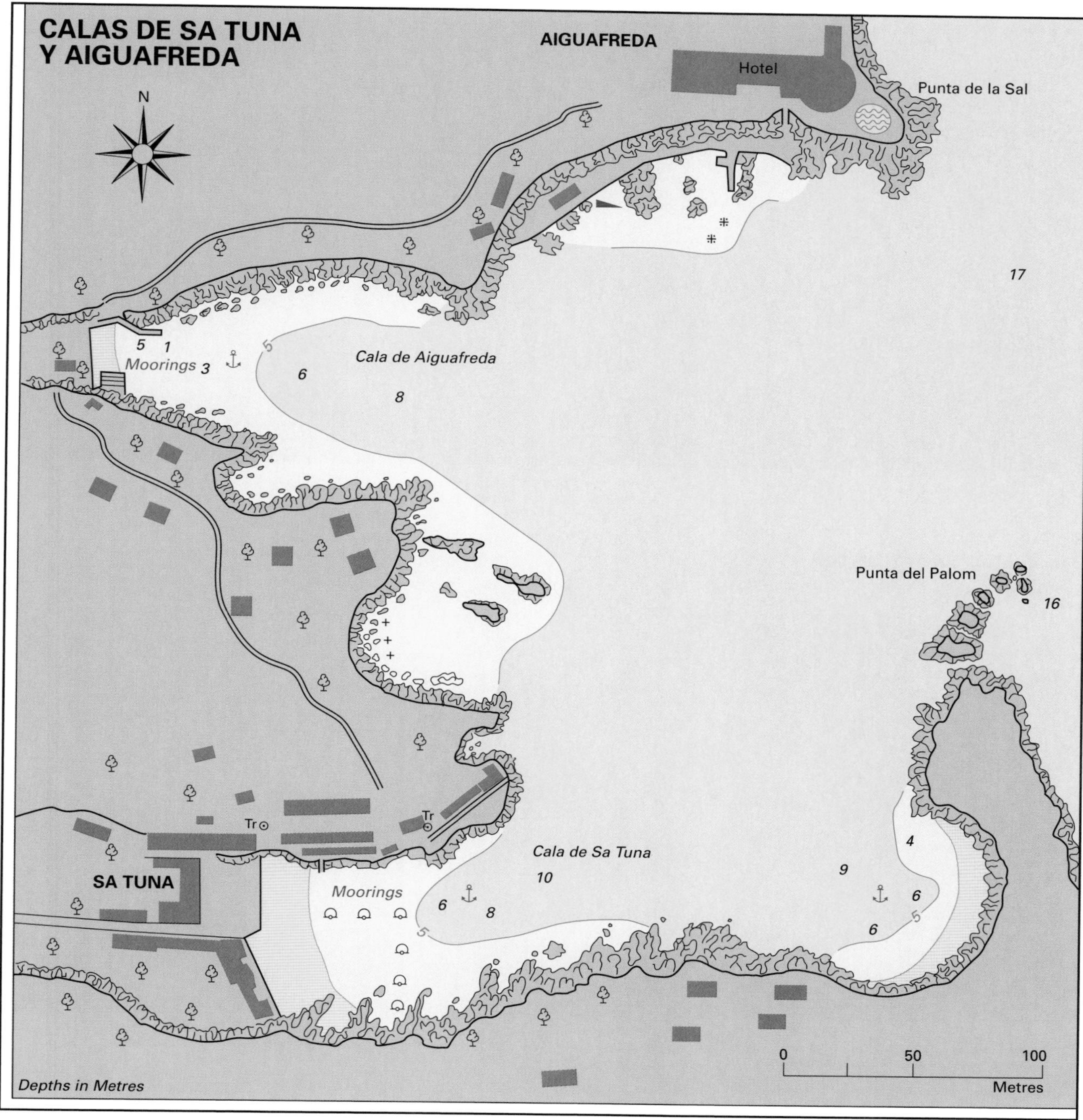

A very large hotel located on the Punta de la Sal at the far side of the entrance to this anchorage, visible over Punta del Palom, is very conspicuous. Round Punta del Palom at 50m and enter.

From the north Cabo Negre can be recognised by the very large hotel on Punta de la Sal just to its S. Round this at 100m and enter the anchorage.

Entrance

This is not difficult as there is deep water up to the cliffs. Cala Aiguafreda lies due W and Cala Sa Tuna to the SW of the outer entrance.

Anchorage

In winter, should an E wind arise, this anchorage should be vacated at once and shelter taken at Palamós. In summer, shelter behind Punta del Palom.

Anchor clear of moorings in 6m, sand and weed, near the centre of the Cala Sa Tuna with the tower bearing NNW. The W half of this *cala* is reserved for bathing and in the season, it is marked with yellow buoys.

In Cala Aiguafreda anchor in the centre of the *cala* about 100m from its head in 5m sand and stone clear of moorings. Alternative anchorages are possible in the little bay to SE and to S of the hotel. It is sometimes necessary to run a line ashore to keep the yacht head to swell, or use two anchors.

Cala de Sa Tuna

Cala Aiguafreda

Quays
There are three small quays and slips on the N side of Cala Sa Tuna and a longer one with 1m depth alongside on the N side of Cala Aiguafreda.

Facilities
There is a spring close to the beach at Cala Aiguafreda. Water is also available from the restaurant at Sa Tuna.
Very limited provisions from two small shops in Sa Tuna, many more in Begur 1M away.

Communications
Bus service to Begur in the season.

⚓ Cala de Sa Riera (Cala de la Rierata)

A *cala* with a sandy beach. Open between N and NE. Small village around the head of the *cala* with the beach. Anchor off the beach in sand. The old town and castle of Begur are 1M up the road.

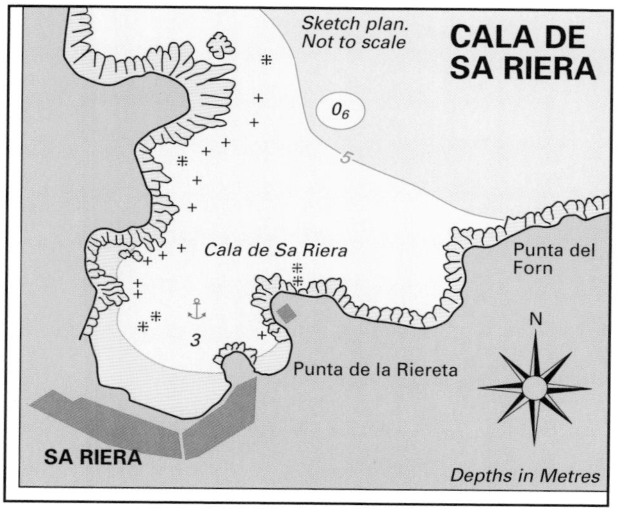

Sketch plan.
Not to scale
CALA DE
SA RIERA
Cala de Sa Riera
Punta del
Forn
Punta de la Riereta
N
SA RIERA
Depths in Metres

⚓ Playa de Pals

The southern end of Playa de Pals, a 2·5M stretch of sandy beach backed by low, flat plains. A group of tall, red and white (F.R) aerial masts are conspicuous at the S end and the mouth of the Río Ter is at the N end. Anchor off the beach in 5m, sand. Open between N and SE.

Puerto de L'Estartit

42°03'N 3°12'E

Charts

British Admiralty *1704, 1705*
French *7008, 7505, 7298*
Spanish *876, 493*
Navicarte *E04, E03*

Lights

To the southeast

0472 **Isla Méda Grande, summit** 42°02'·8N 3°13'·2E Fl(4)24s87m14M Tower on brick building 11m

Harbour

0473·5 **Dique de Levante head** 42°03'·1N 3°12'·5E Fl.G.5s9m5M White tower, green top 4m

0474 **Dique interior head** Fl(2)G.13s4m3M White post, green top 1m

0474·2 **Contradique corner** Fl.R.5s8m5M Red post 4m

0474·4 **Contradique head** Fl(2)R.13s3m3M Red lantern on masonry base 4m

0474·5 **Fuel jetty head** Fl(3)R.13s2m1M White post red top 1m

Port communications

VHF Ch 9, 16. *Capitanía* ☎ 972 751 402 *Fax* 972 751 717.
E mail club.n.estartit@cambrescat.es

General

A fishing and yachting harbour in an attractive setting protected by a breakwater and with reasonable shelter from the NW *tramontana*. Space for visiting yachts on the pontoons is limited. The town and surrounding areas have been developed as a tourist resort and are crowded in the season.

The 14th-century church at Torroella de Montgrí and the 13th-century castle may be visited (2M).

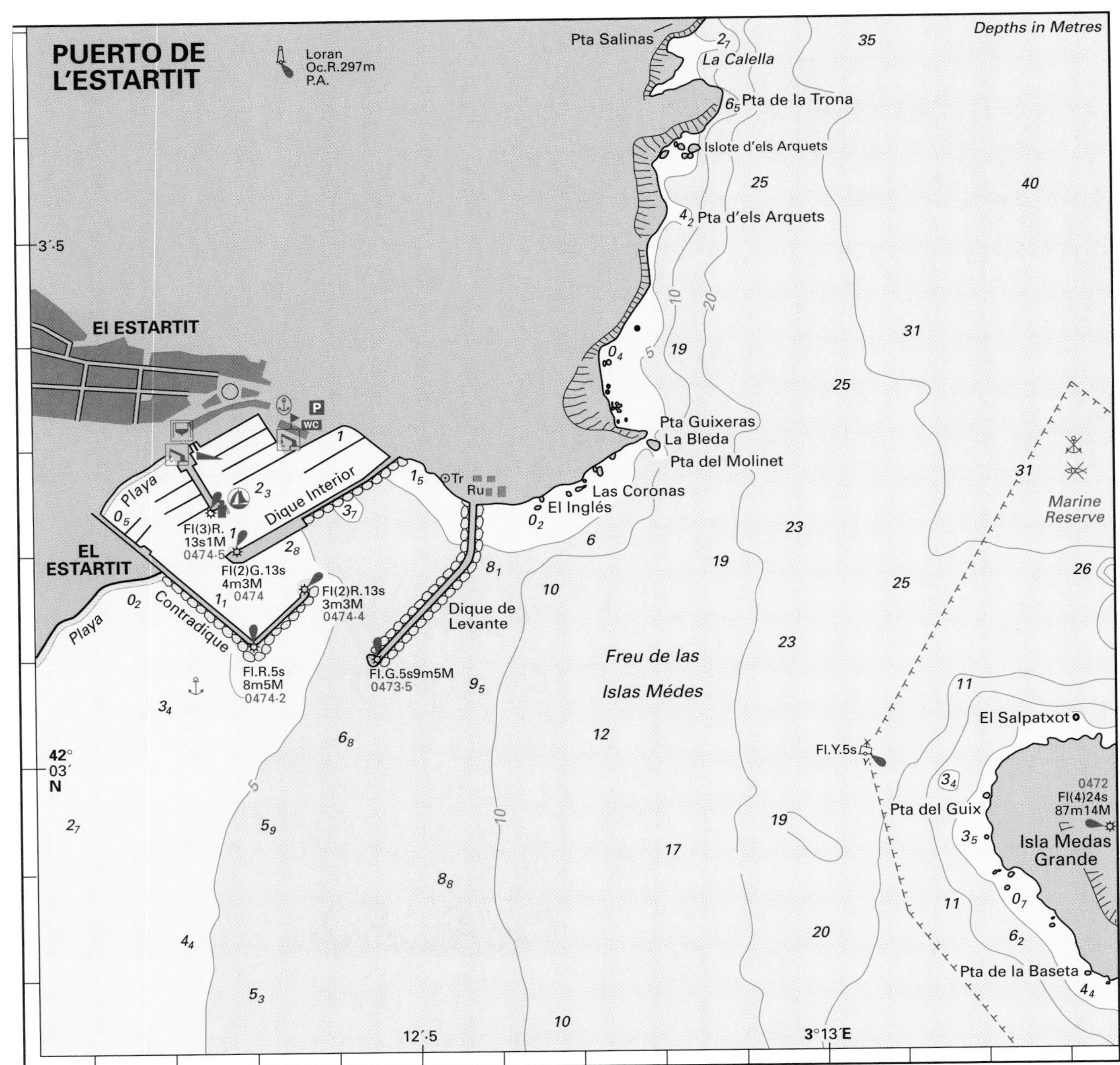

Puerto de L'Estartit

The view from the Castillo de Santa Catalina is spectacular. Excellent sandy beach to SW of the harbour.

Approach

The Río Ter brings down heavy deposits which tend to silt up the harbour and its mouth. Sound carefully. The pontoons on the SW side of the harbour are sometimes removed during winter months.

From the south Cabo Begur with its signal station, Cabo Negre with a large hotel, the group of seven radio masts just to N of it, the Islas Médes close to the harbour and a very tall orange and white radio tower behind it are easily recognisable.

From the north Punta Trenca Braços can be identified by a conspicuous tower and the deep wide Cala Montgó to its S. The coast is very broken but the Islas Médes are easily seen as is the tall orange and white banded radio tower on the top of Montaña de la Barra just to the N of this harbour. Keep over 200m from the shore.

Anchorage in the approach

Anchor 100m to S of the *contradique* in 6m, sand.

Entrance

Straightforward but some sharp manoeuvring once inside.

Berths

On arrival secure to the head of the *espigón* near the fuel berth for allocation of a berth. The inner side of the Dique Interior is reserved for diving vessels whilst the outer side is for local ferries.

Charges

High.

Facilities

Maximum length overall 25m.
Repairs can be carried out to hull and engines by local craftsmen.
Hard-standings in NW corner of harbour.
30-tonne travel-lift.
7·5-tonne and 3-tonne cranes.
Chandlery to NE of the harbour and another to W of the town.
Water taps at the *club náutico* and on quays and pontoons.
Showers.
Gasoleo A and petrol.
220v AC from the Muelle de Ribera and on quays and pontoons.
Ice is available in the season from the *oficina de capitán.*
Club Náutico Estartit with a bar, lounge, terrace, restaurant, showers.
A fair number of shops in the town.
Launderette in the town.
Weather forecast posted at *club náutico* once a day.

Communications

Bus service. Day trips to the Islas Médes by ferry.

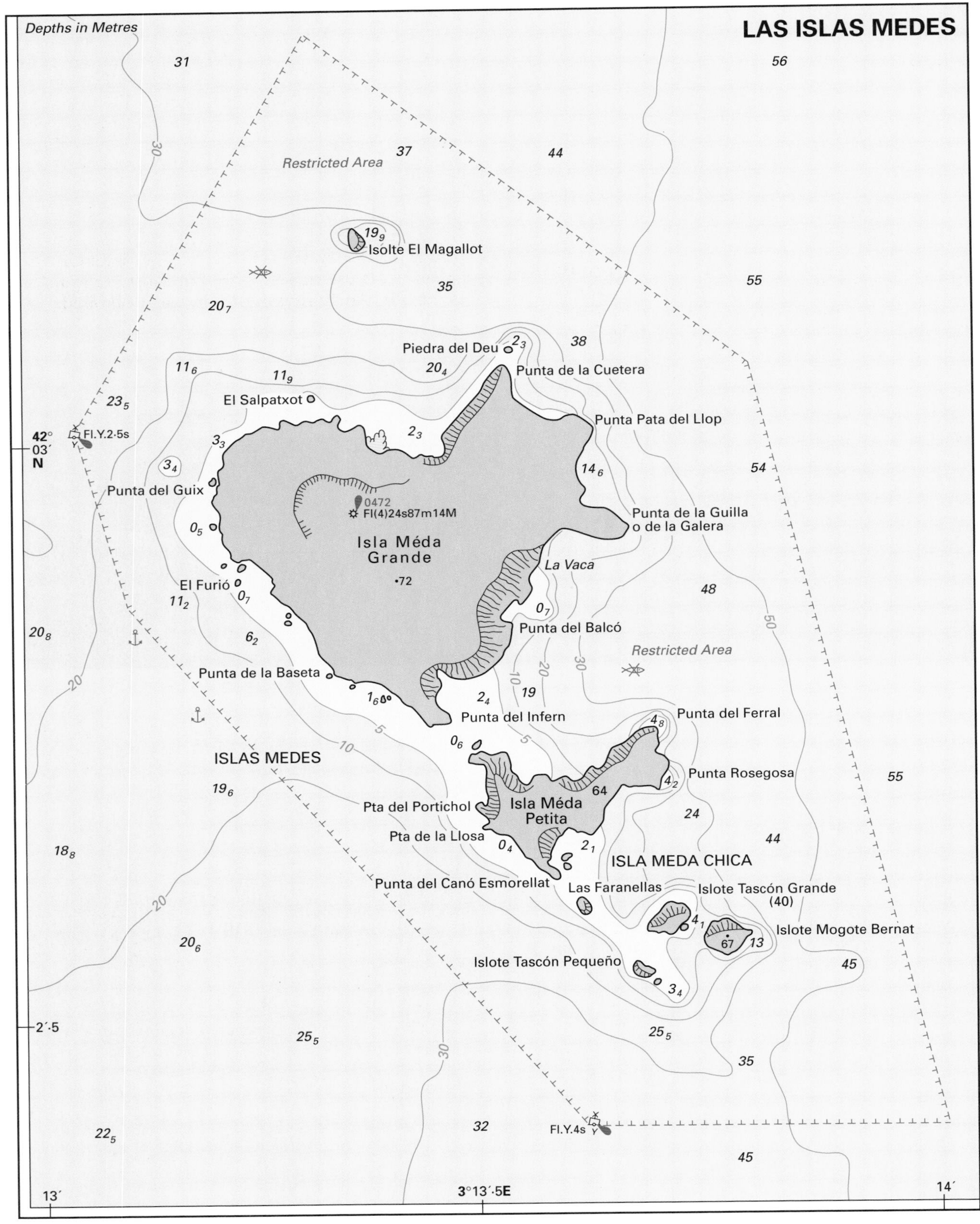
Depths in Metres
LAS ISLAS MEDES
Restricted Area
Isolte El Magallot
Piedra del Deu
Punta de la Cuetera
Punta Pata del Llop
El Salpatxot
Fl.Y.2·5s
42° 03′ N
Punta del Guix
0472
Fl(4)24s87m14M
Isla Méda Grande
Punta de la Guilla o de la Galera
La Vaca
El Furió
Punta del Balcó
Restricted Area
Punta de la Baseta
Punta del Infern
Punta del Ferral
ISLAS MEDES
Punta Rosegosa
Pta del Portichol
Isla Méda Petita
Pta de la Llosa
ISLA MEDA CHICA
Punta del Canó Esmorellat
Las Faranellas
Islote Tascón Grande
(40)
Islote Mogote Bernat
Islote Tascón Pequeño
2′·5
Fl.Y.4s
13′
3°13′·5E
14′

Las Islas Médes

42°03'N 3°13'E

Charts

British Admiralty *1704, 1705*
French *7298, 7505*
Spanish *4931, 876*
Navicarte *E03, E04*

Lights

0472 **Isla Méda Grande, summit** 42°02'·8N 3°13'·2E
Fl(4)24s87m14M Tower on brick building 11m

General

The Islas Médes are a group of uninhabited islands about ½M off Punta del Molinet near L'Estartit. They are a marine reserve with restricted access – see chart. The largest island, Isla Méda Grande is some 500m across and 79m high; there are splendid views from the lighthouse on its summit. To the S of this island lies Isla Méda Petita, 250m long and 67m high. Islote Mogote Bernat, the most SE island, is only 80m across but is 72m high, with almost vertical sides. To the N of the group and nearly 300m away is Islote El Magallot, 24m high. There are a number of low and inconspicuous smaller islets. The islands are in general steep-to but there are some groups of rocky shoals close inshore. The passage between this group of islands and the mainland is deep and clear of obstructions and can be taken under almost any conditions.

The following activities are forbidden inside the reserve:

1. Fishing by line, net or gun
2. Anchoring
3. Collecting animals, plants, flowers, artefacts on land or underwater
4. Visits by night.

Approach

There is no difficulty in navigating the Freu de las Islas Médes as there is a deep-water passage some 600m wide and dangers only exist within 100m of the islands and the mainland shore. The passage is best taken in a NE–SW direction. There is a very narrow passage, 0·6m deep, between Islas Meda Grande and Petita in a NE–SW which is not recommended.

Moorings

Many mooring buoys are laid for visitors inside the restricted area on the SW side of Isla Méda Grande. Small boats use these by day but most are available overnight. Anchoring in this area is prohibited.

Anchorages

The area to the SW of the Isla Méda Grande outside the restricted area is a recognised anchorage. Yachts can anchor 100m to the SW of the landing in 10m weed over sand and stones. Note that there is an isolated rock 50m to SW of this landing which is not shown on all charts. Anchorage is also possible in deep water some 100m further to SE in 16m, sand.

Landing

There is a small landing pier on the SW side of the Isla Méda Grande and one on the NW corner of Isla Méda Petita. These should only be used in calm weather and ferry boats should not be obstructed. Landing from a dinghy in calm weather is also possible on the N and SE sides of the Isla Méda Grande.

⚓ N of Punta Salines

A small anchorage in over 10m rock with high rocky cliffs. Open between N and E. There is foul ground behind the two islets to N of the anchorage.

L'Estartit and Las Islas Médes

Cabo d'Utrera

A double-pointed headland with high rocky cliffs (110m). A small islet off the N point otherwise steep-to.

⚓ Ensenada del Rossinyol

Ensenada del Rossinyol: Anchorage surrounded by rocky cliffs (110m), open between N and E. Anchor in over 10m on rock.

⚓ Golfo de la Morisca

Golfo de la Morisca: anchor in 10m, rock. Open between E and SE. There is foul ground at the NW corner of the bay.

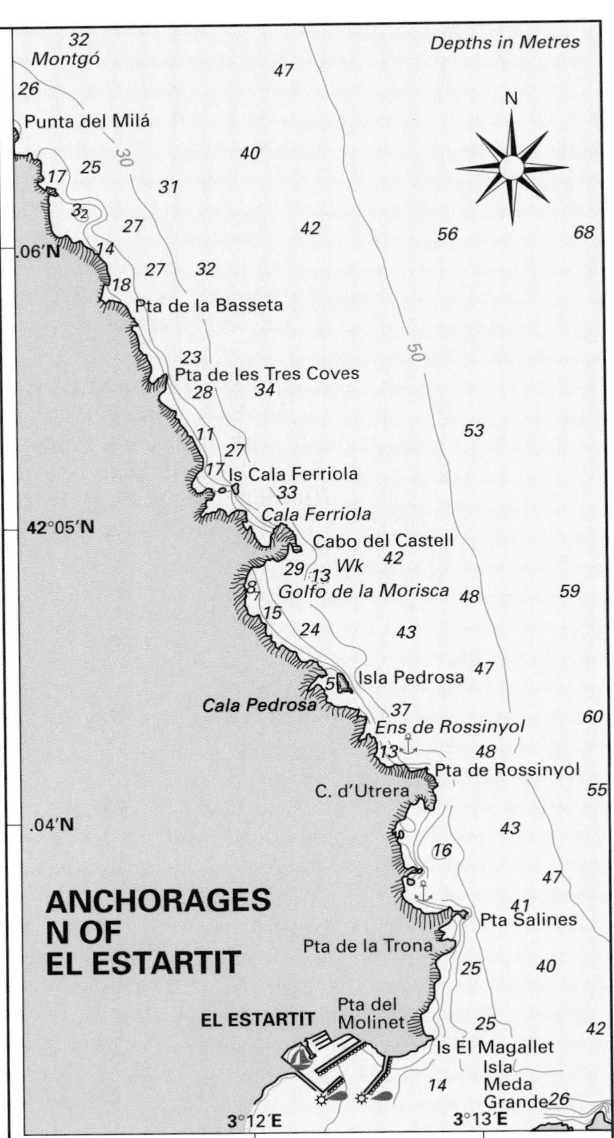

⚓ Cala Ferriola

Cala Ferriola: the anchorage is in 10m behind the two islets. There is a small shingle beach. Open between N and E.

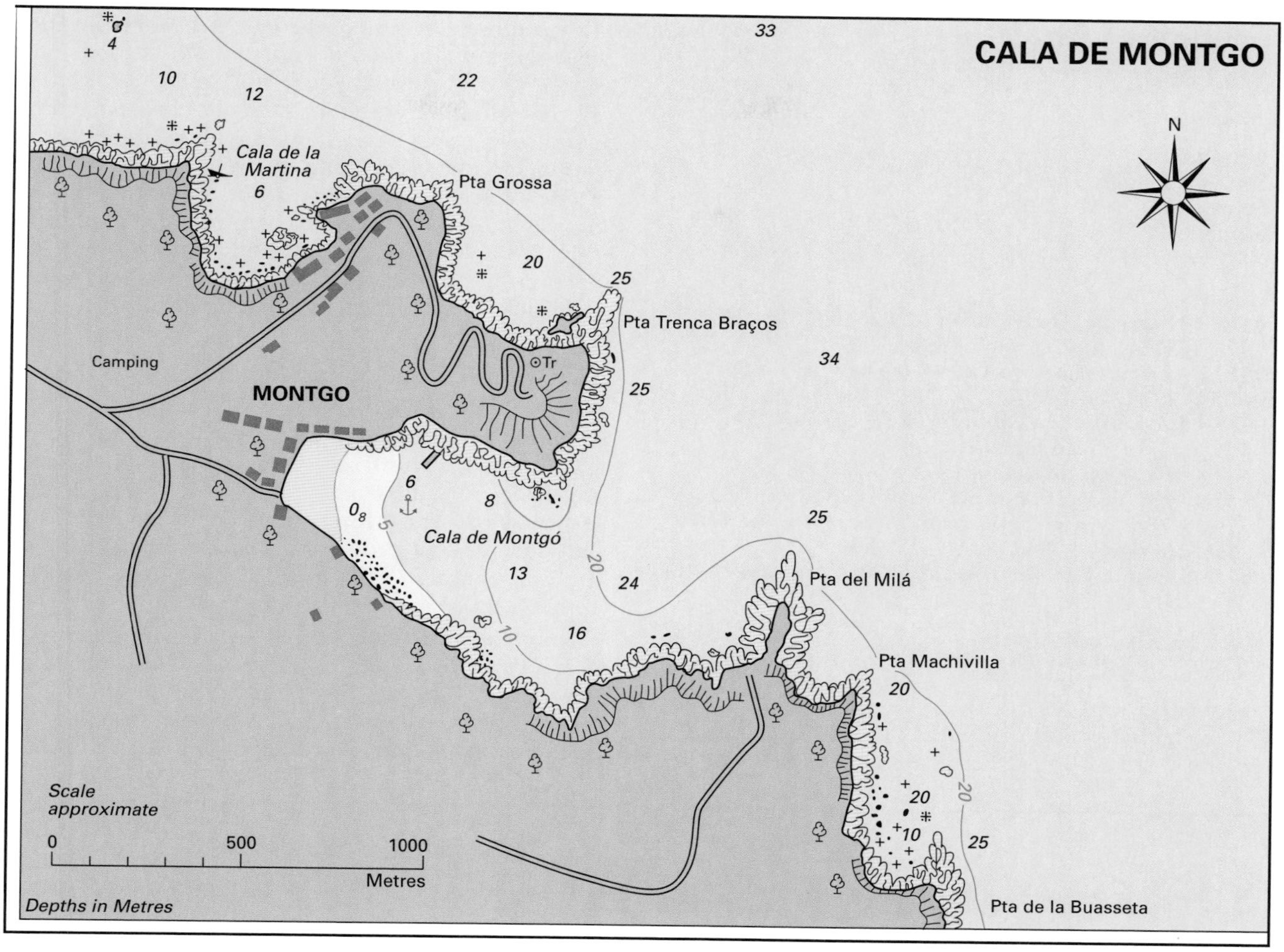
CALA DE MONTGO
N
Cala de la Martina
Pta Grossa
Pta Trenca Braços
Camping
MONTGO
Tr
Cala de Montgó
Pta del Milá
Pta Machivilla
Pta de la Buasseta
33
22
10
12
4
6
20
25
34
25
6
8
25
13
24
16
20
10
25
Scale approximate
0
500
1000
Metres
Depths in Metres

⚓ Cala de Montgó

Cala de Montgó: anchor in 5m off the beach.

Punta Trenca Braços

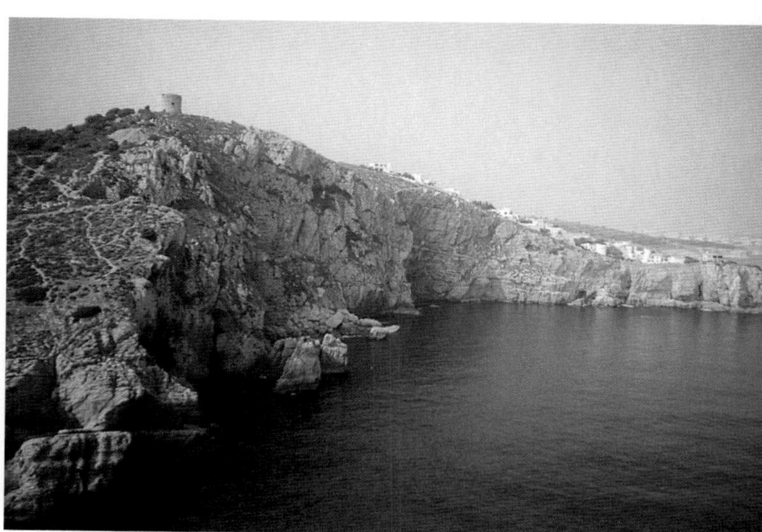

A major steep-to headland (96m), located at the S end of the Golfo de Roses and on the N side of Cala de Montgó. The Torre de Montgó on the crest is conspicuous.

Puerto de L'Escala (La Clota)

42°07'N 3°08'E

Charts

British Admiralty *1704, 1705,*
French *4827, 7008, 7505*
Spanish *876, 493A*
Navicarte *E03*

Lights

0475·3 **Dique de Abrigo head** 42°07'·3N 3°08'·8E Fl(4)R15s12m5M green post 3m
0475·35 **Interior breakwater W corner** Fl.G.3s5m1M
0475·41 Fl.R.3s4m3M
0475·4 **Espigón de la Clota head** Fl(4)G.9s5m3M White post, green top 2m
0475·42 **Espigón de defensa** 42°06'·9N 3°08'·6E Q.6m1M YB post on white base ⬆ card topmark
0475·44 **Dique interior W head** Fl(2+1)G.11s6m3M Green post, red band 3m
0475·45 **Dique interior E head** Fl(4)G.9s6m1M Green post on hut 3m

Port communications

VHF Ch 8 and 9. ☎ 972 770 016 *Fax* 972 770 158.

General

The original fishing and yacht harbour was created by the construction of a breakwater in Cala de la Clota on the east side of the bay. A new breakwater has been built to the north of the old harbour and now houses the fishing fleet and small local craft. Visitors should proceed into the old harbour, which is still susceptible to northerlies which can make the entrance difficult and send in swell.

The Greco-Roman remains at Empuries should be visited as they are unique on this coast and are only 2M away. The old church, Santa Maria de Vilabertran, at L'Escala can also be visited. There are sandy beaches to the W of the harbour.

Approach

The approach and entrance require care due to unmarked off-lying rocky shoals.

From the south the wide and deep Cala de Montgó and Punta Trenca Braços with a tower on its N side are easily recognisable. Punta de la Clota, a low feature with a small fort, is located just to NE of the harbour. Follow round the circular breakwater of the new marina at about 200m until the harbour entrances are clear.

From the north From the massive and mountainous promontory of Cadaqués/Roses the coast becomes low and flat with a gently curving sandy beach. The marinas of Sta Margarita and Ampuriabrava and the inland towns of Sant Pere and Castelló de Empuries

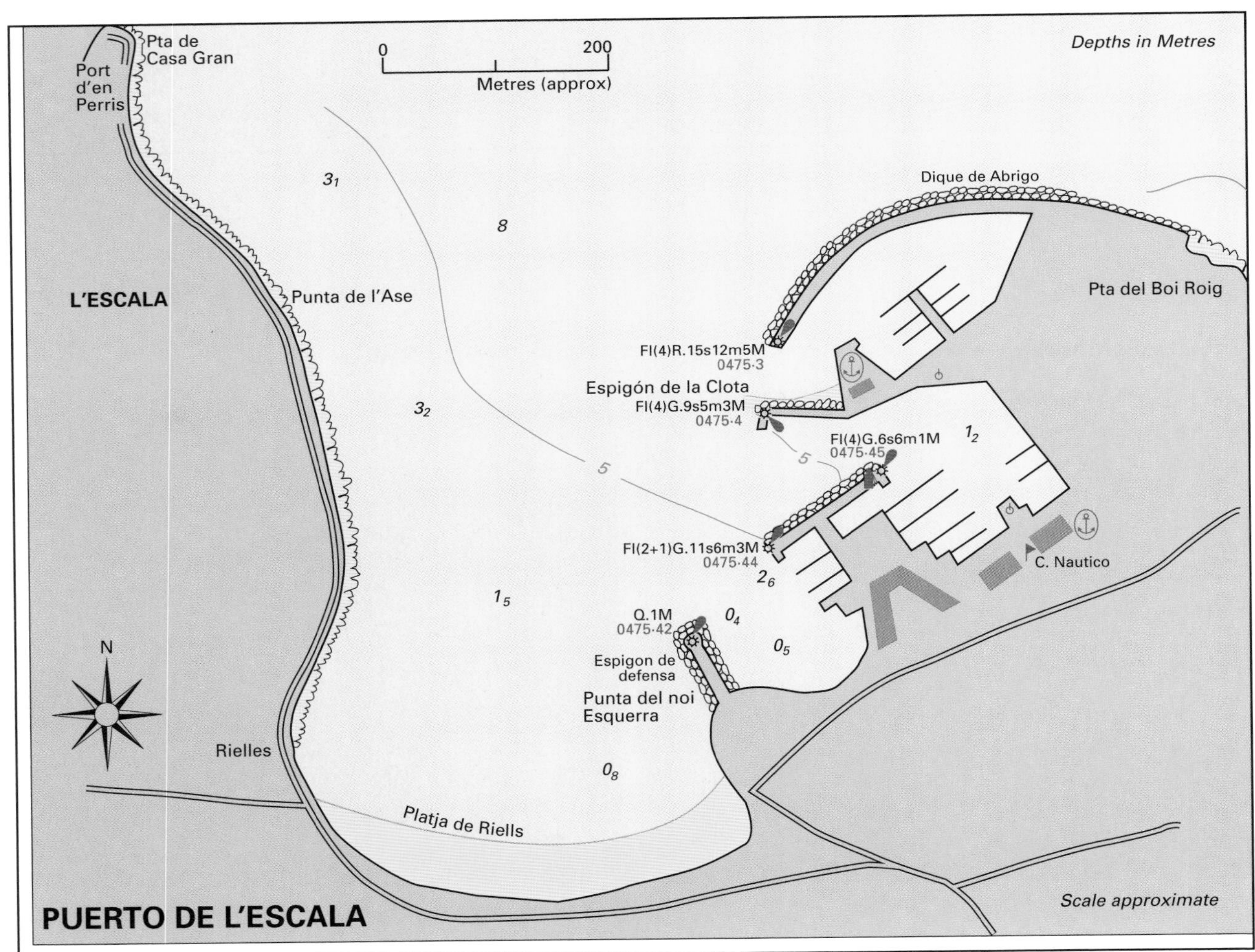

Puerto de L'Escala (La Clota)

will be seen. The coast town of L'Escala will also be recognised.

Do not cut the corner by L'Escala town and, keeping well out from the coast on the west side, make for the head of the Espigón de la Clota on a southerly course.

Anchorage in the approach
Anchor to W of the old harbour near the centre of the *cala* in 10m, sand. An anchor light should be used. It is also possible to anchor off L'Escala in calm weather.

Entrance
Approach the end of the Espigón de la Clota on an easterly heading leaving it 20 to 25 metres to port. Moor to the fuelling point at the E end of the Dique Interior and arrange a berth with the staff there or at the *capitanía* in the club náutico. There is a second *capitanía* (with showers!) being built at the angle of the Espigón de la Clota and one may, in future, be able to moor on the S side of the *espigón* near the new *capitanía* to receive berthing instructions.

Berths
All berths are due to have lazy lines from the quays/pontoons but it is possible that an anchor may have to be used initially on the S side of the Espigón de la Clota. When allocated a berth by the *capitanía* ask as what type of mooring is to be used.

Moorings
Some private moorings to the SW of the harbour, some of which may be available.

Facilities
Maximum length overall 25m.
Mechanics and shipwrights available.
Two cranes of 8 and 10 tonnes and a 5-tonne mobile crane.
Slip to the SW of the harbour.
Water on the quay and the *espigón*.
Gasoleo A and petrol.
220v AC points by the *club náutico* and on pontoons and quays.
Ice from a factory in the NE corner of the harbour or from fuel station at head of Quai Norte.
Club Náutico L'Escala has a bar, lounge, restaurant, showers and WCs.
A limited number of shops near the harbour. Many more are available in L'Escala.
Launderette in the town.
Weather forecast posted twice a day at the *club náutico*.

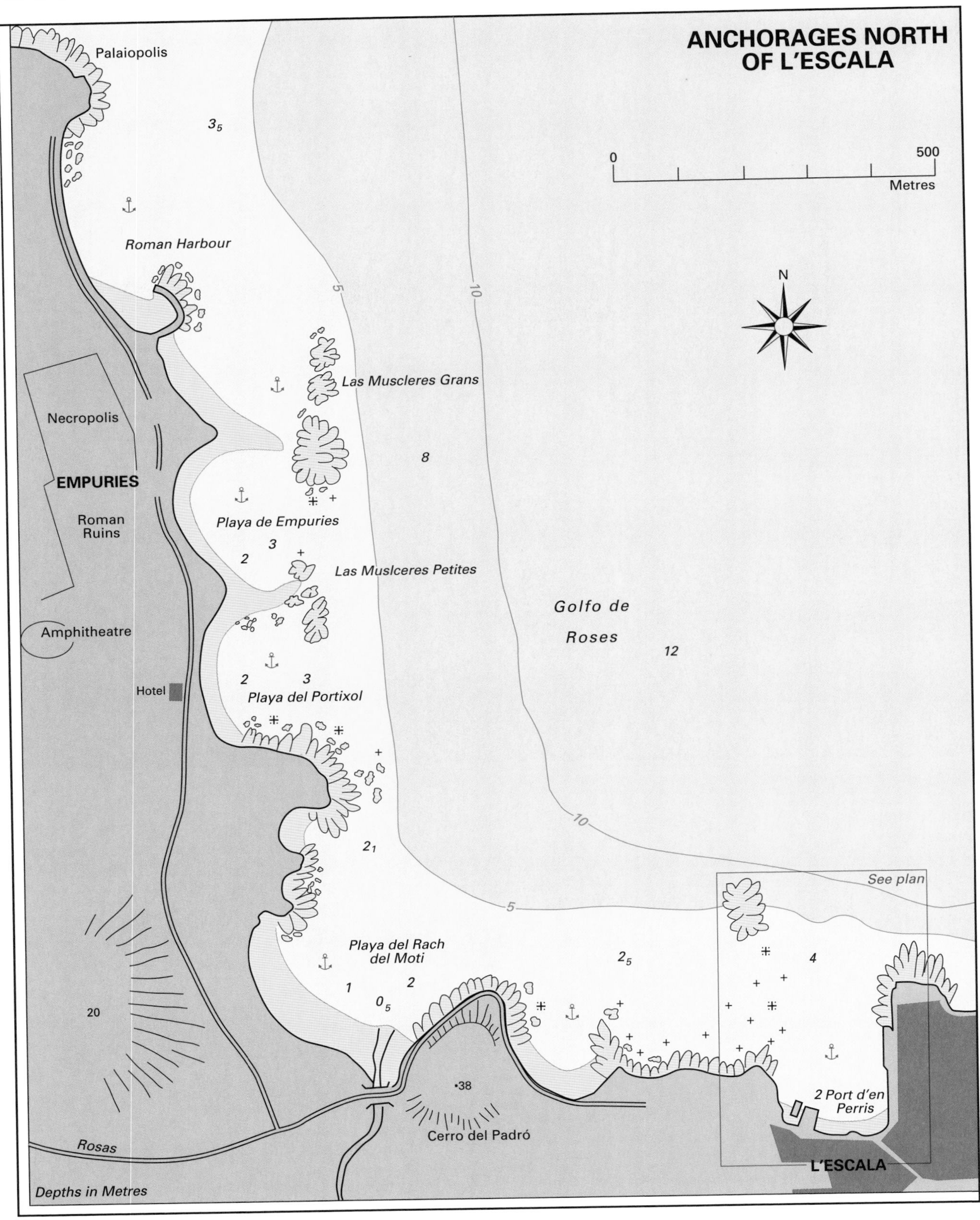
ANCHORAGES NORTH OF L'ESCALA
Palaiopolis
Roman Harbour
Necropolis
EMPURIES
Roman Ruins
Amphitheatre
Hotel
Las Muscleres Grans
Playa de Empuries
Las Muslceres Petites
Playa del Portixol
Golfo de Roses
Playa del Rach del Moti
Cerro del Padró
Rosas
See plan
2 Port d'en Perris
L'ESCALA
0
500
Metres
N
Depths in Metres

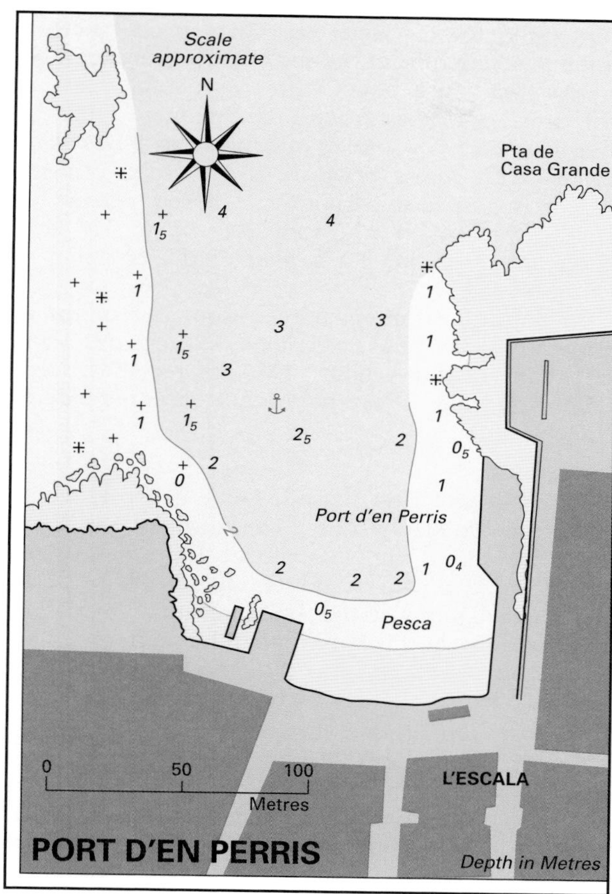

Communications
Bus service ☎ Area code 972. Taxi ☎ 77 09 40.

⚓ Calas de L'Escala (town)

Two small *calas* on the N side of the town of L'Escala, the *cala* to E is used as a harbour for small fishing boats under the name of Port d'en Perris. Anchor in 3m, sand, near the centre of the *cala*, open between N and E. The W *cala* has rocky shallows on the E side and has a sandy beach. Use both *calas* with caution. There is an off-lying rocky islet.

⚓ Las Calas de Empuries

A series of five *calas* lying between natural rocky projections from a sandy coast. The famous ruins of

Playa del Portitxol and Playa de Empuries

Puerto del Rec (Las Calas de Empuries)

the Greco-Roman port and town of Empuries (3rd century BC) lies inland. The beach continues, backed by marshes, to the mouth of the Río Fluviá. Open from N to SE.

Puerto de Empuriabrava (Ampuriabrava)

42°14'N 3°08'E

Charts

British Admiralty *1705*
French *7008, 7505*
Spanish *876, 493, 4932*
Navicarte *E03*

Lights

0475·5 **Dique de Levante head** 42°14'·8N 3°08'·2E Fl(3)G.7s8m5M Green tower, white base 4m
0475·52 **Dique de Poniente head** Fl(3)R.7s8m4M Red tower, white base 4m
0475·53 **Dique Transversal head** Fl(4)R.8s3m3M Red tower, white base 1m
0475·54 **Dique Paralelo head** Fl(4)G.8s4m3M Green tower, white base 1m

Port communications

VHF Ch 8 and 9. *Capitanía* ☎ 972 451 239 *Fax* 972 452 291.

General

Miles of canals lined with blocks of flats, houses, shops and hotels on land reclaimed from the marshes between the Ríos Muga and Salinas. The marine side of the business meets most if not all maintenance requirements. Approach is easy but entering in strong winds between NE and SE is difficult or even dangerous. Once inside there is good protection from the sea but not from the NW *tramontana* which blows with considerable force in this area and eddies around the buildings. Only the first part of this complex of canals can be used by yachts with masts because of low road bridges. There is a special harbour called *port interior* for visiting yachtsmen who may stay up to 15 days. When checking in, get a plan of the complex to locate shops etc.

Visits to the famous Greco-Roman remains at Empuries 6½M, and to Castelló de Empuries 2·5M and Sant Pere Pescador, 4M, are recommended. There are miles of sandy beaches on either side of the entrance.

Approach

From the south Cross the wide Golfo de Roses which has a low flat sandy shore. The towns of Sant Pere Pescador (32m) and Castelló de Empuries (69m) which stand a short distance inland will be seen. The high lighthouse-like building and other high-rise buildings at this harbour can be seen from afar. In the closer approach the breakwaters at the entrance will be seen.

From the north Round the prominent Punta de la Creu which has a small off-lying island and, keeping at least ½M from the shore, round Punta de la Batería onto a W course which leads towards the mass of buildings and a lighthouse-like building at this harbour. In the closer approach the breakwater at the entrance will be seen. Do not mistake Santa Margarita, 1·5M NE which has similar high-rise buildings, for this harbour.

Puerto de Empuriabrava

Anchorage in the approach

Anchor to NE or SW of the entrance in 5m, sand.

Entrance

Approach and enter on a NW course. Inside the entrance, the track is on an S-bend, starting to starboard, round a pier. The corners are blind because of the height of the piers and sand builds up off the pier heads so go slowly and do not cut corners. The waiting dock is to starboard at the start of the entrance canal, immediately after the S bend.

Harbour Charges

High.

Facilities

Maximum length overall 25m.
Shipyard 'Servinav' and engine workshops.
50-tonne travel-lift.
10 and 7-tonne cranes.
Slip.
Several chandlers.
Water points on the quays and pontoons.
220v AC points on quays and pontoons.
Showers and WCs near the *capitanía*.
Gasoleo A and petrol from pumps at the SE corner of the yacht harbour, Port Interior, and at the NW end of the entrance canal.
Ice from the *club náutico*.
Club Náutico Empuriabrava with bar, restaurant, lounge, terrace and showers.

Many shops and a supermarket to SW of the yacht harbour.
Two launderettes within 10 minutes' walk.
Weather forecast posted at the *club náutico* 0900 daily.

Communications
Bus service. Car Hire and Taxi ☎ 972 451 218.

Puerto de Santa Margarida (Margarita)
42°15'N 3°09'E

Charts
British Admiralty *1705*
French *7008, 7505*
Spanish *876, 493A, 4932*
Navicarte *E03*

Lights
0475·6 **Dique de Abrigo** 42°15'·5N 3°09'·1E Q(2)G.4s8m5M White tower, green top 6m
0475·7 **Contradique** Q(2)R.4s6m3M White tower, red top 3m

Buoys
Five red conical buoys mark the port side of the entrance where there is a shoal patch – sometimes red-topped poles are used instead of buoys.

Port communications
☎ 972 257 700 *Fax* 972 151 178.

General
A large development on the flood plain of the Río Muga with buildings along the banks of dredged canals. The marina caters primarily for residents but accepts visitors. The various buildings are run as separate entities with their own offices. The office handling the marina is located at one of the entrances off the main road, at the edge of the complex.

Approach could be dangerous in heavy seas or strong winds between E and S though once inside there is complete protection. The NW *tramontana*, however, is very strong in this area and there is little shelter except in the lee of tower blocks which themselves generate gusts.

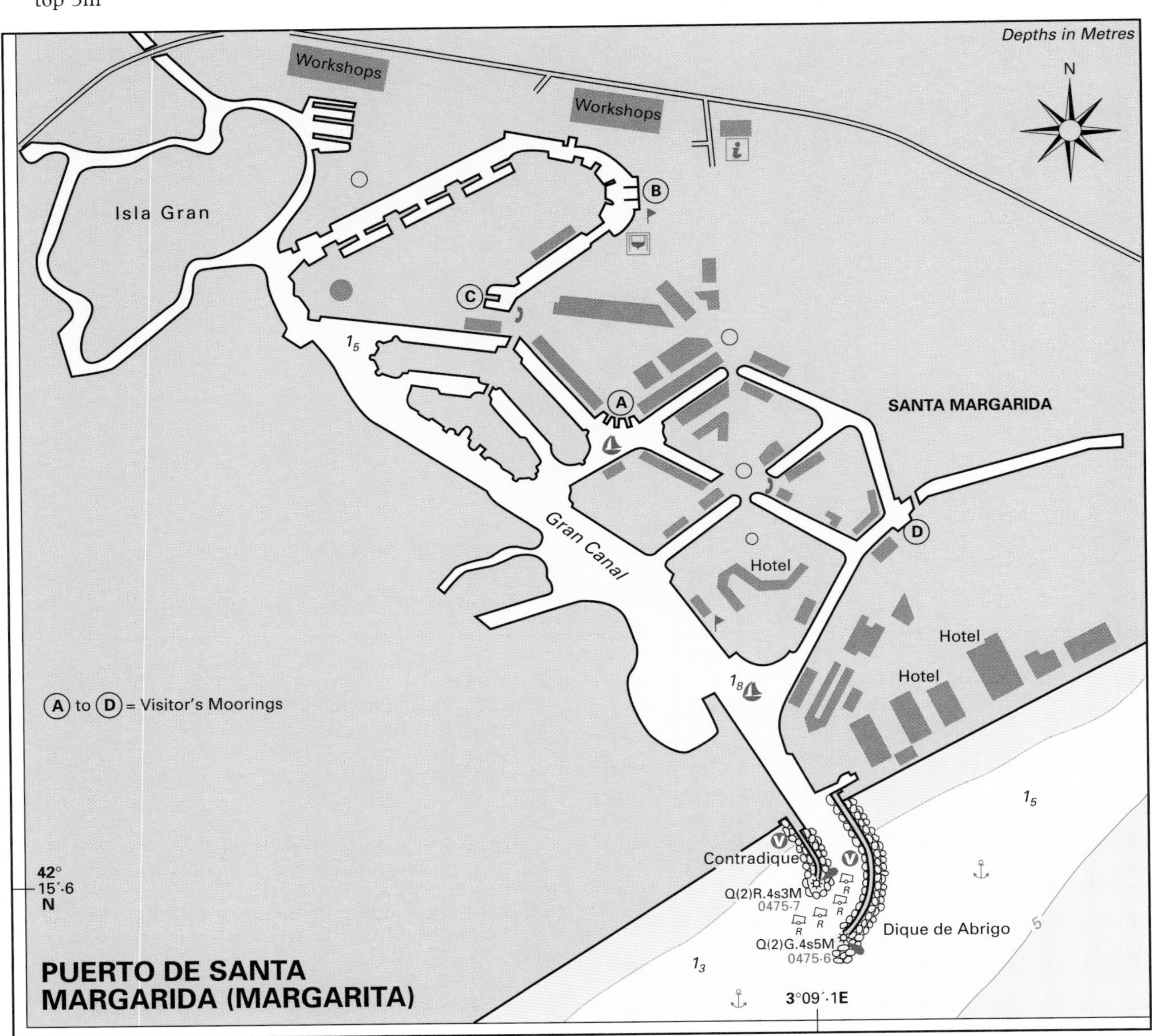

For visits, in addition to Roses, Castelló de Empuries about 3M away has an attractive 11th-century church and other remains. There are miles of sandy beaches on either side of the entrance.

Approach

From the south Cross the wide Golfo de Roses which has a low, flat sandy coast. The two towns of San Pedro Pescador (32m) and Castelló de Empuries (69m) can be recognised as well as the high *torre* at Empuriabrava, to the S of this harbour. The breakwater at the entrance will be seen in the closer approach with a mass of high buildings behind.

From the north Round the prominent Punta de la Creu which has a small off-lying island. Follow the coast round to Punta de la Batería keeping ½M offshore. Set a NW course from this point towards a mass of high buildings. In the closer approach the breakwater will be seen. Do not mistake Empuriabrava for this harbour.

Anchorage in the approach

Anchor to NE or SW of the entrance in 5m, sand.

Entrance

There appears to be no VHF contact. Approach the entrance from a position ½M to the S and enter close to the Dique de Abrigo on the starboard hand, follow it as it curves around the harbour at 20m, leaving red conical buoys and/or red-topped posts to port.

The entrance silts and is periodically dredged. Approach with due caution and sound.

Berths

Secure stern-to the quay by the yacht club area which will be seen ahead or in areas marked A, B, C or D on the plan, with bows-to mooring buoy, or when built, to the pontoons in the yacht harbour on the port hand, just inside the entrance. Then wait developments.

Harbour charges

Low.

Facilities

Maximum length overall 15m.
A shipyard and repair workshop in the repair and maintenance area can carry out minor repairs.
50-tonne travel-lift.
5-tonne crane.
12-tonne slipway.
Slips.
Hard-standing in the repair and maintenance areas.
Chandlery shop.
Water points on the pontoons and quays at A and B.
Showers and WCs.
220v AC at A and B quays.
Club Náutico de Santa Margarida.
A number of shops and supermarkets in the complex.
Ice from supermarket.

Communications

Bus service.

Puerto de Santa Margarida

⚓ Bahía de Roses

There is an anchorage in the N corner of Bahía de Roses, 5–15m in sand, mud and weed, with the ruins of the Ciutadella bearing N to NNW. Open between SE and S.

Puerto de Roses (Rosas)

42°15'N 3°10'E

Charts

British Admiralty *1705*
French *7008, 7505*
Spanish *876, 493, 4932*
Navicarte *E03*

Lights

To the south

0476 **Punta de la Batería** 42°14'·6N 3°10·9E
Oc(4)15s24m12M White round tower on building 11m

Harbour

0479 **Muelle de Abrigo head** 42°15'·0N 3°10'·5E
Fl.G.4s8m5M White tower, green top 4m Fl.Y.3s4M mark marine farm 630m NW

0480 **Muelle de Ribera head** Fl.R.4s6m3M White tower, red top 4m

0481 **Espigón head** Q(6)+LFl.15s3m3M ⧗ card pole 2m

0482 **Playa de Rosas, E pier head**
Q(6)+LFl.15s5m3M ⧗ on black beacon, yellow top

Port communications

VHF Ch 9, 16. *Capitanía* ☎ 972 150 977.
Guarda de puerto ☎ 972 257 087/972 150 408.
Club náutico ☎ 972 256 012.

General

A very old fishing harbour with a mole and an L-shaped breakwater which offer good protection. Approach and entrance are easy and protection from the NW *tramontana* can be obtained but the harbour is subject to swell from winds from S to SW. Construction work is in progress in the

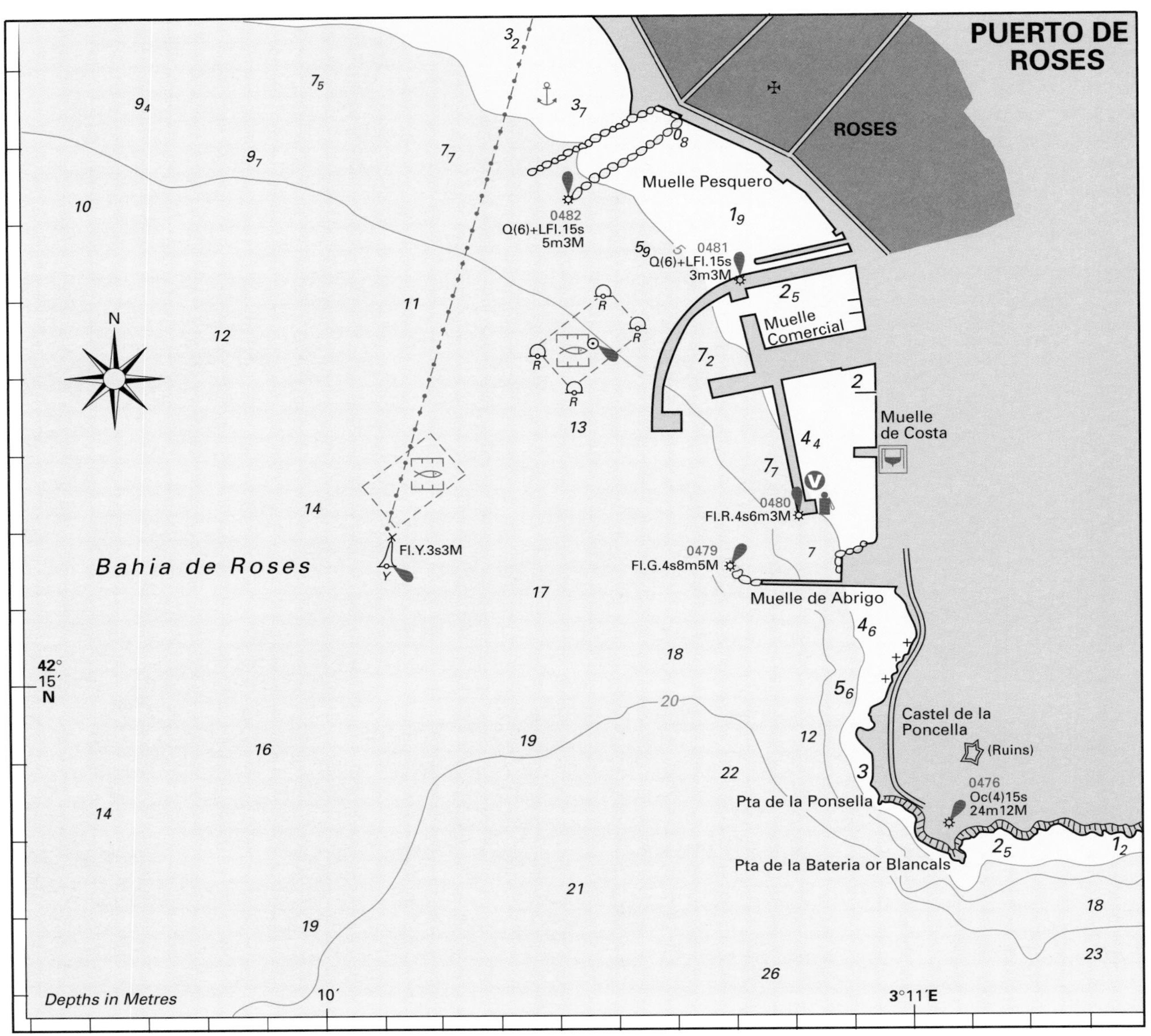

northern basin with breakwaters being built to enclose a pleasure craft harbour. Until this is completed in 2003 it is advised to use other harbours in the vicinity.

Yachts are allowed alongside the east quay opposite the entrance. Space is allotted by the *guarda de puerto* (the *capitán de puerto,* in overall charge, delegates berthing arrangements to the *guarda de puerto*). If a *tramontana* blows up, the quay has to be vacated for the fishing fleet and the *guarda* will suggest alternatives.

Facilities are good. The town which is about ½M away has good shops. The area is under development as a tourist centre.

A harbour has been in use here since the earliest times, its origins being connected with Emporion (Empuries). Greek and Roman records refer to Rhodus which was probably Roses, but there is a long gap in its history from the times of the Visigoths, whose remains have been found, until the Middle Ages when it was known to be a part of the domains of the Counts of Empuries and a naval port. The fort built at this time was blown up by Suchet in 1814 as was the fort on the Punta de la Batería.

There are a number of sites to visit, from Megalithic to more recent times, including a church consecrated in 1022 and the fort that surrounds it which was built in 1543. Excellent sandy beaches to NW of the harbour.

Approach

From the south From the low hills around L'Escala the coast of the wide Golfo de Roses is flat and sandy. The two inland towns of Sant Pere (33m) and Castelló de Empuries (69m) and the marinas of Ampuriabrava and Santa Margarita are the only recognisable landmarks until the massive foothills of the SE end of the Pyrenees that lie behind Roses are visible. The harbour and anchorage are located in the extreme NW corner of this gulf.

From the north After rounding the very prominent but low Cabo Creus the coast is broken with a number of deep *calas* of which Cadaqués is the largest and most easily recognised by virtue of the town at its head. Having rounded Punta de la Creu, which has a small island off its point, keep at least ½M from the coast to avoid rocky shoals. Pay special attention to Los Brancs Canyelles which is over 300m from the shore and has a wide passage

Puerto de Roses. A new breakwater has been built to create a new harbour immediately adjacent to the north side of the existing main harbour. See plan.

inside it. The harbour is not seen until Punta de la Batería has been rounded.

Anchorage in the approach
Anchor 400m to W of the head of the Muelle Comercial in 10m mud and weed, or further to N in more shallow water. Anchor lights should be shown.

Entrance
If going in, straightforward but see below for berths.

Berths
It must be emphasised that this is, first and foremost, a commercial fishing harbour with no real facilities for yachts or other pleasure craft. It is dirty and the fishing fleet take priority for quay space. Storing is not easy so that, unless serious repairs are required, it really would be advisable to moor elsewhere.

It is possible to go alongside the mainland quay opposite the entrance if not occupied by the fishing fleet. In the event of a NW *tramontana* and the space has to be cleared for fishing boats, expect to be advised by the *guarda*. It may be possible to shift to the S side of the Muelle Comercial, to lie stern-to on the on the N side of the Muelle de Abrigo with anchor from the bow if the slipway is not in use, behind the new Muelle de Ribera or to pontoons to the N of the harbour if not in use by fishing or commercial craft.

Charges
Low.

Facilities
Repairs can be carried out by two yards and there are also engine mechanics.
Crane on the S side of the Muelle Comercial.
150-tonne slipway at root of the Muelle Abrigo.
Chandlery shop behind the yard at the head of the Muelle Comercial and two more in the town.
Water from the Club de Mar and taps on the Muelle Comercial and on pontoons.
Ice from the factory located behind the *lonja* and from fuel station.
Club de Mar de Roses has a small clubhouse with bar, lounge and showers.
A fair number of shops of all types in the town about ½M away.
Launderette in the town.

Communications
Bus service.

⚓ Cala de Canyelles Petites

Cala de Canyelles Petites: anchor in 5m, sand, near the centre. There is foul ground around Brancs de Canyelles, ½M to the S.

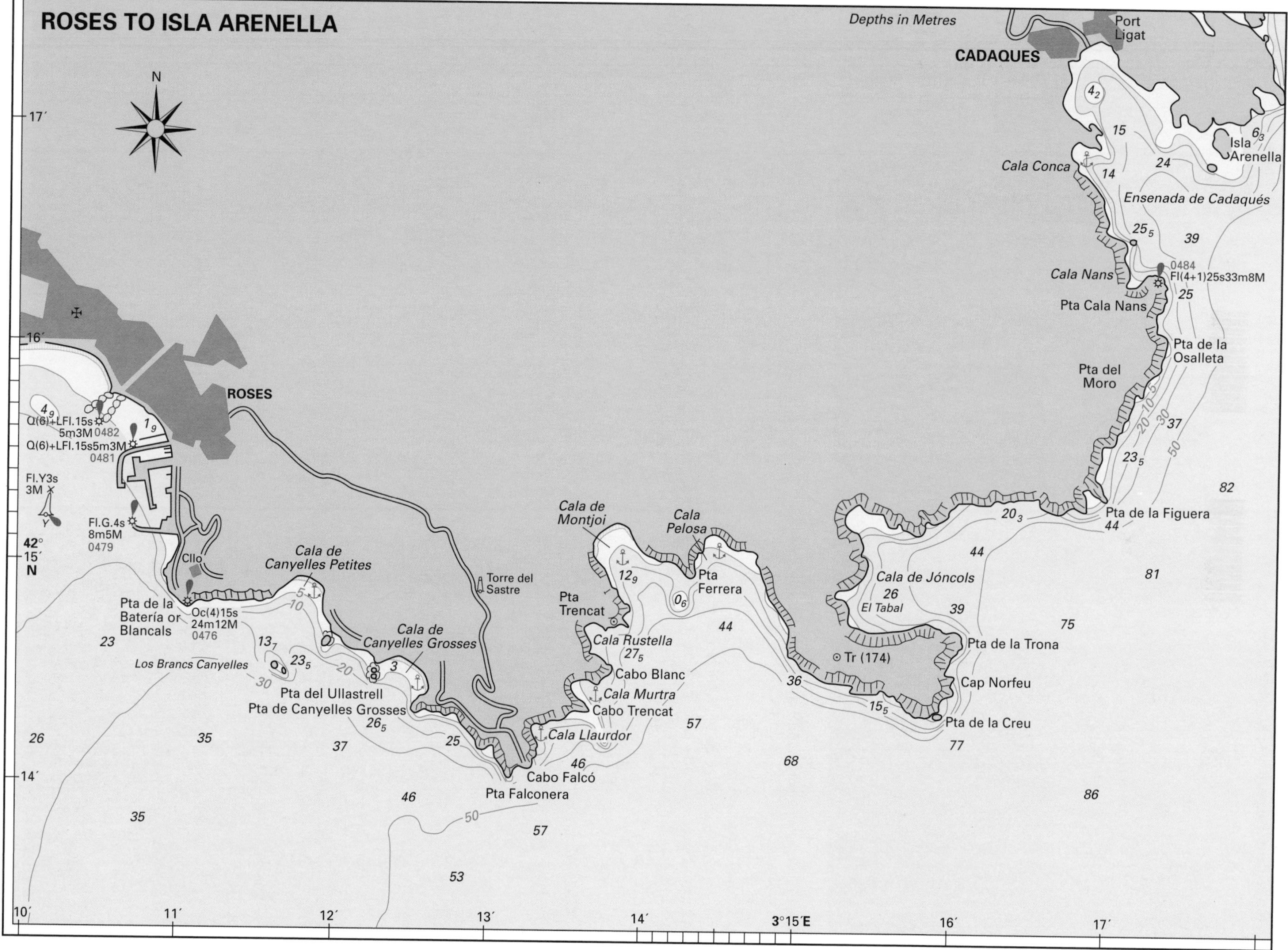
ROSES TO ISLA ARENELLA
Depths in Metres
ROSES
CADAQUES
Port Ligat
Isla Arenella
Ensenada de Cadaqués
Cala Conca
Cala Nans
Pta Cala Nans
Fl(4+1)25s33m8M
0484
Pta de la Osalleta
Pta del Moro
Pta de la Figuera
Pta de la Trona
Cap Norfeu
Pta de la Creu
Cala de Jóncols
El Tabal
Tr (174)
Cala Pelosa
Pta Ferrera
Cala de Montjoi
Pta Trencat
Cala Rustella
Cabo Blanc
Cala Murtra
Cabo Trencat
Cala Llaurdor
Cabo Falcó
Pta Falconera
Torre del Sastre
Cala de Canyelles Grosses
Cala de Canyelles Petites
Pta del Ullastrell
Pta de Canyelles Grosses
Los Brancs Canyelles
Oc(4)15s
24m12M
0476
Pta de la Batería or Blancals
Fl.G.4s
8m5M
0479
Q(6)+LFl.15s
5m3M
0482
Q(6)+LFl.15s5m3M
0481
Fl.Y3s
3M
N
42°
15´
N
3°15´E

⚓ Cala de Canyelles Grosses

Cala de Canyelles Grosses: This *cala* is very similar to Petites except that it is open between SE and W and the foul ground around Brancs Canyelles is ½M to W.

⚓ Cala Llaurador

A small *cala* just to N of Cabo Falcó, similar to Cala Murtra. Enter in mid-*cala*, anchor in 5m, rock and sand. Open between NE and S.

Punta Falconera and Cabo Falcó

A prominent rocky-cliffed headland, steep-to with a small beacon on the Punta. A 5m-deep rocky shoal lies 600m ENE of Cabo Falcó which is usually marked by breakers.

⚓ Cala Murtra

Cala Murtra: anchor in the middle to suit draught. Open between NE and S.

⚓ Cala de Rustella

Cala Rustella: similar to the two previous *calas* but with a larger beach and a road behind it. Open between NE and S.

⚓ Cala de Montjoi

Cala de Montjoi: anchor in 5m, sand and weed, in mid-*cala*. Open between SE and S. There is a shoal (0·5m) 200m to S of Punta Ferrera. Keep to W side of the *cala* when entering but avoid a small rock 200m to SE of Cabo Trencat.

⚓ Cala Pelosa

Cala Pelosa: the bottom is rocky. A tower on Punta de la Creu/Cap Norféu is conspicuous. Beware the shoal (0·5m) off Punta Ferrera.

Punta de la Creu

Punta de la Creu: a large rocky conspicuous headland (148m) with a tower, the Torre de Norféu (174m) 0·7M to NW of the point. A small islet, Carai Bernat, lies off its point, otherwise it is steep-to.

⚓ Cala de Joncols (Jontulls)

Cala de Joncols (Jontulls) with Punta de la Creu at the left. There are two sub-*calas* both with rock and shingle beaches. The N sub-*cala* has a sand bottom and the other stone and rock. Anchor in 10m off the beaches. Open between NE and SE.

⚓ Cala Nans

Cala Nans: anchor in 5m, sand and weed. Open between N and E. The light is Punta de Cala Nans.

⚓ Cala Conca

Cala Conca: keep to the middle and anchor to draught. Open to SE.

Puerto de Cadaqués

42°17'N 3°17'E

Charts

British Admiralty *1705*
French *4827, 7008, 7505, 7298*
Spanish *876, 493*
Navicarte *E03*

Lights

0484 **Punta Cala Nans** 42°16'·1N 3°17'·1E
Fl(4+1)25s33m8M White round tower on house 7m

Beacon

There is a small beacon tower on El Piló in the Els Furallons group of islets.

General

Cadaqués is a large anchorage, easy to approach, with complete protection from the seas created by the NW *tramontana* and partial protection from the wind itself. It is, however, wide open to winds between from E and S. The surroundings are beautiful and impressive and the old town is very attractive. The area has become a very popular place for tourists and holiday-makers.

Once the only route to town was by sea. In the 14th century, with some 600 inhabitants, it was prosperous after a troubled past but in the 16th century the troubles returned. The town was taken over by a succession of masters: Turkish Corsairs, the French, Algerian pirates, the French again in the 17th century followed by the British in the 18th century and again by the French during the Peninsular War. The church of Santa Maria (1662) is rare in that it has not been damaged as were most others in Spain during the various revolutions, wars and invasions. The baroque reredos is quite exceptional and should be seen.

A short walk to Port Lligat, with the summer residence of renowned surrealist Salvador Dali, is worth the effort. As an alternative, there are a number of small sandy beaches at the heads of the *cala*.

Approach

From the south The coast of the wide Golfo de Roses is low, flat and sandy but near Roses it becomes high broken rocky cliffs with many *calas*. This type of coast stretches to Cadaqués and beyond. Punta de la Creu, a prominent point, can be recognised by a small outlying island and the town of Cadaqués with a church spire will be seen at the head of the bay.

From the north The very prominent but low Cabo Creus which has a lighthouse and two smaller towers with off-lying islands can be recognised from afar. The coast to S is very rocky and broken. The Illa Messina, just to the N of the entrance to Cadaqués, is conspicuous and can be passed either side.

From both directions the twin white radomes on the top of Montaña de Cadaqués (610m) 1·5M to W of the town can be seen from far off.

Entrance

Follow the centre line of the bay on a NW course leaving a small beacon tower, El Piló, about 200m to starboard, steering towards the concentration of houses and a church spire at the head of the bay. In a *tramontana,* in order to obtain shelter it is necessary to make nearly 1M to windward inside the bay before the harbour is reached.

Puerto de Cadaqués

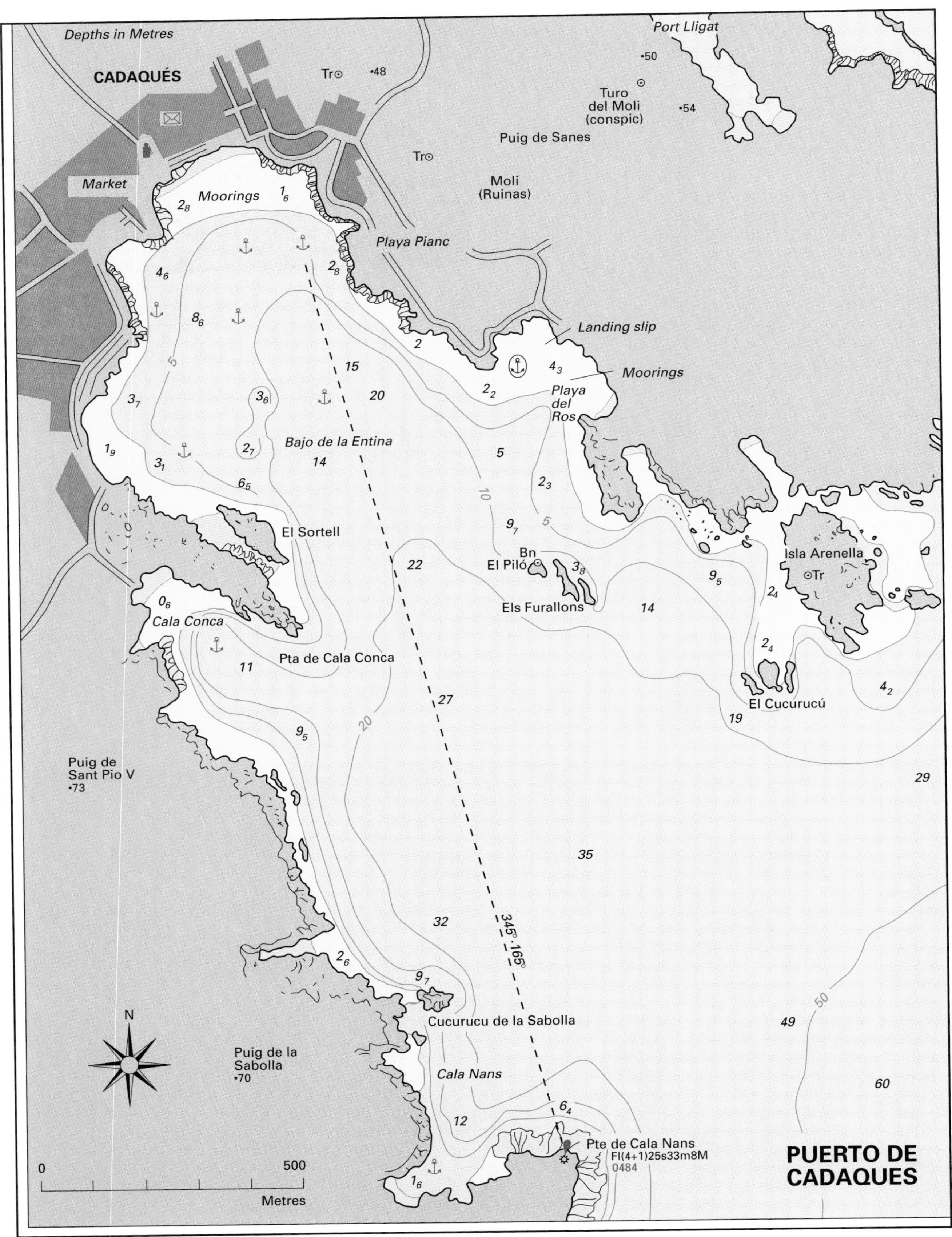
Depths in Metres
CADAQUÉS
Market
Moorings
Playa Pianc
Port Lligat
Turo
del Moli
(conspic)
Puig de Sanes
Moli
(Ruinas)
Landing slip
Moorings
Playa
del
Ros
Bajo de la Entina
El Sortell
Bn
El Piló
Els Furallons
Isla Arenella
Tr
El Cucurucú
Cala Conca
Pta de Cala Conca
Puig de
Sant Pio V
•73
Cucurucu de la Sabolla
Puig de la
Sabolla
•70
Cala Nans
Pte de Cala Nans
Fl(4+1)25s33m8M
0484
345° 165°
N
0
500
Metres
PUERTO DE
CADAQUES

Moorings
Many private moorings will be found near the head of the bay and in the Playa del Ros, some of which may be available.

Anchorages
There are a number of anchorages around the head of the bay which may be used to suit the prevailing wind direction; these are shown on the chart. The bottom is sand, mud and weed with occasional patches of stone; use of a trip-line is advised. In the event of a NW *tramontana*, anchor as close inshore as draught permits opposite the town or in one of the small *calas* such as Cala Conca or Playa del Ros.

Landings
Land by dinghy on sandy beach in front of the town or in Playa del Ros.

Facilities
Water from local bars.
A number of small shops can supply everyday needs. There is also a small open-air market.

Communications
Bus service to Figueres and Roses.

Isla Arenella to Punta Oliguera

This is an interesting area to explore by dinghy. There are many small *calas*, some with stony beaches, and many islets and passages, good for fantastic photos. Use Spanish chart *493*.

⚓ Playa del Ros

Playa del Ros: the *cala* is generally pretty full in summer and it is a matter of anchoring where space is available.

Cala de Port Lligat

42°17'·6N 3°17·5E

Charts

British Admiralty *1705*
French *4827, 7008, 7505, 7298*
Spanish *876, 493*
Navicarte *E03*

General

An attractive anchorage in impressive surroundings where Salvador Dali had a large summer residence. Approach and entrance are simple with good shelter except from NE winds. There is protection from the seas of the NW *tramontana* and limited protection from the effects of the wind itself. Facilities are limited to a small quay for landing from dinghies (0·6m). Many new holiday homes have recently been built around the area and more moorings have been put down. A visit to Cadaqués is worth the short walk.

Puerto Oliguera, Isla de Port Lligat & Cala de Port Lligat.

Isla de Port Lligat and Cala de Port Lligat.

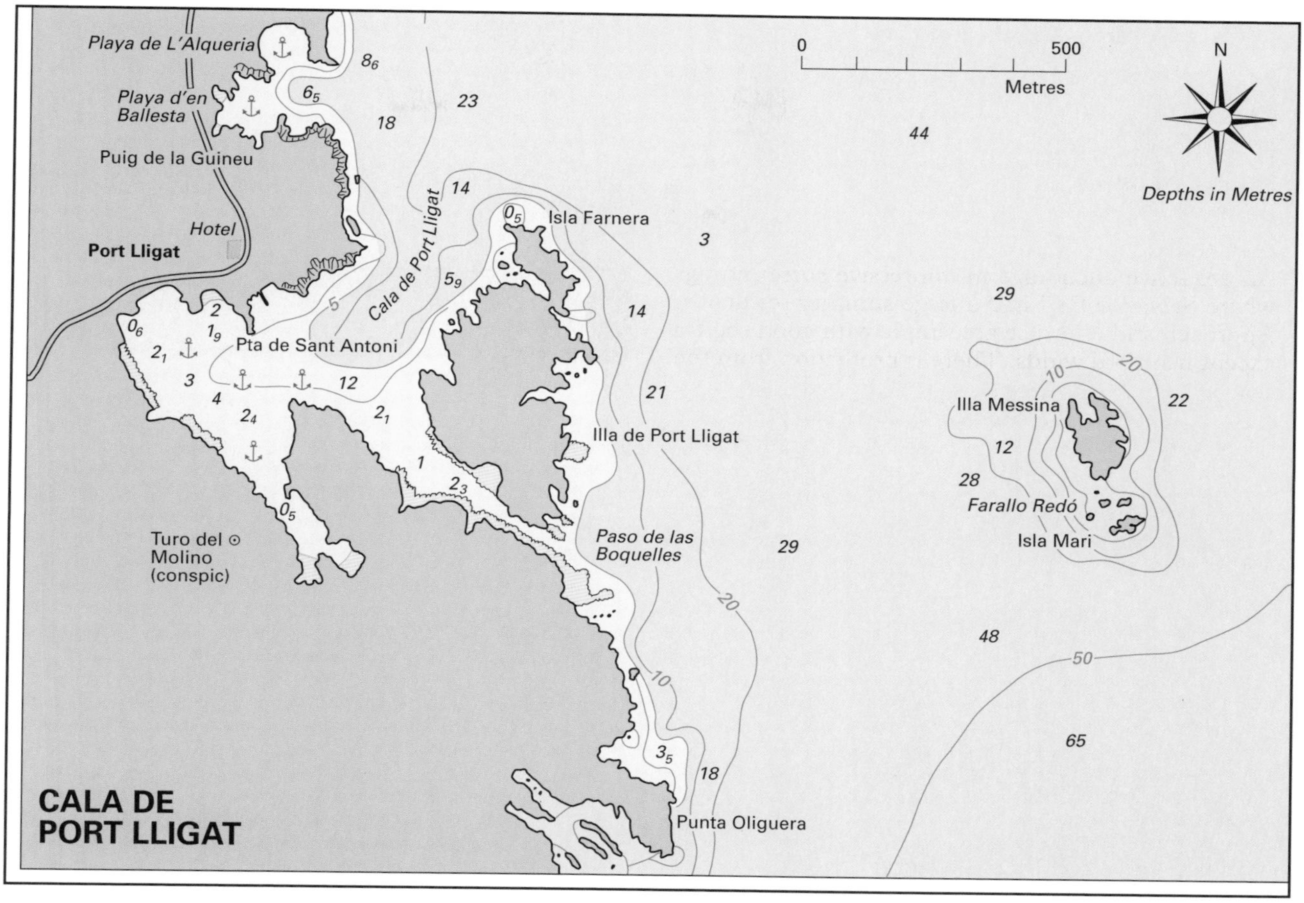

CALA DE PORT LLIGAT

Approach

From the south Round the prominent Punta de la Creu which has a small off-lying island, cross the wide and deep Cala de Cadaqués which has houses at its head. Pass inside the Illa Messina, round Isla de Port Lligat leaving it at least 100m to port to avoid a submerged rock off the N point of Isla Farnera.

Do not attempt the narrow channel Paso de las Boquelles which lies to the S of Isla de Port Lligat. It has isolated and unmarked rocks. The shores of the bay are shallow.

From the north Round the very prominent but low Cabo Creus with its lighthouse, two towers and off-lying islands. The entrance to this cala is wide open from this direction and is to WNW of the Illa Messina. From both directions the two white radomes on Montaña Cadaqués are conspicuous.

Entrance

Enter on a SW course in mid-*cala*, then follow the starboard-hand shore around at 100m into the inner part of the *cala*. The houses are not visible until well inside.

Anchorage

Anchor 100m to SE of Punta de Sant Antoni in 4m, weed over sand and stones. Yachts with less draught may anchor further to the NW.

Facilities

Water from the local small hotel.

⚓ Playa d'en Ballesta y Playa de l'Alqueria

Playa d'en Ballesta y Playa de l'Alqueria: the inner *calas* are banned to boats.

⚓ Cala Guillola & Cala Jonquet

Cala Guillola showing Cala Jonquet, Playa d'en Lluis and Playa Guillola. Anchor in about 3m, stone, rock and sand. Open to the SE with parts open to E and S. See plan page 191.

⚓ Cala Bona

Cala Bona: anchor in 3m, rock and stone. Open to the S. See plan page 191.

⚓ Cala d'Illes

Cala d'Illes: open between E and S. Beware the rocks along the eastern shore. See plan page 191.

⚓ Cala Jugadora

Cala Jugadora, just S of Popa de Vaixell: anchor in 5 to 10m, rock. Open between SE and S. See plan page 191.

⚓ Cala Fredosa (Cova del Infern)

Looking into Cala Fredosa (Cova del Infern), immediately S of Cabo Creus: anchor in 5m, rock, but only in calm weather. There is a much visited rocky tunnel nearby. Cala Jugadora is at the left of the photograph. See plan page 191.

Cabo Creus y Freus

42°19'N 3°19'E

Charts

British Admiralty *1705*
French *4827, 7008, 7505*
Spanish *876, 493*
Navicarte *E03*

Lights

0486 **Cabo Creus** 42°19'·0N 3°18'·9E
Fl(2)10s87m20M White round tower on a house 11m. Aeromarine

Beacons

Two white beacon towers (false lighthouses) are located on this headland, the one furthest to E is very conspicuous.

General

A separate section is devoted to this very prominent headland for several reasons. It is located at the extreme E end of the Pyrenees and represents a major obstacle to be rounded. It is one of the most dangerous points on the whole of the E coast of Spain because it is in the centre of the path of the NW *tramontana* which, with its seas, can be worse here than on any other section of the coast and can arise without warning in a very few minutes. In such circumstances it may be necessary to seek immediate shelter in the local *calas* or harbours described in this section. However in good weather it represents an excellent, unspoilt and attractive cruising ground with many deserted anchorages to visit.

The *cabo* is of dark rock (76m) sloping inland to the two peaks of Els Puigs de Portas (127 and 120m) and on up to Montaña Negra (433m) behind them. To the NE of the *cabo* is the long, thin rocky Illa de Encalladora (38m) separated from the *cabo* by the inner passage which is 90m wide. There is a small rocky islet close to its SE extremity with a rocky reef extending onto SE. Illa de la Massa d'Or (19m) lies 800m to SE of the SE end of Isla La Encalladora. This *islote* has a rocky reef extending 150m to W leaving the middle passage 250m wide between these two reefs.

Readers may wonder why there are 'false' lighthouse towers, one of which is a horn. These were built for a film about 'wreckers'. The situation could not have been bettered.

Currents

A S-going current of up to 1·5 knots is a normal feature of the area though in 1977 it was reported as N-going.

Passages

There are three possible passages round this headland.

Inner passage This passage leads between Isla La Encalladora and the mainland. It is deep but very narrow, being under 90m wide in places. It is shallower at the NW end where the seas break right across it in strong winds between NW and W. The wind buffets and funnels through this passage; be ready to use the engine in emergency. In no circumstance should the passage be attempted in bad weather.

Isla La Encalladora and Cabo Creus

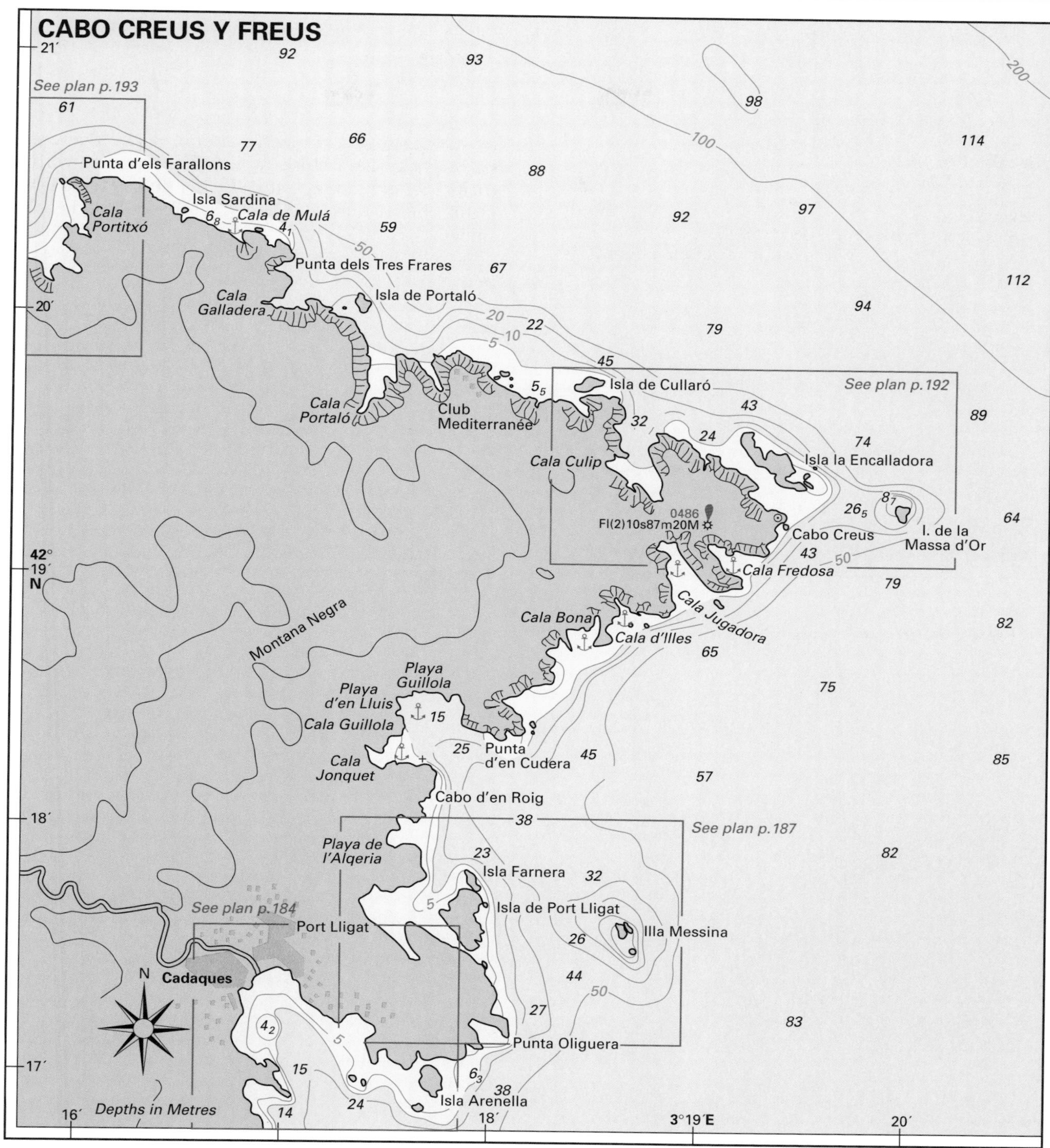

The passage runs WNW–ESE. Approach should be made by closing the mainland coast and following it along into the passage. The outer white beacon tower (one of the false lighthouses) is very conspicuous from either direction.

Middle passage This is between Cabo Creus and Illa de la Massa d'Or passing outside the Isla La Encalladora. It should not be used in very strong winds because the seas break in this area but is quite safe in normal weather. Attention must be paid to the shoal patches which extend into the passage on both sides from the Isla La Encalladora and from the Illa de la Massa d'Or leaving a gap some 250m wide. The passage lies midway between the two islands and should be taken in a N–S direction. It is only about 50m long and is 20 to 30m deep.

Outer passage In bad weather Cabo Creus must be rounded at least 5M out to sea because savage seas can arise close inshore. With very strong SW winds a race develops off the headland. The outer passage is the only safe one to use at night.

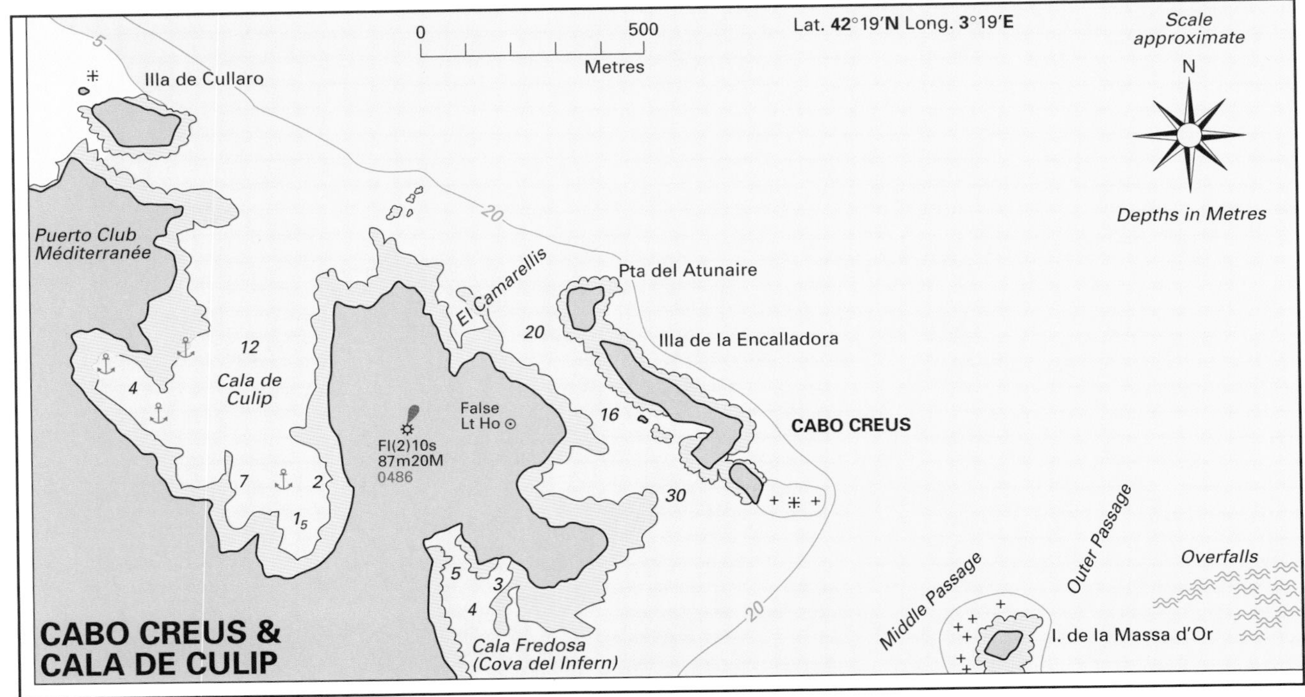

⚓ Cala Culip

Cala Culip: open to the north and susceptible to a *tramontana*. The small crowded harbour on the NW side belongs to the Club Mediterranée.

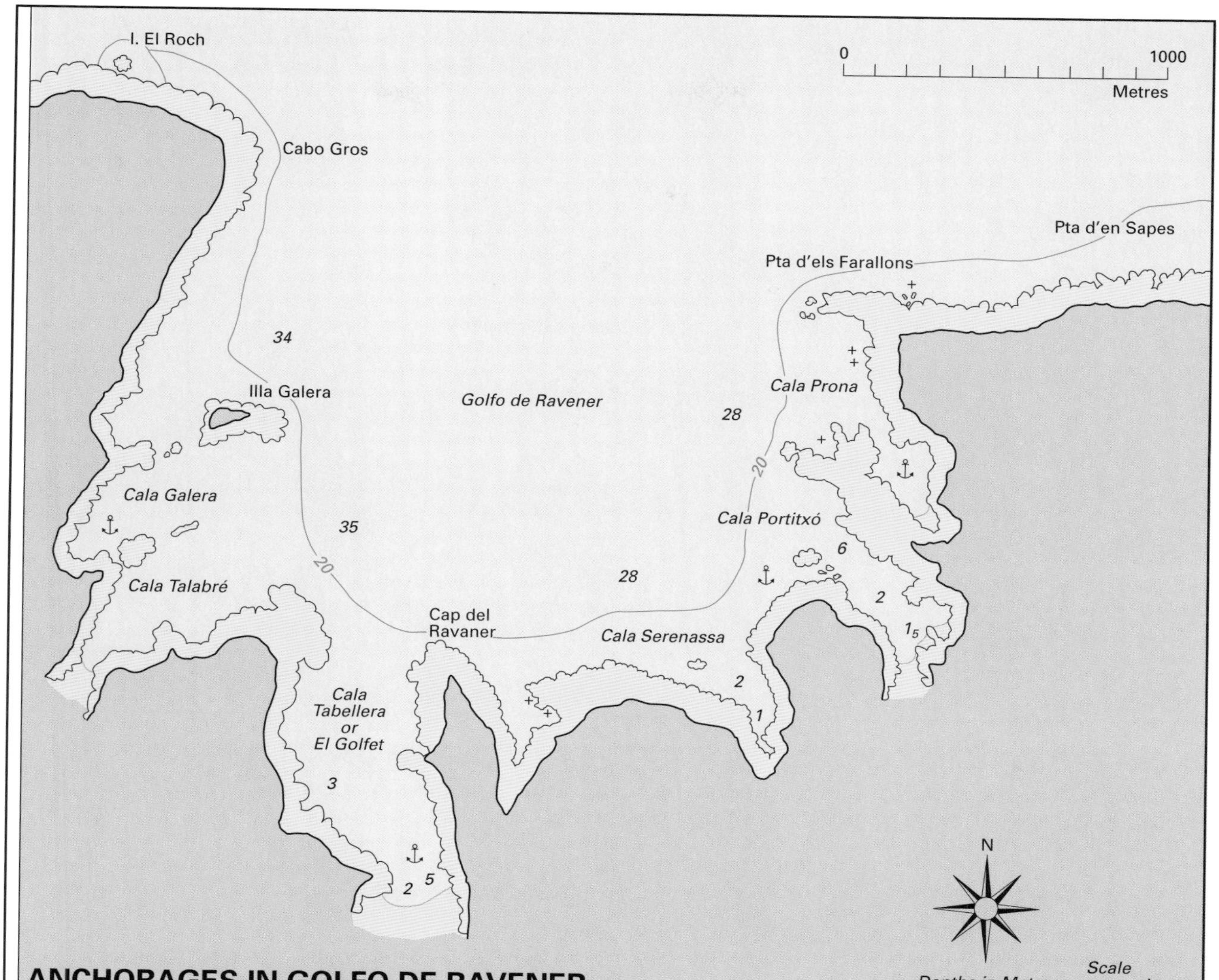

I. El Roch
0 1000 Metres
Cabo Gros
Pta d'en Sapes
Pta d'els Farallons
34
Illa Galera
Golfo de Ravener
Cala Prona
28
Cala Galera
35
Cala Portitxó
6
Cala Talabré
28
Cap del Ravaner
Cala Serenassa
2
Cala Tabellera or El Golfet
3
2
5
N
Depths in Metres
Scale approximate

ANCHORAGES IN GOLFO DE RAVENER

⚓ Cala Portaló

Cala Portaló: anchor in 5 to 10m, rock and sand. Open between N and NE with swell from NW. Club Mediterranée has a holiday village nearby. There is foul ground around Isla del Portaló. See plan on page 191.

⚓ Cala de Galladera

Cala de Galladera: anchor in 5 to 10m, rock and sand. Open between N and E and to swell from N. There is foul ground around Isla del Portaló. See plan on page 191.

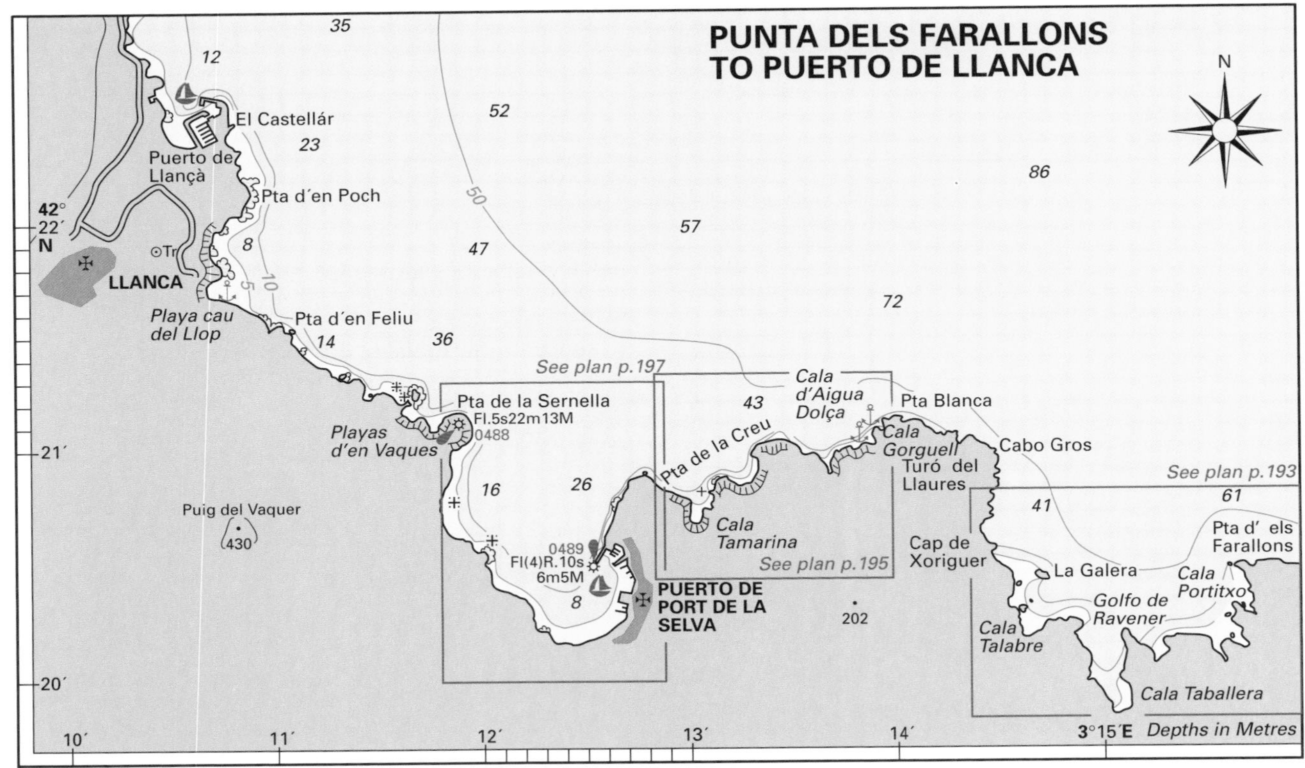

⚓ Cala de Mulá

A small *cala* with rocky-cliffed sides for use with care in calm weather. The bottom is rock. Open between NW and N.

⚓ Cala Portitxó

A pair of sub-*calas* in the SE Golfo de Ravener with high rocky cliffs. Anchor in 5 to 10m. Open between NW and N. See plans above and page 193.

⚓ Cala Taballera

Cala Taballera: anchor in 3 to 10m, rock and sand. Open to the N and to swell between NW and NE. See plan on page 193.

⚓ Cala d'Aigua Dolça

A small *cala* to SW of Punta Blanca with rocky sides. Anchor in 3m sand in mid-*cala*, open between W and N.

⚓ Cala Gorguell

A small *cala* anchorage with rocky cliffs both sides. Anchor in 3m, stone and sand. Open between NW and N.

⚓ Calas Talabré and Galera

Calas Talabré and Galera: anchor in 5 to 10m, rock and sand. Galera is better protected than Talabré; both get swell between NW and NE

⚓ Cala Fornells

A long narrow *cala* with rocky-cliffed sides. Anchor in 5m, rocks, near the head of the *cala* where there is a shingle beach. Open between NW and N. See plan.

⚓ Playa Cativa and Cala Mascorda (Latius)

Two very narrow *calas* with rocky cliffs in a wide bay to E of Cap Mitjá. Enter with care when sea is calm and no onshore wind. Anchor in 3m rocks and sand. Open between NW and N. See plan.

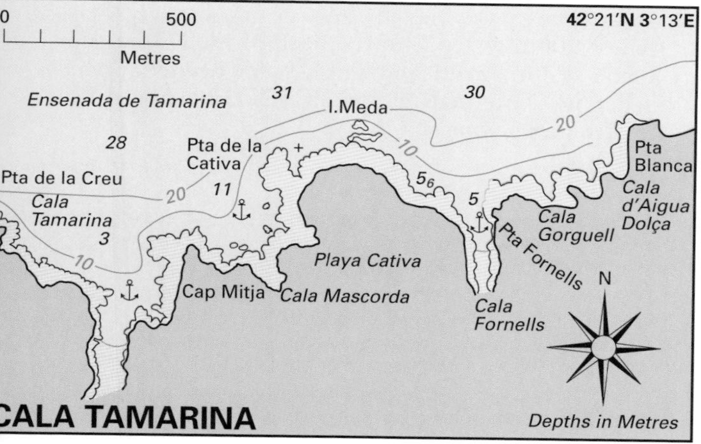

⚓ Cala Tamarina

Cala Tamarina: anchor in 3m, sand, off the beach. Open between NW and NE. See plan.

Port de la Selva

42°20'N 3°12'E

Charts

British Admiralty *1705*
French *7008, 7505, 7298*
Spanish *876, 4934, 493*
Navicarte *E03*

Lights

0489 **Muelle de Punta del Trench** 42°20'·5N 3°12'·0E Fl(4)R.10s6m5M Red concrete tower, white base 5m

To the northwest

0488 **Punta Sernella** 42°20'·9N 3°11'·2E Fl.5s22m13M Grey square tower and building 176°-vis-272° and inside harbour

To the north

0492 **Cap Cebère** 42°26'·4N 3°10'·6E Fl.4s55m15M Grey tower red top 10m

0496 **Cap Béar** 42°30'·9N 3°08'·2E Fl(3)15s80m30M Pale red tower, grey corners 27m 146°-vis-056°

Port communications

VHF Ch 9, 13. *Capitanía* ☎ 972 387 000 *Fax* 972 387 001.

General

A natural shelter on the side of a large bay and surrounded by mountains which has been developed into a fishing and yachting harbour. The approach and entrance are easy. There is very little shelter from the wind of the NW *tramontana* although good shelter from its seas can be had behind the Muelle de Punta del Trenc. Facilities are fair. The town and surrounding area are most attractive but there has been a considerable amount of building, fortunately mostly at low-level, for the tourist market.

The port was named after the extensive forest that surrounded the area in times past. It has been occupied since Neolithic times. Besides Neolithic remains, traces of Greek and Roman settlers have been found. The 11th-century monastery of Sant Pere de Roda, founded by the Benedictines and consecrated in 1022, kept strict control over the area despite constant incursion by the Counts of Ampuries. It was abandoned in 1798 and only recently has restoration commenced.

The local church, partly destroyed in the civil war, is interesting as it is half old and half modern. The monastery of Sant Pere de Roda and Sant Salvadó castle on the Sierra de Roses should be visited. The view from these points is fantastic.

Approach

From the south Round the very prominent Cabo Creus which has a lighthouse, two towers and off-lying islands. The coast is very broken and rocky with three major *calas* and many smaller ones. The wide bay at La Selva is easily recognised and the harbour will be found tucked away on its E side when Punta de la Creu has been rounded.

From the north From Cap Béar (France) with its conspicuous lighthouse, fort, radio and signal station the coast is high and rugged with a series of similar bays and headlands. Follow this coast to S, having passed Punta de la Sernella with its lighthouse, thence into the Bahía de la Selva where the harbour will be found on the E side.

On a clear day the two radomes on Montaña Cadaqués and the monastery Sant Pere de Roda on the mountain behind La Selva will be seen.

Anchorage in the approach
Anchor 200m to SE of the head of the Muelle de Punta del Trenc in 5m, weed over sand, or in deeper water further W. These anchorages are open to the NW *tramontana*.

Entrance
Approach the centre of the Bahía de la Selva on a S course. When level with the head of the Muelle de Punta del Trenc, turn onto an E course and enter leaving the head of the *muelle,* which has foul ground around it, at least 50m to port.

Berths
Secure stern-to pontoon at the SE side of the harbour with anchor ahead or, if available, use a mooring buoy. These berths are often fully occupied. Yachts can also berth at Punta Timba, opposite *lonja* buildings, in comfort though draught is limited and it is a dangerous position during a NW *tramontana*. During this wind vessels secure to the SE side of the Muelle de Punta del Trenc or to vacant pontoons in the inner harbour.

Moorings
Some private moorings may be available; contact *club náutico* officials for advice.

Anchorage
Anchor 200m to the E of the head of the Dique del Muelle in 5m, weed and sand, or in deeper water further W. Note that all anchorages are exposed to the NW *tramontana*.

Port de la Selva

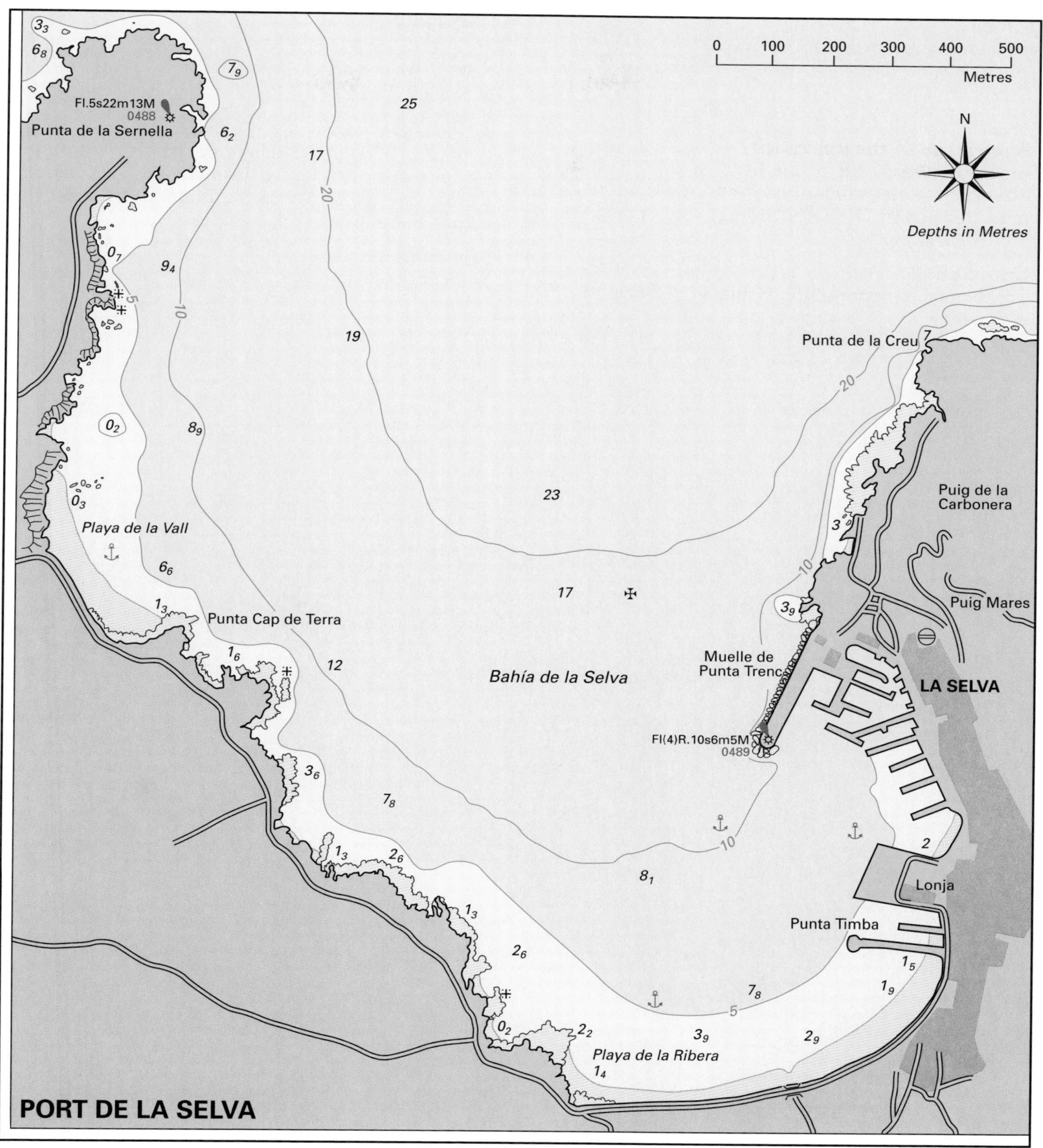
0 100 200 300 400 500
Metres
N
Depths in Metres
Fl.5s22m13M
0488
Punta de la Sernella
Playa de la Vall
Punta Cap de Terra
Punta de la Creu
Puig de la Carbonera
Puig Mares
Muelle de Punta Trenc
LA SELVA
Bahía de la Selva
Fl(4)R.10s6m5M
0489
Lonja
Punta Timba
Playa de la Ribera
PORT DE LA SELVA

Facilities

Maximum length overall 27m.
Minor repairs to hull and engines can be carried out by local craftsmen.
A small crane 1 tonne in the inner harbour and a larger one of 12·5 tonnes on the *muelle*.
A very small slip in the inner harbour and another to S of the harbour.
Chandler near the harbour and another in the town.
Water on the quays and pontoons.
220v AC on quays and pontoons.
Gasoleo A and petrol.
Club Náutico de Puerto de la Selva clubhouse with bar, restaurant, lounge, terrace, swimming pool and showers.
A fair selection of shops in and around the town.
Weather forecasts posted once a day.

Communications

Bus and rail service from Llançá 4M away. Taxi ☎ 972 387 392.

⚓ Playa de La Vall

Playa de La Vall: anchor in 3m, sand. Open between N and E.

⚓ Playa de la Ribera

A long, crescent-shaped sandy beach to S of La Selva. Anchor in 3m, sand, off the beach, open between NW and NE. Road and houses ashore. The W end of the beach has a rocky bottom. Dangerous during a NW *tramontana*.

⚓ Playas de'n Vaqués

Above and below.
Playas de'n Vaqués: two *calas* to N of Punta de la Sernella and largely hidden in this photograph. Anchor in 5m, rock and stone, in mid-*cala*. Open between N and E. See plan page 194.

⚓ Playa Cau del Llop

A large bay with a sandy beach. There is foul ground on the N side of the *cala*. Anchor in the middle, 5m, sand. Open between N and E. See plan page 194.

Puerto de Llançà (Llansá)

42°22'4N 3°09'E

Charts
British Admiralty *1705*
French *6843*
Spanish *876, 493*
Navicarte *E03*

Lights
0489·2 **Breakwater head** 42°22'·3N 3°09'·7E
Fl(3)R.10s8m5M Red concrete tower, white base 3m
0489·3 **Jetty head** Fl(4)R.12s2M White tower, red top
0489·4 **Contradique head** Fl(3)G.10s5m5M White concrete tower, green top 2m

Port communications
VHF Ch 9. ☎ 38 07 10 *Fax* 38 07 06.

General
A former fishing harbour and anchorage now developed as a resort with a good yacht harbour. Approach and entrance are easy and it has better protection than Selva or Portbou. The area is attractive. This harbour was called Deciana in Roman times. In the 17th and 18th centuries it exported a large amount of marble, olive oil and wine. The local wine is still one of the strongest to be found. There is an interesting 18th-century church and it is possible to visit the Benedictine monastery of Sant Pere de Roda and Sant Salvadó Castle, 670m above sea level with a fantastic view. There are also the Dali and the Toy Museums and excellent bathing beaches around the bay.

Approach
All the headlands in this bay have tongues of rocks projecting from the outer ends which are just below sea level.

From the south Cross the mouth of the deep Bahía de la Selva, which has Port de la Selva on its E side, and round Punta de la Sernella which has a lighthouse near the point. Keep at least 500m from the shore until the Ensenada de Llançà is fully opened up, then round El Castellár, which has a small castle on its top and follow the breakwater round.

From the north This harbour lies in the third large bay 3M to the S of Portbou. It can be recognised by El Castellár with its small castle lying just behind the harbour and the houses of the Puerto de Llançà can also be seen from this direction. The harbour lies in the S corner of the bay.

Entrance
Round the breakwater head with caution prepared for a sharp turn to starboard.

Puerto de Llançá

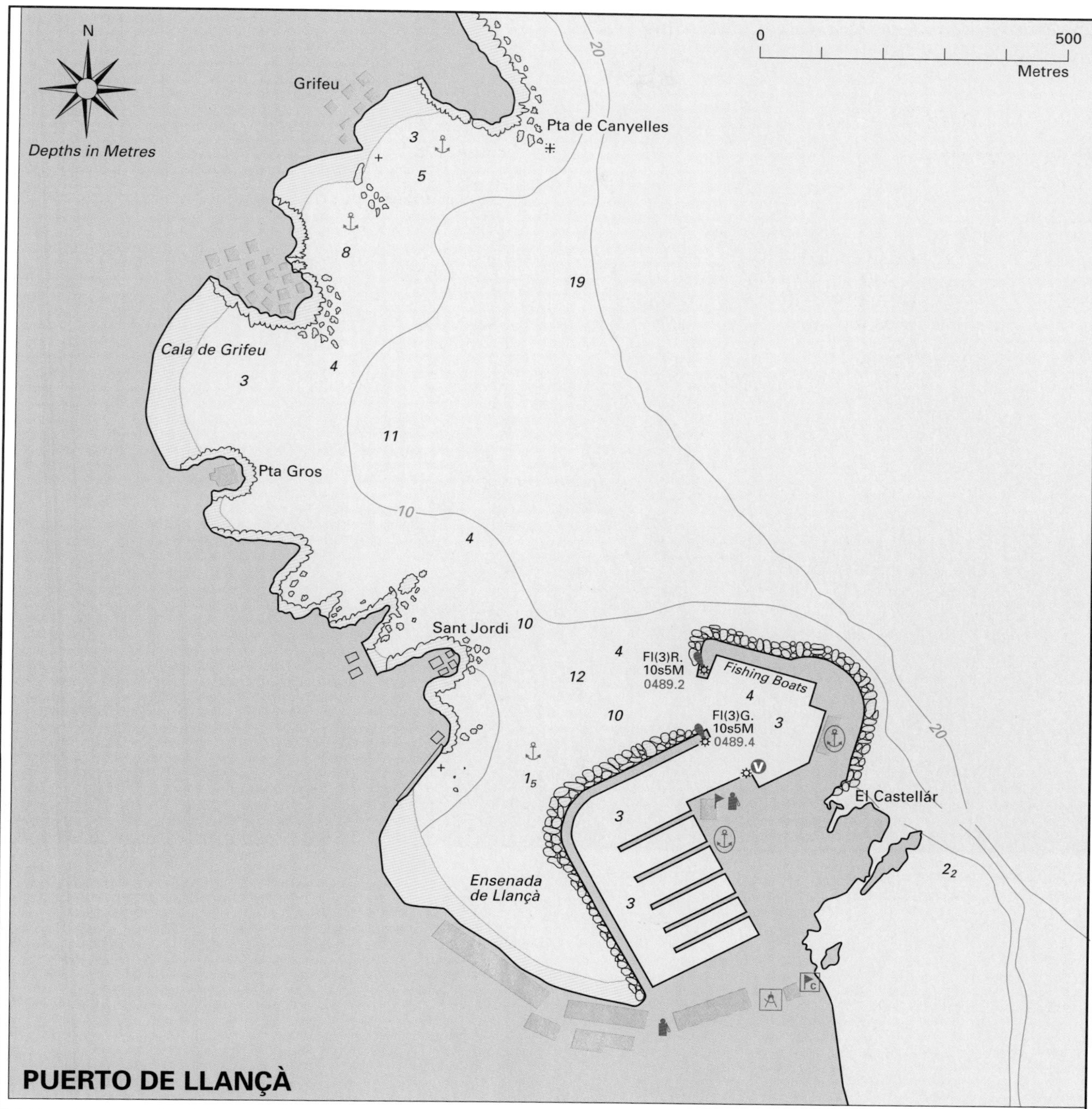

Berths

Go alongside the visitors quay and ask for a berth.

Anchorages

NW of the harbour in 3m, sand and weed, but it is very exposed. Keep clear of the harbour entrance and use an anchor light. There are two other anchorages which may have better shelter on the N side of the *ensenada* (see plan).

Facilities

Maximum length overall 15m.
Mechanics.
12-tonne crane.
Water on the quays.
230v AC on quays.
Gasoleo A and petrol.
Club Náutico de Llançà has the weather forecast posted daily.
Shops in the village and more at Llançá town some ½M away.

Communications

Railway to Barcelona and France. Taxi ☎ 972 381 344/972 380 317.

⚓ Cala Grifeu

Cala Grifeu: anchor in the middle; there is foul ground on both sides. Open between E and SE. See plan on page 201.

⚓ Cala Garbet

Cala Garbet: large bay open between NE and SE. Anchor in 10m, rock and sand. The NW corner of the bay is foul.

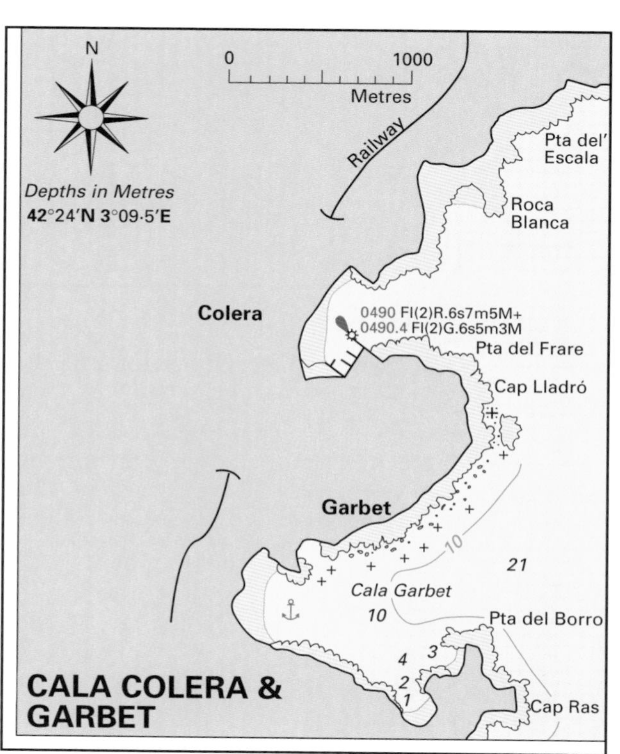

Puerto de Colera

42°24'N 3°9'E

Charts
British Admiralty *1705*
French *7008, 7505*
Spanish *876, 493*
Navicarte *E03*

Lights
0490 **Dique de Levante head** 42°24'·3N 3°09'·3E Fl(2)R.6s7m5M Red structure 3m
0490·4 **Contradique head** Fl(2)G.6s5m3M Green tower white base3m
To the north
0492 **Cap Cerbère** 42°26'·4N 3°10'·6E Fl.4s55m15M Grey tower red top 10m

Port communications
Club Náutico Sant Miquel de Colera ☎ 972 389 095.

General
A small fishing harbour and village originally called St Miquel which was also used as a staging post on the main coast road. It has a small harbour for yachts and fishing craft tucked away on the S side of the *cala*. It is a useful harbour with better protection than the quay at Portbou though a NW *tramontana* creates a chop inside parts of the harbour. The area is impressive with high mountains all around. Harbour facilities are limited. There are a few shops in the village for everyday requirements and a beach of sand and stone to W of the harbour.

Approach
From the south Leave the Bahía de la Selva and follow the coast at 500m to N. The following are easy to identify: Punta Sernella with a lighthouse, Puerto de Llançá which appears behind the Islote and Punta del Castellá, Cabo Rose with the wide Cala Garbet to its N and Cabo Lladró with a detached islet. Cala Colera lies to its N but the harbour remains hidden until mid-*cala* is reached.

Puerto de Colera

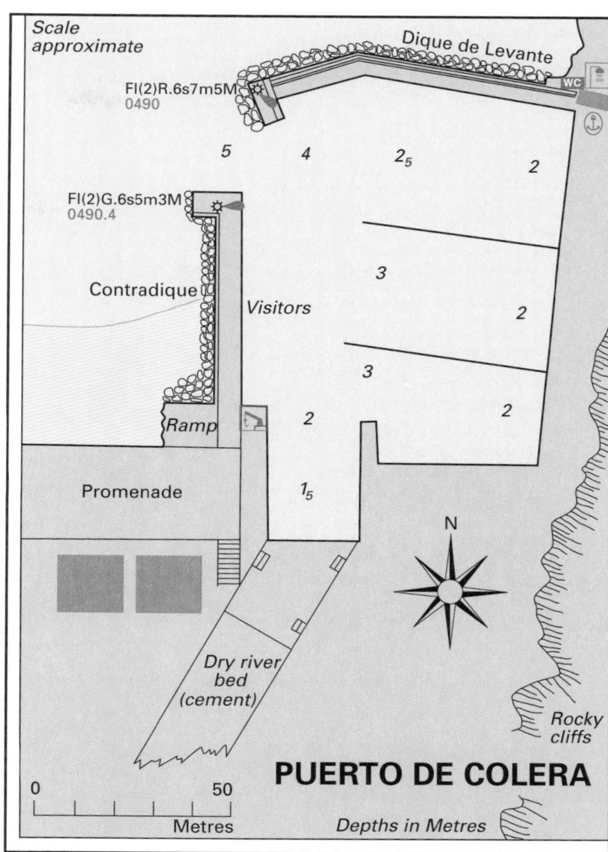

From the north Port de Cerbère, Cap Cerbère with a small white building on its summit and the Cala de Portbou are easily recognised. Cala Colera is the next *cala* to S. From this direction the harbour may be seen in the early approach.

Anchorage in the approach
Anchor in 10m, stone and sand, near the centre of the mouth of Cala Colera. The head of the *cala* is shallow and has outlying spurs either side of the mouth of the river.

Entrance
Go west towards the head of the *cala* and when harbour bears S turn towards the entrance. Round the Dique de Levante at 15m.

Berths
Secure on the inner (E) side of the *contradique* where there is a notice 'Amarres Servicio Publico' and ask the *capitanía* for a berth. Some of the quays have shallow rocky feet.

Facilities
Maximum length overall 15m.
Ramp from beach to *contradique.*
2-tonne crane.
Water taps on quays and pontoons.
Showers and WCs in NE corner of the harbour.
220v AC on quays and pontoons.
Club Náutico Sant Miquel de Colera.
Provisions from village shops in Colera about 500m.

Communications
Buses. Rail to Barcelona and Perpignan.

Puerto de Portbou

42°26'N 3°10'E

Charts

British Admiralty *1705*
French *7008, 7505*
Spanish *876, 493*
Navicarte *E03*

Lights

31860(S) **Dique de Abrigo head** 42°25'·7N 3°10'·0E Q.8m3M ⯅ N card post

To the north

0492 **Cap Cerbère** 42°26'·4N 3°10'·6E Fl.4s55m15M Grey tower red top 10m

0496 **Cap Béar** 42°30'·9N 3°08'·2E Fl(3)15s80m30M Pale red tower, grey corners 27m 146°-vis-056°

Port communications

VHF Ch 9. Club Náutico de Portbou ☎ 972 390 079.
Marina ☎ 972 390 634.

General

This inlet which forms a natural harbour is located close to the frontier with France. Approach and entrance are easy and good protection is offered from all directions except between NE and SE. The force of the NW *tramontana* is somewhat reduced by the ranges of mountains inland but can still descend on the harbour in strong gusts. With a strong wind between NE and SE a heavy swell enters this harbour. Shelter should be taken at Selva or Port Vendres.

A new, much larger, marina is under construction on the west side of the approach, immediately south of the entrance of old Portbou harbour. The breakwaters have been established and it may be possible to anchor within whilst the harbour is being completed.

Facilities at Portbou are limited and the town is not especially attractive but the surrounding countryside is spectacular, with high mountains.

Approach

From the south From the wide and deep Bahía de la Selva, the coast which is rugged and broken consists of a series of deep *calas* with rocky headlands

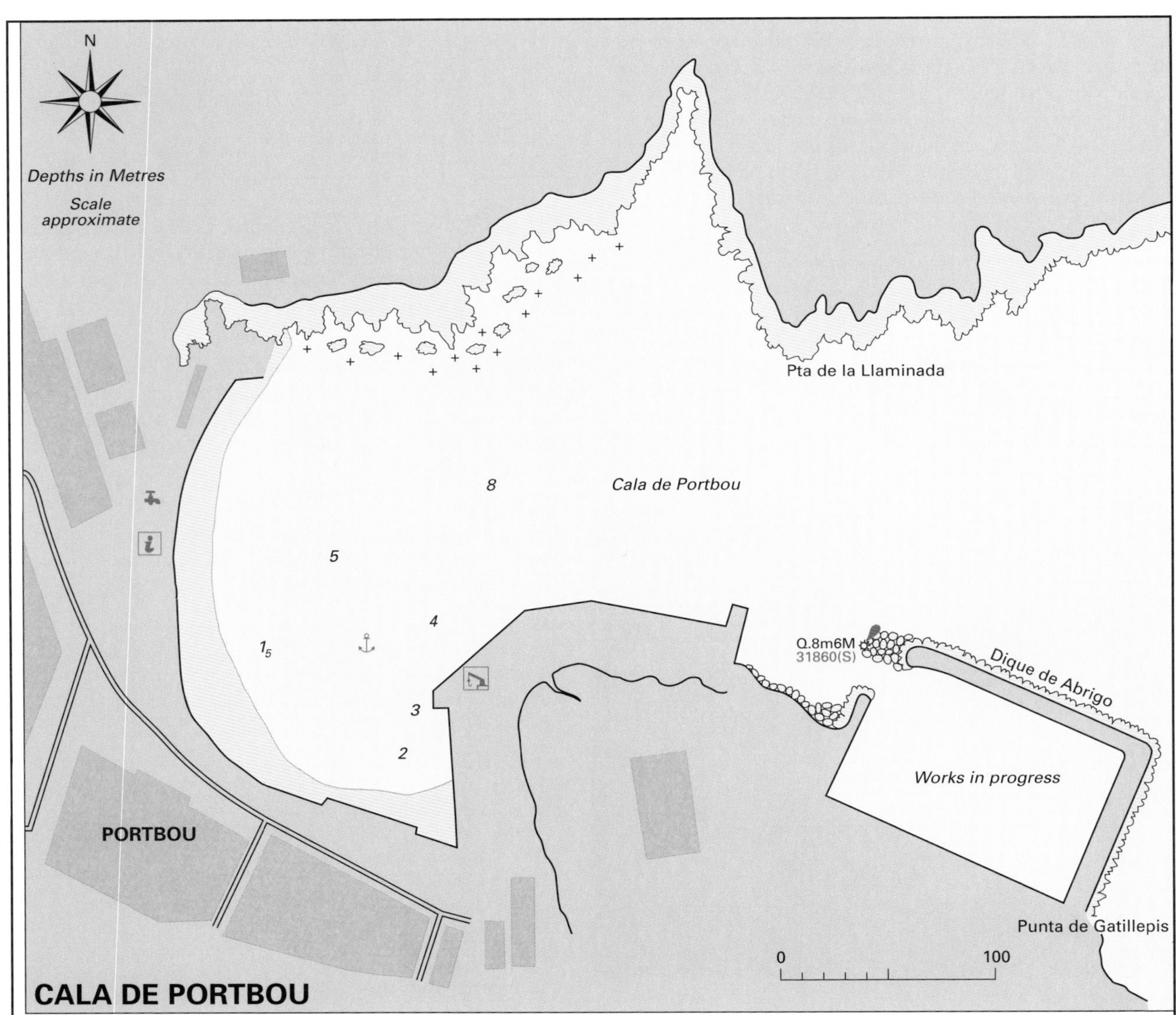

between. These rocks are of a very dark colour just to the S of this harbour. Cap Cerbère which is ½M to N of this harbour is the most prominent of the headlands and can be identified if coasting close in. At the head of the Cala de Portbou can be seen the long railway customs shed on an embankment, the lighthouse-like spire of the church to the N of it, and there is a prominent fort-like building with a small square tower on the inner point on the S side of the harbour.

From the north Round Cap Béar, a prominent point with a lighthouse, signal and radio station and fort. Banyuls-sur-Mer can easily be identified at the head of a wide bay. Port de Cerbère has a multi-arched railway embankment, Cap Cerbère just to S of it will be seen, if coasting close in, as a prominent headland. Cabo Falcó is triangular-shaped and has a small white customs shed on its summit. Portbou will be recognised as detailed in the section above.

Entrance

Enter down the centre of the *cala* on a W course.

Berths

Berth stern-to the quay with anchor and tripping line from the bow. Keep well clear of the quay because of underwater rocky obstructions at its foot.

Anchorages

Anchor near the centre of the head of the *cala* about 100m from the shore in 5m, weed on sand.

Cabo Falcó and Cabo Cerbère

Facilities

Small slip on the S side of the harbour.
Water tap on the NW side of the harbour.
Some small shops in the village.
Club Náutico de Portbou.

Communications

Rail to Barcelona and Perpignan. Bus service. ☎ Area code 972.

Portbou

Appendices

I. CHARTS

Charts and other publications may be corrected annually by reference to the Admiralty *List of Lights and Fog Signals Volume D (NP 77) and E (NP78)* or weekly via the Admiralty *Notices to Mariners.*

Note A few charts appear twice in the following list under different island headings. The index diagrams only shows large-scale charts where the diagram's scale permits.

British Admiralty charts

Note Index references refer to sections in Admiralty World Catalogue NP131 Index E Bay of Biscay, Spain, Portugal and Western Mediterranean

Chart	*Title*	*Scale*
45	Gibraltar harbour	3,600
142	Strait of Gibraltar	100,000
	Tarifa	25,000
144	Gibraltar	10,000
165	Menorca to Sicilia including Malta	1,100,000
469	Puerto de Alicante	10,000
470	Approaches to Puerto de Alicante	27,500
518	Approaches to Puerto de Valencia	27,500
562	Valencia	10,000
773	Strait of Gibraltar to Isla de Alborán	300,000
774	Motril to Cartagena including Isla de Alborán	300,000
	Isla de Alborán	15,000
1180	Barcelona	10,000
1193	Puerto de Tarragona and approaches	10,000
1194	Puerto de Cartagena	12,500
1196	Approaches to Puerto de Barcelona	30,000
1448	Gibraltar bay	25,000
1455	Algeciras	12,500
1458	Plans on the east coast of Spain	
	Puerto de Gandía: Puerto de Vinaroz	10,000
	Puerto de Sagunto: Puerto de Castellón de la Plana:	
	Puerto de Denia	18,000
	Puerto de los Alfaques	30,000
1588	Ports in southern Spain	
	Garrucha	7,500
	Almería	12,000
	Aguilas and El Hornillo: Carboneras	12,500
1700	Cartagena to Cabo de San Antonio including Isla Formentera	300,000
1701	Cabo de San Antonio to Villanueva y Geltrú including Islas de Ibiza and Formentera	300,000
1702	Ibiza, Formentera and southern Mallorca	300,000
1703	Mallorca and Menorca	300,000
1704	Punta de la Bana to Islas Medas	300,000
1705	Cabo de San Sebastian to Îles d'Hyères	300,000
1780	Barcelona to Napoli including Islas Baleares, Corse and Sardegna	1,100,000
1848	Málaga with approaches, Motril, Adra and Estepona	
	Estepona	12,500
	Málaga: Adra	7,500
	Motril	10,000
	Approaches to Málaga	25,000
2717	Strait of Gibraltar to Barcelona and Alger including Islas Baleares	1,100,000
2831	Mallorca: Punta Salinas to Cabo de Formentor including Canal de Menorca	120,000
	Puerto de Alcudia	20,000
2832	Mallorca: Punta Salinas to Punta Beca including Isla de Cabrera	120,000
2833	Menorca	120,000
	Ciudadela	10,000
	Mahón	12,500
	Bahia de Tirant and Cala Fornells	15,000
2834	Ibiza and Formentera	120,000
	Ibiza	10,000
	San Antonio Abad	20,000
	Channels between Ibiza and Formentera	50,000
3036	Approaches to Palma	30,000
	Palma	10,000
3132	Strait of Gibraltar to Arquipélago da Madeira	1,250,000
3578	Eastern approaches to the Strait of Gibraltar	150,000

Spanish charts

6A	Isla de Menorca	96,000
7A	Isla de Ibiza y Formentera	97,500
44	De cabo de San Vicente al Estrecho de Gibraltar	350,000
44C	Costa Sur de España y Norte de Marruecos. De Broa de Sanlúcar a Estepona y de Larache a cabo Mazarí	175,000
45	Estrecho de Gibraltar y Mar de Alborán	350,000
45A	De punta Carnero a cabo Sacratif y de punta Cires a cabo Negro	175,000
45B	De cabo Sacratif a cabo de Gata	175,000
46	De cabo de Gata a cabo de las Huertas y de cabo Milonia a cabo Ivi	350,000
	Plano inserto: Puerto de Gazaouet (Nemours)	10,000
46A	De cabo de Gata a cabo de Palos	175,000
	Plano inserto: Fondeaderos de Palomares y Villaricos	25,000
47	De cabo Tiñoso a cabo Canet, con las islas Ibiza, Formentera, Cabrera y costa SW de Mallorca	350,000
48	De cabo de la Nao a Barcelona con las islas Baleares	425,000
48E	Islas de Mallorca y Menorca	175,000
105	Estrecho de Gibraltar. De cabo Roche a punta de la Chullera y de cabo Espartel a cabo Negro	100,000
215	De cabo Trafalgar a punta Europ y de Ceuta a Kenitra (Port Lyautey)	350,000
287A	Ensenada y puerto de Benidorm	16,400
288A	Ensenada y puerto de Altea	11,600
289A	Puerto y fondeadero de Calpe	17,000

BRITISH ADMIRALTY CHARTS

See list for large scale charts

1704
1705
C. St Sebastian
Barcelona
2717
1701
SPAIN
Menorca
Mallorca
Valencia
1702
Ibiza
1703
C. San Antonio
Alicante
Cartagena
774
1700
Málaga
Almeria
Estepona
Marbella
Gibraltar
142
Tangier
3578
I. de Alboran
Oran
ALGERIA
773
Morocco

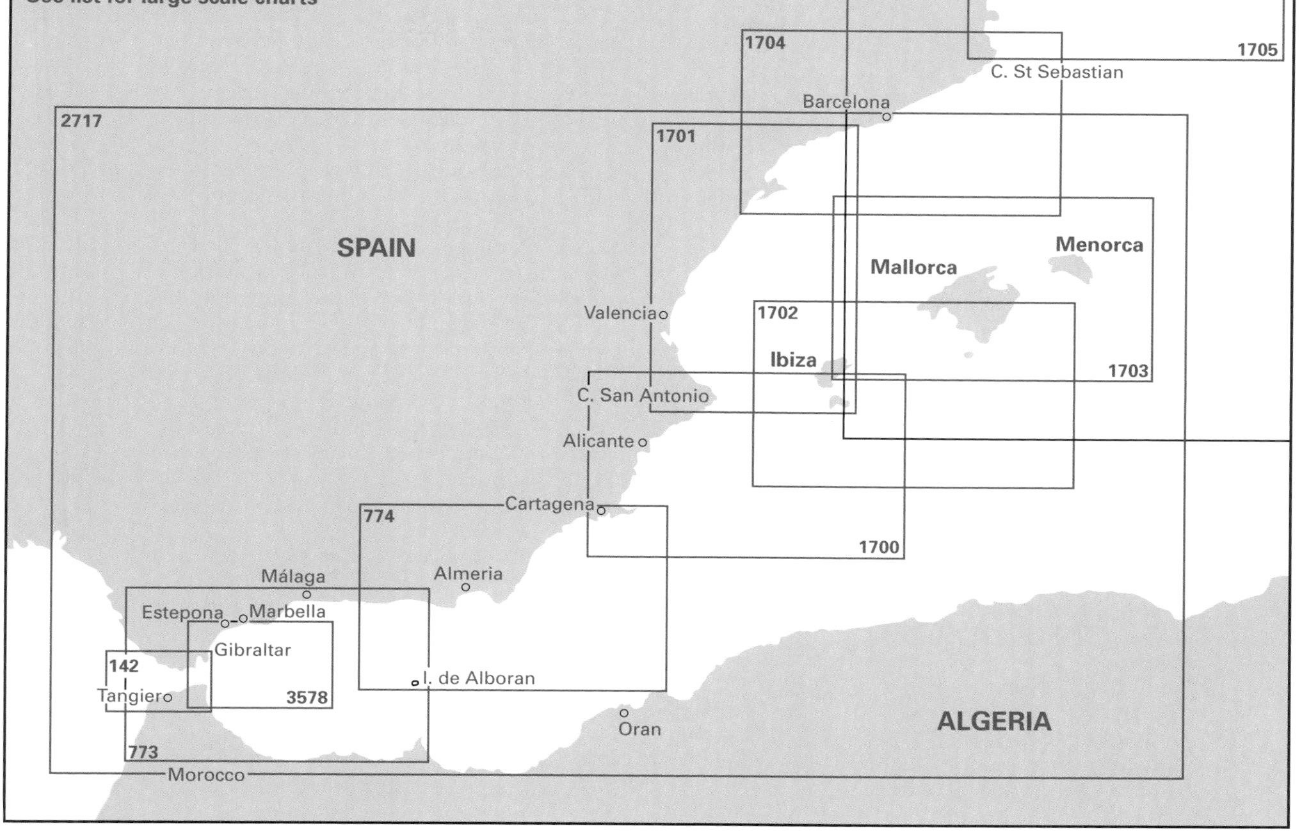

SPANISH CHARTS

See list for large scale charts

C. Creus
876
48
Barcelona
873
Tarragona
871
837
838
C. Tortosa
836
Menorca
ESPÃNA
Valencia
Palma
Mallorca
835
834
Ibiza
833
C. San Antonio
46
Alicante
832
Cartagena
C. Palos
45
Málaga
Almeria
C. de Gata
46A
Gibraltar
I. de Alborán
45B
105
45A
Oran
ARGELIA
Marruecos
44C

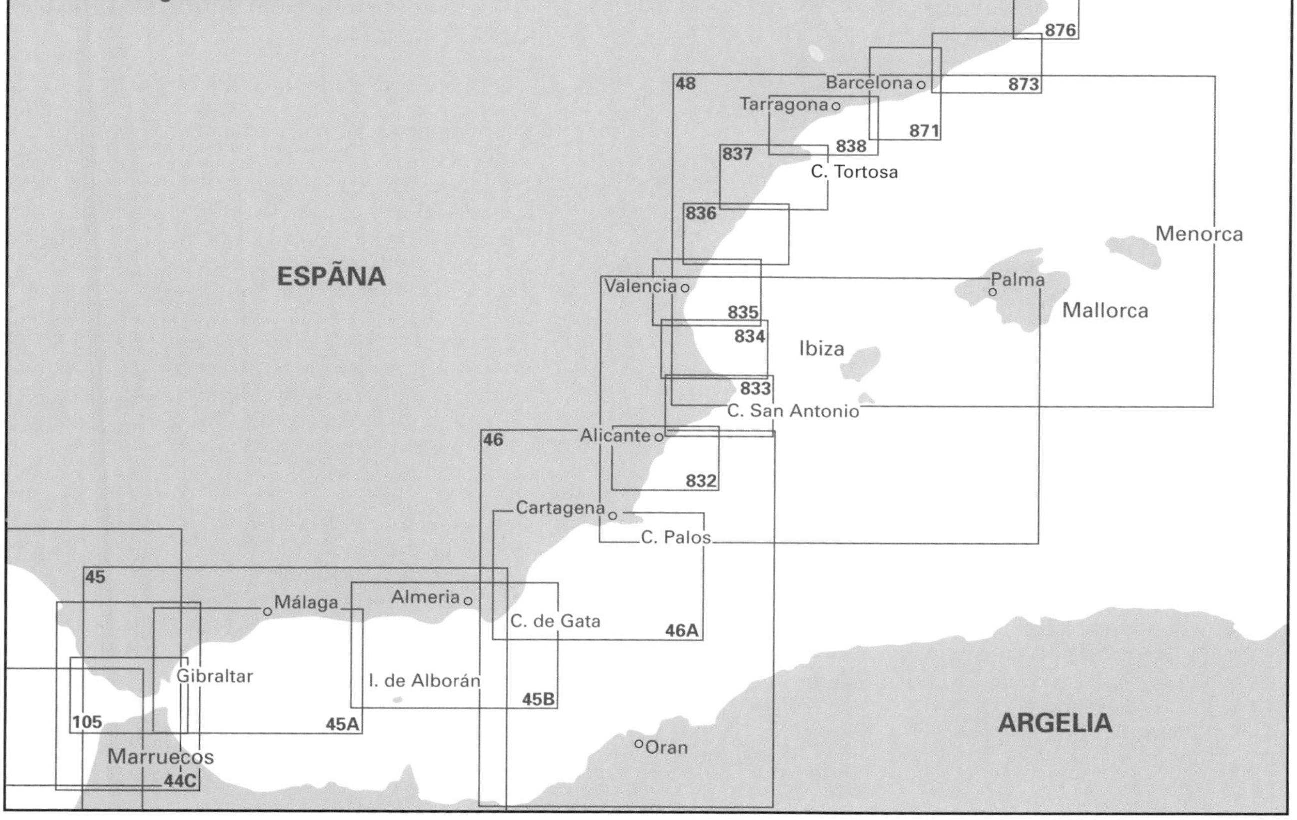

Chart	Title	Scale
291A	Ensenada de Morayra	11,700
292A	Ensenada y puerto de Jávea	13,000
301A	Fondeadero de Mataró	10,000
309A	Puerto de Cadaqués	10,000
421	De isla Dragonera a cabo Blanco	50,000
421A	Bahía de Palma. De Islote El Toro a cabo Regana	25,000
422	De Cabo Regana a punta Salinas	50,000
422A	Freu de Cabrera	25,000
423	De punta Plana a Porto Colom con la isla de Cabrera y adyacentes	50,000
424	De cala Llonga a cabo Farrutx	50,000
425	De cabo Pera a cabo Formentor	50,000
425A	Bahía de Alcudia	25,000
426	De la bahía de Alcudia al puerto de Sóller	50,000
427	De cala de la Calobra a Isla Dragonera	50,000
428A	De punta Binibeca a cabo Favaritx	25,000
435	Isla de Alboran	50,000
445	Estrecho de Gibraltar. De punta Camarinal a punta Europa y de cabo Espartel a punta Almina	60,000
445A	Bahía de Algeciras	25,000
451	De punta Leona a cabo Mazarí	50,000
453	De Punta Europa a la torre de las Bóvedas	50,000
	Planos insertos: Fondeadero de Estepona	12,500
	Fondeadero de la Sabinilla	12,500
454	De Estepona a punta de Calaburras	50,000
	Plano inserto: Fondeadero de Marbella	10,000
455	De punta de Calaburras a la ensenada de Vélez Málaga	50,000
	Plano inserto: Fondeadero y puerto de Fuengirola	10,000
455A	Aproches del puerto de Malaga	25,000
456	De punta de Torrox a cabo Sacratif	50,000
457	De Motril a Adra	50,000
458	De Adra a Almería	50,000
459	Golfo de Almería. De punta del Sabinal a cabo de Gata	50,000
	Plano inserto: Roquetas de Mar	5,000
461	De cabo de Gata a Mesa de Roldán	50,000
	Planos insertos: Puerto Genovés y ensenada de San José	15,000
	Ensenada de los Escullos	25,000
	Cala de San Pedro	25,000
462	De Mesa de Roldán a isla de los Terreros	50,000
	Plano inserto: Puerto de Garrucha	7,500
463	De punta de Sarriá a cabo Tiñoso	50,000
	Plano inserto: Puertos de Aguilas y el Hornillo	12,500
463A	De monte Cope a punta de la Azohía	30,000
464	De cabo Tiñoso a cabo de Palos	50,000
464A	Del puerto de Mazarrón a cabo del Agua	30,000
471	De cabo de Palos a cabo Cervera	50,000
471A	De cabo de Palos a punta de la Horadada	40,000
	Planos insertos: San Pedro del Pinatar	7,500
	Cabo de Palos	15,000
	Puerto de Tomás Maestre	10,000
472	Bahías de Santa Pola y Alicante	50,000

Chart	Title	Scale
472A	Aproches del puerto de Alicante	25,000
476	De cabo Culleria al puerto de Valencia	50,000
478	De cabo Negret a cabo Berbería	50,000
479	De cabo Berbería a punta Arabí	50,000
479A	Freus entre Ibiza y Formentera	25,000
481	Del puerto de Valencia al puerto de Sagunto	50,000
481A	Aproches del puerto de Valencia	25,000
482	Del puerto de Sagunto al cabo de Oropesa	60,000
482A	Aproches del puerto de Casellón	25,000
483A	Aproches de les Islas Columbretes	25,000
485	De puerto de Vinaroz a puerto de La Ampolla	60,000
485A	De Vinaroz al puerto de los Alfaques	30,000
485B	Delta del río Ebro, puerto del Fangal y golfo de La Ampolla	30,000
487A	Aproches del puerto de Tarragona	85,000
488	Del puerto de Villanueva y Geltrú al puerto de Barcelona	50,000
488A	De puerto de Villanueva y Geltrú a puerto de Garraf	25,000
	Planos insertos: Puerto de Vallcarca	5,000
	Puerto de Garraf	5,000
489	Del puerto de Barcelona al puerto de Arenys de Mar	50,000
489A	Aproches del puerto de Barcelona	25,000
491	De puerto de Arenys de Mar a puerto de San Feliú de Guixols	50,000
492	De cabo de Tossa a cabo Begur	50,000
493	De cap Negre a cap Cerbere	10,000
	Planos insertos: Puerto de Llançà	10,000
	Fondeadero de Cadaqués	20,000
493A	Golfo de Rosas	25,000
729	Puerto de Villajoyosa	9,450
772	De cabo Callera al puerto de Valencia	35,600
832	De cabo Roig a cabo de las Huerta	99,000
833	De cabo de las Huertas a cabo de San Antonio	98,500
834	De cabo de San Antonio a la Albufera de Valencia	97,800
835	De la Albufera de Valencia al Grao de Moncófar	97,000
836	De Moncófar a Alcocebre	96,300
837	De cabo de Irta a cabo Tortosa	95,600
838	De cabo Tortosa a punta Paloma	94,900
871	De punta Paloma al río Llobregat	94,700
	Plano inserto: Puerto de Vallcarca	4,500
873	Del rio Llobregat a cabo de Tossa	94,000
876	De cabo de Tossa a cabo Cerbére	93,700
900	De Cabo Blanco a punta de Amer	100,000
965	De punta de Amer al Morro de la Vaca	100,000
970	De Morro de la Vaca a cabo Blanco	100,000
	Plano inserto: Surgidero de la Foradada de Miramar	12,000
3550	Puerto de Motril	5,000
	Fondeadero de Calahonda	5,000
	Puerto de Adra	5,000
	Ensenada de las Entinas	25,000
3713	Puerto de San Carlos de la Rápita	5,000
4211	Bahía de Palma. De las Illetas a islote Galera	10,000
4212	Puerto de Palma	5,000
4213	Freu de Dragonera	10,000
4214	Puerto de Andraitx	10,000
4215	Ensenada de Santa Ponsa	10,000
4221	Isla de Cabrera y adyacentes	12,500

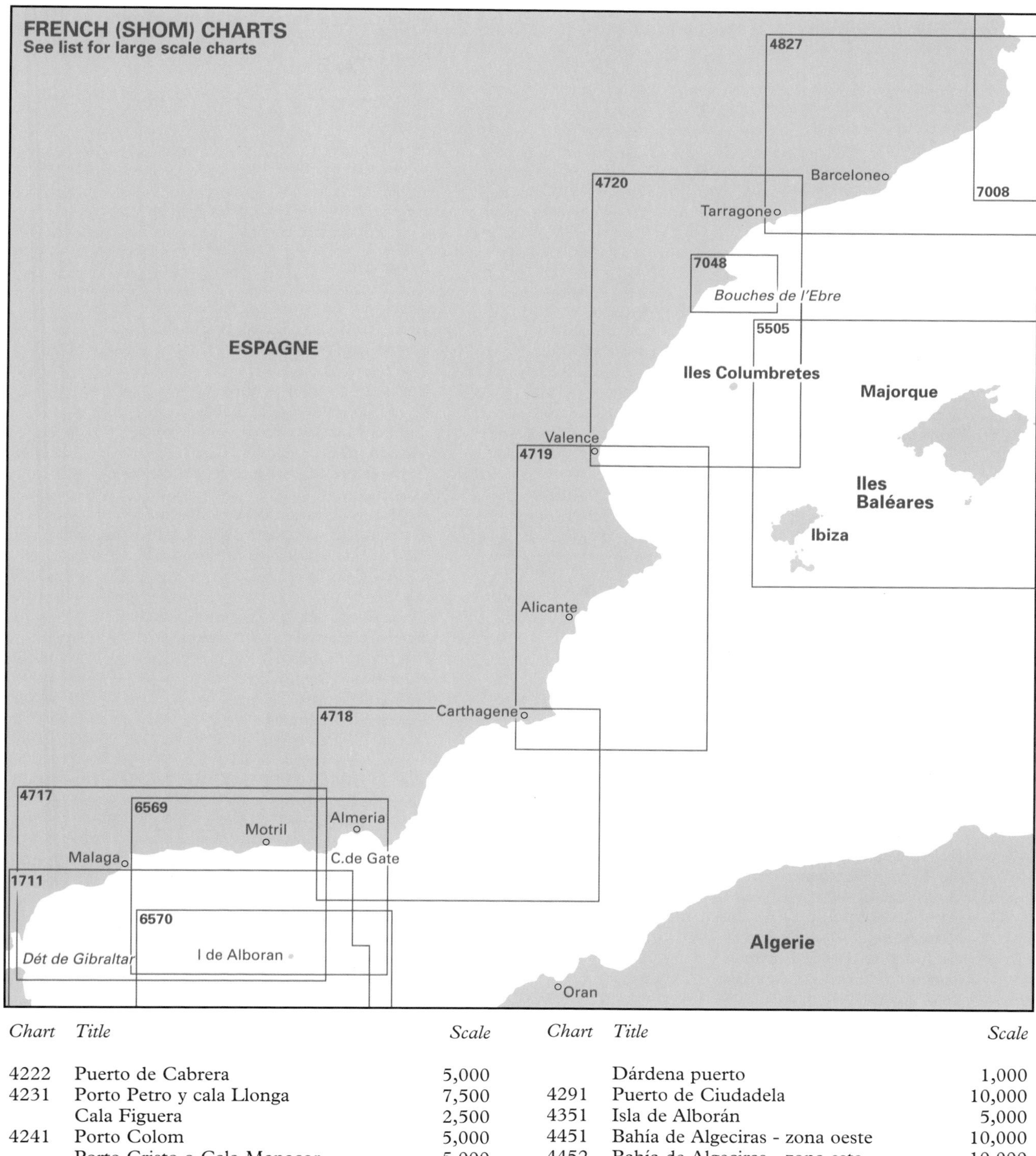

Chart	Title	Scale
4222	Puerto de Cabrera	5,000
4231	Porto Petro y cala Llonga	7,500
	Cala Figuera	2,500
4241	Porto Colom	5,000
	Porto Cristo o Cala Manacor	5,000
	Cala Ratjada	5,000
4251	Puerto de Pollensa	7,500
4252	Bahía de Alcudia. De playa de Sas Escortjas a isla de Aucunada	12,500
4253	Bahía de Alcudia. De cabo Farrutx a playa de Sas Escortjas	12,500
4254	Puerto de Alcudia	5,000
4271	Puerto de Sóller	5,000
4281	Puerto de Mahón	7,500
4282	Cala Mesquida	5,000
4283	Ensenada de Tirant y cala Fornells	7,500
	Planos insertos: Puerto Nitge	10,000
	Dárdena puerto	1,000
4291	Puerto de Ciudadela	10,000
4351	Isla de Alborán	5,000
4451	Bahía de Algeciras - zona oeste	10,000
4452	Bahía de Algeciras - zona este	10,000
4551	Puerto de Málaga	5,000
4591	Puerto de Almería	10,000
4621	Puertos de Carboneras y Hornos Ibéricos	7,500
4631	De punta de Calnegre al puerto de Mazarrón	12,500
4632	Rada de Mazarrón	12,500
4642	Puertos de Cartagena y Escombreras	10,000
4711	Puerto de Torrevieja	50,000
4721	Bahía de Santa Pola	10,000
4722	Puerto de Alicante	10,000
4751	Puerto de Denia	10,000
4752	Puerto de Gandía	10,000

4781	Puerto de San Antonio Abad	5,000
4791	Puerto de Ibiza	10,000
4811	Puerto de Valencia	10,000
4812	Puerto de Sagunto	7,500
4821	Puerto de Castellón	10,000
4822	Puerto de Burriana	10,000
4831	Islas Columbretes	10,000
4841	Puertos de Banicarló y Peñíscola	10,000
4842	Puerto de Vinaroz	10,000
4861	Rada de Salou y Pto Cambrils	10,000
4871	Puerto de Tarragona	10,000
4881	Puerto de Villanueva y Geltrú	7,500
4882	Puerto de Sitges	10,000
4891	Puerto de Barcelona	10,000
4892	De Puerto de Masnou al Puerto de Premiá de Mar	10,000
4911	Puerto de Arenys de Mar	10,000
4913	Puerto de Blanes	10,000
4922	Ensenada y puerto de San Feliú de Guixols	10,000
4923	Fondeadero y puerto de Palamós	10,000
4924	Cabo San Sebastián e islas Hormigas	10,000
4931	Fondeadero de las islas Medas y puerto de El Estartit	10,000
4932	Bahia de Rosas	10,000
4934	Puerto de la Selva	10,000

French charts

Service Hydrographique et Oceanographique de la Marine (SHOM)

4033	Iles Columbretes	18,000
4717	De Gibraltar à la pointe del Sabinal	250,000
	Cartouche: Port de Motril	10,000
	Mouillages de la Herradura, Los Berengueles, Almunecar, Belilla et Salobrena	80,000
4718	De la Pointe del Sabinal à Carthagène	247,000
	Cartouche: Port Genoves et anse de San Jose	25,000
	Cartouche: Anse de los Escullos	25,000
	Cartouche: Port de San Pedro	25,000
4719	De Carthagène à Valence	242,000
4720	De Valence a Tarragone	236,000
4827	De Tarragone au cap de Creux	231,000
5505	Iles Baléares	319,000
6341	Ports de la côte Sud d'Espagne, anse de Mazarron	25,000
	Cartouche: Port de Portman	10,000
	Cartouche: Ports de Aguilas et de el Hornillo	15,000
6515	Ports de la côte Est d'Espagne – Port d'Alicante	10,000
	Cartouche: Port de Torrevieja	15,000
6569	Mer d'Alboran, feuille Nord	202,000
6570	Mer d'Alboran, feuille Sud	203,000
6775	Baie de Palma, de las Illetas a l'ilot Galera	10,000
6843	Du Cabo Creus à Port-Bacarès	50,000
7008	Du Cabo de San Sébastian à Fos-sur-Mer	25,000
7026	Baie de Algeciras	25,000
7042	Détroit de Gibraltar	100,000
7046	Port de Barcelona	10,000
7047	Du Cabo de Salou à Tarragona	10,000
7048	Du port de Vinaroz au port de la Ampolla – Delta de l'Ebre (Ebro)	60,000
7114	Ibiza Formentera	
	Cartouche: Ibiza et Formentera	100,000
	Cartouche: Puerto de San Antonio Abad	20,000
	Cartouche: Puerto de Ibiza	10,000
	Cartouche: Passages entre Ibiza et Espalmador Abords de Puerto de Ibiza	30,000
7115	Mallorca – Partie Ouest – De Punta Beca à Punta Salinas	100,000
7116	Mallorca – Partie Est – De Punta Salinas à Cabo Formentor	100,000
7117	Menorca – Ports et Mouillages de Menorca, Ciudadela, Tiranet Cala Fornells, Máhon	100,000
7118	Abords de Palma – De Isla Dragoner à Cabo Blanco, Andraitx, Santa Ponsa	40,000
7119	Ports et Mouillages de Mallorca et Cabrèra Pollensa, Alcudia, Soller, Colom Ratjada, Surgidero de, Foradada, Figuera, Cristó ou Calá Manacor, Cala Llonga	12,500
7276	Abords de Valencia	25,000
7294	Puerto de Malaga	10,000
7295	Ports et Mouillages entre Cabo de la Nao et Cabo de Palos Tomás Maestre, Palos, Villajoyosa, Mar Menor	15,000
7296	Ports et mouillages entre Tarragona et Alicante Peñiscola, Castellón de la Plana, Burriana, Jávea, Benìcarlo, Sagunto, Denia, San Carlos de la Rápita, Calpe, Gandia	15,000
	Altea	20,000
7298	Ports et mouillages entre la frontière franco-espagnole et Tarragona	
	Puerto de la Selva	10,000
	Puerto de Cadaqués	15,000
	Bahía de Rosas	15,000
	Puerto de El Estartit	15,000
	Puerto de Palamos	15,000
	Puerto de Arenys de Mar	10,000
	Puerto de San Feliú de Guíxols	10,000
	Cala de Llafranc	10,000
	Puerto de Blanes	15,000
	Puerto de Villanueva y Geltrú	15,000
	Sitges et puerto Vallcarca	20,000
	Puerto de Garraf	5,000
7304	Abords de Alicante	10,000
7504	Abords de Almeria	25,000
7505	Du Cabo de Tossa au Cap Cerbère	93,700
7642	Ports de Carthagène et d'Escombreras	10,000

Imray M series charts

M1 Southeast Spain
Gibraltar to Cabo de San Antonio
Plans Strait of Gibraltar, Fuengirola, Marbella, Almería, Alicante 1:685,000

M2 Northeast Spain
Cabo de San Antonio to Cabo Creus
Plans Valencia, Tarragona, Barcelona 1:590,000

M3 Islas Baleares
Formentera, Ibiza, Mallorca, Menorca
Plans Ibiza, Puerto de Colom, Puerto de Palma, Máhon, San Antonio-Abad 1:350,000

M10 Western Mediterranean 1:2,750,000

II. FURTHER READING

Many navigational publications are reprinted annually, in which case the latest edition should be carried. Others, including most cruising guides, are updated by means of supplements available from the publishers (see *Correctional Supplements*, page ii). Further corrections or amendments are always welcome (see *Corrections*, page ii).

Admiralty publications

Mediterranean Pilot Vol I (NP 45) and *Supplement* covers the south and east coasts of Spain, the Islas Baleares, Sardinia, Sicily and the north coast of Africa

List of Lights and Fog Signals, Vol E (NP 78) (Mediterranean, Black and Red Seas)

List of Radio Signals

Vol 1, Part 1 (NP281/1) Coast Radio Stations (Europe, Africa and Asia)

Vol 2 (NP 282) Radio Navigational Aids, Electronic Position Fixing Systems and Radio Time Signals

Vol 3, Part 1 (NP 283/1) Radio Weather Services and Navigational Warnings (Europe, Africa and Asia)

Vol 4 (NP 284) Meteorological Observation Stations

Vol 5 (NP 285) Global Maritime Distress and Safety Systems (GMDSS)

Vol 6, Part 2 (NP 286/2) Vessel Traffic Services, Port Operations and Pilot Services (The Mediterranean, Africa and Asia)

Yachtsmen's guides, almanacs etc
English language

Imray Mediterranean Almanac, Rod Heikell (Imray Laurie Norie & Wilson Ltd). A biennial almanac with second year supplement, packed with information. Particularly good value for yachts on passage when not every cruising guide is likely to be carried.

Mediterranean Cruising Handbook, Rod Heikell (Imray Laurie Norie & Wilson Ltd, 1998). Useful information on techniques such as berthing bow or stern-to, clothing, storing up etc. General information on cruising areas, passages etc.

Islas Baleares RCC Pilotage Foundation - Robin Brandon - Revised by Anne Hammick (Imray Laurie Norie & Wilson Ltd, 2000).

Mediterranean Spain – Costas del Sol and Blanca, RCC Pilotage Foundation - Robin Brandon (Imray Laurie Norie & Wilson Ltd, 2001).

Mediterranean France and Corsica Pilot, Rod Heikell (Imray Laurie Norie & Wilson Ltd, 2002).

North Africa, Hans van Rijn (Imray Laurie Norie & Wilson Ltd, 1999). The only yachtsman's guide to the coast between the Strait of Gibraltar and Tunisia.

Spanish

La Guia del Navegante – La Costa de España y el Algarve (The Yachtsman's Guide). Spanish and English, revised annually.(PubliNáutic Rilnvest SL,). Not a full scale pilot book, but an excellent source of up-to-date information on local services and facilites (partly via the advertisements) with phone numbers etc.

Guia Náutica Turistica y Deportiva de España by the *Asamblea de Capitánes de Yate.* An expensive and colourful guide book covering all the Spanish coasts and including some useful data on harbours but no pilotage information. The plans are in outline only. Written in Spanish with a partial English translation. Because symbols are lavishly used, much of it can be understood with only a limited knowledge of Spanish.

Guia Náutica de España. Tomo II, Costa del Azahar, Blanca and Baleares. One of a series of books featuring attractive colour pictures, some of which are out of date, and some text. Written in Spanish but an English version is sometimes available.

El Mercado Nautico (The Boat Market). A free newspaper published every two or three months and available from yacht clubs, marina offices etc. Written in Spanish, English and German it includes, amongst other things, a useful (though by no means comprehensive) listing of current marina prices.

French

Votre Livre de Bord – Méditerranée (Bloc Marine). French almanac covering the Mediterranean, including details of weather forecasts transmitted from France and Monaco. An English/French version is also published which translates some, though by no means all, the text. Published annually.

German

Spanische Gewässer, Lissabon bis Golfe du Lion, K Neumann (Delius Klasing). A seamanlike guide and semi-pilot book, which includes sketch plans of most harbours. Harbour data is limited but it contains much good general advice on sailing in this area.

Background

The Birth of Europe, Michael Andrew (BBC Books). An excellent and comprehensive work which explains in simple terms how the Mediterranean and surrounding countries developed over the ages from 3000 BC.

The First Eden, David Attenborough (William Collins). A fascinating study of 'The Mediterranean World and Man'.

The Inner Sea, Robert Fox (Sinclair-Stevenson, 1991). An account of the countries surrounding the Mediterranean and the forces which shaped them, written by a well known BBC journalist.

Sea of Seas, H Scott (van Nostrand). A half-guidebook half-storybook on the western Mediterranean. Very out of date and now out of print, but a delight to read.

III. SPANISH GLOSSARY

The following limited glossary relates to the weather, the abbreviations to be found on Spanish charts and some words likely to be useful on entering port. For a list containing many words commonly used in connection with sailing, see Webb & Manton, *Yachtsman's Ten Language Dictionary* (Adlard Coles Nautical).

Weather

On the radio, if there is a storm warning the forecast starts *aviso temporal.* If, as usual, there is no storm warning, the forecast starts *no hay temporal.* Many words are similar to the English and their meanings can be guessed. The following may be less familiar:

Viento **Wind**

calma calm
ventolina light air
flojito light breeze
flojo gentle breeze
bonancible moderate breeze
fresquito fresh breeze
fresco strong breeze
frescachón near gale
temporal fuerte gale
temporal duro strong gale
temporal muy duro storm
borrasca violent storm
huracán, temporal huracanado hurricane
tempestad, borrasca thunderstorm

***El Cielo* The sky**
nube cloud
nubes altas, bajas high, low clouds
nubloso cloudy
cubierto covered, overcast
claro, despejado clear

Names of cloud types in Spanish are based on the same Latin words as the names used in English.

***Visibilidad* Visibility**
buena good
regular moderate
mala poor
calima haze
neblina mist
bruma sea mist
niebla fog

***Precipitación* Precipitation**
aguacero shower
llovizna drizzle
lluvia rain
aguanieve sleet
nieve snow
granizada hail

***Sistemas del Tiempo* Weather Systems**
anticiclón anticyclone
depresión, borrasca depression
vaguada trough
cresta, dorsal ridge
cuna wedge
frente front
frio cold
cálido warm
ocluido occluded
bajando falling
subiendo rising

Lights and Charts – major terms and abbreviations:

A	*amarilla*	yellow
Alt	*alternativa*	alternative
Ag Nv	*aguas navegables*	navegable waters
Ang	*angulo*	angle
Ant	*anterior*	anterior, earlier, forward
Apag	*apagado*	extinguished
Arrc	*arrecife*	reef
At	*atenuada*	attenuated
B	*blanca*	white
Ba	*bahía*	bay
	bajamar escorada	chart datum
Bal	*baliza*	buoy, beacon
Bal. E	*baliza elástica*	plastic (elastic) buoy
Bco	*banco*	bank
Bo	*bajo*	shoal, under, below, low
Boc	*bocina*	horn, trumpet
Br	*babor*	port (ie. left)
C	*campana*	bell
Card	*cardinal*	cardinal
Cañ	*cañon*	canyon
	boya de castillete	pillar buoy
cil	*cilíndrico*	cylindrical
C	*cabo*	cape
Cha	*chimenea*	chimney
Cno	*castillo*	castle
cón	*cónico*	conical
Ct	*centellante*	quick flashing (50-80/minute)
CtI	*centellante interrumpida*	interrupted quick flashing
cuad	*cuadrangular*	quadrangular
D	*destello*	flash
Desap	*desaparecida*	disappeared
Dest	*destruida*	destroyed
	dique	breakwater, jetty
Dir	*direccional*	directional
DL	*destello largo*	long flash
E	*este*	east
edif	*edificio*	building
	ensenada	cove, inlet
Er	*estribor*	starboard
Est	*esférico*	spherical
Esp	*especial*	special
Est sñ	*estación de señales*	signal station
ext	*exterior*	exterior
Extr	*extremo*	end, head (of pier etc.)
F	*fija*	fixed
Fca	*fabrica*	factory
FD	*fija y destello*	fixed and flashing
FGpD	*fija y grupo de destellos*	fixed and group flashing
Flot	*flotador*	float
Fondn	*fondeadero*	anchorage
GpCt	*grupo de centellos*	group quick flashing
GpD	*grupo de destellos*	group flashing
GpOc	*grupo de ocultaciones*	group occulting
GpRp	*grupo de centellos rápidos*	group very quick flashing
hel	*helicoidales*	helicoidal
hor	*horizontal*	horizontal
Hund	*hundida*	submerged, sunk
I	*interrumpido*	interrupted
Igla	*iglesia*	church
Inf	*inferior*	inferior, lower
Intens	*intensificado*	intensified
Irreg	*irregular*	irregular
Iso	*isofase*	isophase
L	*luz*	light
La	*lateral*	lateral
	levante	eastern
M	*millas*	miles
Mte	*monte*	mountain
Mto	*monumento*	monument
N	*norte*	north
Naut	*nautófono*	foghorn
NE	*nordeste*	northeast
No	*número*	number
NW	*noroeste*	northwest
Obst	*obstrucción*	obstruction
ocas	*ocasional*	occasional
oct	*octagonal*	octagonal
oc	*oculta*	obscured
Oc	*ocultatión sectores*	obscured sectors
Pe A	*peligro aislado*	isolated danger
	poniente	western
Post	*posterior*	posterior, later
Ppal	*principal*	principal
	prohibido	prohibited
Obston	*obstrucción*	obstruction
Prov	*provisional*	provisional
prom	*prominente*	prominent, conspicuous
Pta	*punta*	point
Pto,	*puerto*	port[1]
PTO	*puerto deportivo*	yacht harbour
	puerto pesquero	fishing harbour
	puerto de Marina de Guerra	naval harbour
R	*roja*	red

Ra	*estación radar*	radar station
Ra+	*radar + suffix*	radar + suffix (Ra Ref etc.)
RC	*radiofaro circular*	non-directional radiobeacon
RD	*radiofaro dirigido*	directional radiobeacon
rect	*rectangular*	rectangular
Ra	*rocas*	rocks
Rp	*centeneallante rápida*	very quick flashing (80-160/min)
RpI	*cent. rápida interrumpida*	interrupted very quick flashing
RW	*radiofaro giratorio*	rotating radiobeacon
s	*sugundos*	seconds
S	*sur*	south
SE	*sudeste*	southeast
sil	*silencio*	silence
Silb	*silbato*	whistle
Sincro	*sincronizda con*	syncronized with
Sir	*sirena*	siren
son	*sonido*	sound, noise, report
Sto/a	*Santo, Santa*	Saint
SW	*sudoeste*	southwest
T	*temporal*	temporary
Te	*torre*	tower
trans	*transversal*	transversal
triang	*triangular*	triangular
troncoc	*troncocónico*	truncated cone
troncop	*troncopiramidal*	truncated pyramid
TSH	*antena de radio*	radio mast
TV	*antena de TV*	TV mast
U	*centellante ultra-rápida*	ultra quick flashing (+160/min)
UI	*cent. ultra-rápida interrumpido*	interrupted ultra quick flashing
V	*verde*	green
Vis	*visible*	visible
	vivero	shellfish raft or bed
W	*oeste*	west

1. 'puerto' can be applied to any landing place from a beach to a container port.

Ports and Harbours

a popa stern-to
a proa bows-to
abrigo shelter
al costado alongside
amarrar to moor
amarradero mooring
ancho breadth (see also manga)
anclar to anchor
botar to launch (a yacht)
boya de amarre mooring buoy
cabo warp, line (also cape)
calado draught
compuerta lock, basin
dársena dock, harbour
dique breakwater, jetty
escala ladder
escalera steps
esclusa lock
escollera jetty
eslora total length overall
espigón spur, spike, mole
fábrica factory
ferrocarril railway
fondear to anchor or moor
fondeadero anchorage
fondeo mooring buoy
fondo depth (bottom)
grua crane
guia mooring lazy-line (lit. guide)
nudo knot (ie. speed)
longitud length (see also eslora), longitude
lonja fish market (wholesale)
manga beam (ie. width)
muelle mole, jetty, quay
noray bollard
pantalán jetty, pontoon
parar to stop
pila estaca pile
pontón pontoon
práctico pilot (ie. pilot boat)
profundidad depth
rampa slipway
rompeolas breakwater
varadero slipway, hardstanding
varar to lift (a yacht)
vertedero (verto) spoil ground

Direction

babor port (ie. left)
estribor starboard
norte north
este east
sur south
oeste west

Phrases useful on arrival

¿Donde puedo amarrar?	Where can I moor?
¿A donde debo ir?	Where should I go?
¿Que es la profundidad?	What is the depth?
¿Que es su eslora	What is your length?
¿Cuantos metros?	How many metres?
¿Para cuantas noches?	For how many nights?

Administration and stores

aceite oil (including engine oil)
aduana customs
agua potable drinking water
aseos toilet block
astillero shipyard
capitán de puerto harbour master
derechos dues, rights
duchas showers
dueño, propietario owner
efectos navales chandlery
electricidad electricity
gasoleo, diesel diesel
guardia civil police
hielo (cubitos) ice (cubes)
lavandería laundry
lavandería automática launderette
luz electricity (lit. light)
manguera hosepipe
parafina, petróleo, keroseno paraffin, kerosene
patrón skipper (not owner)
gasolina petrol
título certificate
velero sailmaker (also sailing ship)

IV. CERTIFICATE OF COMPETENCE

1. Given below is a transcription of a statement made by the Counsellor for Transport at the Spanish Embassy, London in March 1996. It is directed towards citizens of the UK but doubtless the principles apply to other EU citizens. One implication is that in a particular circumstance (paragraph 2a below) a UK citizen does not need a Certificate of Competence during the first 90 days of his visit.
2. a. British citizens visiting Spain in charge of a UK registered pleasure boat flying the UK flag need only fulfil UK law.
   b. British citizens visiting Spain in charge of a Spanish registered pleasure boat flying the Spanish flag has one of two options:
   i. To obtain a Certificate of Competence issued by the Spanish authorities. See *Normas reguladore para la obtención de titulos para el gobierno de embarcaciones de recreo* issued by the Ministerio de Obras Publicas, Transportes y Medio Ambiente.
   ii. To have the Spanish equivalent of a UK certificate issued. The following equivalencies are used by the Spanish Maritime Administration:
   Yachtmaster Ocean *Capitan de Yate*
   Yachtmaster Offshore *Patron de Yate de altura*
   Coastal Skipper *Patron de Yate*
   Day Skipper *Patron de Yate embarcaciones de recreo*
   Helmsman Overseas[1] *Patron de embarcaciones de recreo restringido a motor*

   1. The Spanish authorities have been informed that this certificate has been replaced by the International Certificate of Competence.
3. The catch to para 2(a) above is that, in common with other EU citizens, after 90 days a UK citizen is technically no longer a visitor, must apply for a *permiso de residencia* and must equip his boat to Spanish rules and licensing requirements.

   In practice the requirement to apply for a *permiso de residencia* does not appear to be enforced in the case of cruising yachtsmen who live aboard rather than ashore and are frequently on the move. By the same token, the requirement for a British skipper in charge of a UK registered pleasure boat flying the UK flag to carry a Certificate of Competence after their first 90 days in Spanish waters also appears to be waived. Many yachtsmen have reported cruising Spanish waters for extended periods with no documentation beyond that normally carried in the UK.
4. The RYA suggests the following technique to obtain an equivalent Spanish certificate:
   a. Obtain two photocopies of your passport
   b. Have them notarised by a Spanish notary
   c. Obtain a copy of the UK Certificate of Competence and send it to the Consular Department, The Foreign and Commonwealth Office, Clive House, Petty France, London SW1H 9DH, with a request that it be stamped with the Hague Stamp (this apparently validates the document). The FCO will probably charge a fee so it would be best to call the office first (☎ 0207 270 3000).
   d. Have the stamped copy notarized by a UK notary.
   e. Send the lot to the Spanish Merchant Marine for the issue of the Spanish equivalent.

It may be both quicker and easier to take the Spanish examination.

V. VALUE ADDED TAX

The Spanish phrase for Value Added Tax (VAT) is *Impuesto sobre el valor añadido* (IVA), levied at 16% in 1996. Note that for VAT purposes the Canaries, Gibraltar, the Channel Islands and the Isle of Man are outside the EU fiscal area.

Subject to certain exceptions, vessels in EU waters are liable for VAT. One exception is a boat registered outside the EU fiscal area and owned by a non EU citizen which remains in EU waters for less than six months.

For a boat built within the EU fiscal area after 1985 the following documents taken together will show VAT status:

a. An invoice listing VAT or receipt if available
b. Registration Certificate
c. Bill of Sale

For a boat built prior to 1985 the following documentation is required:

e. Evidence of age and of ownership. The full Registration Certificate will serve but the Small Ship Registry Certificate will not.
f. Evidence that it was moored in EU fiscal waters at midnight on 31 December 1992 or, in the case of Austrian, Finnish and Swedish waters, 31 December 1994.

Any boat purchased outside the EU by an EU resident is liable for VAT on import to the EU.

EU owners of boats built within the EU, exported by them and which were outside EU fiscal waters at the cut-off date may be entitled to Returned Goods Relief. In the latter case, HM Customs and Excise may be able to issue a 'tax opinion letter'. The office has no public counter but may be approached by letter or fax. The address is: HM Customs and Excise, Dover Yacht Unit, Parcel Post Depot, Charlton Green, Dover, Kent CT16 1EH (☎ (01304) 224421, *Fax* (01304) 215786).

All the rules change when a yacht is used commercially – most commonly for chartering.

VI. CHARTER REGULATIONS

Any EU-flag yacht applying to charter in Spanish waters must be either VAT paid or exempt (the latter most commonly due to age). Non-EU flag vessels must have a valid Temporary Import Licence and may also have to conform to other regulations.

Applying for a charter licence can be a tortuous business. Firstly the *Director General de Transportes* at the *Conselleria d'Obres Publiques i Ordenacio del Territori* must be approached with a pre-authorisation application. This obtained, the application itself is sent to the *Capitanias Maritimas* together with ships' papers and proof of passenger insurance and registration as a commercial activity. A safety and seaworthiness inspection will be carried out. Finally a fiscal representative must be appointed and tax paid on revenue generated.

It will probably be found simpler to make the application through one of the companies specialising in this type of work.

Index